• THE BARNES & NOBLE LIBRARY OF ESSENTIAL READING •

RECOLLECTIONS AND LETTERS

Robert E. Lee

Introduction by Ben Wynne

BARNES & NOBLE BOOKS

NEW YORK

THE BARNES & NOBLE
LIBRARY OF ESSENTIAL READING

Introduction and Suggested Reading Copyright © 2004 by Barnes & Noble Books

Originally published in 1904

This edition published by Barnes & Noble Publishing, Inc.

All rights reserved. No part of this book may be used
or reproduced in any manner whatsoever without
written permission of the Publisher.

Cover Design by Pronto Design, Inc.

2004 Barnes & Noble Publishing, Inc.

ISBN 0-7607-5919-7

Printed and bound in the United States of America

3 5 7 9 10 8 6 4 2

2

RECOLLECTIONS AND LETTERS

GENERAL ROBERT E. LEE
Photographed in 1869–his last sitting

To My Daughters
Anne Carter
And
Mary Custis

CONTENTS

LIST OF ILLUSTRATIONS

INTRODUCTION

JUST as its subject, General Robert E. Lee, was no ordinary man, *The Recollections and Letters* is no ordinary book. In the South, Robert E. Lee's legend is unrivaled. Generations have revered him to the point of outright deification. In defeat, the formal Confederate general *became* the South, or at least the personification of an image that the South desperately wanted to project onto itself. Lee's name became synonymous with chivalry, humility, dignity, and all that was right within the human spirit. Southern counties and towns were named in his honor, as were schools, bridges, buildings, parks, and even many children. His birthday became a holiday in the states of the old Confederacy. Lee's larger-than-life persona eventually grew to such an extent that he became not just a Southern icon, but an American icon as well—an American hero. This was a remarkable evolution for a man who in 1861 took up arms against the nation of his birth and subsequently led an army to a devastating end. Lee's transformation from defeated general to American hero was due in part to Robert E. Lee, Jr.'s, dedication to his father's memory. In 1904, the younger Lee produced *The Recollections and Letters,* a book made up primarily of the general's personal correspondence, much of which was written to his wife and children. The book provided touching insights into the general's family life, allowing already admiring readers to connect with him on a more human level. In historical perspective, the work offers personal insights into Lee that should not be ignored by anyone interested in the man, the South, the Civil War, or American history. Without *Recollections and Letters,* any study of Robert E. Lee is incomplete.

Lee's life and military career have been well chronicled. The son of Revolutionary hero Henry "Lighthorse Harry" Lee, the future Confederate general was born in Stratford, Virginia, in 1807. He was educated at the United States Military Academy in West Point where in 1829 he graduated second in his class. As an army officer, Lee distinguished himself during the Mexican War and was wounded during the storming of Chapultepec in 1847. He later served as superintendent of the U.S. Military Academy and commanded the combined force of soldiers and marines that captured John Brown at Harper's Ferry in 1859. In 1861, Abraham Lincoln offered Lee field command of all Federal forces but the Virginian declined, choosing instead to leave the Union with his home state. Though he realized the inherent dangers of secession, he said that he could never take part in an invasion of the South. Lee served as a military advisor to Confederate president Jefferson Davis and led the Army of Northern Virginia. He orchestrated a number of stunning victories during the conflict, but his 1863 defeat at Gettysburg marked the beginning of the end for the Confederacy. In February 1865, Lee was finally given command of all Confederate forces, but the move came far too late. Overwhelmed, he surrendered two months later to Ulysses S. Grant at Appomattox Courthouse and the Civil War ended. After the war and in poor health, Lee accepted a position as president of Washington College (later Washington and Lee University), and under his leadership the institution prospered. In 1870, the former general succumbed to heart disease that had plagued him since the war years, and he was entombed in Lexington, Virginia. The entire South mourned his passing.

Lee united two of the great American families of the Revolutionary era in 1831 when he married Mary Custis, the daughter of Washington Parke Custis and granddaughter of Martha Washington. The union produced seven children, three sons and four daughters. Robert E. Lee, Jr., known as "Rob" to his family, was the general's youngest son. He was born in 1843, and later wrote "[t]he first vivid recollection I have of my father is his arrival at Arlington, after his return from the Mexican War." Though he seemed to give little thought to a military career before the Civil War, Rob left the University of Virginia in 1862 and joined the "Rockbridge Artillery" as a private. He was later appointed to the rank of captain and served as an aid to his brother Custis. Rob survived the war and afterward returned to Virginia and entered private business. Like his siblings, he revered his father, and was determined to preserve his father's memory for future generations. With this in mind, the publication of his father's correspondence was as much a celebration of the general's life and legend as it was an attempt to preserve the historical record.

While the publication of *Recollections and Letters* was a tribute by a son to his father, it was also part of a larger phenomenon that was beginning to peak by the turn of the twentieth century. Although Lee died just a few years after the Civil War ended, many other Confederate veterans did not, and as they recovered from their ordeal the seeds of Southern mythology regarding their collective military service began to take root. Defeated militarily, the South in the decades following 1865 struggled to vindicate the ideals and decisions that had led it into a conflict that cost so many men their lives. From the ashes of war and the turbulence of the Reconstruction period, a cultural identity took shape grounded in ideas and attitudes referred to collectively as the Lost Cause. Celebrations of the Lost Cause took many forms: annual civil and religious services honoring the Confederate dead, veterans' reunions, the deification of Confederate military leaders, the erection of Confederate monuments, and the emergence of groups such as the United Confederate Veterans, United Sons of Confederate Veterans, and United Daughters of the Confederacy. Politicians on the stump used the language of the Lost Cause—language denoting moral superiority based on abstract notions of honor and chivalry—to garner votes, and ministers espoused Lost

Cause virtues from the pulpit. Textbooks "educated" generations of white Southern school children on the nature of the war as a noble struggle of principle, lost only in the face of superior Northern resources. For a century after the war, the Lost Cause salved the psychological wounds of defeat and gave cultural authority to Confederate symbols, most prominently the "stars and bars" rebel flag. As they entered the twentieth century, the states of the old Confederacy did their best to maintain this cultural identity by accenting the New South with many of the cosmetic trappings of an idealized Old South. The Confederate memoir also became fashionable during the period. Some major figures produced books, but across the South common soldiers were also encouraged to put pen to paper and record their recollections. More than a generation removed from the bloody consequences of actual fighting, many of these first-hand accounts were more romantic in nature, emphasizing Confederate valor and minimizing those aspects of war that might be less attractive. By the time the generation of Southern males that had fought the war began passing from the scene, their exploits as Confederate soldiers had already entered the realm of legend. In the South every veteran, regardless of rank, became a larger-than-life hero and every battle—large or small, won or lost—drew comparisons with the great battles of history.

In this atmosphere there was no greater hero than Robert E. Lee, and the publication of his letters helped propagate his legend. *Recollections and Letters* concentrated more on Lee's character than on his military career. Only about one-third of the book featured correspondence from the general's years in the service of the Confederacy, and this was undoubtedly by design. Lee's military career alone was a story of defeat, but by concentrating on his character, the story changed to one of perseverance and triumph over adversity. Not only did this help make Lee more popular than ever, it mirrored what many white Southerners wanted to believe about their region. In short, Lee's story became the South's story in the minds of many Southerners. Just as Lee's character prevailed after a terrible defeat, the South would persevere in kind.

The letters and other correspondence in the book were arranged chronologically, and commentary by Rob Lee placed the material in context. The younger Lee's affection for his father was evident through his words, and through the themes of the letters chosen for inclusion in the book. Indeed, he titled one of the book's chapters "An Ideal Father." Many of the elder Lee's letters were written to his wife and children, highlighting a devotion to family at an emotional level not previously associated with the stately general. Lee wrote letters of encouragement to his family, expressed concern over his sons who were serving in the Confederate army, and lamented the death of his daughter during the war years. However, devotion to family was only one of the themes of the work. While Lee's image as a commanding general is a familiar one, much of *Recollections and Letters* dealt with Lee as a private citizen. Devotion to duty was a constant theme in the letters, particularly after Lee assumed the presidency of Washington College. Lee turned down more lucrative offers and shunned politics to dedicate all of his energies to the school. He refused to profit from his status and seemed acutely aware that many ex-Confederates across the defeated South looked to him as an example of how they should behave. Lee's letters also emphasized the personal attention that he paid to the students under his care, particularly in the chapter of the book that Rob Lee titled "An Advisor to Young Men."

The myth of Robert E. Lee as we recognize it today was certainly enhanced with the original publication of *Recollections and Letters*. The book was well received by the American public and by the national press. *The New York Times* told its readers that Lee's true character was unknown before the book's publication, and that in the work Lee's modesty, courage, humility, and "grandeur of soul" were recorded "so beautifully that scorners were subdued to contrition." Other widely read publications expressed similar sentiments, as if a holy grail had been discovered, a blueprint for both the Southern and the American conscience. Soon other writers began emphasizing Lee's character as well as his military acumen, heaping praise upon the general until actual memory intertwined with myth. The result was an ideal that no human being could ever live up to. Lee's faults were erased from public memory and he was transformed into a man of perfect character, placed upon a pedestal as the epitome of grace and dignity.

Lee moved from Southern icon to national icon in part due to his conduct after the war. From his post at Washington College he advocated reconciliation between the North and the South, serving as a role model for all former Confederates struggling to find their place in a reconstructed United States. He urged the South to accept defeat, counseled moderation and, in so doing, helped facilitate sectional reunion. For this Lee was revered in a way that many other Confederate generals, and certainly most Confederate politicians, were not. Unlike men such as James Ewell Brown "Jeb" Stuart or Thomas J. "Stonewall" Jackson, who achieved cultural sainthood in the South after death on the battlefield, Lee became a true national figure. His postwar prestige, both national and international, was unlike that of any other figure from the Civil War. "The people of Virginia and of the entire South," Rob Lee remembered, "were continually giving evidence of their intense love for General Lee. From all nations, even from the Northern states, came to him marks of admiration and respect." While the younger Lee composed these words a century ago, the sentiment that they reflected remains today in the hearts and minds of many Americans. Lee is, oddly enough, a quintessential American hero to many despite the fact that he took up arms against the United States, an act that we now consider one of the definitions of treason. But Robert E. Lee remains a rebel rather than a traitor, a man to be admired in defeat rather than pitied. A century later, Rob Lee's affection for his father is still apparent in the pages of *Recollections and Letters*. More important, the book brings the general back to life today just as it did the day it was first published. Robert E. Lee's words still resonate, and he continues to demand attention as a larger-than-life figure in American history.

Ben Wynne is a member of the history faculty at Florida State University. He holds a Ph.D. in history from the University of Mississippi, and he writes frequently on the Civil War era as well as on the history of his native Mississippi.

CHAPTER I

SERVICES IN THE UNITED STATES ARMY

CAPTAIN LEE, OF THE ENGINEERS, A HERO TO HIS
CHILD — THE FAMILY PETS — HOME FROM THE MEXICAN
WAR — THREE YEARS IN BALTIMORE — SUPERINTENDENT
OF THE WEST POINT MILITARY ACADEMY — LIEUTENANT-
COLONEL OF SECOND CAVALRY — SUPPRESSES "JOHN
BROWN RAID" AT HARPER'S FERRY — COMMANDS THE
DEPARTMENT OF TEXAS

THE first vivid recollection I have of my father is his arrival at
Arlington, after his return from the Mexican War. I can remember some events of which he seemed a part, when we lived at
Fort Hamilton, New York, about 1846, but they are more like
dreams, very indistinct and disconnected—naturally so, for I
was at that time about three years old. But the day of his return
to Arlington, after an absence of more than two years, I have
always remembered. I had a frock or blouse of some light wash
material, probably cotton, a blue ground dotted over with white
diamond figures. Of this I was very proud, and wanted to wear it
on this important occasion. Eliza, my "mammy," objecting, we
had a contest and I won. Clothed in this, my very best, and with
my hair freshly curled in long golden ringlets, I went down into
the large hall where the whole household was assembled,

eagerly greeting my father, who had just arrived on horseback from Washington, having missed in some way the carriage which had been sent for him.

There was visiting us at this time Mrs. Lippitt, a friend of my mother's, with her little boy, Armistead, about my age and size, also with long curls. Whether he wore as handsome a suit as mine I cannot remember, but he and I were left together in the background, feeling rather frightened and awed. After a moment's greeting to those surrounding him, my father pushed through the crowd, exclaiming:

"Where is my little boy?"

He then took up in his arms and kissed—not me, his own child in his best frock with clean face and well-arranged curls—but my little playmate, Armistead! I remember nothing more of any circumstances connected with that time, save that I was shocked and humiliated. I have no doubt that he was at once informed of his mistake and made ample amends to me.

A letter from my father to his brother Captain S. S. Lee, United States Navy, dated "Arlington, June 30, 1848," tells of his coming home:

"Here I am once again, my dear Smith, perfectly surrounded by Mary and her precious children, who seem to devote themselves to staring at the furrows in my face and the white hairs in my head. It is not surprising that I am hardly recognisable to some of the young eyes around me and perfectly unknown to the youngest. But some of the older ones gaze with astonishment and wonder at me, and seem at a loss to reconcile what they see and what was pictured in their imaginations. I find them, too, much grown, and all well, and I have much cause for thankfulness, and gratitude to that good God who has once more united us."

My next recollection of my father is in Baltimore, while we were on a visit to his sister, Mrs. Marshall, the wife of Judge Marshall. I remember being down on the wharves, where my father had taken me to see the landing of a mustang pony which he had gotten for me in Mexico, and which had been shipped from Vera Cruz to Baltimore in a sailing vessel. I was all eyes for the pony, and a very miserable, sad-looking object he was. From his long voyage, cramped quarters and unavoidable lack of grooming, he was rather a disappointment to me, but I soon got over all that. As I grew older, and was able to ride and appreciate him, he became the joy and pride of my life. I was taught to ride on him by Jim Connally, the faithful Irish servant of my father, who had been with him in Mexico. Jim used often to tell me, in his quizzical way, that he and "Santa Anna" (the pony's name) were the first men on the walls of Chepultepec. This pony was pure white, five years old and about fourteen hands high. For his inches, he was as good a horse as I ever have seen. While we lived in Baltimore, he and "Grace Darling," my father's favourite mare, were members of our family.

Grace Darling was a chestnut of fine size and of great power, which he had bought in Texas on his way out to Mexico, her owner having died on the march out. She was with him during the entire campaign, and was shot seven times; at least, as a little fellow I used to brag about that number of bullets being in her, and since I could point out the scars of each one, I presume it was so. My father was very much attached to and proud of her, always petting her and talking to her in a loving way, when he rode her or went to see her in her stall. Of her he wrote on his return home:

"I only arrived yesterday, after a long journey up the Mississippi, which route I was induced to take, for the better accommodation of my horse, as I wished to spare her as much annoyance and fatigue as possible, she already having undergone so much suffering in my service. I landed her at Wheeling and left her to come over with Jim."

Santa Anna was found lying cold and dead in the park at Arlington one morning in the winter of '60–'61. Grace Darling was taken in the spring of '62 from the White House[1] by some Federal quartermaster, when McClellan occupied that place as his base of supplies during his attack on Richmond. When we lived in Baltimore, I was greatly struck one day by hearing two ladies who were visiting us saying:

3

"Everybody and everything—his family, his friends, his horse, and his dog—loves Colonel Lee."

The dog referred to was a black-and-tan terrier named "Spec," very bright and intelligent and really a member of the family, respected and beloved by ourselves and well known to all who knew us. My father picked up his mother in the "Narrows" while crossing from Fort Hamilton to the fortifications opposite on Staten Island. She had doubtless fallen overboard from some passing vessel and had drifted out of sight before her absence had been discovered. He rescued her and took her home, where she was welcomed by his children and made much of. She was a handsome little thing, with cropped ears and a short tail. My father named her "Dart." She was a fine ratter, and with the assistance of a Maltese cat, also a member of the family, the many rats which infested the house and stables were driven away or destroyed. She and the cat were fed out of the same plate, but Dart was not allowed to begin the meal until the cat had finished.

Spec was born at Fort Hamilton and was the joy of us children, our pet and companion. My father would not allow his tail and ears to be cropped. When he grew up, he accompanied us everywhere and was in the habit of going into church with the family. As some of the little ones allowed their devotions to be disturbed by Spec's presence, my father determined to leave him at home on those occasions. So the next Sunday morning, he was sent up to the front room of the second story. After the family had left for church he contented himself for awhile looking out of the window, which was open, it being summer time. Presently impatience overcame his judgment and he jumped to the ground, landed safely notwithstanding the distance, joined the family just as they reached the church, and went in with them as usual, much to the joy of the children. After that he was allowed to go to church whenever he wished. My father was very fond of him, and loved to talk to him and about him as if he were really one of us. In a letter to my mother, dated Fort Hamilton, January 18, 1846, when she and her children were on a visit to Arlington, he thus speaks of him:

". . . I am very solitary, and my only company is my dog and cats. But 'Spec' has become so jealous now that he will hardly let me look at the cats. He seems to be afraid that I am going off from him, and never lets me stir without him. Lies down in the office from eight to four without moving, and turns himself before the fire as the side from it becomes cold. I catch him sometimes sitting up looking at me so intently that I am for a moment startled. . . ."

In a letter from Mexico written a year later—December 25, '46, to my mother, he says:

". . . Can't you cure poor 'Spec.' Cheer him up—take him to walk with you and tell the children to cheer him up. . . ."

In another letter from Mexico to his eldest boy, just after the capture of Vera Cruz, he sends this message to Spec. . . .

"Tell him I wish he was here with me. He would have been of great service in telling me when I was coming upon the Mexicans. When I was reconnoitering around Vera Cruz, their dogs frequently told me by barking when I was approaching them too nearly. . . ."

When he returned to Arlington from Mexico, Spec was the first to recognise him, and the extravagance of his demonstrations of delight left no doubt that he knew at once his kind master and loving friend, though he had been absent three years. Sometime during our residence in Baltimore, Spec disappeared, and we never knew his fate.

From that early time I began to be impressed with my father's character, as compared with other men. Every member of the household respected, revered and loved him as a matter of course, but it began to dawn on me that every one else with whom I was thrown held him high in their regard. At forty-five years of age he was active, strong, and as handsome as he had ever been. I never remember his being ill. I presume he was indisposed at times; but no impressions of that kind remain. He was always bright and gay with us little folk, romping, playing, and joking with us. With the older children, he was just as companionable, and I have seen him join my elder brothers and their friends when they would try their powers at a high jump put up in our yard. The two younger children he petted a great deal, and our greatest treat was to get into his bed in the morning and lie close to him, listening while he talked to us in his bright, entertaining way. This custom we kept up until I was ten years old and over. Although he was so joyous and familiar with us, he was very firm on all proper occasions, never indulged us in anything that was not good for us, and exacted the most implicit obedience. I always knew that it was impossible to disobey my father. I felt it in me, I never thought why, but was perfectly sure when he gave an order that it had to be obeyed. My mother I could sometimes circumvent, and at times took liberties with her orders, construing them to suit myself; but exact obedience to every mandate of my father was a part of my life and being at that time. He was very fond of having his hands tickled, and, what was still more curious, it pleased and delighted him to take off his slippers and place his feet in our laps in order to have them tickled. Often, as little things, after romping all day, the enforced sitting would be too much for us, and our drowsiness would soon show itself in continued nods. Then, to arouse us, he had a way of stirring us up with his foot—laughing heartily at and with us. He would often tell us the most delightful stories, and then there was no nodding. Sometimes, however, our interest in his wonderful tales became so engrossing that we would forget to do our duty—when he would declare, "No tickling, no story!" When we were a little older, our elder sister told us one winter the ever-delightful "Lady of the Lake." Of course, she told it in prose and arranged it to suit our mental capacity. Our father was generally in his corner by the fire, most probably with a foot in either the lap of myself or

ROBERT E. LEE
Photographed in 1850 or '51, when he was
Brevet Lieutenant-Colonel of Engineers

youngest sister—the tickling going on briskly—and would come in at different points of the tale and repeat line after line of the poem—much to our disapproval—but to his great enjoyment.

In January, 1849, Captain Lee was one of a board of army officers appointed to examine the coasts of Florida and its defenses and to recommend locations for new fortifications. In April he was assigned to the duty of the construction of Fort Carroll, in the Patapsco River below Baltimore. He was there, I think, for three years, and lived in a house on Madison Street, three doors above Biddle. I used to go down with him to the Fort quite often. We went to the wharf in a "bus," and there we were met by a boat with two oarsmen, who rowed us down to Sollers Point, where I was generally left under the care of the people who lived there, while my father went over to the Fort, a short distance out in the river. These days were very happy ones for me. The wharves, the shipping, the river, the boat and oarsmen, and the country dinner we had at the house at Sollers Point, all made a strong impression on me; but above all I remember my father, his gentle, loving care of me, his bright talk, his stories, his maxims and teachings. I was very proud of him and of the evident respect for and trust in him every one showed. These impressions, obtained at that time, have never left me. He was a great favourite in Baltimore, as he was everywhere, especially with ladies and little children. When he and my mother went out in the evening to some entertainment, we were often allowed to sit up and see them off; my father, as I remember, always in full uniform, always ready and waiting for my mother, who was generally late. He would chide her gently, in a playful way and with a bright smile. He would then bid us good-bye, and I would go to sleep with this beautiful picture in my mind, the golden epaulets and all—chiefly the epaulets.

In Baltimore, I went to my first school, that of a Mr. Rollins on Mulberry Street, and I remember how interested my father was in my studies, my failures, and my little triumphs. Indeed, he was so always, as long as I was at school and college, and I only wish that all of the kind, sensible, useful letters he wrote me had been preserved.

My memory as to the move from Baltimore, which occurred in 1852, is very dim. I think the family went to Arlington to remain until my father had arranged for our removal to the new home at West Point.

My recollection of my father as Superintendent of the West Point Military Academy is much more distinct. He lived in the house which is still occupied by the Superintendent. It was built of stone, large and roomy, with gardens, stables, and pasture lots. We, the two youngest children, enjoyed it all. "Grace Darling" and "Santa Anna" were there with us, and many a fine ride did I have with my father in the afternoons, when, released from his office, he would mount his old mare and, with Santa Anna carrying me by his side, take a five- or ten-mile trot. Though the pony cantered delightfully, he would make me keep him in a trot, saying playfully that the hammering I sustained was good for me. We rode the dragoon-seat, no posting, and until I became accustomed to it I used to be very tired by the time I got back.

My father was the most punctual man I ever knew. He was always ready for family prayers, for meals, and met every engagement, social or business, at the moment. He expected all of us to be the same, and taught us the use and necessity of forming such habits for the convenience of all concerned. I never knew him late for Sunday service at the Post Chapel. He used to appear some minutes before the rest of us, in uniform, jokingly rallying my mother for being late, and for forgetting something at the last moment. When he could wait no longer for her, he would say that he was off and would march along to church by himself, or with any of the children who were ready. There he sat very straight— well up the middle aisle—and, as I remember, always became very sleepy, and sometimes even took a little nap during the sermon. At that time, this drowsiness of my father's was something awful to me, inexplicable. I know it was very hard for me to keep awake, and frequently I did not; but why he, who to my mind could do everything that was right, without any effort, should sometimes be overcome, I could not understand, and did not try to do so.

It was against the rules that the cadets should go beyond certain limits without permission. Of course they did go sometimes, and when caught were given quite a number of "demerits." My father was riding out one afternoon with me, and, while rounding a turn in the mountain road with a deep woody ravine on one side, we came suddenly upon three cadets far beyond the limits. They immediately leaped over a low wall on the side of the road and disappeared from our view. We rode on for a minute in silence; then my father said: "Did you know those young men? But no; if you did, don't say so. I wish boys would do what is right, it would be so much easier for all parties!"

He knew he would have to report them, but, not being sure of who they were, I presume he wished to give them the benefit of the doubt. At any rate, I never heard any more about it. One of the three asked me next day if my father had recognised them, and I told him what had occurred.

By this time I had become old enough to have a room to myself, and, to encourage me in being useful and practical, my father made me attend to it, just as the cadets had to do with their quarters in barracks and in camp. He at first even went through the form of inspecting it, to see if I had performed my duty properly, and I think I enjoyed this until the novelty wore off. However, I was kept at it, becoming in time very proficient, and the knowledge so acquired has been of great use to me all through life.

My father always encouraged me in every healthy outdoor exercise and sport. He taught me to ride, constantly giving me minute instructions, with the reasons for them. He gave me my first sled, and sometimes used to come out where we boys were coasting to look on. He gave me my first pair of skates, and placed me in the care of a trustworthy person, inquiring regularly how I progressed. It was the same with swimming, which he was very anxious I should learn in a proper manner. Professor Bailey had a son about my age, now himself a professor at Brown University, Providence, Rhode Island, who became my great chum. I took my first lesson in the water with him, under the direction and supervision of his father.

My father inquired constantly how I was getting along, and made me describe exactly my method and stroke, explaining to me what he considered the best way to swim, and the reasons therefor.

I went to a day-school at West Point, and had always a sympathetic helper in my father. Often he would come into the room where I studied at night, and, sitting down by me, would show me how to overcome a hard sentence in my Latin reader or a difficult sum in arithmetic, not by giving me the translation of the troublesome sentence or the answer to the sum, but by showing me, step by step, the way to the right solutions. He was very patient, very loving, very good to me, and I remember trying my best to please him in my studies. When I was able to bring home a good report from my teacher, he was greatly pleased, and showed it in his eye and voice, but he always insisted that I should get the "maximum," that he would never be perfectly satisfied with less. That I did sometimes win it, deservedly, I know was due to his judicious and wise method of exciting my ambition and perseverance. I have endeavoured to show how fond my father was of his children, and as the best picture I can offer of his loving, tender devotion to us all, I give here a letter from him written about this time to one of his daughters who was staying with our grandmother, Mrs. Custis, at Arlington:

"WEST POINT, February 25, 1853.

"*My Precious Annie*: I take advantage of your gracious permission to write to you, and there is no telling how far my feelings might carry me were I not limited by the conveyance furnished by the Mim's[2] letter, which lies before me, and which must, the Mim says so, go in this morning's mail. But my limited time does not diminish my affection for you, Annie, nor prevent my thinking of you and wishing for you. I long to see you through the dilatory nights. At dawn when I rise, and all day, my thoughts revert to you in expressions that you cannot hear or I repeat. I hope you will always appear to me as you are now painted on my heart, and that you will endeavour to improve and so conduct yourself as to make you happy and me joyful all our lives. Diligent and earnest attention to *all* your duties can only accomplish this. I am told you are growing very tall, and I hope very straight. I do not know what the Cadets will say if the Superintendent's *children* do not practice what he demands of them. They will naturally say he had better attend to his own before he corrects other people's children, and as he permits his to stoop it is hard he will not allow them. You and Agnes[3] must not, therefore, bring me into discredit with my young friends, or give them reason to think that I require more of them than of my own. I presume your mother has told all about us, our neighbours and our affairs. And indeed she may have done that and not said much either, so far as I know. But we are all well and have much to be grateful for. To-morrow we anticipate the pleasure of your brother's[4] company, which is always a source of pleasure to us. It is the only time we see him, except when the Corps come under my view at some of their exercises, when my eye is sure to distinguish him among his comrades and follow him over the plain. Give much love to your dear grandmother, grandfather, Agnes, Miss Sue, Lucretia, and all friends, including the servants. Write sometimes, and think always of your

Affectionate father,

R. E. LEE."

In a letter to my mother written many years previous to this time, he says:

"I pray God to watch over and direct our efforts in guarding our dear little son. . . . Oh, what pleasure I lose in being separated from my children! Nothing can compensate me for that. . . ."

In another letter of about the same time:

"You do not know how much I have missed you and the children, my dear Mary. To be alone in a crowd is very solitary. In the woods, I feel sympathy with the trees and birds, in whose company I take delight, but experience no pleasure in a strange crowd. I hope you are all well and will continue so, and, therefore, must again urge

11

you to be very prudent and careful of those dear children. If I could only get a squeeze at that little fellow, turning up his sweet mouth to 'keese baba!' You must not let him run wild in my absence, and will have to exercise firm authority over all of them. This will not require severity or even strictness, but constant attention and an unwavering course. Mildness and forbearance will strengthen their affection for you, while it will maintain your control over them."

In a letter to one of his sons he writes as follows:

"I cannot go to bed, my dear son, without writing you a few lines, to thank you for your letter, which gave me great pleasure. . . . You and Custis must take great care of your kind mother and dear sisters when your father is dead. To do that you must learn to be good. Be true, kind and generous, and pray earnestly to God to enable you to keep His Commandments 'and walk in the same all the days of your life.' I hope to come on soon to see that little baby you have got to show me. You must give her a kiss for me, and one to all the children, to your mother, and grandmother."

The expression of such sentiments as these was common to my father all through his life, and to show that it was all children, and not his own little folk alone that charmed and fascinated him, I quote from a letter to my mother:

". . . I saw a number of little girls all dressed up in their white frocks and pantalets, their hair plaited and tied up with ribbons, running and chasing each other in all directions. I counted twenty-three nearly the same size. As I drew up my horse to admire the spectacle, a man appeared at the door with the twenty-fourth in his arms.

"'My friend,' said I, 'are all these your children?'

"'Yes,' he said, 'and there are nine more in the house, and this is the youngest.'

"Upon further inquiry, however, I found that they were only temporarily his, and that they were invited to a party at his house.

He said, however, he had been admiring them before I came up, and just wished that he had a million of dollars, and that they were all his in reality. I do not think the eldest exceeded seven or eight years old. It was the prettiest sight I have seen in the west, and, perhaps, in my life. . . ."

As Superintendent of the Military Academy at West Point my father had to entertain a good deal, and I remember well how handsome and grand he looked in uniform, how genial and bright, how considerate of everybody's comfort of mind and body. He was always a great favourite with the ladies, especially the young ones. His fine presence, his gentle, courteous manners and kindly smile put them at once at ease with him.

Among the cadets at this time were my eldest brother, Custis, who graduated first in his class in 1854, and my father's nephew, Fitz. Lee, a third classman, besides other relatives and friends. Saturday being a half-holiday for the cadets, it was the custom for all social events in which they were to take part to be placed on that afternoon or evening. Nearly every Saturday a number of these young men were invited to our house to tea, or supper, for it was a good, substantial meal. The misery of some of these lads, owing to embarrassment, possibly from awe of the Superintendent, was pitiable and evident even to me, a boy of ten or eleven years old. But as soon as my father got command, as it were, of the situation, one could see how quickly most of them were put at their ease. He would address himself to the task of making them feel comfortable and at home, and his genial manner and pleasant ways at once succeeded.

In the spring of '53 my grandmother, Mrs. Custis, died. This was the first death in our immediate family. She was very dear to us, and was admired, esteemed and loved by all who had ever known her. Bishop Meade, of Virginia, writes of her:

"Mrs. Mary Custis, of Arlington, the wife of Mr. Washington Custis, grandson of Mrs. General Washington, was the daughter of Mr. William Fitzhugh, of Chatham. Scarcely is there a Christian lady in our land more honoured than she was, and none more loved and esteemed. For good sense, prudence, sincerity, benevolence, unaffected piety, disinterested zeal in every good work, deep humarity and retiring modesty—for all the virtues which adorn the wife, the mother, and the friend—I never knew her superior."

In a letter written to my mother soon after this sad event my father says:

"May God give you strength to enable you to bear and say, 'His will be done.' She has gone from all trouble, care and sorrow to a holy immortality, there to rejoice and praise forever the God and Saviour she so long and truly served. Let that be our comfort and that our consolation. May our death be like hers, and may we meet in happiness in Heaven."

In another letter about the same time he writes:

"She was to me all that a mother could be, and I yield to none in admiration for her character, love for her virtues, and veneration for her memory."

At this time, my father's family and friends persuaded him to allow R. S. Weir, Professor of Painting and Drawing at the Academy, to paint his portrait. As far as I remember, there was only one sitting, and the artist had to finish it from memory or from the glimpses he obtained of his subject in the regular course of their daily lives at "The Point." This picture shows my father in the undress uniform of a Colonel of Engineers,[5] and many think it a very good likeness. To me, the expression of strength peculiar to his face is wanting, and the mouth fails to portray that sweetness of disposition so characteristic of his countenance. Still, it was like him at that time. My father never could bear to have his picture taken, and there are no likenesses of him that really give his sweet expression. Sitting for a picture was such a serious business with him that he never could "look pleasant."

In 1855 my father was appointed to the lieutenant-colonelcy of the Second Cavalry, one of the two regiments just raised. He left West Point to enter upon his new duties, and his family went to Arlington to live. During the fall and winter of 1855 and '56, the Second Cavalry was recruited and organised at Jefferson Barracks, Missouri, under the direction of Colonel Lee, and in the following spring was marched to western Texas, where it was assigned the duty of protecting the settlers in that wild country.

I did not see my father again until he came to my mother at Arlington after the death of her father, G. W. P. Custis, in October, 1857. He took charge of my mother's estate after her father's death, and commenced at once to put it in order—not an easy task, as it consisted of several plantations and many negroes. I was at a boarding-school, after the family returned to Arlington, and saw my father only during the holidays, if he happened to be at home. He was always fond of farming, and took great interest in the improvements he immediately began at Arlington relating to the cultivation of the farm, to the buildings, roads, fences, fields, and stock, so that in a very short time the appearance of everything on the estate was improved. He often said that he longed for the time when he could have a farm of his own, where he could end his days in quiet and peace, interested in the care and improvement of his own land. This idea was always with him. In a letter to his son, written in July, '65, referring to some proposed indictments of prominent Confederates, he says:

". . . As soon as I can ascertain their intention toward me, if not prevented, I shall endeavour to procure some humble, but quiet abode for your mother and sisters, where I hope they can be happy. As I before said, I want to get in some grass country where the natural product of the land will do much for my subsistence. . . ."

Again in a letter to his son, dated October, 1865, after he had accepted the presidency of Washington College, Lexington, Virginia:

"I should have selected a more quiet life and a more retired abode than Lexington. I should have preferred a small farm, where I could have earned my daily bread."

About this time I was given a gun of my own and was allowed to go shooting by myself. My father, to give me an incentive, offered a reward for every crow-scalp I could bring him, and, in order that I might get to work at once, advanced a small sum with which to buy powder and shot, this sum to be returned to him out of the first scalps obtained. My industry and zeal were great, my hopes high, and by good luck I did succeed in bagging two crows about the second time I went out. I showed them with great pride to my father, intimating that I should shortly be able to return him his loan, and that he must be prepared to hand over to me very soon further rewards for my skill. His eyes twinkled, and his smile showed that he had strong doubts of my making an income by killing crows, and he was right, for I never killed another, though I tried hard and long.

I saw but little of my father after we left West Point. He went to Texas, as I have stated, in '55 and remained until the fall of '57, the time of my grandfather's death. He was then at Arlington about a year. Returning to his regiment, he remained in Texas until the autumn of '59, when he came again to Arlington, having applied for leave in order to finish the settling of my grandfather's estate. During this visit he was selected by the Secretary of War to suppress the famous "John Brown Raid," and was sent to Harper's Ferry in command of the United States troops.

From his memorandum book the following entries are taken:

"October 17, 1859. Received orders from the Secretary of War in person, to repair in evening train to Harper's Ferry.

"Reached Harper's Ferry at 11 P. M. . . . Posted marines in the United States Armory. Waited until daylight, as a number of citizens were held as hostages, whose lives were threatened. Tuesday about sunrise, with twelve marines, under Lieutenant Green, broke in the door of the engine-house, secured the insurgents, and relieved the prisoners unhurt. All the insurgents killed or mortally wounded, but four, John Brown, Stevens, Coppie, and Shields."

Brown was tried and convicted and sentenced to be hanged on December 2, 1859. Colonel Lee writes as follows to his wife:

"HARPER'S FERRY, December 1, 1859.

"I arrived here, dearest Mary, yesterday about noon, with four companies from Fort Monroe, and was busy all the evening and night getting accommodation for the men, etc., and posting sentinels and piquets to insure timely notice of the approach of the enemy. The night has passed off quietly. The feelings of the community seem to be calmed down, and I have been received with every kindness. Mr. Fry is among the officers from Old Point. There are several young men, former acquaintances of ours, as cadets, Mr. Bingham of Custis's class, Sam Cooper, etc., but the senior officers I never met before, except Captain Howe, the friend of our Cousin Harriet R———.

"I presume we are fixed here till after the 16th. To-morrow will probably be the last of Captain Brown. There will be less interest for the others, but still I think the troops will not be withdrawn till they are similarly disposed of.

"Custis will have informed you that I had to go to Baltimore the evening I left you, to make arrangements for the transportation for the troops. . . . This morning I was introduced to Mrs. Brown, who, with a Mrs. Tyndall and a Mr. and Mrs. McKim, all from Philadelphia, had come on to have a last interview with her husband. As it is a matter over which I have no control I referred them to General Taliaferro.[6]

"You must write to me at this place. I hope you are all well. Give love to everybody. Tell Smith[7] that no charming women have insisted on taking care of me as they are always doing of him—I am left to my own resources. I will write you again soon, and will always be truly and affectionately yours,

"Mrs. M. C. Lee.   R. E. LEE."

In February, 1860, he was ordered to take command of the Department of Texas. There he remained a year. The first months after his arrival were spent in the vain pursuit of the famous brigand, Cortinez, who was continually stealing across the Rio Grande, burning the homes, driving off the stock of the ranchmen, and then retreating into Mexico. The summer months he spent in San Antonio, and while there interested himself with the good people of that town in building an Episcopal church, to which he contributed largely.

CHAPTER II

THE CONFEDERATE GENERAL

RESIGNS FROM COLONELCY OF FIRST U. S. CAVALRY—
MOTIVES FOR THIS STEP—CHOSEN TO COMMAND VIRGINIA
FORCES—ANXIETY ABOUT HIS WIFE, FAMILY AND POSSES-
SIONS—CHIEF ADVISER TO PRESIDENT DAVIS—BATTLE OF
MANASSAS—MILITARY OPERATIONS IN WEST VIRGINIA—
LETTER TO STATE GOVERNOR

IN February, 1861, after the secession of Texas, my father was
ordered to report to General Scott, the Commander-in-Chief of
the United States Army. He immediately relinquished the command of his regiment, and departed from Fort Mason, Texas, for
Washington. He reached Arlington March 1st. April 17th, Virginia
seceded. On the 18th Colonel Lee had a long interview with
General Scott. On April 20th he tendered his resignation of his
commission in the United States Army. The same day he wrote to
General Scott the following letter:

"ARLINGTON, Virginia, April 20, 1861.

"*General:* Since my interview with you on the 18th inst. I have felt
that I ought no longer to retain my commission in the Army. I therefore tender my resignation, which I request you will recommend for
acceptance. It would have been presented at once but for the struggle it has cost me to separate myself from a service to which I have
devoted the best years of my life, and all the ability I possessed.

"During the whole of that time—more than a quarter of a century—I have experienced nothing but kindness from my superiors and a most cordial friendship from my comrades. To no one, General, have I been as much indebted as to yourself for uniform kindness and consideration, and it has always been my ardent desire to merit your approbation. I shall carry to the grave the most grateful recollections of your kind consideration, and your name and fame shall always be dear to me.

"Save in the defense of my native State, I never desire again to draw my sword.

"Be pleased to accept my most earnest wishes for the continuance of your happiness and prosperity, and believe me most truly yours,

"(Signed)
"R. E. Lee."

His resignation was written the same day.

"Arlington, Washington City P. O., April 20, 1861.
"Honourable Simon Cameron, Secretary of War.

"*Sir:* I have the honour to tender the resignation of my command as Colonel of the First Regiment of Cavalry.

"Very respectfully your obedient servant,
"R. E. Lee,
"Colonel First Cavalry."

To show further his great feeling in thus having to leave the army with which he had been associated so long, I give two more letters, one to his sister, Mrs. Anne Marshall, of Baltimore, the other to his brother, Captain Sydney Smith Lee, of the United States Navy:

"Arlington, Virginia, April 20, 1861.
"*My Dear Sister:* I am grieved at my inability to see you. . . . I have been waiting for a 'more convenient season,' which has brought to many before me deep and lasting regret. Now we are in a state of war which will yield to nothing. The whole South is in a state of

revolution, into which Virginia, after a long struggle, has been drawn; and though I recognise no necessity for this state of things, and would have forborne and pleaded to the end for redress of grievances, real or supposed, yet in my own person I had to meet the question whether I should take part against my native State.

"With all my devotion to the Union and the feeling of loyalty and duty of an American citizen, I have not been able to make up my mind to raise my hand against my relatives, my children, my home. I have therefore resigned my commission in the Army, and save in defense of my native State, with the sincere hope that my poor services may never be needed, I hope I may never be called on to draw my sword. I know you will blame me; but you must think as kindly of me as you can, and believe that I have endeavoured to do what I thought right.

"To show you the feeling and struggle it has cost me, I send you a copy of my letter of resignation. I have no time for more. May God guard and protect you and yours, and shower upon you everlasting blessings, is the prayer of your devoted brother,   R. E. Lee."

"Arlington, Virginia, April 20, 1860.

"*My Dear Brother Smith:* The question which was the subject of my earnest consultation with you on the 18th inst. has in my own mind been decided. After the most anxious inquiry as to the correct course for me to pursue, I concluded to resign, and sent in my resignation this morning. I wished to wait till the Ordinance of Secession should be acted on by the people of Virginia; but war seems to have commenced, and I am liable at any time to be ordered on duty which I could not conscientiously perform. To save me from such a position, and to prevent the necessity of resigning under orders, I had to act at once, and before I could see you again on the subject, as I had wished. I am now a private citizen, and have no other ambition than to remain at home. Save in defense of my native State, I have no desire ever again to draw my sword. I send you my warmest love.

"Your affectionate brother,

"R. E. Lee."

I will give here one of my father's letters, written after the war, in which is his account of his resignation from the United States Army:

"LEXINGTON, Virginia, February 25, 1868.
"HONOURABLE REVERDY JOHNSON,
"UNITED STATES SENATE, WASHINGTON, D. C.

"*My Dear Sir:* My attention has been called to the official report of the debate in the Senate of the United States, on the 19th instant, in which you did me the kindness to doubt the correctness of the statement made by the Honourable Simon Cameron, in regard to myself. I desire that you may feel certain of my conduct on the occasion referred to, so far as my individual statement can make you. I never intimated to any one that I desired the command of the United States Army; nor did I ever have a conversation with but one gentleman, Mr. Francis Preston Blair, on the subject, which was at his invitation, and, as I understood, at the instance of President Lincoln. After listening to his remarks, I declined the offer he made me, to take command of the army that was to be brought into the field; stating, as candidly and as courteously as I could, that, though opposed to secession and deprecating war, I could take no part in an invasion of the Southern States. I went directly from the interview with Mr. Blair to the office of General Scott; told him of the proposition that had been made to me, and my decision. Upon reflection after returning to my home, I concluded that I ought no longer to retain the commission I held in the United States Army, and on the second morning thereafter I forwarded my resignation to General Scott. At the time, I hoped that peace would have been preserved; that some way would have been found to save the country from the calamities of war; and I then had no other intention than to pass the remainder of my life as a private citizen. Two days afterward, upon the invitation of the Governor of Virginia, I repaired to Richmond; found that the Convention then in session had passed the ordinance withdrawing the State from the Union; and accepted the commission of commander of its forces, which was tendered me.

"These are the ample facts of the case, and they shew that Mr. Cameron has been misinformed.

"I am with great respect,

"Your obedient servant,
"R. E. LEE."

My father reached Richmond April 22, 1861. The next day he was introduced to the Virginia Convention, and offered by them the command of the military forces of his State. In his reply to Mr. John Janney, the President, who spoke for the Convention, he said:

"*Mr. President and Gentlemen of the Convention:* Deeply impressed with the solemnity of the occasion on which I appear before you, and profoundly grateful for the honour conferred upon me, I accept the position your partiality has assigned me, though I would greatly have preferred your choice should have fallen on one more capable.

"Trusting to Almighty God, an approving conscience, and the aid of my fellow-citizens, I will devote myself to the defense and service of my native State, in whose behalf alone would I have ever drawn my sword."

On April 26th, from Richmond, he wrote to his wife:

". . . I am very anxious about you. You have to move and make arrangements to go to some point of safety, which you must select. The Mount Vernon plate and pictures ought to be secured. Keep quiet while you remain and in your preparation. War is inevitable, and there is no telling when it will burst around you. Virginia, yesterday, I understand, joined the Confederate States. What policy they may adopt I cannot conjecture. May God bless and preserve you, and have mercy upon all our people, is the constant prayer of your affectionate husband,

"R. E. LEE."

On April 30th:

"On going to my room last night I found my trunk and sword there, and opening them this morning discovered the package of letters and was very glad to learn you were all well and as yet peaceful. I fear the latter state will not continue long. . . . I think therefore you had better prepare all things for removal, that is, the plate, pictures, etc., and be prepared at any moment. Where to go is the difficulty. When the war commences no place will be exempt, in my opinion, and indeed all the avenues into the State will be the scenes of military operations.

"There is no prospect or intention of the Government to propose a truce. Do not be deceived by it. . . . May God preserve you all and bring peace to our distracted country."

Again to my mother at Arlington:

"RICHMOND, May 2, 1861.

"*My dear Mary:* I received last night your letter of the 1st, with contents. It gave me great pleasure to learn that you were all well and in peace. You know how pleased I should be to have you and my dear daughters with me. That I fear cannot be. There is no place that I can expect to be but in the field, and there is no rest for me to look to. But I want you to be in a place of safety. . . . We have only to be resigned to God's will and pleasure, and do all we can for our protection. . . . I have just received Custis's letter of the 30th, inclosing the acceptance of my resignation. It is stated that it will take effect April 25th. I resigned on the 20th, and wished it to take effect that day. I cannot consent to its running on further, and he must receive no pay, if they tender it, beyond that day, but return the whole, if need be. . . ."

From another letter to my mother, dated May 8th:

". . . I grieve at the necessity that drives you from your home. I can appreciate your feelings on the occasion, and pray that you may receive comfort and strength in the difficulties that surround you. When I reflect upon the calamity impending over the country, my own sorrows sink into insignificance. . . . Be content and resigned to God's will. I shall be able to write seldom. Write to me, as your letters will be my greatest comfort. I send a check for $500; it is all I have in bank. Pay the children's school expenses. . . ."

To my mother, still at Arlington:

"RICHMOND, May 11, 1861.
"I have received your letter of the 9th from Arlington. I had supposed you were at Ravensworth. . . . I am glad to hear that you are at peace, and enjoying the sweet weather and beautiful flowers. You had better complete your arrangements and retire further from the scene of war. It may burst upon you at any time. It is sad to think of the devastation, if not ruin, it may bring upon a spot so endeared to us. But God's will be done. We must be resigned. May He guard and keep you all, is my constant prayer."

All this time my father was very hard at work organising and equipping the volunteers who were pouring into Richmond from the Southern States, but he was in constant correspondence with my mother, helping her all he could in her arrangements for leaving her home. His letters show that he thought of everything, even the least, and he gave the most particular directions about his family, their effects, the servants, the horses, the farm, pictures, plate, and furniture. Being called to Norfolk suddenly, before going he wrote to my mother:

"RICHMOND, May 16, 1861.
"*My Dear Mary:* I am called down to Norfolk and leave this afternoon. I expect to return Friday, but may be delayed. I write to advise you of my absence, in case you should not receive answers

to any letters that may arrive. I have not heard from you since I last wrote; nor have I anything to relate. I heard from my dear little Rob, who had an attack of chills and fever. He hoped to escape the next paroxysm. . . . I witnessed the opening of the convention[1] yesterday, and heard the good Bishop's[2] sermon, being the 50th anniversary of his ministry. It was a most impressive scene, and more than once I felt the tears coming down my cheek. It was from the text, 'and Pharaoh said unto Jacob, how old art thou?' It was full of humility and self-reproach. I saw Mr. Walker, Bishop Johns, Bishop Atkinson, etc. I have not been able to attend any other services, and presume the session will not be prolonged. I suppose it may be considered a small attendance. Should Custis arrive during my absence, I will leave word for him to take my room at the Spotswood till my return. Smith[3] is well and enjoys a ride in the afternoon with Mrs. Stannard. The charming women, you know, always find him out. Give much love to Cousin Anna, Nannie, and dear daughters. When Rob leaves the University take him with you.

"Truly and affectionately,   R. E. Lee."

By this time my mother and all the family had left Arlington. My brother, Custis, had joined my father in Richmond, the girls had gone to Fauquier county, to visit relatives, and my mother to Ravensworth, about ten miles from Arlington towards Fairfax Court House, where her aunt, Mrs. A. M. Fitzhugh, lived. Always considerate of the happiness and comfort of others, my father feared that his wife's presence at Ravensworth might possibly bring annoyance to "Cousin Anna," as he called our aunt, and he wrote to my mother, urging her not to remain there. He sympathised with her in having to leave her home, which she never saw again.

"Richmond, May 25, 1861.

"I have been trying, dearest Mary, ever since the receipt of your letter by Custis, to write to you. I sympathise deeply in your feelings at leaving your dear home. I have experienced them myself, and they are constantly revived. I fear we have not been grateful enough for the happiness there within our reach, and our heavenly Father has found it necessary to deprive us of what He has given us. I acknowledge my ingratitude, my transgressions, and my unworthiness, and submit with resignation to what he thinks proper to inflict upon me. We must trust all then to him, and I do not think it prudent or right for you to return there, while the United States troops occupy that country. I have gone over all this ground before, and have just written to Cousin Anna on the subject.

"While writing, I received a telegram from Cousin John Goldsborough[4], urging your departure 'South.' I suppose he is impressed with the risk of your present position, and in addition to the possibility, or probability, of personal annoyance to yourself, I fear your presence may provoke annoyance to Cousin Anna. But unless Cousin Anna goes with you, I shall be distressed about her being there alone. If the girls went to 'Kinloch' or 'Eastern View,' you and Cousin Anna might take care of yourselves, because you could get in the carriage and go off in an emergency. But I really am afraid that you may prove more harm than comfort to her. Mr. Wm. C. Rives has just been in to say that if you and Cousin Anna will go to his house, he will be very glad for you to stay as long as you please. That his son has a commodious house just opposite his, unoccupied, partially furnished; that you could, if you prefer, take that, bring up servants and what you desire, and remain there as independent as at home. . . . I must now leave the matter to you, and pray that God may guard you. I have no time for more. I know and feel the discomfort of your position, but it cannot be helped, and we must bear our trials like Christians. . . . If you and Cousin Anna choose to come here, you know how happy we shall be to see you. I shall take the field as soon now as I can. . . .

"Ever yours truly and devotedly,

"R. E. LEE."

Three days later he was at Manassas, only a short distance from Ravensworth, and he sent her this short note:

"MANASSAS, May 28, 1861.

"I reached here, dearest Mary, this afternoon. I am very much occupied in examining matters, and have to go out to look over the ground. Cousin John tempts me strongly to go down, but I never visit for many reasons. If for no other, to prevent compromising the house, for my visit would certainly be known.

"I have written to you fully and to Cousin Anna. I am decidedly of the opinion that it would be better for you to leave, on your account and Cousin Anna's. My only objection is the leaving Cousin Anna alone, if she will not go with you. If you prefer Richmond, go with Nannie. Otherwise, go to the upper country, as John indicates. I fear I cannot be with you anywhere. I do not think Richmond will be permanent.

"Truly,   R."

I may as well say here, that "Cousin Anna" never did leave "Ravensworth" during the war. She remained there, with only a few faithful servants, and managed to escape any serious molestation. "Nannie" was Mrs. S. S. Lee, who shortly after this time went to Richmond.

On May 25th my father was transferred, with all the Virginia troops, to the Confederate States Army. He ceased to be a Major-General, and became a Brigadier, no higher rank having been created as yet in the Confederate service. Later, when the rank was created, he was made a full general.

By the end of May, to quote from General Long,

"Lee had organised, equipped, and sent to the field more than thirty thousand men, and various regiments were in a forward state of preparation."

When the Confederate government moved from Montgomery to Richmond, and President Davis took charge of all military movements, my father was kept near him as his constant and trusted adviser. His experience as an engineer was of great service to the young Confederacy, and he was called upon often for advice for the location of batteries and troops on our different defensive lines. In a letter to my mother he speaks of one of these trips to the waters east of Richmond.

"RICHMOND, June 9, 1861.

". . . I have just returned from a visit to the batteries and troops on James and York rivers, etc., where I was some days. I called a few hours at the White House. Saw Charlotte and Annie. Fitzhugh was away, but got out of the cars as I got in. Our little boy looked very sweet and seemed glad to kiss me a good-bye. Charlotte said she was going to prepare to leave for the summer, but had not determined where to go. I could only see some of the servants about the house and the stables. They were all well. . . . You may be aware that the Confederate Government is established here. Yesterday I turned over to it the command of the military and naval forces of the State, in accordance with the proclamation of the Government and the agreement between the State and the Confederate States. I do not know what my position will be. I should like to retire to private life, if I could be with you and the children, but if I can be of any service to the State or her cause I must continue. Mr. Davis and all his Cabinet are here. . . . Good-bye. Give much love to kind friends. May God guard and bless you, them, and our suffering country, and enable me to perform my duty. I think of you constantly. Write me what you will do. Direct here.

"Always yours,
"R. E. LEE."

To my mother, who was now in Fauquier County, staying at "Kinloch," Mr. Edward Turner's home, he writes on June 24th, from Richmond:

". . . Your future arrangements are the source of much anxiety to me. No one can say what is in the future, nor is it wise to anticipate evil. But it is well to prepare for what may reasonably happen and be provided for the worst. There is no saying when you can return to your home or what may be its condition when you do return. What, then, can you do in the meantime? To remain with friends may be incumbent, and where can you go? . . . My movements are very uncertain, and I wish to take the field as soon as certain arrangements can be made. I may go at any moment, and to any point where it may be necessary. . . . Many of our old friends are dropping in. E. P. Alexander is here, Jimmy Hill, Alston, Jenifer, etc., and I hear that my old colonel, A. S. Johnston, is crossing the plains from California. . . .

"As ever,   R. E. LEE."

I again quote from a letter to my mother, dated Richmond, July 12, 1861:

". . . I am very anxious to get into the field, but am detained by matters beyond my control. I have never heard of the appointment, to which you allude, of Commander-in-Chief of the Confederate States Army, nor have I any expectation or wish for it. President Davis holds that position. Since the transfer of the military operations in Virginia to the authorities of the Confederate States, I have only occupied the position of a general in that service, with the duties devolved on me by the President. I have been labouring to prepare and get into the field the Virginia troops, and to strengthen, by those from the other States, the threatened commands of Johnston, Beauregard, Huger, Garnett, etc. Where I shall go I do not know, as that will depend upon President Davis. As usual in getting through with a thing, I have broken down a little and had to take my bed last evening, but am at my office this morning and hope will soon be right again. . . . My young friend Mr. Vest has just returned from a search in the city for 'Dixie,' and says he has visited every place in Richmond without finding it. I suppose it is exhausted. Always yours,

"R. E. LEE."

"The booksellers say 'Dixie' is not to be had in Virginia. R. E. L."

On July 21st occurred the battle of Manassas. In a letter to my mother written on the 27th, my father says:

". . . That indeed was a glorious victory and has lightened the pressure upon our front amazingly. Do not grieve for the brave dead. Sorrow for those they left behind—friends, relatives, and families. The former are at rest. The latter must suffer. The battle will be repeated there in greater force. I hope God will again smile on us and strengthen our hearts and arms. I wished to partake in the former struggle, and am mortified at my absence, but the President thought it more important I should be here. I could not have done as well as has been done, but I could have helped, and taken part in the struggle for my home and neighbourhood. So the work is done I care not by whom it is done. I leave to-morrow for the Northwest Army. I wished to go before, as I wrote you, and was all prepared, but the indications were so evident of the coming battle, and in the uncertainty of the result, the President forbade my departure. Now it is necessary and he consents. I cannot say for how long, but will write you. . . . I inclose you a letter from Markie.[5] Write to her if you can and thank her for her letter to me. I have not time. My whole time is occupied, and all my thoughts and strength are given to the cause to which my life, be it long or short, will be devoted. Tell her not to mind the reports she sees in the papers. They are made to injure and occasion distrust. Those that know me will not believe them. Those that do not will not care for them. I laugh at them. Give love to all, and for yourself accept the constant prayers and love of truly yours,

"R. E. LEE."

It was thought best at this time to send General Lee to take command of military operations in West Virginia. The ordinary difficulties of a campaign in this country of mountains and bad roads were greatly increased by incessant rains, sickness of all kinds amongst the new troops, and the hostility of many of the inhabitants to the Southern cause. My father's letters, which I will give here, tell of his trials and troubles, and describe at the same time the beauty of scenery and some of the military movements.

About August 1st he started for his new command and he writes to my mother on his arrival at Huntersville, Pocahontas County, now West Virginia:

"HUNTERSVILLE, August 4, 1861.

"I reached here yesterday, dearest Mary, to visit this portion of the army. The day after my arrival at Staunton, I set off for Monterey, where the army of General Garnett's command is stationed. Two regiments and a field-battery occupy the Alleghany Mountains in advance, about thirty miles, and this division guards the road to Staunton. The division here guards the road leading by the Warm Springs to Milboro and Covington. Two regiments are advanced about twenty-eight miles to Middle Mountain. Fitzhugh[6] with his squadron is between that point and this. I have not seen him. I understand he is well. South of here again is another column of our enemies, making their way up the Kanawha Valley, and, from General Wise's report, are not far from Lewisburgh. Their object seems to be to get possession of the Virginia Central Railroad and the Virginia and Tennessee Railroad. By the first they can approach Richmond; by the last interrupt our reinforcements from the South. The points from which we can be attacked are numerous, and their means are unlimited. So we must always be on the alert. My uneasiness on these points brought me out here. It is so difficult to get our people, unaccustomed to the necessities of war, to comprehend and promptly execute the measures required for the occasion. General Jackson of Georgia commands on the Monterey line, General Loring on this line, and General Wise, supported by General Floyd, on the Kanawha line. The soldiers everywhere are sick. The measles are prevalent throughout the whole army, and you know that disease leaves unpleasant results, attacks on the lungs, typhoid, etc., especially in camp, where accommodations for the sick are poor. I travelled from Staunton on horseback. A part of the road, as far as Buffalo Gap, I passed over in the summer of 1840, on my return to St. Louis, after bringing you home. If any one had then told me that the next time I travelled that road would have been on my present errand, I should have supposed him insane. I enjoyed the mountains, as I rode along. The views are magnificent—the valleys so beautiful, the scenery so peaceful. What a glorious world Almighty God has given us. How thankless and ungrateful we are, and how we labour to mar his gifts. I hope you received my letters from Richmond. Give love to daughter and Mildred. I did not see Rob as I passed through Charlottesville. He was at the University and I could not stop."

A few days later there is another letter:

"CAMP AT VALLEY MOUNTAIN, August 9, 1861.

"I have been here, dear Mary, three days, coming from Monterey to Huntersville and thence here. We are on the dividing ridge looking north down the Tygart's river valley, whose waters flow into the Monongahela and South towards the Elk River and Greenbrier, flowing into the Kanawha. In the valley north of us lie Huttonsville and Beverly, occupied by our invaders, and the Rich Mountains west, the scene of our former disaster, and the Cheat Mountains east, their present stronghold, are in full view.

"The mountains are beautiful, fertile to the tops, covered with the richest sward of bluegrass and white clover, the inclosed fields waving with the natural growth of timothy. The habitations are few and population sparse. This is a magnificent grazing country, and all it needs is labour to clear the mountain-sides of its great growth of timber. There surely is no lack of moisture at this time. It has rained, I believe, some portion of every day since I left Staunton. Now it is pouring, and the wind, having veered around to every point of the compass, has settled down to the northeast. What that portends in these regions I do not know. Colonel Washington[7],

Captain Taylor, and myself are in one tent, which as yet protects us. I have enjoyed the company of Fitzhugh since I have been here. He is very well and very active, and as yet the war has not reduced him much. He dined with me yesterday and preserves his fine appetite. To-day he is out reconnoitring and has the full benefit of this rain. I fear he is without his overcoat, as I do not recollect seeing it on his saddle. I told you he had been promoted to a major in cavalry, and is the commanding cavalry officer on this line at present. He is as sanguine, cheerful, and hearty as ever. I sent him some corn-meal this morning and he sent me some butter—a mutual interchange of good things. There are but few of your acquaintances in this army. I find here in the ranks of one company Henry Tiffany. The company is composed principally of Baltimoreans—George Lemmon and Douglas Mercer are in it. It is a very fine company, well drilled and well instructed. I find that our old friend, J. J. Reynolds, of West Point memory, is in command of the troops immediately in front of us. He is a brigadier-general. You may recollect him as the Assistant Professor of Philosophy, and lived in the cottage beyond the west gate, with his little, pale-faced wife, a great friend of Lawrence and Markie. He resigned on being relieved from West Point, and was made professor of some college in the West. Fitzhugh was the bearer of a flag the other day, and he recognised him. He was very polite and made kind inquiries of us all. I am told they feel very safe and are very confident of success. Their numbers are said to be large, ranging from 12,000 to 30,000, but it is impossible for me to get correct information either as to their strength or position. Our citizens beyond this are all on their side. Our movements seem to be rapidly communicated to them, while theirs come to us slowly and indistinctly. I have two regiments here, with others coming up. I think we shall shut up this road to the Central Railroad which they strongly threaten. Our supplies come up slowly. We have plenty of beef and can get some bread. I hope you are well and are content. I have heard nothing of you or the children since I left Richmond. You must write there. . . . The men are suffering from the measles, etc., as elsewhere, but are cheerful and light-hearted. The atmosphere, when it is not raining, is delightful. You must give much love to daughter and 'Life.'[8] I want to see you all very much, but I know not when that can be. May God guard and protect you all. In Him alone is our hope. Remember me to Ned[9] and all at 'Kinloch' and Avenel.[10] Send word to Miss Lou Washington[11] that her father is sitting on his blanket sewing the strap on his haversack. I think she ought to be here to do it.　　　　Always yours,

"R. E. LEE."

In a letter to his two daughters who were in Richmond, he writes:

"VALLEY MOUNTAIN, August 29, 1861.

"*My Precious Daughters:* I have just received your letters of the 24th and am rejoiced to hear that you are well and enjoying the company of your friends. . . . It rains here all the time, literally. There has not been sunshine enough since my arrival to dry my clothes. Perry[12] is my washerman, and socks and towels suffer. But the worst of the rain is that the ground has become so saturated with water that the constant travel on the roads has made them almost impassable, so that I cannot get up sufficient supplies for the troops to move. It is raining now. Has been all day, last night, day before, and day before that, etc., etc. But we must be patient. It is quite cool, too. I have on all my winter clothes and am writing in my overcoat. All the clouds seem to concentrate over this ridge of mountains, and by whatever wind they are driven, give us rain. The mountains are magnificent. The sugar-maples are beginning to turn already, and the grass is luxuriant.

"'Richmond'[13] has not been accustomed to such fare or such treatment. But he gets along tolerably, complains some, and has not much superfluous flesh. There has been much sickness among the men—measles, etc.—and the weather has been unfavourable. I hope their attacks are nearly over, and that they will come out with the sun. Our party has kept well. . . . Although we may be too weak to break through the lines, I feel well satisfied that the enemy cannot at present reach Richmond by either of these routes, leading to Staunton, Milborough or Covington. He must find some other way. . . . God bless you, my children, and preserve you from all harm is the constant prayer of

"Your devoted father,

"R. E. LEE."

On account of rheumatism, my mother was anxious to go to the Hot Springs in Bath County. She was now staying at "Audley," Clarke County, Virginia, with Mrs. Lorenzo Lewis, who had just sent her six sons into the army. Bath County was not very far from the seat of war in western Virginia, and my father was asked as to the safety of the Hot Springs from occupation by the enemy. He writes as follows to my mother:

"VALLEY MOUNTAIN, September 1, 1861.

"I have received, dearest Mary, your letter of August 18th from Audley, and am very glad to get news of your whereabouts. . . . I am very glad you are enabled to see so many of your friends. I hope you have found all well in your tour, and am very glad that our cousin Esther bears the separation from all her sons so bravely. I have no doubt they will do good service in our Southern cause, and wish they could be placed according to their fancies. . . . I fear you have postponed your visit to the Hot too late. It must be quite cold there now, judging from the temperature here, and it has been raining in these mountains since July 24th. . . . I see Fitzhugh quite often, though he is encamped four miles from me. He is very well and not at all harmed by the campaign.

"We have a great deal of sickness among the soldiers, and now those on the sick-list would form an army. The measles is still among them, though I hope it is dying out. But it is a disease which though light in childhood is severe in manhood, and prepares the system for other attacks. The constant cold rains, with no shelter but tents, have aggravated it. All these drawbacks, with impassable roads, have paralysed our efforts.

Still I think you will be safe at the Hot, for the present. We are right up to the enemy on the three lines, and in the Kanawha he has been pushed beyond the Gauley. . . . My poor little Rob I never hear from scarcely. He is busy, I suppose, and knows not where to direct. . . .

"With much affection,

"R. E. LEE."

From the same camp, to my mother, on September 9th:

". . . I hope from the tone of your letter that you feel better, and wish I could see you and be with you. I trust we may meet this fall somewhere, if only for a little time. I have written to Robert telling him if, after considering what I have previously said to him on the subject of his joining the company he desires under Major Ross, he still thinks it best for him to do so, I will not withhold my consent. It seems he will be eighteen; I thought seventeen. I am unable to judge for him and he must decide for himself. In reply to a recent letter from him to me on the same subject, I said to him all I could. I pray God to bring him to a right conclusion. . . . For military news, I must refer you to the papers. You will see there more than ever occurs, and what does occur the relation must be taken with some allowance. Do not believe anything you see about me. There has been no battle, only skirmishing with the outposts, and nothing done of any moment. The weather is still unfavourable to us. The roads, or rather tracks of mud, are almost impassable and the number of sick large. . . .

"Truly and devotedly yours,

"R. E. LEE."

My mother was at the Hot Springs—I had taken her there and was with her. I don't now remember why, but it was decided that I should return to the University of Virginia, which opened October 1st, and continue my course there. While at the Springs my mother received this letter from my father:

"VALLEY MOUNTAIN, September 17, 1861.

"I received, dear Mary, your letter of the 5th by Beverly Turner,[14] who is a nice young soldier. I am pained to see fine young men like him, of education and standing, from all the old and respectable families in the State, serving in the ranks. I hope in time they will receive their reward. I met him as I was returning from an expedition to the enemy's works, which I had hoped to have surprised on the morning of the 12th, both at Cheat Mountain and on Valley River. All the attacking parties with great labour had reached their destination, over mountains considered impassable to bodies of troops, notwithstanding a heavy storm that set in the day before and raged all night, in which they had to stand up till daylight. Their arms were then unserviceable, and they in poor condition for a fierce assault against artillery and superior numbers. After waiting till 10 o'clock for the assault on Cheat Mountain, which did not take place, and which was to have been the signal for the rest, they were withdrawn, and, after waiting three days in front of the enemy, hoping he would come out of his trenches, we returned to our position at this place. I can not tell you my regret and mortification at the untoward events that caused the failure of the plan. I had taken every precaution to ensure success and counted on it. But the Ruler of the Universe willed otherwise and sent a storm to disconcert a well-laid plan, and to destroy my hopes. We are no worse off now than before, except the disclosure of our plan, against which they will guard. We met with one heavy loss which grieves me deeply: Colonel Washington accompanied Fitzhugh on a reconnoitering expedition, and I fear they were carried away by their zeal and approached within the enemy's pickets. The first they knew was a volley from a concealed party within a few yards of them. Their balls passed through the Colonel's body, then struck Fitzhugh's horse, and the horse of one of the men was killed. Fitzhugh mounted the Colonel's horse and brought him off. I am much grieved. He was always anxious to go on these expeditions. This was the first day I assented. Since I had been thrown into such intimate relations with him, I had learned to appreciate him very highly. Morning and evening have I seen him on his knees praying to his Maker.

"'The righteous perisheth and no man layeth it to heart, and merciful men are taken away, none considering that the righteous is taken away from the evil to come.' May God have mercy on us all! I suppose you are at the Hot Springs and will direct to you there. Our poor sick, I know, suffer much. They bring it on themselves by not doing what they are told. They are worse than children, for the latter can be forced. . . .

"Truly yours,

"R. E. LEE."

On the same day he wrote to the Governor of Virginia:

"VALLEY MOUNTAIN, September 17, 1861.

"*My Dear Governor:* I received your very kind note of the 5th instant, just as I was about to accompany General Loring's command on an expedition to the enemy's works in front, or I would have before thanked you for the interest you take in my welfare, and your too flattering expressions of my ability. Indeed, you overrate me much, and I feel humbled when I weigh myself by your standard. I am, however, very grateful for your confidence, and I can answer for my sincerity in the earnest endeavour I make to advance the cause I have so much at heart, though conscious of the slow progress I make. I was very sanguine of taking the enemy's works on last Thursday morning. I had considered the subject well. With great effort the troops intended for the surprise had reached their destination, having traversed twenty miles of steep, rugged mountain paths; and the last day through a terrible storm, which lasted all night, and in which they had to stand drenched to the skin in cold rain. Still, their spirits were good. When morning broke, I could see the enemy's tents on Valley River, at the point on the Huttonsville road just below me. It was a tempting sight. We waited for the attack on Cheat Mountain, which was to be the signal. Till 10 A. M. the men were cleaning their unserviceable arms. But the signal did not come. All chance for a surprise was gone. The provisions of the men had been destroyed the preceding day by the storm. They had nothing to eat that morning, could not hold out another day, and were obliged to be withdrawn. The party sent to Cheat Mountain to take that in rear had also to be withdrawn. The attack to come off from the east side failed from the difficulties in the way; the opportunity was lost, and our plan discovered. It is a grievous disappointment to me, I assure you. But for the rain-storm, I have no doubt it would have succeeded. This, Governor, is for your own eye. Please do not speak of it; we must try again. Our greatest loss is the death of my dear friend, Colonel Washington. He and my son were reconnoitering the front of the enemy. They came unawares upon a concealed party, who fired upon them within twenty yards, and the Colonel fell pierced by three balls. My son's horse received three shots, but he escaped on the Colonel's horse. His zeal for the cause to which he had devoted himself carried him, I fear, too far. We took some seventy prisoners, and killed some twenty-five or thirty of the enemy. Our loss was small besides what I have mentioned. Our greatest difficulty is the roads. It has been raining in these mountains about six weeks. It is impossible to get along. It is that which has paralysed all our efforts. With sincere thanks for your good wishes,

"I am very truly yours,

"R. E. LEE.

"His Excellency, Governor John Letcher."

CHAPTER III

LETTERS TO WIFE AND DAUGHTERS

FROM CAMP ON SEWELL'S MOUNTAIN—QUOTATION FROM
COLONEL TAYLOR'S BOOK—FROM PROFESSOR WM. P. TRENT—
FROM MR. DAVIS'S MEMORIAL ADDRESS—DEFENSE OF
SOUTHERN PORTS—CHRISTMAS, 1861—THE GENERAL VISITS
HIS FATHER'S GRAVE—COMMANDS, UNDER THE PRESIDENT,
ALL THE ARMIES OF THE CONFEDERATE STATES

THE season being too far advanced to attempt any further movements away from our base of supplies, and the same reasons preventing any advance of the Federal forces, the campaign in this
part of Virginia ended for the winter. In the Kanawha Valley, however, the enemy had been and were quite active. Large reinforcements under General Rosecrans were sent there to assist General
Cox, the officer in command at that point. General Loring, leaving a sufficient force to watch the enemy at Cheat Mountain,
moved the rest of his army to join the commands of Generals
Floyd and Wise, who were opposing the advance of Cox. General
Lee, about September 20th, reached General Floyd's camp, and
immediately proceeded to arrange the lines of defense. Shortly
after his arrival there he wrote to my mother at the Hot Springs:

"CAMP ON SEWELL'S MOUNTAIN,
"September 26, 1861.

"I have just received, dear Mary, your letters of the 17th and 19th instants, with one from Robert. I have but little time for writing to-night, and will, therefore, write to you. . . . Having now disposed of business matters, I will say how glad I am to hear from you, and to learn that you have reached the Hot in safety, with daughter and Rob. I pray that its healing waters may benefit you all. I am glad to hear of Charlotte and the girls, and hope all will go well with them. I infer you received my letter written before leaving Valley Mountain, though you did not direct your letter 'via Lewisburg, Greenbrier County,' and hence its delay. I told you of the death of Colonel Washington. I grieve for his loss, though trust him to the mercy of our Heavenly Father. May He have mercy on us all.

"It is raining heavily. The men are all exposed on the mountain, with the enemy opposite to us. We are without tents, and for two nights I have lain buttoned up in my overcoat. To-day my tent came up and I am in it. Yet I fear I shall not sleep for thinking of the poor men. I wrote about socks for myself. I have no doubt the yarn ones you mention will be very acceptable to the men here or elsewhere. If you can send them here, I will distribute them to the most needy. Tell Rob I could not write to him for want of time. My heart is always with you and my children. May God guard and bless you all is the constant prayer of

"Your devoted husband,

"R. E. Lee."

To my mother, still at the Hot Springs:

"Sewell's Mountain, October 7, 1861.

"I received, dear Mary, your letter by Doctor Quintard, with the cotton socks. Both were very acceptable, though the latter I have not yet tried. At the time of their reception the enemy was threatening an attack, which was continued till Saturday night, when under cover of darkness he suddenly withdrew. Your letter of the 2d, with the yarn socks, four pairs, was handed to me when I was preparing to follow, and I could not at the time attend to either. But I have since, and as I found Perry in desperate need, I bestowed a couple of pairs on him, as a present from you. The others I have put in my trunk and suppose they will fall to the lot of Meredith,[1] into the state of whose hose I have not yet inquired. Should any sick man require them first, he shall have them, but Meredith will have no one near to supply him but me, and will naturally expect that attention. I hope, dear Mary, you and daughter, as well as poor little Rob, have derived some benefit from the sanitary baths of the Hot. What does daughter intend to do during the winter? And, indeed, what do you? It is time you were determining. There is no prospect of your returning to Arlington. I think you had better select some comfortable place in the Carolinas or Georgia, and all board together. If Mildred goes to school at Raleigh, why not go there? It is a good opportunity to try a warmer climate for your rheumatism. If I thought our enemies would not make a vigorous move against Richmond, I would recommend to rent a house there. But under these circumstances I would not feel as if you were permanently located if there. I am ignorant where I shall be. In the field somewhere, I suspect, so I have little hope of being with you, though I hope to be able to see you. . . . I heard from Fitzhugh the other day. He is well, though his command is greatly reduced by sickness. I wished much to bring him with me; but there is too much cavalry on this line now, and I am dismounting them. I could not, therefore, order more. The weather is almost as bad here as in the mountains I left. There was a drenching rain yesterday, and as I had left my overcoat in camp I was thoroughly wet from head to foot. It has been raining ever since and is now coming down with a will. But I have my clothes out on the bushes and they will be well washed.

"The force of the enemy, by a few prisoners captured yesterday and civilians on the road, is put down from 17,000 to 20,000. Some went as high as 22,000. General Floyd thinks 18,000. I do not think it exceeds 9,000 or 10,000, though it exceeds ours. I wish he had attacked us, as I believe he would have been repulsed with great loss. His plan was to attack us at all points at the same time. The rumbling of his wheels, etc., was heard by our pickets, but as that was customary at night in the moving and placing of his cannon, the officer of the day to whom it was reported paid no particular attention to it, supposing it to be a preparation for attack in the morning. When day appeared, the bird had flown, and the misfortune was that the reduced condition of our horses for want of provender, exposure to cold rains in these mountains, and want of provisions for the men prevented the vigorous pursuit and following up that was proper. We can only get up provisions from day to day—which paralyses our operations.

"I am sorry, as you say, that the movements of the armies cannot keep pace with the expectations of the editors of papers. I know they can regulate matters satisfactorily to themselves on paper. I wish they could do so in the field. No one wishes them more success than I do and would be happy to see them have full swing. I hope something will be done to please them. Give much love to the children and everybody, and believe me

"Always yours,

"R. E. Lee."

Colonel Taylor, in his "Four Years with General Lee," says:

"We had now reached the latter days of October. The lateness of the season and the condition of the roads precluded the idea of earnest, aggressive operations, and the campaign in western Virginia was virtually concluded.

"Judged from its results, it must be confessed that this series of operations was a failure. At its conclusion, a large portion of the State was in possession of the Federals, including the rich valleys of the Ohio and Kanawha rivers, and so remained until the close of the war. For this, however, General Lee cannot reasonably be held accountable. Disaster had befallen the Confederate arms, and the worst had been accomplished before he had reached the theatre of operations; the Alleghanies there constituted the dividing line between the hostile forces, and in this network of mountains,

sterile and rendered absolutely impracticable by a prolonged season of rain, Nature had provided an insurmountable barrier to
operations in this transmontane country. . . . It was doubtless
because of similar embarrassments that the Federal general retired,
in the face of inferior numbers, to a point near his base of supplies."

Professor William P. Trent, in his "Robert E. Lee," after describing briefly the movements of the contending armies, writes:

"There was, then, nothing to do but to acknowledge the campaign a failure. The Confederate Government withdrew its troops
and sent them elsewhere. Lee, whom the press abused and even
former friends began to regard as overrated, was assigned to command the Department of South Carolina, Georgia, and Florida;
and her western counties were lost to the Old Dominion forever. It
must have been a crushing blow to Lee at the time, but he bore it
uncomplainingly. . . . And when all is said, no commander, however great, can succeed against bad roads, bad weather, sickness of
troops, lack of judgment and harmony among subordinates, and a
strong, alert enemy. Yet this is what Lee was expected to do."

Mr. Davis, in an address before a memorial meeting at
Richmond in 1870, speaking of General Lee in this campaign, said:

"He came back, carrying the heavy weight of defeat, and unap-
preciated by the people whom he served, for they could not
know, as I knew, that, if his plans and orders had been carried
out, the result would have been victory rather than retreat. You
did not know it; for I should not have known it had he not
breathed it in my ear only at my earnest request, and begging that
nothing be said about it. The clamour which then arose followed
him when he went to South Carolina, so that it became necessary
on his departure to write a letter to the Governor of that State,
telling him what manner of man he was. Yet, through all this, with
a magnanimity rarely equalled, he stood in silence, without

defending himself or allowing others to defend him, for he was unwilling to offend any one who was wearing a sword and striking blows for the Confederacy."

After returning to Richmond, my father resumed his position as adviser and counsellor to Mr. Davis. From there he writes to my mother, who had left the Hot Springs and gone on a visit to "Shirley," on James River:

"RICHMOND, November 5, 1861.
"*My Dear Mary:* I received last night your letter of the 2d, and would have answered it at once, but was detained with the Secretary till after 11 P. M. I fear now I may miss the mail. Saturday evening I tried to get down to you to spend Sunday, but could find no government boat going down, and the passenger boats all go in the morning. I then went to the stable and got out my horse, but it was near night then and I was ignorant both of the road and distance and I gave it up. I was obliged to be here Monday, and as it would have consumed all Sunday to go and come, I have remained for better times. The President said I could not go to-day, so I must see what can be done to-morrow. I will come, however, wherever you are, either Shirley or the White House, as soon as possible, and if not sooner, Saturday at all events. . . . I am, as ever,   Yours,
"R. E. LEE."

The day after this letter was written, my father was ordered to South Carolina for the purpose of directing and supervising the construction of a line of defense along the southern coast. I give here several letters to members of his family which tell of his duties and manner of life:

"SAVANNAH, November 18, 1861.
"*My Dear Mary:* This is the first moment I have had to write to you, and now am waiting the call to breakfast, on my way to Brunswick, Fernandina, etc. This is my second visit to Savannah.

Night before last, I returned to Coosawhatchie, South Carolina, from Charleston, where I have placed my headquarters, and last night came here, arriving after midnight. I received in Charleston your letter from Shirley. It was a grievous disappointment to me not to have seen you, but better times will come, I hope. . . . You probably have seen the operations of the enemy's fleet. Since their first attack they have been quiescent apparently, confining themselves to Hilton Head, where they are apparently fortifying.

"I have no time for more. Love to all.

"Yours very affectionately and truly,

"R. E. Lee."

"Charleston, November 15, 1861.

"*My Precious Daughter:* I have received your letter forwarded to Richmond by Mr. Powell, and I also got, while in the West, the letter sent by B. Turner. I can write but seldom, but your letters always give me great pleasure. I am glad you had such a pleasant visit to 'Kinloch.' I have passed a great many pleasant days there myself in my young days. Now you must labour at your books and gain knowledge and wisdom. Do not mind what Rob says. I have a beautiful white beard. It is much admired. At least, much remarked on. You know I have told you not to believe what the young men tell you. I was unable to see your poor mother when in Richmond. Before I could get down I was sent off here. Another forlorn hope expedition. Worse than West Virginia. . . . I have much to do in this country. I have been to Savannah and have to go again. The enemy is quiet after his conquest of Port Royal Harbor and his whole fleet is lying there. May God guard and protect you, my dear child, prays your

"Affectionate father,

"R. E. Lee."

The above letter was written to his youngest daughter, Mildred, who was at school in Winchester, Virginia. Two of my sisters were in King George County, Virginia, at "Clydale," the summer home of Dr. Richard Stuart, with whose family we had been a long time intimate. From there they had driven to "Stratford," in Westmoreland County, about thirty miles distant, where my father was born. They had written him of this trip, and this is his reply:

"SAVANNAH, November 22, 1861.

"*My Darling Daughters:* I have just received your joint letter of October 24th, from 'Clydale.' It was very cheering to me, and the affection and sympathy you expressed were very grateful to my feelings. I wish indeed I could see you, be with you, and never again part from you. God only can give me that happiness. I pray for it night and day. But my prayers I know are not worthy to be heard. I received your former letter in western Virginia, but had no opportunity to reply to it. I enjoyed it, nevertheless. I am glad you do not wait to hear from me, as that would deprive me of the pleasure of hearing from you often. I am so pressed with business. I am much pleased at your description of Stratford and your visit. It is endeared to me by many recollections, and it has been always a great desire of my life to be able to purchase it. Now that we have no other home, and the one we so loved has been so foully polluted, the desire is stronger with me than ever. The horse-chestnut you mention in the garden was planted by my mother. I am sorry the vault is so dilapidated. You did not mention the spring, one of the objects of my earliest recollections. I am very glad, my precious Agnes, that you have become so early a riser. It is a good habit, and in these times for mighty works advantage should be taken of every hour. I much regretted being obliged to come from Richmond without seeing your poor mother. . . . This is my second visit to Savannah. I have been down the coast to Amelia Island to examine the defenses. They are poor indeed, and I have laid off work enough to employ our people a month. I hope our enemy will be polite enough to wait for us. It is difficult to get our people to realise their position. . . . Good-bye, my dear daughters.

"Your affectionate father,

"R. E. LEE."

To his daughter Annie:

"COOSAWHATCHIE, South Carolina,
"December 8, 186.

"*My Precious Annie:* I have taken the only quiet time I have been able to find on this holy day to thank you for your letter of the 29th ulto. One of the miseries of war is that there is no Sabbath, and the current of work and strife has no cessation. How can we be pardoned for all our offenses! I am glad that you have joined your mamma again and that some of you are together at last. It would be a great happiness to me were you all at some quiet place, remote from the vicissitudes of war, where I could consider you safe. You must have had a pleasant time at 'Clydale.' I hope indeed that 'Cedar Grove' may be saved from the ruin and pillage that other places have received at the hands of our enemies, who are pursuing the same course here as they have practised elsewhere. Unfortunately, too, the numerous deep estuaries, all accessible to their ships, expose the multitude of islands to their predatory excursions, and what they leave is finished by the negroes whose masters have deserted their plantations, subject to visitations of the enemy. I am afraid Cousin Julia[2] will not be able to defend her home if attacked by the vandals, for they have little respect for anybody, and if they catch the Doctor[2] they will certainly send him to Fort Warren or La Fayette. I fear, too, the Yankees will bear off their pretty daughters. I am very glad you visited 'Chatham.'[3] I was there many years ago, when it was the residence of Judge Coulter, and some of the avenues of poplar, so dear to your grandmama, still existed. I presume they have all gone now. The letter that you and Agnes wrote from 'Clydale' I replied to and sent to that place. You know I never have any news. I am trying to get a force to make headway on our defenses, but it comes in very slow. The people do not seem to realise that there is a war.

"It is very warm here, if that is news, and as an evidence I inclose some violets I plucked in the yard of a deserted house I occupy. I wish I could see you and give them in person. . . . Good-bye, my precious child. Give much love to everybody, and believe me,

"Your affectionate father,

"R. E. LEE."

From the same place, on December 2d, he writes to my mother:

"I received last night, dear Mary, your letter of the 12th, and am delighted to learn that you are all well and so many of you are together. I am much pleased that Fitzhugh has an opportunity to be with you all and will not be so far removed from his home in his new field of action. I hope to see him at the head of a fine regiment and that he will be able to do good service in the cause of his country. If Mary and Rob get to you Christmas, you will have quite a family party, especially if Fitzhugh is not obliged to leave his home and sweet wife before that time. I shall think of you all on that holy day more intensely than usual, and shall pray to the great God of Heaven to shower His blessings upon you in this world, and to unite you all in His courts in the world to come. With a grateful heart I thank Him for His preservation thus far, and trust to His mercy and kindness for the future. Oh, that I were more worthy, more thankful for all He has done and continues to do for me! Perry and Meredith[4] send their respects to all. . . .

"Truly and affectionately,

"R. E. LEE."

From the same place, on Christmas Day, he writes to my mother:

"I cannot let this day of grateful rejoicing pass, dear Mary, without some communication with you. I am thankful for the many among the past that I have passed with you, and the remembrance

of them fills me with pleasure. For those on which we have been separated we must not repine. If it will make us more resigned and better prepared for what is in store for us, we should rejoice. Now we
must be content with the many blessings we receive. If we can only
become sensible of our transgressions, so as to be fully penitent and
forgiven, that this heavy punishment under which we labour may
with justice be removed from us and the whole nation, what a gracious consummation of all that we have endured it will be!

"I hope you had a pleasant visit to Richmond. . . . If you were to
see this place, I think you would have it, too. I am here but little
myself. The days I am not here I visit some point exposed to the
enemy, and after our dinner at early candle-light, am engaged in
writing till eleven or twelve o'clock at night. . . . As to our old
home, if not destroyed, it will be difficult ever to be recognised.
Even if the enemy had wished to preserve it, it would almost have
been impossible. With the number of troops encamped around it,
the change of officers, etc., the want of fuel, shelter, etc., and all
the dire necessities of war, it is vain to think of its being in a habitable condition. I fear, too, books, furniture, and the relics of
Mount Vernon will be gone. It is better to make up our minds to a
general loss. They cannot take away the remembrance of the spot,
and the memories of those that to us rendered it sacred. That will
remain to us as long as life will last, and that we can preserve. In
the absence of a home, I wish I could purchase 'Stratford.' That is
the only other place that I could go to, now accessible to us, that
would inspire me with feelings of pleasure and local love. You and
the girls could remain there in quiet. It is a poor place, but we
could make enough corn-bread and bacon for our support, and
the girls could weave us clothes. I wonder if it is for sale and at how
much. Ask Fitzhugh to try to find out, when he gets to
Fredericksburg. You must not build your hopes on peace on
account of the United States going into a war with England.[5] She
will be very loath to do that, notwithstanding the bluster of the
Northern papers. Her rulers are not entirely mad, and if they find
England is in earnest, and that war or a restitution of their captives

must be the consequence, they will adopt the latter. We must make up our minds to fight our battles and win our independence alone. No one will help us. We require no extraneous aid, if true to ourselves. But we must be patient. It is not a light achievement and cannot be accomplished at once. . . . I wrote a few days since, giving you all the news, and have now therefore nothing to relate. The enemy is still quiet and increasing in strength. We grow in size slowly but are working hard. I have had a day of labour instead of rest, and have written at intervals to some of the children. I hope they are with you, and inclose my letters. . . .

"Affectionately and truly,

"R. E. LEE."

In the next letter to my mother he describes a visit to the grave of his father at Dungeness, on Cumberland Island, Georgia. Dungeness was presented to General Nathaniel Green by the State of Georgia for services rendered her in the Revolution. General Henry Lee, returning from the West Indies, where he had been for some months on account of his health, landed there, and in a few days died, March 15, 1818. He was most kindly cared for by the daughter of his old commander, and was buried there in the garden of Dungeness. At the time of my father's visit the place belonged to a great-nephew of General Green, Mr. Nightingale.

"COOSAWHATCHIE, South Carolina,

"January 18, 1862.

"On my return, day before yesterday, from Florida, dear Mary, I received your letter of the 1st inst. I am very glad to find that you had a pleasant family meeting Christmas, and that it was so large. I am truly grateful for all the mercies we enjoy, notwithstanding the miseries of war, and join heartily in the wish that the next year may find us at peace with all the world. I am delighted to hear that our little grandson[6] is improving so fast and is becoming such a perfect gentleman. May his path be strewn with flowers and his life with happiness. I am very glad to hear also that his dear papa is promoted. It will be gratifying to him and increase, I hope, his means of usefulness. Robert wrote me he saw him on his way through Charlottesville with his squadron, and that he was well. While at Fernandina I went over to Cumberland Island and walked up to 'Dungeness,' the former residence of General Green. It was my first visit to the house, and I had the gratification at length of visiting my father's grave. He died there, you may recollect, on his way from the West Indies, and was interred in one corner of the family cemetery. The spot is marked by a plain marble slab, with his name, age, and date of his death. Mrs. Green is also buried there, and her daughter, Mrs. Shaw, and her husband. The place is at present owned by Mr. Nightingale, nephew of Mrs. Shaw, who married a daughter of Mr. James King. The family have moved into the interior of Georgia, leaving only a few servants and a white gardener on the place. The garden was beautiful, inclosed by the finest hedge I have ever seen. It was of the wild olive. The orange trees were small, and the orange grove, which, in Mrs. Shaw's lifetime, during my tour of duty in Savannah in early life, was so productive, had been destroyed by an insect that has proved fatal to the orange on the coast of Georgia and Florida. There was a fine grove of olives, from which, I learn, Mr. Nightingale procures oil. The garden was filled with roses and beautiful vines, the names of which I do not know. Among them was the tomato-vine in full bearing, with the ripe fruit on it. There has yet been no frost in that region of country this winter. I went in the dining-room and parlour, in which the furniture still remained. . . . The house has never been finished, but is a fine, large one and beautifully located. A magnificent grove of live-oaks envelops the road from the landing to the house. . . . Love to everybody and God bless you all.

"Truly and faithfully yours,

"R. E. LEE."

From the same place there is another letter to my mother:

"Coosawhatchie, South Carolina,
"January 28, 1862.

"I have just returned from Charleston, and received your letter of the 14th, dear Mary. . . . I was called to Charleston by the appearance off the bar of a fleet of vessels the true character and intent of which could not be discerned during the continuance of the storm which obscured the view. Saturday, however, all doubt was dispelled, and from the beach on Sullivan's Island the preparations for sinking them were plainly seen. Twenty-one were visible the first day of my arrival, but at the end of the storm, Saturday, only seventeen were seen. Five of these were vessels of war: what became of the other four is not known. The twelve old merchantmen were being stripped of their spars, masts, etc., and by sunset seven were prepared apparently for sinking across the mouth of the Maffitt Channel. They were placed in a line about two hundred yards apart, about four miles from Fort Moultrie. They will do but little harm to the channel, I think, but may deter vessels from running out at night for fear of getting on them. There now seem to be indications of a movement against Savannah. The enemy's gunboats are pushing up the creek to cut off communication between the city and Fort Pulaski on Cockspur Island. Unless I have better news, I most go there to-day. There are so many points of attack, and so little means to meet them on water, that there is but little rest. . . . Perry and Meredith are well and send regards to everybody. . . .

"Very truly and sincerely yours,
"R. E. Lee."

It was most important that the defenses of Charleston and Savannah should be made as strong as possible. The difficulties in the way were many and great, but General Lee's perseverance overcame most of them. The result was that neither of those cities fell till the close of the war, and a region of country was preserved to the Confederacy necessary for the feeding of its armies. Of course all of this was not accomplished by my father alone in the four months he was there; but the plans of defense he laid down were successfully followed.

While in Savannah, he writes to my mother:

"SAVANNAH, February 8, 1862.

"I wrote to you, dear Mary, the day I left Coosawhatchie for this place. I have been here ever since, endeavouring to push forward the work for the defense of the city, which has lagged terribly and which ought to have been finished. But it is difficult to arouse ourselves from ease and comfort to labour and self-denial.

"Guns are scarce, as well as ammunition, and I shall have to break up batteries on the coast to provide, I fear, for this city. Our enemies are endeavouring to work their way through the creeks that traverse the impassable and soft marshes stretching along the interior of the coast and communicating with the sounds and sea, through which the Savannah flows, and thus avoid the entrance of the river commanded by Fort Pulaski. Their boats require only seven feet of water to float them, and the tide rises seven feet, so that at high water they can work their way and rest on the mud at low. They are also provided with dredges and appliances for removing obstructions through the creeks in question, which cannot be guarded by batteries. I hope, however, we shall be able to stop them, and I daily pray to the Giver of all victories to enable us to do so. . . . I trust you are all well and doing well, and wish I could do anything to promote either. I have more here than I can do, and more, I fear, than I can well accomplish. It is so very hard to get anything done, and while all wish well and mean well, it is so different to get them to act energetically and promptly. . . . The news from Kentucky and Tennessee is not favourable, but we must make up our minds to meet with reverses and overcome them. I hope God will at last crown our efforts with success. But the contest must be long and severe, and the whole country has to go through much suffering. It is necessary we should be humbled and taught to be less boastful, less selfish, and more devoted to right and justice to all the world. . . . Always yours,

"R. E. LEE."

To my mother:

"SAVANNAH, February 23, 1862.

"I have been wishing, dear Mary, to write to you for more than a week, but every day and every hour seem so taken up that I have found it impossible. . . . The news from Tennessee and North Carolina is not all cheering, and disasters seem to be thickening around us. It calls for renewed energies and redoubled strength on our part, and, I hope, will produce it. I fear our soldiers have not realised the necessity for the endurance and labour they are called upon to undergo, and that it is better to sacrifice themselves than our cause. God, I hope, will shield us and give us success. Here the enemy is progressing slowly in his designs, and does not seem prepared, or to have determined when or where to make his attack. His gunboats are pushing up all the creeks and marshes of the Savannah, and have attained a position so near the river as to shell the steamers navigating it. None have as yet been struck. I am engaged in constructing a line of defense at Fort Jackson which, if time permits and guns can be obtained, I hope will keep them out. They can bring such overwhelming force in all their movements that it has the effect to demoralise our new troops. The accounts given in the papers of the quantity of cotton shipped to New York are, of course, exaggerated. It is cotton in the seed and dirt, and has to be ginned and cleaned after its arrival. It is said that the negroes are employed in picking and collecting it, and are paid a certain amount. But all these things are gathered from rumour, and can only be believed as they appear probable, which this seems to be. . . . I went yesterday to church, being the day appointed for fasting and prayer. I wish I could have passed it more devoutly. The bishop (Elliott) gave a most beautiful prayer for the President, which I hope may be heard and answered. . . .

Here the yellow jasmine, red-bud, orange-tree, etc., perfume the whole woods, and the japonicas and azaleas cover the garden. Perry and Meredith are well. May God bless and keep you always is the constant prayer of your husband,

"R. E. LEE."

To his daughter Annie:

"SAVANNAH, March 2, 1862.

"*My Precious Annie:* It has been a long time since I have written to you, but you have been constantly in my thoughts. I think of you all, separately and collectively, in the busy hours of the day and the silent hours of the night, and the recollection of each and every one whiles away the long night, in which my anxious thoughts drive away sleep. But I always feel that you and Agnes at those times are sound asleep, and that it is immaterial to either where the blockaders are or what their progress is in the river. I hope you are all well, and as happy as you can be in these perilous times to our country. They look dark at present, and it is plain we have not suffered enough, laboured enough, repented enough, to deserve success. But they will brighten after awhile, and I trust that a merciful God will arouse us to a sense of our danger, bless our honest efforts, and drive back our enemies to their homes. Our people have not been earnest enough, have thought too much of themselves and their ease, and instead of turning out to a man, have been content to nurse themselves and their dimes, and leave the protection of themselves and families to others. To satisfy their consciences, they have been clamorous in criticising what others have done, and endeavoured to prove that they ought to do nothing. This is not the way to accomplish our independence. I have been doing all I can with our small means and slow workmen to defend the cities and coast here. Against ordinary numbers we are pretty strong, but against the hosts our enemies seem able to bring everywhere there is no calculating. But if our men will stand to their work, we shall give them trouble and damage them yet. They have worked their way across the marshes, with their dredges, under cover of their gunboats, to the Savannah River, about Fort Pulaski. I presume they will endeavour to reduce the fort and thus open a way for their vessels up the river. But we have an interior line they must force before reaching the city. It is on this line we are working, slowly to my anxious mind, but as fast as I can drive them. . . . Goodbye, my dear child. May God bless you and our poor country.

"Your devoted father,
"R. E. LEE."

Soon after this letter was written my father was recalled to Richmond, "and was assigned on the 13th of March, under the direction of the President, to the conduct of the military operations of all the armies of the Confederate States."[7] My mother was still at the White House, my brother's place on the Pamunkey, and there my father wrote to her:

"RICHMOND, March 14, 1862.
"*My Dear Mary:* I have been trying all the week to write to you, but have not been able. I have been placed on duty here to conduct operations under the direction of the President. It will give me great pleasure to do anything I can to relieve him and serve the country, but I do not see either advantage or pleasure in my duties. But I will not complain, but do my best. I do not see at present either that it will enable me to see much more of you. In the present condition of affairs no one can foresee what may happen, nor in my judgment is it advisable for any one to make arrangements with a view to permanency or pleasure. We must all do what promises the most usefulness. The presence of some one at the White House is necessary as long as practicable. How long it will be practicable for you and Charlotte to remain there I cannot say. The enemy is pushing us back in all directions, and how far he will be successful depends much upon our efforts and the mercy of Providence. I shall, in all human probability, soon have to take the field, so for the present I think things had better remain as they

are. Write me your views. If you think it best for you to come to Richmond I can soon make arrangements for your comfort and shall be very glad of your company and presence. We have experienced a great affliction both in our private and public relations. Our good and noble Bishop Meade died last night. He was very anxious to see you, sent you his love and kindest remembrances, and had I known in time yesterday I should have sent expressly for you to come up. But I did not know of his wish or condition till after the departure of the cars yesterday. Between 6 and 7 P. M. yesterday he sent for me, said he wished to bid me good-bye, and to give me his blessing, which he did in the most affecting manner. Called me Robert and reverted to the time I used to say the catechism to him. He invoked the blessing of God upon me and the country. He spoke with difficulty and pain, but was perfectly calm and clear. His hand was then cold and pulseless, yet he shook mine warmly. 'I ne'er shall look upon his like again.' He died during the night. I presume the papers of to-morrow will tell you all. . . .

"Very truly and sincerely,

"R. E. LEE."

The next day he again writes to my mother.

"RICHMOND, March 15, 1862.

"*My Dear Mary:* I wrote you yesterday by mail. On returning to my quarters last night after 11 P. M. Custis informed me Robert had arrived and had made up his mind to go into the army. He stayed at the Spottswood, and this morning I went with him to get his overcoat, blankets, etc. There is great difficulty in procuring what is good. They all have to be made, and he has gone to the office of the adjutant-general of Virginia to engage in the service. God grant it may be for his good as He has permitted it. I must be resigned. I told him of the exemption granted by the Secretary of War to the professors and students of the university, but he expressed no desire to take advantage of it. It would be useless for him to go, if he did not improve himself, nor would I wish him to go merely for exemption. As I have done all in the matter that seems proper and right, I must now leave the rest in the hands of our merciful God. I hope our son will do his duty and make a good soldier. . . . I had expected yesterday to go to North Carolina this morning, but the President changed his mind. I should like to go to see you to-morrow, but in the present condition of things do not feel that I ought to be absent. . . I may have to go to North Carolina or Norfolk yet. New Berne, N. C., has fallen into the hands of the enemy. In Arkansas our troops under Van Dorn have had a hard battle, but nothing decisive gained. Four generals killed—McIntosh, McCullogh, Herbert, and Slack. General Price wounded. Loss on both sides said to be heavy. . . .

"Very truly yours,

"R. E. LEE."

CHAPTER IV

ARMY LIFE OF ROBERT THE YOUNGER

VOLUNTEER IN ROCKBRIDGE ARTILLERY— "FOUR YEARS WITH
GENERAL LEE" QUOTED—MEETINGS BETWEEN FATHER AND
SON—PERSONAL CHARACTERISTICS OF THE GENERAL—
DEATH OF HIS DAUGHTER, ANNIE—HIS SON ROBERT RAISED
FROM THE RANKS—THE HORSES, "GRACE DARLING" AND
"TRAVELLER"—FREDERICKSBURG—FREEING SLAVES

LIKE all the students at the university, I was wild to go into the
army, and wrote my father that I was afraid the war would be over
before I had a chance to serve. His reply was that I need have no
fear of that contingency, that I must study hard and fit myself to be
useful to my country when I was old enough to be of real service to
her; so, very properly, I was not allowed to have my wish then. In a
letter to my mother written April, '61, he says:

"I wrote to Robert that I could not consent to take boys from
their schools and young men from their colleges and put them in
the ranks at the beginning of a war, when they are not wanted and
when there were men enough for that purpose. The war may last
ten years. Where are our ranks to be filled from then? I was willing
for his company to continue at their studies, to keep up its organisation, and to perfect themselves in their military exercises, and to

perform duty at the college; but *not* to be called into the field. I therefore wished him to remain. If the exercises at the college are suspended, he can then come home. . . ."

But in the spring of '62 he allowed me to volunteer, and I having selected the company I wished to join, the Rockbridge Artillery, he gave his approval, and wrote me to come to Richmond, where he would give me my outfit. He was just as sweet and loving to me then as in the old days. I had seen so little of him during the last six years that I stood somewhat in awe of him. I soon found, however, that I had no cause for such a feeling. He took great pains in getting what was necessary for me. The baggage of a private in a Confederate battery was not extensive. How little was needed my father, even at that time, did not know, for though he was very careful in providing me with the least amount he thought necessary, I soon found by experience that he had given me a great deal too much. It was characteristic of his consideration for others and the unselfishness of his nature, that at this time, when weighed down, harassed and burdened by the cares incident to bringing the untrained forces of the Confederacy into the field, and preparing them for a struggle the seriousness of which he knew better than any one, he should give his time and attention to the minute details of fitting out his youngest son as a private soldier. I think it worthy of note that the son of the commanding general enlisting as a private in his army was not thought to be anything remarkable or unusual. Neither my mother, my family, my friends nor myself expected any other course, and I do not suppose it ever occurred to my father to think of giving me an office, which he could easily have done. I know it never occurred to me, nor did I ever hear, at that time or afterwards, from anyone, that I might have been entitled to better rank than that of a private because of my father's prominence in Virginia and in the Confederacy. With the good advice to be obedient to all authority, to do my duty in everything, great or small, he bade me good-bye, and sent me off to the Valley of Virginia, where the command in which I was about to enlist were serving under "Stonewall Jackson."

Of my father's military duties at this time, Colonel Taylor, in his "Four Years with General Lee," says:

"Exercising a constant supervision over the condition of affairs at each important point, thoroughly informed as to the resources and necessities of the several commanders of armies in the field, as well as of the dangers which respectively threatened them, he was enabled to give them wise counsel, to offer them valuable suggestions, and to respond to their demands for assistance and support to such extent as the limited resources of the government would permit. It was in great measure due to his advice and encouragement that General Magruder so stoutly and so gallantly held his lines on the Peninsula against General McClellan until troops could be sent to his relief from General Johnston's army. I recollect a telegraphic despatch received by General Lee from General Magruder, in which he stated that a council of war which he had convened had unanimously determined that his army should retreat, in reply to which General Lee urged him to maintain his lines, and to make as bold a front as possible, and encouraged him with the prospect of being early reinforced. No better illustration of the nature and importance of the duty performed by General Lee, while in this position, can be given than the following letter—one of a number of similar import—written by him to General Jackson, the 'rough' or original draft of which is still in my possession:

"'HEADQUARTERS, RICHMOND, Virginia,
"'April 29, 1862.
"'MAJOR-GENERAL T. J. JACKSON, commanding, etc., Swift Run Gap, Virginia.
"'*General:* I have had the honour to receive your letter of yesterday's date. From the reports that reach me that are entitled to credit, the force of the enemy opposite Fredericksburg is represented as too large to admit of any diminution whatever of our army in that vicinity at present, as it might not only invite an

attack on Richmond, but jeopard the safety of the army in the Peninsula. I regret, therefore, that your request to have five thousand men sent from that army to reinforce you cannot be complied with. Can you not draw enough from the command of General Edward Johnson to warrant you in attacking Banks? The last return received from that army show a present force of upward of thirty-five hundred, which, it is hoped, has since increased by recruits and returned furloughs. As he does not appear to be pressed, it is suggested that a portion of his force might be temporarily removed from its present position and made available for the movement in question. A decisive and successful blow at Banks's column would be fraught with the happiest results, and I deeply regret my inability to send you the reinforcements you ask. If, however, you think the combined forces of Generals Ewell and Johnson, with your own, inadequate for the move, General Ewell might, with the assistance of General Anderson's army near Fredericksburg, strike at McDowell's army between that city and Acquia, with much promise of success; provided you feel sufficiently strong alone to hold Banks in check.

"'Very truly yours,

"'R. E. LEE.'

"The reader will observe that this letter bears the date 'April 29, 1862.' On May 5th or 6th, General Jackson formed a junction between his own command and that of General Edward Johnson; on May 8th, he defeated Milroy at McDowell. Soon thereafter, the command of General Ewell was united to that already under Jackson, and on the 25th of the same month Banks was defeated and put to flight. Other incidents might be cited to illustrate this branch of the important service rendered at this period by General Lee. The line of earthworks around the city of Richmond, and other preparations for resisting an attack, testified to the immense care and labour bestowed upon the defense of the capital, so seriously threatened by the army of General McClellan."

On May 31st, the battle of Seven Pines was fought, and General Joseph E. Johnston, commanding the Confederate Army, was severely wounded. The next day, by order of the President, General Lee took command of the Army of Northern Virginia.

The day after the battle of Cold Harbor, during the "Seven Days" fighting around Richmond, was the first time I met my father after I had joined General Jackson. The tremendous work Stonewall's men had performed, including the rapid march from the Valley of Virginia, the short rations, the bad water, and the great heat, had begun to tell upon us, and I was pretty well worn out. On this particular morning, my battery had not moved from its bivouac ground of the previous night, but was parked in an open field all ready, waiting orders. Most of the men were lying down, many sleeping, myself among the latter number. To get some shade and to be out of the way, I had crawled under a caisson, and was busy making up many lost hours of rest. Suddenly I was rudely awakened by a comrade, prodding me with a sponge-staff as I had failed to be aroused by his call, and was told to get up and come out, that some one wished to see me. Half awake, I staggered out, and found myself face to face with General Lee and his staff. Their fresh uniforms, bright equipments and well-groomed horses contrasted so forcibly with the war-worn appearance of our command that I was completely dazed. It took me a moment or two to realise what it all meant, but when I saw my father's loving eyes and smile it became clear to me that he had ridden by to see if I was safe and to ask how I was getting along. I remember well how curiously those with him gazed at me, and I am sure that it must have struck them as very odd that such a dirty, ragged, unkempt youth could have been the son of this grand-looking victorious commander.

I was introduced recently to a gentleman, now living in Washington, who, when he found out my name, said he had met me once before and that it was on this occasion. At that time he was a member of the Tenth Virginia Infantry, Jackson's Division, and was camped near our battery. Seeing General Lee and staff approach, he, with others, drew near to have a look at them, and thus witnessed the meeting between father and son. He also said that he had often told of this incident as illustrating the peculiar composition of our army.

After McClellan's change of base to Harrison's Landing on James River, the army lay inactive around Richmond. I had a short furlough on account of sickness, and saw my father; also my mother and sisters, who were then living in Richmond. He was the same loving father to us all, as kind and thoughtful of my mother, who was an invalid, and of us, his children, as if our comfort and happiness were all he had to care for. His great victory did not elate him, so far as one could see. In a letter of July 9th, to my mother, he says:

". . . I have returned to my old quarters and am filled with gratitude to our Heavenly Father for all the mercies He has extended to us. Our success has not been so great or complete as we could have desired, but God knows what is best for us. Our enemy met with a heavy loss, from which it must take him some time to recover, before he can recommence his operations. . . ."

The Honourable Alexander H. Stephens, Vice-President of the Confederate States, says of General Lee:

"What I had seen General Lee to be at first—child-like in simplicity and unselfish in his character—he remained, unspoiled by praise and by success."

He was the same in victory or defeat, always calm and contained. Jackson, having had a short rest, was now moved up to Gordonsville. I rejoined my command and went with him, supplied with new clothes and a fresh stock of health. In a letter to his three daughters who were in North Carolina, dated Richmond, July 18, 1862, he writes describing my condition:

"Rob came out to see me one afternoon. He had been much worn down by his marching and fighting, and had gone to his mamma to get a little rest. He was thin but well, but, not being able to get a clean shirt, has not got to see Miss Norvell. He has rejoined his company and gone off with General Jackson, as good as new again, I hope, inasmuch as your mother thought, by means of a bath and a profusion of soap, she had cleansed the outward man considerably, and replenished his lost wardrobe."

From Gordonsville we were moved on to Orange County, and then commenced that series of manœuvres by the Army of Northern Virginia, beginning with the battle of Cedar Mountain and ending with second Manassas.

When I again saw my father, he rode at the head of Longstreet's men on the field of Manassas, and we of Jackson's corps, hard pressed for two days, welcomed him and the divisions which followed him with great cheers. Two rifle-guns from our battery had been detached and sent to join Longstreet's advance artillery, under General Stephen D. Lee, moving into action on our right. I was "Number 1" at one of these guns. We advanced rapidly, from hill to hill, firing as fast as we could, trying to keep ahead of our gallant comrades, just arrived. As we were ordered to cease firing from the last position we took, and the breathless cannoneers were leaning on their guns, General Lee and staff galloped up, and from this point of vantage scanned the movements of the enemy and of our forces. The general reined in "Traveller" close by my gun, not fifteen feet from me. I looked at them all some few minutes, and then went up and spoke to Captain Mason of the staff, who had not the slightest idea who I was. When he found me out he was greatly amused, and introduced me to several others whom I already knew. My appearance was even less prepossessing than when I had met my father at Cold Harbour, for I had been marching night and day for four days, with no opportunity to wash myself or my clothes; my face and hands were blackened with powder-sweat, and the few garments I had on were ragged and stained with the red soil of that section. When the General, after a moment or two, dropped his glass to his side, and turned to his staff, Captain Mason said:

"General, here is some one who wants to speak to you."

The General, seeing a much-begrimed artillery-man, sponge-staff in hand, said:

"Well, my man, what can I do for you?" I replied:

"Why, General, don't you know me?" and he, of course, at once recognised me, and was very much amused at my appearance and most glad to see that I was safe and well.

We, of the ranks, used to have our opinions on all subjects. The armies, their generals, and their manœuvres were freely discussed. If there was one point on which the entire army was unanimous— I speak of the rank and file—it was that we were not in the least afraid of General Pope, but were perfectly sure of whipping him whenever we could meet him. The passages I quote here from two of General Lee's letters indicate that this feeling may possibly have extended to our officers. In a letter to my mother, from near Richmond, dated July 28, 1862, he says:

". . . When you write to Rob, tell him to catch Pope for me, and also bring in his cousin, Louis Marshall, who, I am told, is on his staff. I could forgive the latter's fighting against us, but not his joining Pope."

And again:

". . . Johnny Lee[1] saw Louis Marshall after Jackson's last battle, who asked him kindly after his old uncle, and said his mother was well. Johnny said Louis looked wretched himself. I am sorry he is in such bad company, but I suppose he could not help it."

As one of the Army of Northern Virginia, I occasionally saw the commander-in-chief, on the march, or passed the headquarters close enough to recognise him and members of his staff, but a private soldier in Jackson's corps did not have much time, during that campaign, for visiting, and until the battle of Sharpsburg I had no opportunity of speaking to him. On that occasion our battery had been severely handled, losing many men and horses. Having three guns disabled, we were ordered to withdraw, and while moving back we passed General Lee and several of his staff, grouped on a little knoll near the road. Having no definite orders where to go, our captain, seeing the commanding general, halted us and rode over to get some instructions. Some others and myself went along to see and hear. General Lee was dismounted with some of his staff around him, a courier holding his horse. Captain Poague, commanding our battery, the Rock-bridge Artillery, saluted, reported our condition, and asked for instructions. The General, listening patiently, looked at us—his eyes passing over me without any sign of recognition—and then ordered Captain Poague to take the most serviceable horses and men, man the uninjured gun, send the disabled part of his command back to refit, and report to the front for duty. As Poague turned to go, I went up to speak to my father. When he found out who I was, he congratulated me on being well and unhurt. I then said:

"General, are you going to send us in again?"

"Yes, my son," he replied, with a smile; "you all must do what you can to help drive these people back."

This meeting between General Lee and his son has been told very often and in many different ways, but the above is what I remember of the circumstances.

He was much on foot during this part of the campaign, and moved about either in an ambulance or on horseback, with a courier leading his horse. The accident which temporarily disabled him happened before he left Virginia. He had dismounted, and was sitting on a fallen log, with the bridle reins hung over his arm. Traveller, becoming frightened at something, suddenly dashed away, threw him violently to the ground, spraining both hands and breaking a small bone in one of them. A letter written some weeks afterward to my mother alludes to this meeting with his son, and to the condition of his hands:

". . . I have not laid eyes on Rob since I saw him in the battle of Sharpsburg—going in with a single gun of his for the second time, after his company had been withdrawn in consequence of three of its guns having been disabled. Custis has seen him and says he is very well, and apparently happy and content. My hands are improving slowly, and, with my left hand, I am able to dress and undress myself, which is a great comfort. My right is becoming of some assistance, too, though it is still swollen and sometimes painful. The bandages have been removed. I am now able to sign my name. It has been six weeks to-day since I was injured, and I have at last discarded the sling."

After the army recrossed the Potomac into Virginia, we were camped for some time in the vicinity of Winchester. One beautiful afternoon in October, a courier from headquarters rode up to our camp, found me out, and handed me a note from my father. It told me of the death of my sister Annie. As I have lost this letter to me, I quote from one to my mother about the same time. It was dated October 26, 1862:

". . . I cannot express the anguish I feel at the death of our sweet Annie. To know that I shall never see her again on earth, that her place in our circle, which I always hoped one day to enjoy, is forever vacant, is agonising in the extreme. But God in this, as in all things, has mingled mercy with the blow, in selecting that one best prepared to leave us. May you be able to join me in saying 'His will be done!'. . . I know how much you will grieve and how much she will be mourned. I wish I could give you any comfort, but beyond our hope in the great mercy of God, and the belief that He takes her at the time and place when it is best for her to go, there is none. May that same mercy be extended to us all, and may we be prepared for His summons."

In a letter to my sister Mary, one month later, from "Camp near Fredericksburg":

". . . The death of my dear Annie was, indeed, to me a bitter pang, but 'the Lord gave and the Lord has taken away: blessed be the name of the Lord.' In the quiet hours of the night, when there is nothing to lighten the full weight of my grief, I feel as if I should be over-whelmed. I have always counted, if God should spare me a few days after this Civil War was ended, that I should have her with me, but year after year my hopes go out, and I must be resigned. . . ."

To this daughter whose loss grieved him so he was specially devoted. She died in North Carolina, at the Warren White Sulphur Springs. At the close of the war, the citizens of the county erected over her grave a handsome monument. General Lee was invited to be present at the ceremonies of the unveiling. In his reply, he says:

". . . I have always cherished the intention of visiting the tomb of her who never gave me aught but pleasure; . . . Though absent in person, my heart will be with you, and my sorrow and devotions will be mingled with yours. . . . I inclose, according to your request, the date of my daughter's birth and the inscription proposed for the monument over her tomb. The latter are the last lines of the hymn which she asked for just before her death."

A visitor to her grave, some years after the war, thus describes it:

"In the beautiful and quiet graveyard near the Springs, a plain shaft of native granite marks the grave of this beloved daughter. On one side is cut in the stone, 'Annie C. Lee, daughter of General R. E. Lee and Mary C. Lee'—and on the opposite— 'Born at Arlington, June 18, 1839, and died at White Sulphur Springs, Warren County, North Carolina, Oct. 20, 1862.' On another side are the lines selected by her father,

"'Perfect and true are all His ways
Whom heaven adores and earth obeys.'"

That autumn I was offered the position of Lt. and A. D. C. on the staff of my brother, W. H. F. Lee, just promoted from the colonelcy of the 9th Virginia Cavalry to the command of a brigade in the same arm of the service. My father had told me when I joined the army to do my whole duty faithfully, not to be rash about volunteering for any service out of my regular line, and always to accept promotion. After consulting him, it was decided that I should take the position offered, and he presented me with a horse and one of his swords. My promotion necessitated my having an honourable discharge as a private, from the ranks, and this I obtained in the proper way from General "Stonewall" Jackson, commanding the corps of which my company was a part, and was thus introduced for the first time to that remarkable man. Having served in his command since my enlistment, I had been seeing him daily. "Old Jack," at a distance, was as familiar to me as one of the battery guns, but I had never met him, and felt much awe at being ushered into his presence. This feeling, however, was groundless, for he was seemingly so much embarrassed by the interview that I really felt sorry for him before he dismissed me with my discharge papers, properly made out and signed.

I had received a letter from my father telling me to come to him as soon as I had gotten my discharge from my company, so I proceeded at once to his headquarters, which were situated near Orange Court House, on a wooded hill just east of the village. I found there the horse which he gave me. She was a daughter of his mare, "Grace Darling," and, though not so handsome as her mother, she inherited many of her good qualities, and carried me well until the end of the war and for thirteen years afterward. She was four years old, a solid bay, and never failed me a single day during three years' hard work. The General was on the point of moving his headquarters down to Fredericksburg, some of the army having already gone forward to that city. I think the camp was struck the day after I arrived, and as the General's hands were not yet entirely well, he allowed me, as a great favour, to ride his horse "Traveller." Amongst the soldiers this horse was as well known as was his master. He was a handsome iron-gray with black points—mane and tail very dark—sixteen hands high, and five years old. He was born near the White Sulphur Springs, West Virginia, and attracted the notice of my father when he was in that part of the State in 1861. He was never known to tire, and, though quiet and sensible in general and afraid of nothing, yet if not regularly exercised, he fretted a good deal, especially in a crowd of horses. But there can be no better description of this famous horse than the one given by his master. It was dictated to his daughter Agnes at Lexington, Virginia, after the war, in response to some artist who had asked for a description, and was corrected in his own handwriting:

"If I were an artist like you I would draw a true picture of Traveller—representing his fine proportions, muscular figure, deep chest and short back, strong haunches, flat legs, small head, broad forehead, delicate ears, quick eye, small feet, and black mane and tail. Such a picture would inspire a poet, whose genius could then depict his worth and describe his endurance of toil, hunger, thirst, heat, cold, and the dangers and sufferings through which he passed. He could dilate upon his sagacity and affection, and his invariable response to every wish of his rider. He might even imagine his thoughts, through the long night marches and days of battle through which he has passed. But I am no artist; I can only say he is a Confederate gray. I purchased him in the mountains of Virginia in the autumn of 1861, and he has been my patient follower ever since—to Georgia, the Carolinas, and back to Virginia. He carried me through the Seven Days battle around Richmond, the second Manassas, at Sharpsburg, Fredericksburg, the last day at Chancellorsville, to Pennsylvania, at Gettysburg, and back to the Rappahannock. From the commencement of the campaign in 1864 at Orange, till its close around Petersburg, the saddle was scarcely off his back, as he passed through the fire of the Wildemesss, Spottsylvania, Cold Harbour, and across the James River. He was almost in daily requisition in the winter of 1864-65 on the long line of defenses from Chickahominy, north of Richmond, to Hatcher's Run, south of the Appomattox. In the campaign of 1865, he bore me from Petersburg to the final days at Appomattox Court House. You must know the comfort he is to me in my present retirement. He is well supplied with equipments. Two sets have been sent to him from England, one from the ladies of Baltimore, and one was made for him in Richmond; but I think his favourite is the American saddle from St. Louis. Of all his companions in toil, 'Richmond,' 'Brown Roan,' 'Ajax,' and quiet 'Lucy Long,' he is the only one that retained his vigour. The first two expired under their onerous burden, and the last two failed. You can, I am sure, from what I have said, paint his portrait."

The general had the strongest affection for Traveller, which he showed on all occasions, and his allowing me to ride him on this long march was a great compliment. Possibly he wanted to give me a good hammering before he turned me over to the cavalry. During my soldier life, so far, I had been on foot, having backed nothing more lively than a tired artillery horse; so I mounted with some misgivings, though I was very proud of my steed. My misgivings were fully realised, for Traveller would not walk a step. He took a short, high trot—a buck-trot, as compared with a buck-jump—and kept it up to Fredericksburg, some thirty miles. Though young, strong, and tough, I was glad when the journey ended. This was my first introduction to the cavalry service. I think I am safe in saying that I could have walked the distance with much less discomfort and fatigue. My father having thus given me a horse and presented me with one of his swords, also supplied my purse so that I could get myself an outfit suitable to my new position, and he sent me on to join my command, stationed not far away on the Rappahannock, southward from Fredericksburg.

As an officer in the cavalry on the staff, I had more frequent opportunities of seeing my father than as a private in the artillery. In the course of duty, I was sometimes sent to him to report the condition of affairs at the front, or on the flank of the army, and I also, occasionally, paid him a visit. At these times, he would take me into his tent, talk to me about my mother and sisters, about my horse and myself, or the people and the country where my command happened to be stationed. I think my presence was very grateful to him, and he seemed to brighten up when I came. I remember, he always took it as a matter of course that I must be hungry (and I was for three years), so he invariably made his mess-steward, Bryan, give me something to eat, if I did not have time to wait for the regular meal. His headquarters at this time, just before the battle of Fredericksburg and after, were at a point on the road between Fredericksburg and Hamilton's Crossing, selected on account of its accessibility. Notwithstanding there was near-by a good house vacant, he lived in his tents. His quarters were very unpretentious, consisting of three or four "wall-tents" and several more common ones. They were pitched on the edge of an old pine field, near a grove of forest trees from which he drew his supply of fire-wood, while the pines helped to shelter his tents and horses from the cold winds. Though from the outside they were rather dismal, especially through the dreary winter time, within they were cheerful, and the surroundings as neat and comfortable as possible under the circumstances.

On November 24, 1862, in a letter to his daughter Mary, he writes:

". . . General Burnside's whole army is apparently opposite Fredericksburg, and stretches from the Rappahannock to the Potomac. What his intentions are he has not yet disclosed. I am sorry he is in position to oppress our friends and citizens of the Northern Neck. He threatens to bombard Fredericksburg, and the noble spirit displayed by its citizens, particularly the women and children, has elicited my highest admiration. They have been abandoning their homes, night and day, during all this inclement weather, cheerfully and uncomplainingly, with only such assistance as our wagons and ambulances could afford, women, girls, children, trudging through the mud and bivouacking in the open fields."

How the battle of Fredericksburg was fought and won all the world has heard, and I shall not attempt to describe it. On December 11th, the day Burnside commenced his attack, General Lee wrote to my mother:

". . . The enemy, after bombarding the town of Fredericksburg, setting fire to many houses and knocking down nearly all those along the river, crossed over a large force about dark, and now occupies the town. We hold the hills commanding it, and hope we shall be able to damage him yet. His position and heavy guns command the town entirely."

On December 16th, in another letter to my mother, he tells of the recrossing of the Federals:

"I had supposed they were just preparing for battle, and was saving our men for the conflict. Their hosts crown the hill and plain beyond the river, and their numbers to me are unknown. Still I felt the confidence we could stand the shock, and was anxious for the blow that is to fall on some point, and was prepared to meet it here. Yesterday evening I had my suspicions that they might return during the night, but could not believe they would relinquish their hopes after all their boasting and preparation, and when I say that the latter is equal to the former you will have some idea of the magnitude. This morning they were all safe on the north side of the Rappahannock. They went as they came—in the night. They suffered heavily as far as the battle went, but it did not go far enough to satisfy me. Our loss was comparatively slight, and I think will not exceed two thousand. The contest will have now to be renewed, but on what field I cannot say."

I did not see my father at any time during the fighting. Some days after it was all over, I saw him, as calm and composed as if nothing unusual had happened, and he never referred to his great victory, except to deplore the loss of his brave officers and soldiers or the sufferings of the sick and wounded. He repeatedly referred to the hardships so bravely endured by the inhabitants of Fredericksburg, who had been obliged to flee from the town, the women and children, the old and the feeble, whose sufferings cut him to the heart. On Christmas Day he writes to his youngest daughter, Mildred, who was at school in North Carolina:

". . . I cannot tell you how I long to see you when a little quiet occurs. My thoughts revert to you, your sisters, and your mother; my heart aches for our reunion. Your brothers I see occasionally. This morning Fitzhugh rode by with his young aide-de-camp (Rob) at the head of his brigade, on his way up the Rappahannock. You must study hard, gain knowledge, and learn your duty to God and your neighbour: that is the great object of life. I have no news, confined constantly to camp, and my thoughts occupied with its necessities and duties. I am, however, happy in the knowledge that General Burnside and army will not eat their promised Christmas dinner in Richmond to-day."

On the next day he writes as follows to his daughter Agnes, who was with her mother in Richmond:

"CAMP FREDERICKSBURG, December 26, 1862.

"*My Precious Little Agnes:* I have not heard of you for a long time. I wish you were with me, for, always solitary, I am sometimes weary, and long for the reunion of my family once again. But I will not speak of myself, but of you. . . . I have seen the ladies in this vicinity only when flying from the enemy, and it caused me acute grief to witness their exposure and suffering. But a more noble spirit was never displayed anywhere. The faces of old and young were wreathed with smiles, and glowed with happiness at their sacrifices for the good of their country. Many have lost *everything*. What the fire and shells of the enemy spared, their pillagers destroyed. But God will shelter them, I know. So much heroism will not be unregarded. I can only hold oral communication with your sister[2], and have forbidden the scouts to bring any writing, and have taken back some that I had given them for her. If caught, it would compromise them. They only convey messages. I learn in that way she is well.

"Your devoted father,

"R. E. LEE."

I give another letter he wrote on Christmas Day, besides the one quoted above, to his daughter, Mildred. It was written to his wife, and is interesting as giving an insight into his private feelings and views regarding this great victory:

". . . I will commence this holy day by writing to you. My heart is filled with gratitude to Almighty God for His unspeakable mercies with which He has blessed us in this day, for those He has granted us from the beginning of life, and particularly for those He has vouchsafed us during the past year. What should have become of us without His crowning help and protection? Oh, if our people would only recognise it and cease from vain self-boasting and adulation, how strong would be my belief in final success and happiness to our country! But what a cruel thing is war; to separate and destroy families and friends, and mar the purest joys and happiness God has granted us in this world; to fill our hearts with hatred instead of love for our neighbours, and to devastate the fair face of this beautiful world! I pray that, on this day when only peace and good-will are preached to mankind, better thoughts may fill the hearts of our enemies and turn them to peace. Our army was never in such good health and condition since I have been attached to it. I believe they share with me my disappointment that the enemy did not renew the combat on the 13th. I was holding back all day and husbanding our strength and ammunition for the great struggle, for which I thought I was preparing. Had I divined that was to have been his only effort, he would have had more of it. My heart bleeds at the death of every one of our gallant men."

GENERAL ROBERT E. LEE
Photographed in 1862 or '63

One marked characteristic of my father was his habit of attending to all business matters promptly. He was never idle, and what he had to do he performed with care and precision. Mr. Custis, my grandfather, had made him executor of his will, wherein it was directed that all the slaves belonging to the estate should be set free after the expiration of so many years. The time had now arrived, and, notwithstanding the exacting duties of his position, the care of his suffering soldiers, and his anxiety about their future, immediate and distant, he proceeded according to the law of the land to carry out the provisions of the will, and had delivered to every one of the servants, where it was possible, their manumission papers. From his letters written at this time I give a few extracts bearing on this subject:

". . . As regards the liberation of the people, I wish to progress in it as far as I can. Those hired in Richmond can still find employment there if they choose. Those in the country can do the same or remain on the farms. I hope they will all do well and behave themselves. I should like, if I could, to attend to their wants and see them placed to the best advantage. But that is impossible. All that choose can leave the State before the war closes. . . .

". . . I executed the deed of manumission sent me by Mr. Caskie, and returned it to him. I perceived that John Sawyer and James's names, among the Arlington people, had been omitted, and inserted them. I fear there are others among the White House lot which I did not discover. As to the attacks of the Northern papers, I do not mind them, and do not think it wise to make the publication you suggest. If all the names of the people at Arlington and on the Pamunkey are not embraced in this deed I have executed, I should like a supplementary deed to be drawn up, containing all those omitted. They are entitled to their freedom and I wish to give it to them. Those that have been carried away, I hope are free and happy; I cannot get their papers to them, and they do not require them. I will give them if they ever call for them. It will be useless to ask their restitution to manumit them. . . ."

CHAPTER V

THE ARMY OF NORTHERN VIRGINIA

THE GENERAL'S SYMPATHY FOR HIS SUFFERING SOLDIERS—
CHANCELLORSVILLE—DEATH OF "STONEWALL" JACKSON—
GENERAL FITZHUGH LEE WOUNDED AND CAPTURED—ESCAPE OF
HIS BROTHER ROBERT—GETTYSBURG—RELIGIOUS REVIVAL—
INFANTRY REVIEW—UNSATISFACTORY COMMISSARIAT

DURING this winter, which was a very severe one, the sufferings of General Lee's soldiers on account of insufficient shelter and clothing, the scant rations for man and beast, the increasing destitution throughout the country, and his inability to better these conditions, bore heavily upon him. But he was bright and cheerful to those around him, never complaining of any one nor about anything, and often indulging in his quaint humour, especially with the younger officers, as when he remarked to one of them, who complained of the tough biscuit at breakfast:

"You ought not to mind that; they will stick by you the longer!"

His headquarters continued all the winter at the same place, and with stove and fire-places in the tents, the General and his military family managed to keep fairly comfortable. On February 6, 1863, he wrote to his daughter, Agnes, from this camp:

"CAMP FREDERICKSBURG, February 6, 1863.

". . . I read yesterday, my precious daughter, your letter, and grieved very much when last in Richmond at not seeing you. My movements are so uncertain that I cannot be relied on for anything. The only place I am to be found is in camp, and I am so cross now that I am not worth seeing anywhere. Here you will have to take me with the three stools—the snow, the rain, and the mud. The storm of the last twenty-four hours has added to our stock of all, and we are now in a floating condition. But the sun and the wind will carry all off in time, and then we shall appreciate our relief. Our horses and mules suffer the most. They have to bear the cold and rain, tug through the mud, and suffer all the time with hunger. The roads are wretched, almost impassable. I heard of Mag lately. One of our scouts brought me a card of Margaret Stuart's with a pair of gauntlets directed to 'Cousin Robert.'. . . I have no news. General Hooker is obliged to do something. I do not know what it will be. He is playing the Chinese game, trying what frightening will do. He runs out his guns, starts his wagons and troops up and down the river, and creates an excitement generally. Our men look on in wonder, give a cheer, and all again subsides *in statu quo ante bellum.* I wish you were here with me to-day. You would have to sit by this little stove, look out at the rain, and keep yourself dry. But here come, in all the wet, the adjutants-general with the papers. I must stop and go to work. See how kind God is; we have plenty to do in good weather and bad. . . . "

"Your devoted father,

"R. E. LEE."

On February 23d, he writes to Mrs. Lee:

"CAMP FREDERICKSBURG, February 23, 1863.

"The weather is now very hard upon our poor bushmen. This morning the whole country is covered with a mantle of snow fully a foot deep. It was nearly up to my knees as I stepped out this morning, and our poor horses were enveloped. We have dug them out and opened our avenues a little, but it will be terrible and the roads impassable. No cars from Richmond yesterday. I fear our short rations for man and horse will have to be curtailed. Our enemies have their troubles too. They are very strong immediately in front, but have withdrawn their troops above and below us back toward Acquia Creek. I owe Mr. F. J. Hooker[1] no thanks for keeping me here. He ought to have made up his mind long ago what to do——24th. The cars have arrived and brought me a young French officer, full of vivacity, and ardent for service with me. I think the appearance of things will cool him. If they do not, the night will, for he brought no blankets.

"R. E. LEE."

The dreary winter gradually passed away. Toward the last of April, the two armies, which had been opposite each other for four months, began to move, and, about the first of May, the greatest of General Lee's battles was fought. My command was on the extreme left, and, as Hooker crossed the river, we followed a raiding party of the enemy's cavalry over toward the James River above Richmond; so I did not see my father at any time during the several days' fighting. The joy of our victory at Chancellorsville was saddened by the death of "Stonewall" Jackson. His loss was the heaviest blow the Army of Northern Virginia ever sustained. To Jackson's note telling him he was wounded, my father replied:

"I cannot express my regret at the occurrence. Could I have directed events, I should have chosen for the good of the country to have been disabled in your stead. I congratulate you on the victory, which is due to your skill and energy."

Jackson said, when this was read to him,
"Better that ten Jacksons should fall than one Lee."
Afterward, when it was reported that Jackson was doing well, General Lee playfully sent him word:

"You are better off than I am, for while you have only lost your *left*, I have lost my *right* arm."

Then, hearing that he was worse, he said:

"Tell him that I am praying for him as I believe I have never prayed for myself."

After his death, General Lee writes to my mother, on May 11th:

". . . In addition to the deaths of officers and friends consequent upon the late battles, you will see that we have to mourn the loss of the great and good Jackson. Any victory would be dear at such a price. His remains go to Richmond to-day. I know not how to replace him. God's will be done! I trust He will raise up some one in his place. . . . "

Jones, in his Memoirs, says: "To one of his officers, after Jackson's death, he [General Lee] said: 'I had such implicit confidence in Jackson's skill and energy that I never troubled myself to give him detailed instructions. The most general suggestions were all that he needed.'"

To one of his aides, who came to his tent, April 29th, to inform him that the enemy had crossed the Rappahannock River in heavy force, General Lee made the playful reply:

"Well, I heard firing, and I was beginning to think it was time some of you lazy young fellows were coming to tell me what it was all about. Say to General Jackson that he knows just as well what to do with the enemy as I do."

Jackson said of Lee, when it was intimated by some, at the time he first took command, that he was slow:

"He is cautious. He ought to be. But he is *not* slow. Lee is a phenomenon. He is the only man whom I would follow blindfold."

As the story of these great men year by year is made plainer to the world, their love, trust, and respect for each other will be better understood. As commander and lieutenant they were exactly suited. When General Lee wanted a movement made and gave

Jackson an outline of his plans and the object to be gained, it was performed promptly, well, and thoroughly, if it was possible for flesh and blood to do it.

At the end of May, the Army of Northern Virginia, rested and strengthened, was ready for active operations. On May 31st General Lee writes to Mrs. Lee:

". . . General Hooker has been very daring this past week, and quite active. He has not said what he intends to do, but is giving out by his movements that he designs crossing the Rappahannock. I hope we may be able to frustrate his plans, in part, if not in whole. . . . I pray that our merciful Father in Heaven may protect and direct us! In that case, I fear no odds and no numbers."

About June 5th most of the army was gathered around Culpeper. Its efficiency, confidence, and *morale* were never better. On June 7th the entire cavalry corps was reviewed on the plain near Brandy Station in Culpeper by General Lee. We had been preparing ourselves for this event for some days, cleaning, mending and polishing, and I remember we were very proud of our appearance. In fact, it was a grand sight—about eight thousand well-mounted men riding by their beloved commander, first passing him in a walk and then in a trot. He writes to my mother next day—June 8, 1863:

". . . I reviewed the cavalry in this section yesterday. It was a splendid sight. The men and horses looked well. They have recuperated since last fall. Stuart[2] was in all his glory. Your sons and nephews[3] were well and flourishing. The country here looks very green and pretty, notwithstanding the ravages of war. What a beautiful world God, in His loving kindness to His creatures, has given us! What a shame that men endowed with reason and knowledge of right should mar His gifts. . . ."

The next day, June 9th, a large force of the enemy's cavalry, supported by infantry, crossed the Rappahannock and attacked General Stuart. The conflict lasted until dark, when

"The enemy was compelled to recross the river, with heavy loss, leaving about five hundred prisoners, three pieces of artillery, and several colours in our hands."

During the engagement, about 3 P. M., my brother, General W. H. F. Lee, my commanding officer, was severely wounded. In a letter dated the 11th of the month, my father writes to my mother:

". . . My supplications continue to ascend for you, my children, and my country. When I last wrote I did not suppose that Fitzhugh would be so soon sent to the rear disabled, and I hope it will be for a short time. I saw him the night after the battle—indeed, met him on the field as they were bringing him from the front. He is young and healthy, and I trust will soon be up again. He seemed to be more concerned about his brave men and officers, who had fallen in the battle, than about himself. . . ."

It was decided, the next day, to send my brother to "Hickory Hill," the home of Mr. W. F. Wickham, in Hanover County, about twenty miles from Richmond, and I was put in charge of him to take him there and to be with him until his wound should heal. Thus it happened that I did not meet my father again until after Gettysburg had been fought, and the army had recrossed into Virginia, almost to the same place I had left it. My father wrote my brother a note the morning after he was wounded, before he left Culpeper. It shows his consideration and tenderness:

"*My Dear Son:* I send you a despatch, received from C. last night. I hope you are comfortable this morning. I wish I could see you, but I cannot. Take care of yourself, and make haste and get well and return. Though I scarcely ever saw you, it was a great comfort to know that you were near and with me. I could think of you and hope to see you. May we yet meet in peace and happiness. . . ."

In a letter to my brother's wife, written on the 11th, his love and concern for both of them are plainly shown:

"I am so grieved, my dear daughter, to send Fitzhugh to you wounded. But I am so grateful that his wound is of a character to give us full hope of a speedy recovery. With his youth and strength to aid him, and your tender care to nurse him, I trust he will soon be well again. I know that you will unite with me in thanks to Almighty God, who has so often sheltered him in the hour of danger, for his recent deliverance, and lift up your whole heart in praise to Him for sparing a life so dear to us, while enabling him to do his duty in the station in which He had placed him. Ask him to join us in supplication that He may always cover him with the shadow of His almighty arm, and teach him that his only refuge is in Him, the greatness of whose mercy reacheth unto the heavens, and His truth unto the clouds. As some good is always mixed with the evil in this world, you will now have him with you for a time, and I shall look to you to cure him soon and send him back to me. . . ."

My brother reached "Hickory Hill" quite comfortably, and his wound commenced to heal finely. His wife joined him, my mother and sisters came up from Richmond, and he had all the tender care he could wish. He occupied "the office" in the yard, while I slept in the room adjoining and became quite an expert nurse. About two weeks after our arrival, one lovely morning as we all came out from the breakfast table, stepping into the front porch with Mrs. Wickham, we were much surprised to hear two or three shots down in the direction of the outer gate, where there was a large grove of hickory trees. Mrs. Wickham said some one must be after her squirrels, as there were many in those woods, and she asked me to run down and stop whoever was shooting them. I got my hat, and at once started off to do her bidding. I had not gone over a hundred yards toward the grove, when I saw, coming up at a gallop to the gate I was making for, five or six Federal cavalrymen.

86

I knew what it meant at once, so I rushed back to the office and told my brother. He immediately understood the situation and directed me to get away—said I could do no good by staying, that the soldiers could not and would not hurt him, and there was nothing to be gained by my falling into their hands; but that, on the contrary, I might do a great deal of good by eluding them, making my way to "North Wales," a plantation across the Pamunkey River, and saving our horses.

So I ran out, got over the fence and behind a thick hedge, just as I heard the tramp and clank of quite a body of troopers riding up. Behind this hedge I crept along until I reached a body of woods, where I was perfectly safe. From a hill near by I ascertained that there was a large raiding party of Federal cavalry in the main road, and the heavy smoke ascending from the Court House, about three miles away, told me that they were burning the railroad buildings at that place. After waiting until I thought the coast was clear, I worked my way very cautiously back to the vicinity of the house to find out what was going on. Fortunately, I took advantage of the luxuriant shrubbery in the old garden at the rear of the house, and when I looked out from the last box bush that screened me, about twenty yards from the back porch, I perceived that I was too soon, for there were standing, sitting and walking about quite a number of the bluecoats. I jumped back behind the group of box trees, and, flinging myself flat under a thick fir, crawled close up to the trunk under the low-hanging branches, and lay there for some hours.

I saw my brother brought out from the office on a mattress, and placed in the "Hickory Hill" carriage, to which was hitched Mr. Wickham's horses, and then saw him driven away, a soldier on the box and a mounted guard surrounding him. He was carried to the "White House" in this way, and then sent by water to Fortress Monroe. This party had been sent out especially to capture him, and he was held as a hostage (for the safety of some Federal officers we had captured) for nine long, weary months.

The next day I found out that all the horses but one had been saved by the faithfulness of our servants. The one lost, my brother's favourite and best horse, was ridden straight into the column by Scott, a negro servant, who had him out for exercise. Before he knew our enemies, he and the horse were prisoners. Scott watched his opportunity, and, not being guarded, soon got away. By crawling through a culvert, under the road, while the cavalry was passing along, he made his way into a deep ditch in the adjoining field, thence succeeded in reaching the farm where the rest of the horses were, and hurried them off to a safe place in the woods, just as the Federal cavalry rode up to get them.

In a letter dated Culpeper, July 26th, to my brother's wife, my father thus urges resignation:

"I received, last night, my darling daughter, your letter of the 18th from 'Hickory Hill.' . . . You must not be sick while Fitzhugh is away, or he will be more restless under his separation. Get strong and hearty by his return, that he may the more rejoice at the sight of you. . . . I can appreciate your distress at Fitzhugh's situation. I deeply sympathise with it, and in the lone hours of the night I groan in sorrow at his captivity and separation from you. But we must bear it, exercise all our patience, and do nothing to aggravate the evil. This, besides injuring ourselves, would rejoice our enemies and be sinful in the eyes of God. In His own good time He will relieve us and make all things work together for our good, if we give Him our love and place in Him our trust. I can see no harm that can result from Fitzhugh's capture, except his detention. I feel assured that he will be well attended to. He will be in the hands of old army officers and surgeons, most of whom are men of principle and humanity. His wound, I understand, has not been injured by his removal, but is doing well. Nothing would do him more harm than for him to learn that you were sick and sad. How could he get well? So cheer up and prove your fortitude and patriotism. . . . You may think of Fitzhugh and love him as much as you please, but do not grieve over him or grow sad."

From Williamsport, to my mother, he thus writes of his son's capture:

"I have heard with great grief that Fitzhugh has been captured by the enemy. Had not expected that he would be taken from his bed and carried off, but we must bear this additional affliction with fortitude and resignation, and not repine at the will of God. It will eventuate in some good that we know not of now. We must bear our labours and hardships manfully. Our noble men are cheerful and confident. I constantly remember you in my thoughts and prayers."

On July 12th, from near Hagerstown, he writes again about him:

"The consequences of war are horrid enough at best, surrounded by all the ameliorations of civilisation and Christianity. I am very sorry for the injuries done the family at Hickory Hill, and particularly that our dear old Uncle Williams, in his eightieth year, should be subjected to such treatment. But we cannot help it, and must endure it. You will, however, learn before this reaches you that our success at Gettysburg was not so great as reported—in fact, that we failed to drive the enemy from his position, and that our army withdrew to the Potomac. Had the river not unexpectedly risen, all would have been well with us; but God, in His all-wise providence, willed otherwise, and our communications have been interrupted and almost cut off. The waters have subsided to about four feet, and, if they continue, by to-morrow, I hope, our communications will be open. I trust that a merciful God, our only hope and refuge, will not desert us in this hour of need, and will deliver us by His almighty hand, that the whole world may recognise His power and all hearts be lifted up in adoration and praise of His unbounded loving-kindness. We must, however, submit to His almighty will, whatever that may be. May God guide and protect us all is my constant prayer."

In 1868, in a letter to Major Wm. M. McDonald, of Berryville, Clarke County, Virginia, who was intending to write a school history, and had written to my father, asking for information about some of his great battles, the following statement appears:

"As to the battle of Gettysburg, I must again refer you to the official accounts. Its loss was occasioned by a combination of circumstances. It was commenced in the absence of correct intelligence. It was continued in the effort to overcome the difficulties by which we were surrounded, and it would have been gained could one determined and united blow have been delivered by our whole line. As it was, victory trembled in the balance for three days, and the battle resulted in the infliction of as great an amount of injury as was received and in frustrating the Federal campaign for the season."

After my brother's capture I went to Richmond, taking with me his horses and servants. After remaining there a short time, I mounted my mare and started back to the army, which I found at its old camping-ground in Culpeper. I stopped at first for a few days with my father. He was very glad to see me, and I could tell him all about my mother and sisters, and many other friends whom I had just left in Richmond. He appeared to be unchanged in manner and appearance. The disappointment in the Gettysburg campaign, to which he alludes in his letter to my mother, was not shown in anything he said or did. He was calm and dignified with all, at times bright and cheerful, and always had a playful smile and a pleasant word for those about him. The army lay inactive, along the line of the Rappahannock and the Rapidan for two months, watching the enemy, who was in our front. We were very anxious to attack or to be attacked, but each general desired to fight on ground of his own choosing.

During this period, and indeed at all times, my father was fully employed. Besides the care of his own immediate command, he advised with the President and Secretary of War as to the movements and dispositions of the other armies in the Confederacy. In looking over his correspondence one is astonished at the amount of it and at its varied character. He always answered all letters addressed to him, from whatever source, if it was possible. During this winter he devoted himself especially to looking after the welfare of his troops, their clothing, shoes, and rations, all three of which were becoming very scarce. Often, indeed, his army had only a few days' rations in sight. Here are some letters written to the authorities, showing how he was hampered in his movements by the deficiencies existing in the quartermaster's and commissary departments. To the Quartermaster-General, at Richmond, he writes, October, 1863, after his movement around General Meade's right, to Manassas:

". . . The want of the supplies of shoes, clothing and blankets is very great. Nothing but my unwillingness to expose the men to the hardships that would have resulted from moving them into Loudoun in their present condition induced me to return to the Rappahannock. But I was averse to marching them over the rough roads of that region, at a season, too, when frosts are certain and snows probable, unless they were better provided to encounter them without suffering. I should, otherwise, have endeavoured to detain General Meade near the Potomac, if I could not throw him to the north side."

In a letter of the same time to the Honourable James A. Seddon, Secretary of War:

". . . If General Meade is disposed to remain quiet where he is, it was my intention, provided the army could be supplied with clothing, again to advance and threaten his position.

Nothing prevented my continuing in his front but the destitute condition of the men, thousands of whom are barefooted, a greater number partially shod, and nearly all without overcoats, blankets, or warm clothing. I think the sublimest sight of war was the cheerfulness and alacrity exhibited by this army in the pursuit of the enemy under all the trials and privations to which it was exposed. . . ."

Later on, in January, when the severe weather commenced, he again writes to the Quartermaster-General on the same subject:

"*General:* The want of shoes and blankets in this army continues to cause much suffering and to impair its efficiency. In one regiment I am informed that there are only fifty men with serviceable shoes, and a brigade that recently went on picket was compelled to leave several hundred men in camp, who were unable to bear the exposure of duty, being destitute of shoes and blankets. . . . The supply, by running the blockade, has become so precarious that I think we should turn our attention chiefly to our own resources, and I should like to be informed how far the latter can be counted upon. . . . I trust that no efforts will be spared to develop our own resources of supply, as a further dependence upon those from abroad can result in nothing but increase of suffering and want. I am, with great respect,

"Your obedient servant,

"R. E. LEE, General."

There was at this time a great revival of religion in the army. My father became much interested in it, and did what he could to promote in his camps all sacred exercises. Reverend J. W. Jones, in his "Personal Reminiscences of General R. E. Lee," says:

"General Lee's orders and reports always gratefully recognised 'The Lord of Hosts' as the 'Giver of Victory,' and expressed an humble dependence upon and trust in Him."

All his correspondence shows the same devout feeling. On August 13, 1863, he issued the following order:

"HEADQUARTERS, ARMY NORTHERN VIRGINIA,
"August 13, 1863.

"The President of the Confederate States has, in the name of the people, appointed August 21st as a day of fasting, humiliation, and prayer. A strict observance of the day is enjoined upon the officers and soldiers of this army. All military duties, except such as are absolutely necessary, will be suspended. The commanding officers of brigades and regiments are requested to cause divine services, suitable to the occasion, to be performed in their respective commands. Soldiers! we have sinned against Almighty God. We have forgotten His signal mercies, and have cultivated a revengeful, haughty, and boastful spirit. We have not remembered that the defenders of a just cause should be pure in His eyes; that 'our times are in His hands,' and we have relied too much on our own arms for the achievement of our independence. God is our only refuge and our strength. Let us humble ourselves before Him. Let us confess our many sins, and beseech Him to give us a higher courage, a purer patriotism, and more determined will; that He will convert the hearts of our enemies; that He will hasten the time when war, with its sorrows and sufferings, shall cease, and that He will give us a name and place among the nations of the earth.

"R. E. LEE, General."

His was a practical, every-day religion, which supported him all through his life, enabled him to bear with equanimity every reverse of fortune, and to accept her gifts without undue elation. During this period of rest, so unusual to the Army of Northern Virginia, several reviews were held before the commanding general. I remember being present when that of the Third Army Corps, General A. P. Hill commanding, took place. Some of us young cavalrymen, then stationed near the Rappahannock, rode over to Orange Court House to see this grand military pageant.

From all parts of the army, officers and men who could get leave came to look on, and from all the surrounding country the people, old and young, ladies and children, came in every pattern of vehicle and on horseback, to see twenty thousand of that "incomparable infantry" of the Army of Northern Virginia pass in review before their great commander.

The General was mounted on Traveller, looking very proud of his master, who had on sash and sword, which he very rarely wore, a pair of new cavalry gauntlets, and, I think, a new hat. At any rate, he looked unusually fine, and sat his horse like a perfect picture of grace and power. The infantry was drawn up in column by divisions, with their bright muskets all glittering in the sun, their battle-flags standing straight out before the breeze, and their bands playing, awaiting the inspection of the General, before they broke into column by companies and marched past him in review. When all was ready, General Hill and staff rode up to General Lee, and the two generals, with their respective staffs, galloped around front and rear of each of the three divisions standing motionless on the plain. As the cavalcade reached the head of each division, its commanding officer joined in and followed as far as the next division, so that there was a continual infusion of fresh groups into the original one all along the lines. Traveller started with a long lope, and never changed his stride. His rider sat erect and calm, not noticing anything but the gray lines of men whom he knew so well. The pace was very fast, as there were nine good miles to go, and the escort began to become less and less, dropping out one by one from different causes as Traveller raced along without a check. When the General drew up, after this nine-mile gallop, under the standard at the reviewing-stand, flushed with the exercise as well as with pride in his brave men, he raised his hat and saluted. Then arose a shout of applause and admiration from the entire assemblage, the memory of which to this day moistens the eye of every old soldier. The corps was then passed in review at a quick-step, company front. It was a most imposing sight. After it was all over, my father rode up to several carriages whose occupants he knew and gladdened them by a smile, a word, or a shake of the hand. He found several of us young officers with some pretty cousins of his from Richmond, and he was very bright and cheerful, joking us young people about each other. His letters to my mother and sister this summer and fall help to give an insight into his thoughts and feelings. On July 15th, from Bunker Hill, in a letter to his wife, he says:

". . . The army has returned to Virginia. Its return is rather sooner than I had originally contemplated, but, having accomplished much of what I proposed on leaving the Rappahannock—namely, relieving the valley of the presence of the enemy and drawing his army north of the Potomac—I determined to recross the latter river. The enemy, after centering his forces in our front, began to fortify himself in his position and bring up his troops, militia, etc.—and those around Washington and Alexandria. This gave him enormous odds. It also circumscribed our limits for procuring subsistence for men and animals, which, with the uncertain state of the river, rendered it hazardous for us to continue on the north side. It has been raining a great deal since we first crossed the Potomac, making the roads horrid and embarrassing our operations. The night we recrossed it rained terribly, yet we got all over safe, save such vehicles as broke down on the road from the mud, rocks, etc. We are all well. I hope we will yet be able to damage our adversaries when they meet us. That it should be so, we must implore the forgiveness of God for our sins, and the continuance of His blessings. There is nothing but His almighty power that can sustain us. God bless you all. . . ."

Later, July 26th, he writes from Camp Culpeper:

". . . After crossing the Potomac, finding that the Shenandoah was six feet above the fording-stage, and, having waited for a week for it to fall, so that I might cross into Loudoun, fearing that the enemy might take advantage of our position and move upon Richmond, I determined to ascend the Valley and cross into Culpeper. Two corps are here with me. The third passed Thornton's Gap, and I hope will be in striking distance to-morrow. The army has laboured hard, endured much, and behaved nobly. It has accomplished all that could be reasonably expected. It ought not to have been expected to perform impossibilities, or to have fulfilled the anticipations of the thoughtless and unreasonable."

On August 2d, from the same camp, he again writes to my mother:

". . . I have heard of some doctor having reached Richmond, who had seen our son at Fortress Monroe. He said that his wound was improving, and that he himself was well and walking about on crutches. The exchange of prisoners that had been going on has, for some cause, been suspended, owing to some crotchet or other, but I hope will soon be resumed, and that we shall have him back soon. The armies are in such close proximity that frequent collisions are common along the outposts. Yesterday the enemy laid down two or three pontoon bridges across the Rappahannock and crossed his cavalry, with a big force of his infantry. It looked at first as if it were the advance of his army, and, as I had not intended to deliver battle, I directed our cavalry to retire slowly before them and to check their too rapid pursuit. Finding, later in the day, that their army was not following, I ordered out the infantry and drove them back to the river. I suppose they intended to push on to Richmond by this or some other route. I trust, however, they will never reach there. . . ."

On August 23d, from the camp near Orange Court House, General Lee writes to Mrs. Lee:

". . . My camp is near Mr. Erasmus Taylor's house, who has been very kind in contributing to our comfort. His wife sends us, every day, buttermilk, loaf bread, ice, and such vegetables as she has. I cannot get her to desist, though I have made two special visits to that effect. All the brides have come on a visit to the army: Mrs. Ewell, Mrs. Walker, Mrs. Heth, etc. General Meade's army is north of the Rappahannock along the Orange and Alexandria Railroad. He is very quiet. . . ."

"September 4, 1863.

". . . You see I am still here. When I wrote last, the indications were that the enemy would move against us any day; but this past week he has been very quiet, and seems at present to continue so. I was out looking at him yesterday, from Clarke's Mountain. He has spread himself over a large surface and looks immense. . . . "

And on September 18th, from the same camp:

". . . The enemy state that they have heard of a great reduction in our forces here, and are now going to drive us back to Richmond. I trust they will not succeed; but our hope and our refuge is in our merciful Father in Heaven. . . ."

On October 9th, the Army of Northern Virginia was put in motion, and was pushed around Meade's right. Meade was gradually forced back to a position near the old battlefield at Manassas. Although we had hard marching, much skirmishing, and several severe fights between the cavalry of both armies, nothing permanent was accomplished, and in about ten days we were back on our old lines. In a letter of October 19, 1863, to his wife, my father says:

". . . I have returned to the Rappahannock. I did not pursue with the main army beyond Bristoe or Broad Run. Our advance went as far as Bull Run, where the enemy was entrenched, extending his right as far as 'Chantilly,' in the yard of which he was building a redoubt. I could have thrown him farther back, but saw no chance of bringing him to battle, and it would only have served to fatigue our troops by advancing farther. I should certainly have endeavored to throw them north of the Potomac; but thousands were barefooted, thousands with fragments of shoes, and all without overcoats, blankets, or warm clothing. I could not bear to expose them to certain suffering and an uncertain issue. . . ."

On October 25th, from "Camp Rappahannock," he writes again to my mother:

". . . I moved yesterday into a nice pine thicket, and Perry is to-day engaged in constructing a chimney in front of my tent, which will make it warm and comfortable. I have no idea when Fitzhugh[4] will be exchanged. The Federal authorities still resist all exchanges, because they think it is to our interest to make them. Any desire expressed on our part for the exchange of any individual magnifies the difficulty, as they at once think some great benefit is to result to us from it. His detention is very grievous to me, and, besides, I want his services. I am glad you have some socks for the army. Send them to me. They will come safely. Tell the girls[5] to send all they can. I wish they could make some shoes, too. We have thousands of barefooted men. There is no news. General Meade, I believe, is repairing the railroad, and I presume will come on again. If I could only get some shoes and clothes for the men, I would save him the trouble. . . ."

One can see from these letters of my father how deeply he felt for the sufferings of his soldiers, and how his plans were hindered by inadequate supplies of food and clothing. I heard him constantly allude to these troubles; indeed, they seemed never absent from his mind.

CHAPTER VI

THE WINTER OF 1863-4

THE LEE FAMILY IN RICHMOND—THE GENERAL'S LETTERS TO
THEM FROM CAMPS RAPPAHANNOCK AND RAPIDAN—DEATH OF
MRS. FITZHUGH LEE—PREPARATIONS TO MEET GENERAL
GRANT—THE WILDERNESS—SPOTT-SYLVANIA COURT HOUSE—
DEATH OF GENERAL STUART—GENERAL LEE'S ILLNESS

My mother had quite recently rented a house on Clay Street in
Richmond which, though small, gave her a roof of her own, and it
also enabled her at times to entertain some of her many friends.
Of this new home, and of a visit of a soldier's wife to him, the
General thus writes:

"CAMP RAPPAHANNOCK, November 1, 1863.

"I received yesterday, dear Mary, your letter of the 29th, and am
very glad to learn that you find your new abode so comfortable and
so well arranged. The only fault I find in it is that it is not large
enough for you all, and that Charlotte, whom I fear requires much
attention, is by herself. Where is 'Life' to go, too, for I suppose she is
a very big personage? But you have never told me where it is situated,
or how I am to direct to you. Perhaps that may be the cause of delay
in my letters. I am sorry you find such difficulty in procuring yarn for
socks, etc. I fear my daughters have not taken to the spinning-wheel
and loom, as I have recommended. I shall not be able to recommend

them to the brave soldiers for wives. I had a visit from a soldier's wife to-day, who was on a visit to her husband. She was from Abbeville district, S. C. Said she had not seen her husband for more than two years, and, as he had written to her for clothes, she herself thought she would bring them on. It was the first time she had travelled by railroad, but she got along very well by herself. She brought an entire suit of her own manufacture for her husband. She spun the yarn and made the clothes herself. She clad her three children in the same way, and had on a beautiful pair of gloves she had made for herself. Her children she had left with her sister. She said she had been here a week and must return to-morrow, and thought she could not go back without seeing me. Her husband accompanied her to my tent, in his nice gray suit. She was very pleasing in her address and modest in her manner, and was clad in a nice, new alpaca. I am certain she could not have made that. Ask Misses Agnes and Sally Warwick what they think of that. They need not ask me for permission to get married until they can do likewise. She, in fact, was an admirable woman. Said she was willing to give up everything she had in the world to attain our independence, and the only complaint she made of the conduct of our enemies was their arming our servants against us. Her greatest difficulty was to procure shoes. She made them for herself and children of cloth with leather soles. She sat with me about ten minutes and took her leave—another mark of sense—and made no request for herself or husband. I wrote you about my wants in my former letter. My rheumatism I hope is a little better, but I have had to-day, and indeed always have, much pain. I trust it will pass away. . . . I have just had a visit from my nephews, Fitz, John, and Henry.[1] The former is now on a little expedition. The latter accompanies him. As soon as I was left alone, I committed them in a fervent prayer to the care and guidance of our Heavenly Father. . . . I pray you may be made whole and happy.

"Truly and devotedly yours,

"R. E. LEE."

Another letter from the same camp is interesting:

"Camp Rappahannock, November 5, 1863.

"I received last night, dear Mary, your letter of the 2d. . . . I am glad to hear that Charlotte is better. I hope that she will get strong and well, poor child. The visit of her 'grandpa' will cheer her up. I trust, and I know, he gave her plenty of good advice. Tell Mrs. Atkinson that her son Nelson is a very good scout and a good soldier. I wish I had some way of promoting him. I received the bucket of butter she was so kind as to send me, but have had no opportunity of returning the vessel, which I hope to be able to do. I am sorry Smith does not like your house. I have told you my only objection to it, and wish it were large enough to hold Charlotte. It must have reminded you of old times to have your brother Carter and Uncle Williams[2] to see you. I think my rheumatism is better to-day. I have been through a great deal with comparatively little suffering. I have been wanting to review the cavalry for some time, and appointed to-day with fear and trembling. I had not been on horseback for five days previously and feared I should not get through. The governor was here and told me Mrs. Letcher had seen you recently. I saw all my nephews looking very handsome, and Rob too. The latter says he has written to you three times since he crossed the river. Tell "Chas." I think F's old regiment, the 9th, made the best appearance in review.

"While on the ground, a man rode up to me and said he was just from Alexandria and had been requested to give me a box, which he handed me, but did not know who sent it. It contained a handsome pair of gilt spurs. Good-night. May a kind heavenly Father guard you all.

"Truly and affectionately,

"R. E. Lee."

When our cavalry was reviewed the preceding summer, it happened that we engaged the next day, June 9th, the enemy's entire force of that arm, in the famous battle of Brandy Station. Since then there had been a sort of superstition amongst us that if we wanted a fight all that was necessary was to have a review. We were now on the same ground we had occupied in June, and the enemy was in force just across the river. As it happened, the fighting did take place, though the cavalry was not alone engaged. Not the day after the review, but on November 7th, Meade advanced and crossed the Rappahannock, while our army fell back and took up our position on the line of the Rapidan.

Before the two armies settled down into winter quarters, General Meade tried once more to get at us, and on the 26th of November, with ten days' rations and in light marching order, he crossed the Rapidan and attempted to turn our right. But he was unable to do anything, being met at every point by the Army of Northern Virginia, heavily entrenched and anxious for an attack. Long says:

"Meade declared that the position could not be carried without the loss of thirty thousand men. This contingency was too terrible to be entertained—yet the rations of the men were nearly exhausted, and nothing remained but retreat. This was safely accomplished on the night of December 1st. . . ."

Lee was more surprised at the retreat of Meade than he had been at his advance, and his men, who had been in high spirits at the prospect of obliterating the memory of Gettysburg, were sadly disappointed at the loss of the opportunity. To my mother, General Lee wrote on December 4th, from "Camp Rapidan":

". . . You will probably have seen that General Meade has retired to his old position on the Rappahannock, without giving us battle. I had expected from his movements, and all that I had heard, that it was his intention to do so, and after the first day, when I thought it necessary to skirmish pretty sharply with him, on both flanks, to ascertain his views, I waited, patiently, his attack. On Tuesday, however, I thought he had changed his mind, and that night made preparations to move around his left next morning and attack him. But when day dawned he was nowhere to be seen. He had commenced to withdraw at dark Tuesday evening. We pursued to the Rapidan, but he was over. Owing to the nature of the ground, it was to our advantage to receive rather than to make the attack. I am greatly disappointed at his getting off with so little damage, but we do not know what is best for us. I believe a kind God has ordered all things for our good. . . ."

About this time the people of the City of Richmond, to show their esteem for my father, desired to present him with a home. General Lee, on hearing of it, thus wrote to the President of the Council:

". . . I assure you, sir, that no want of appreciation of the honour conferred upon me by this resolution—or insensibility to the kind feelings which prompted it—induces me to ask, as I most respectfully do, that no further proceedings be taken with reference to the subject. The house is not necessary for the use of my family, and my own duties will prevent my residence in Richmond. I should therefore be compelled to decline the generous offer, and I trust that whatever means the City Council may have to spare for this purpose may be devoted to the relief of the families of our soldiers in the field, who are more in want of assistance, and more deserving it, than myself. . . ."

My brother was still in prison, and his detention gave my father great concern. In a letter to my mother, written November 21st, he says:

". . . I see by the papers that our son has been sent to Fort Lafayette. Any place would be better than Fort Monroe, with Butler in command. His long confinement is very grievous to me, yet it may all turn out for the best. . . . "

To his daughter-in-law my father was devotedly attached. His love for her was like that for his own children, and when her husband was captured and thrown, wounded, into prison, his great tenderness for her was shown on all occasions. Her death about this time, though expected, was a great blow to him. When news came to Gen. W. H. F. Lee, at Fortress Monroe, that his wife Charlotte was dying in Richmond, he made application to General Butler, commanding that post, that he be allowed to go to her for 48 hours, his brother Custis Lee, of equal rank with himself, having formally volunteered in writing to take his place, as a hostage, until he should return to his captivity. This request was curtly and peremptorily refused.

In his letter to my mother, of December 27th, my father says:

". . . Custis's despatch which I received last night demolished all the hopes, in which I had been indulging during the day, of dear Charlotte's recovery. It has pleased God to take from us one exceedingly dear to us, and we must be resigned to His holy will. She, I trust, will enjoy peace and happiness forever, while we must patiently struggle on under all the ills that may be in store for us. What a glorious thought it is that she has joined her little cherubs and our angel Annie[3] in Heaven. Thus is link by link the strong chain broken that binds us to earth, and our passage soothed to another world. Oh, that we may be at last united in that heaven of rest, where trouble and sorrow never enter, to join in an everlasting chorus of praise and glory to our Lord and Saviour! I grieve for our lost darling as a father only can grieve for a daughter, and my sorrow is heightened by the thought of the anguish her death will cause our dear son and the poignancy it will give to the bars of his prison. May God in His mercy enable him to bear the blow He has so suddenly dealt, and sanctify it to his everlasting happiness!"

After Meade's last move, the weather becoming wintry, the troops fixed up for themselves winter quarters, and the cavalry and artillery were sent back along the line of the Chesapeake & Ohio Railroad, where forage could be more easily obtained for their horses. On January 24, 1864, the General writes to my mother:

". . . I have had to disperse the cavalry as much as possible, to obtain forage for their horses, and it is that which causes trouble. Provisions for the men, too, are very scarce, and, with very light diet and light clothing, I fear they suffer, but still they are cheerful and uncomplaining. I received a report from one division the other day in which it stated that over four hundred men were barefooted and over a thousand without blankets."

Lee was the idol of his men. Colonel Charles Marshall, who was his A. D. C. and military secretary, illustrates this well in the following incident:

"While the Army was on the Rapidan, in the winter of 1863–4, it became necessary, as was often the case, to put the men on very short rations. Their duty was hard, not only on the outposts during the winter, but in the construction of roads, to facilitate communication between the different parts of the army. One day General Lee received a letter from a private soldier, whose name I do not now remember, informing him of the work that he had to do, and stating that his rations were not sufficient to enable him to undergo the fatigue. He said, however, that if it was absolutely necessary to put him upon such short allowance, he would make the best of it, but that he and his comrades wanted to know if General Lee was aware that his men were getting so little to eat, because if he was aware of it he was sure there must be some necessity for it. General Lee did not reply directly to the letter, but issued a general order in which he informed the soldiers of his efforts in their behalf, and that their privation was beyond his means of present relief, but assured them that he was making every effort to procure sufficient supplies. After that there was not a murmur in the army, and the hungry men went cheerfully to their hard work."

When I returned to the army in the summer, I reported to my old brigade, which was gallantly commanded by John R. Chambliss, Colonel of the 13th Virginia Cavalry, the senior officer of the brigade. Later, I had been assigned to duty with General Fitz Lee and was with him at this time. My mother was anxious that I should be with my father, thinking, I have no doubt, that my continued presence would be a comfort to him. She must have written him to that effect, for in a letter to her, dated February, 1864, he says:

". . . In reference to Rob, his company would be a great pleasure and comfort to me, and he would be extremely useful in various ways, but I am opposed to officers surrounding themselves with their sons and relatives. It is wrong in principle, and in that case selections would be made from private and social relations, rather than for the public good. There is the same objection to his going with Fitz Lee. I should prefer Rob's being in the line, in an independent position, where he could rise by his own merit and not through the recommendation of his relatives. I expect him soon, when I can better see what he himself thinks. The young men have no fondness for the society of the old general. He is too heavy and sombre for them. . . ."

If anything was said to me on this occasion by my father, I do not remember it. I rather think that something prevented the interview, for I cannot believe that it could have entirely escaped my memory. At any rate, I remained with General Fitz Lee until my brother's return from prison in April of that year. Fitz Lee's brigade camped near Charlottesville, on the Chesapeake & Ohio Rilroad, in January, in order that forage could be more readily obtained. The officers, to amuse themselves and to return in part the courtesies and kindnesses of the ladies of the town, gave a ball. It was a grand affair for those times. Committees were appointed and printed invitations issued. As a member of the invitation committee, I sent one to the general commanding the army. Here is his opinion of it, in a letter to me:

". . . I inclose a letter for you, which has been sent to my care. I hope you are well and all around you are so. Tell Fitz I grieve over the hardships and sufferings of his men, in their late expedition. I should have preferred his waiting for more favourable weather.

He accomplished much under the circumstances, but would have done more in better weather. I am afraid he was anxious to get back to the ball. This is a bad time for such things. We have too grave subjects on hand to engage in such trivial amusements. I would rather his officers should entertain themselves in fattening their horses, healing their men, and recruiting their regiments. There are too many Lees on the committee. I like all to be present at battles, but can excuse them at balls. But the saying is, 'Children will be children.' I think he had better move his camp farther from Charlottesville, and perhaps he will get more work and less play. He and I are too old for such assemblies. I want him to write me how his men are, his horses, and what I can do to fill up the ranks. . . ."

In this winter and spring of 1864, every exertion possible was made by my father to increase the strength of his army and to improve its efficiency. He knew full well that the enemy was getting together an enormous force, and that his vast resources would be put forth to crush us in the spring. His letters at this time to President Davis and the Secretary of War show how well he understood the difficulties of his position.

"In none of them," General Long says, "does he show a symptom of despair or breathe a thought of giving up the contest. To the last, he remained full of resources, energetic and defiant, and ready to bear upon his shoulders the whole burden of the conduct of the war."

In a letter to President Davis, written March, 1864, he says:

"*Mr. President:* Since my former letter on the subject, the indications that operations in Virginia will be vigorously prosecuted by the enemy are stronger than they then were. General Grant has returned from the army in the West. He is, at present, with the Army of the Potomac, which is being organised and recruited. . . . Every train brings recruits, and it is stated that every available regiment at the North is added to it. . . . Their plans are not sufficiently developed to discover them, but I think we can assume that, if General Grant is to direct operations on this frontier, he will concentrate a large force on one or more lines, and prudence dictates that we should make such preparations as are in our power. . . ."

On April 6th he again writes to the President:

". . . All the information I receive tends to show that the great effort of the enemy in this campaign will be made in Virginia. . . . Reinforcements are certainly daily arriving to the Army of the Potomac. . . . The tone of the Northern papers, as well as the impression prevailing in their armies, go to show that Grant with a large force is to move against Richmond. . . . The movements and reports of the enemy may be intended to mislead us, and should therefore be carefully observed. But all the information that reaches me goes to strengthen the belief that General Grant is preparing to move against Richmond."

The question of feeding his army was ever before him. To see his men hungry and cold, and his horses ill fed, was a great pain to him. To Mr. Davis he thus writes on this subject:

"HEADQUARTERS, April 12, 1864.

"*Mr. President:* My anxiety on the subject of provisions for the army is so great that I cannot refrain from expressing it to Your Excellency. I cannot see how we can operate with our present supplies. Any derangement in their arrival or disaster to the railroad would render it impossible for me to keep the army together, and might force a retreat into North Carolina. There is nothing to be had in this section for men or animals. We have rations for the troops to-day and to-morrow. I hope a new supply arrived last night, but I have not yet had a report. Every exertion should be made to supply the depots at Richmond and at other points. All pleasure travel should cease, and everything be devoted to necessary wants.

"I am, with great respect, your obedient servant,

"R. E. LEE, General."

In a letter written to our cousin, Margaret Stuart, of whom he was very fond, dated March 29th, he says:

". . . The indications at present are that we shall have a hard struggle. General Grant is with the Army of the Potomac. All the officers' wives, sick, etc., have been sent to Washington. No ingress into or egress from the lines is now permitted and no papers are allowed to come out—they claim to be assembling a large force. . . ."

Again, April 28th, he writes to this same young cousin:

". . . I dislike to send letters within reach of the enemy, as they might serve, if captured, to bring distress on others. But you must sometimes cast your thoughts on the Army of Northern Virginia, and never forget it in your prayers. It is preparing for a great struggle, but I pray and trust that the great God, mighty to deliver, will spread over it His almighty arms, and drive its enemies before it. . . ."

One perceives from these letters how clearly my father foresaw the storm that was so soon to burst upon him. He used every means within his power to increase and strengthen his army to meet it, and he continually urged the authorities at Richmond to make preparations in the way of supplies of ammunition, rations, and clothing.

I shall not attempt to describe any part of this campaign except in a very general way. It has been well written up by both sides, and what was done by the Army of Northern Virginia we all know. I saw my father only once or twice, to speak to him, during the thirty odd days from the Wilderness to Petersburg, but, in common with all his soldiers, I felt that he was ever near, that he could be entirely trusted with the care of us, that he would not fail us, that it would all end well. The feeling of trust that we had in him was simply sublime.

When I say "we," I mean the men of my age and standing, officers and privates alike. Older heads may have begun to see the "beginning of the end" when they saw that slaughter and defeat did not deter our enemy, but made him the more determined in his "hammering" process; but it never occurred to me, and to thousands and thousands like me, that there was any occasion for uneasiness. We firmly believed that "Marse Robert," as his soldiers lovingly called him, would bring us out of this trouble all right.

When Grant reached Spottsylvania Court House, he sent all of his cavalry, under Sheridan, to break our communications. They were met at Yellow Tavern, six miles from Richmond, by General Stuart, with three brigades of Confederate cavalry, and were attacked so fiercely that they were held there nearly all day, giving time for the troops around and in Richmond to concentrate for the defense of the city.

In this fight General Stuart fell mortally wounded, and he died the next day in Richmond. The death of our noted cavalry leader was a great blow to our cause—a loss second only to that of Jackson.

Captain W. Gordon McCabe writes me:

"I was sitting on my horse very near to General Lee, who was talking to my colonel, William Johnson Pegram, when a courier galloped up with the despatch announcing that Stuart had been mortally wounded and was dying. General Lee was evidently greatly affected, and said slowly, as he folded up the despatch, 'General Stuart has been mortally wounded: a most valuable and able officer.' Then, after a moment, he added in a voice of deep feeling, '*He never brought me a piece of false information*'—turned and looked away. What praise dearer to a soldier's heart could fall from the lips of the commanding general touching his Chief of Cavalry! These simple words of Lee constitute, I think, the fittest inscription for the monument that is soon to be erected to the memory of the great cavalry leader of the 'Army of Northern Virginia.'"

In a letter from my father to my mother, dated Spottsylvania Court House, May 16th, he says:

"... As I write I am expecting the sound of the guns every moment. I grieve over the loss of our gallant officers and men, and miss their aid and sympathy. A more zealous, ardent, brave, and devoted soldier than Stuart the Confederacy cannot have. Praise be to God for having sustained us so far. I have thought of you very often in these eventful days. God bless and preserve you."

General Lee, in his order announcing the death of Stuart, thus speaks of him:

"... Among the gallant soldiers who have fallen in this war, General Stuart was second to none in valour, in zeal, and in unflinching devotion to his country. His achievements form a conspicuous part of the history of this army, with which his name and services will be forever associated. To military capacity of a high order and to the noble virtues of the soldier he added the brighter graces of a pure life, guided and sustained by the Christian's faith and hope. The mysterious hand of an all-wise God has removed him from the scene of his usefulness and fame. His grateful countrymen will mourn his loss and cherish his memory. To his comrades in arms he has left the proud recollections of his deeds and the inspiring influence of his example."

Speaking of the operations around Spottsylvania Court House, Swinton, the historian of the Army of the Potomac, says:

"Before the lines of Spottsylvania, the Army of the Potomac had for twelve days and nights engaged in a fierce wrestle in which it had done all that valour may do to carry a position by nature and art impregnable. In this contest, unparalleled in its continuous fury, and swelling to the proportions of a campaign, language is inadequate to convey an impression of the labours, fatigues, and sufferings of the troops, who fought by day, only to march by night, from point to point of the long line, and renew the fight on the morrow. Above forty thousand men had already fallen in the bloody encounters of the Wilderness and Spottsylvania, and the exhausted army began to lose its spirits. It was with joy, therefore, that it at length turned its back upon the lines of Spottsylvania."

General Long, in his "Memoirs of General Lee," speaking of our army at this time, says:

"In no previous operations did the Army of Northern Virginia display higher soldierly qualities. Regardless of numbers, every breach was filled, and, with unparalleled stubbornness, its lines were maintained. The soldiers of that army not only gratified their countrymen, but by their gallantry and vigour won the admiration of their enemies. Wherever the men in blue appeared they were met by those in gray, and muzzle to muzzle and point to point they measured their foeman's strength."

When we learned that General Lee was ill—confined for a day or two to his tent, at the time he was confronting General Grant on the North Anna—this terrible thought forced itself upon us: Suppose disease should disable him, even for a time, or, worse, should take him forever from the front of his men! It could not be! It was too awful to consider! And we banished any such possibility from our minds. When we saw him out again, on the lines, riding Traveller as usual, it was as if some great crushing weight had been suddenly lifted from our hearts. Colonel Walter H. Taylor, his adjutant-general, says:

"The indisposition of General Lee . . . was more serious than was generally supposed. Those near him were very apprehensive lest he should be compelled to give up."

General Early also writes of this circumstance:

"One of his three corps commanders[4] had been disabled by wounds at the Wilderness, and another was too unwell to command his corps[5], while he (General Lee) was suffering from a most annoying and weakening disease. In fact, nothing but his own determined will enabled him to keep the field at all; and it was then rendered more manifest than ever that he was the head and front, the very life and soul of the army."

CHAPTER VII

FRONTING THE ARMY OF THE POTOMAC

BATTLE OF COLD HARBOUR—SIEGE OF PETERSBURG—THE
GENERAL INTRUSTS A MISSION TO HIS SON, ROBERT—
BATTLE OF THE CRATER—GRANT CROSSES THE JAMES
RIVER—GENERAL LONG'S PEN-PICTURE OF LEE—KNITTING
SOCKS FOR THE SOLDIERS—A CHRISTMAS DINNER—INCIDENTS
OF CAMP LIFE

FROM the North Anna River the Federal Army moved by its left flank, seeking to find its adversary unprepared, but the Army of Northern Virginia steadily confronted it, ever ready to receive any attack. At Cold Harbour they paused, facing each other, and General Grant, having received sixteen thousand men from Butler by way of Yorktown on June 1st, made an attack, but found our lines immovable. In his "Memoirs" he writes:

"June 2d was spent in getting troops into position for attack on the 3d. On June 3d, we again assaulted the enemy's work in the hope of driving him from his position. In this attempt our loss was heavy, while that of the enemy, I have reason to believe, was comparatively light."

This assault was repelled along the whole line, with the most terrible slaughter yet recorded in our war. Yet in a few hours these beaten men were ordered to move up to our lines again. Swinton, the historian of the Army of the Potomac, thus describes what happened when this order was sent to the men:

"The order was issued through these officers" (the corps commanders) "to their subordinate commanders, and from them descended through the wonted channels; but no man stirred, and the immobile lines pronounced a verdict, silent, yet emphatic, against further slaughter. The loss on the Union side in this sanguinary action was more than thirteen thousand, while on the part of the Confederates it is doubtful whether it reached that many hundreds."

Colonel Walter H. Taylor, in his "Four Years with General Lee," says:

"Soon after this, he (Grant) abandoned his chosen line of operations, and moved his army to the south side of the James River. The struggle from the Wilderness to this point covers a period of about one month, during which time there had been an almost daily encounter of hostile arms, and the Army of Northern Virginia had placed *hors de combat* of the army under General Grant a number equal to its entire numerical strength at the commencement of the campaign, and, notwithstanding its own heavy losses and the reinforcements received by the enemy, still presented an impregnable front to its opponent, and constituted an insuperable barrier to General Grant's 'On to Richmond.'"

Thus after thirty days of marching, starving, fighting, and with a loss of more than sixty thousand men, General Grant reached the James River, near Petersburg, which he could have done at any time he so desired without the loss of a single man. The baffling of our determined foe so successfully raised the spirits of our rank and file, and their confidence in their commander knew no bounds.

The two armies now commenced a contest which could end only one way. If General Lee had been permitted to evacuate Petersburg and Richmond, to fall back upon some interior point, nearer supplies for man and beast and within supporting distance of the remaining forces of the Confederacy, the surrender would certainly have been put off—possibly never have taken place—and the result of the war changed. The Army of the Potomac placed itself on the James, through whose channel it had easy access to the wide world whence to secure for itself an unlimited supply of men and munitions of war. General Lee, with a line thirty miles long to defend and with only 35,000 men to hold it, with no chance of reinforcements, no reserves with which to fill up the ranks lessened daily by death in battle and by disease, had to sit still and see his army, on half rations or less, melt away because it was deemed advisable by his government, for political and other purposes, to hold Richmond, the Confederacy's capital.

In an article by Lord Wolseley, in *Macmillan's Magazine*, he says:

"Lee was opposed to the final defense of Richmond that was urged upon him for political, not military reasons. It was a great strategic error. General Grant's large army of men was easily fed, and its daily losses easily recruited from a near base; whereas, if it had been drawn far into the interior after the little army with which Lee endeavoured to protect Richmond, its fighting strength would have been largely reduced by the detachments required to guard a long line of communications through a hostile country."

During the nine months the siege of Petersburg lasted, I saw my father but seldom. His headquarters were near the town, my command was on the extreme right of the army, and during the winter, in order to get forage, we were moved still further away, close to the border of North Carolina. During this summer, I had occasion, once or twice, to report to him at his headquarters, once about July 1st by his special order. I remember how we all racked our brains to account for this order, which was for me to report "at once to the commanding general," and many wild guesses were made by my young companions as to what was to become of me. Their surmises extended from my being shot for unlawful foraging to my being sent on a mission abroad to solicit the recognition of our independence. I reported at once, and found my father expecting me, with a bed prepared. It was characteristic of him that he never said a word about what I was wanted for until he was ready with full instructions. I was fed at once, for I was still hungry, my bed was shown me, and I was told to rest and sleep well, as he wanted me in the morning, and that I would need all my strength.

The next morning he gave me a letter to General Early, who, with his command, was at that time in Maryland, threatening Washington. My mission was to carry this letter to him. As Early had cut loose from his communications with Virginia, and as there was a chance of any messenger to him being caught by raiding parties, my father gave me verbally the contents of his letter, and told me that if I saw any chance of my capture to destroy it, then, if I did reach the General, I should be able to tell him what he had written. He cautioned me to keep my own counsel, and to say nothing to any one as to my destination. Orders for a relay of horses from Staunton, where the railroad terminated, to the Potomac had been telegraphed, and I was to start at once. This I did, seeing my sisters and mother in Richmond while waiting for the train to Staunton, and having very great difficulty in keeping from them my destination. But I did, and, riding night and day, came up with General Early at a point in Maryland some miles beyond the old battlefield of Sharpsburg. I delivered the letter to him, returned to Petersburg, and reported to my father. Much gratified by the evident pleasure of the General at my diligence and at the news I had brought from Early and his men, after a night's rest and two good meals I returned to my command, never telling my comrades until long afterward what had been done to me by the commanding general.

My father's relations with the citizens of Petersburg were of the kindest description. The ladies were ever trying to make him more comfortable, sending him of their scanty fare more than they could well spare. He always tried to prevent them, and when he could do so without hurting their feelings he would turn over to the hospitals the dainties sent him—much to the disgust of his mess-steward, Bryan. Bryan was an Irishman, perfectly devoted to my father, and, in his opinion, there was nothing in the eatable line which was too good for the General. He was an excellent caterer, a good forager, and, but for my father's frowning down anything approaching lavishness, the headquarters' table would have made a much better show. During this period of the war, Bryan was so handicapped by the universal scarcity of all sorts of provisions that his talents were almost entirely hidden. The ladies not only were anxious to feed the General, but also to clothe him. From Camp Petersburg he writes to my mother, June 24th:

". . . The ladies of Petersburg have sent me a nice set of shirts. They were given to me by Mrs. James R. Branch and her mother, Mrs. Thomas Branch. In fact, they have given me everything, which I fear they cannot spare—vegetables, bread, milk, ice-cream. To-day one of them sent me a nice peach—the first one I think I have seen for two years. I sent it to Mrs. Shippen[1]. Mr. Platt had services again to-day under the trees near my camp. We had quite a large congregation of citizens, ladies and gentlemen, and our usual number of soldiers. During the services, I constantly heard the shells crashing among the houses of Petersburg. Tell 'Life'[2] I send her a song composed by a French soldier. As she is so learned in the language, I want her to send me a reply in verse."

June 30, 1864, the anniversary of his wedding day, he thus writes to my mother:

". . . I was very glad to receive your letter yesterday, and to hear that you were better. I trust that you will continue to improve and soon be as well as usual. God grant that you may be entirely restored in His own good time. Do you recollect what a happy day thirty-three years ago this was? How many hopes and pleasures it gave birth to! God has been very merciful and kind to us, and how thankless and sinful I have been. I pray that He may continue His mercies and blessings to us, and give us a little peace and rest together in this world, and finally gather us and all He has given us around His throne in the world to come. The President has just arrived, and I must bring my letter to a close."

My mother had been quite ill that summer, and my father's anxiety for her comfort and welfare, his desire to be with her to help her, was very great. The sick in the Confederacy at this period of universal scarcity suffered for want of the simplest medicines. All that could be had were given to hospitals. To his youngest daughter the General writes, and sends to Mrs. Lee what little he could find in the way of fruit:

". . . I received this morning by your brother your note of the 3d, and am glad to hear that your mother is better. I sent out immediately to try to find some lemons, but could only procure two, sent to me by a kind lady, Mrs. Kirkland, in Petersburg. These were gathered from her own trees. There are none to be purchased. I found one in my valise, dried up, which I also send, as it may prove of some value. I also put up some early apples which you can roast for your mother, and one pear. This is all the fruit I can get. You must go to market every morning and see if you cannot find some fruit for her. There are no lemons to be had. Tell her lemonade is not as palatable or digestible as buttermilk. Try to get some good buttermilk for her. With ice, it is delicious and very nutritious."

My sister Mildred had a pet squirrel which ran about the house in Richmond. She had named it "Custis Morgan," after her brother Custis, and General John Morgan, the great cavalry leader of the western army. He ventured out one day to see the city, and never returned. In a letter to Mildred, July 10th, my father alludes to his escape, and apparently considers it a blessing:

". . . I was pleased on the arrival of my little courier to learn that you were better, and that 'Custis Morgan' was still among the missing. I think the farther he gets from you the better you will be. The shells scattered the poor inhabitants of Petersburg so that many of the churches are closed. Indeed, they have been visited by the enemy's shells. Mr. Platt, pastor of the principal Episcopal church, had services at my headquarters to-day. The services were under the trees, and the discourse on the subject of salvation. . . ."

About this time, the enemy, having been at work on a mine for nearly a month, exploded it, and attacked our lines with a large force. The ensuing contest was called the Battle of the Crater. General Lee, having suspected that a mine was being run under his works, was partly prepared for it, and the attack was repulsed very quickly with great loss to the enemy. In the address of Capt. W. Gordon McCabe before the Association of the Army of Northern Virginia—November 2, 1876—speaking of this event, he says:

"From mysterious paragraphs in the Northern papers, and from reports of deserters, though those last were vague and contradictory, Lee and Beauregard suspected that the enemy was mining in front of some one of the three salients on Beauregard's front, and the latter officer had in consequence directed counter-mines to be sunk from all three, meanwhile constructing gorge-lines in the rear upon which the troops might retire in case of surprise or disaster. . . . But the counter-mining on the part of the Confederates was after a time discontinued, owing to the lack of proper tools, the inexperience of the troops in such work, and the arduous nature of their service in the trenches."

The mine was sprung July 30th. On the 31st, the General writes:

". . . Yesterday morning the enemy sprung a mine under one of our batteries on the line and got possession of a portion of our intrenchments. It was the part defended by General Beauregard's troops. I sent General Mahone with two brigades of Hill's corps, who charged into them handsomely, recapturing the intrenchments and guns, twelve stands of colours, seventy-three officers, including General Bartlett, his staff, three colonels, and eight hundred and fifty enlisted men. There were upward of five hundred of his dead unburied in the trenches, among them many officers and blacks. He suffered severely. He has withdrawn his troops from the north side of the James. I do not know what he will attempt next. He is mining on other points along our line. I trust he will not succeed in bettering his last attempt. . . . "

Grant, by means of a pontoon bridge, permanently established across the James, was able to move his troops very quickly from one side to the other, and could attack either flank, while making a feint on the opposite one. This occurred several times during the summer, but General Lee seemed always to have anticipated the movement and to be able to distinguish the feint from the real attack. On August 14th, he speaks of one of these movements in a letter to my mother:

". . . I have been kept from church to-day by the enemy's crossing to the north side of the James River and the necessity of moving troops to meet him. I do not know what his intentions are. He is said to be cutting a canal across the Dutch Gap, a point in the river—but I cannot, as yet, discover it. I was up there yesterday, and saw nothing to indicate it. We shall ascertain in a day or two. I received to-day a kind letter from Reverend Mr. Cole, of Culpeper Court House. He is a most excellent man in all the relations of life. He says there is not a church standing in all that country, within the lines formerly occupied by the enemy. All are razed to the ground, and the materials used often for the vilest purposes. Two of the churches at the Court House barely escaped destruction. The pews were all taken out to make seats for the theatre. The fact was reported to the commanding officer by their own men of the Christian Commission, but he took no steps to rebuke or arrest it. We must suffer patiently to the end, when all things will be made right. . . ."

To oppose this movement (of August 14th), which was in heavy force, our cavalry division was moved over to the north side, together with infantry and artillery, and we had a very lively time for several days. In the engagement on the 15th of August I was shot in the arm and disabled for about three weeks. The wound was a very simple one—just severe enough to give me a furlough, which I enjoyed intensely. Time heals all wounds, it is said. I remember it cured mine all too soon, for, being on a wounded leave, provided it did not keep one in bed, was the best luck a soldier could have. I got back the last of September, and in passing stopped to see my father. I take from General Long a pen-picture of him at this time, which accords with my own recollection of his appearance:

". . . General Lee continued in excellent health and bore his many cares with his usual equanimity. He had aged somewhat in appearance since the beginning of the war, but had rather gained than lost in physical vigour, from the severe life he had led. His hair had grown gray, but his face had the ruddy hue of health, and his eyes were as clear and bright as ever. His dress was always a plain, gray uniform, with cavalry boots reaching to his knees, and a broad-brimmed gray felt hat. He seldom wore a weapon, and his only mark of rank was the stars on his collar. Though always abstemious in diet, he seemed able to bear any amount of fatigue, being capable of remaining in his saddle all day and at his desk half the night."

I cannot refrain from further quoting from the same author this beautiful description of the mutual love, respect, and esteem existing between my father and his soldiers:

"No commander was ever more careful, and never had care for the comfort of an army given rise to greater devotion. He was constantly calling the attention of the authorities to the wants of his soldiers, making every effort to provide them with food and clothing. The feeling for him was one of love, not of awe or dread. They could approach him with the assurance that they would be received with kindness and consideration, and that any just complaint would receive proper attention. There was no condescension in his manner, but he was ever simple, kind, and sympathetic, and his men, while having unbounded faith in him as a leader, almost worshipped him as a man. These relations of affection and mutual confidence between the army and its commander had much to do with the undaunted bravery displayed by the men, and bore a due share in the many victories they gained."

Colonel Charles Marshall, in his address before the "Association of the Army of Northern Virginia," also alludes to this "wonderful influnce over the troops under his command. I can best describe that influence by saying that such was the love and veneration of the men for him that they came to look upon the cause as General Lee's cause, and they fought for it because they loved him. To them he represented cause, country, and all."

All persons who were ever thrown into close relations with him had somewhat these same feelings. How could they help it? Here is a letter to his youngest daughter which shows his beautiful love and tenderness for us all. Throughout the war, he constantly took the time from his arduous labours to send to his wife and daughters such evidences of his affection for them:

"CAMP PETERSBURG, November 6, 1864.
"*My Precious Life:* This is the first day I have had leisure to answer your letter. I enjoyed it very much at the time of its reception, and have enjoyed it since, but I have often thought of you in the meantime, and have seen you besides. Indeed, I may say, you are never out of my thoughts. I hope you think of me often, and if you could know how earnestly I desire your true happiness, how ardently I pray you may be directed to every good and saved from every evil, you would as sincerely strive for its accomplishment. Now in your youth you must be careful to discipline your thoughts, words, and actions. Habituate yourself to useful employment, regular improvement, and to the benefit of all those around

you. You have had some opportunity of learning the rudiments of your education—not as good as I should have desired, but I am much cheered by the belief that you availed yourself of it—and I think you are now prepared by diligence and study to learn whatever you desire. Do not allow yourself to forget what you have spent so much time and labour in acquiring, but increase it every day by extended application. I hope you will embrace in your studies all useful acquisitions. I was much pleased to hear that while at 'Bremo' you passed much of your time in reading and music. All accomplishments will enable you to give pleasure, and thus exert a wholesome influence. Never neglect the means of making yourself useful in the world. I think you will not have to complain of Rob again for neglecting your schoolmates. He has equipped himself with a new uniform from top to toe, and, with a new and handsome horse, is cultivating a marvellous beard and preparing for conquest. I went down on the lines to the right, Friday, beyond Rowanty Creek, and pitched my camp within six miles of Fitzhugh's last night. Rob came up and spent the night with me, and Fitzhugh appeared early in the morning. They rode with me till late that day. I visited the battlefield in that quarter, and General Hampton in describing it said there had not been during the war a more spirited charge than Fitzhugh's division made that day up the Boydton plank road, driving cavalry and infantry before him, in which he was stopped by night. I did not know before that his horse had been shot under him. Give a great deal of love to your dear mother, and kiss your sisters for me. Tell them they must keep well, not talk too much, and go to bed early.

"Ever your devoted father,

"R. E. Lee."

He refers in this letter to his coming down near our command, and my brother's visit and mine to him. Everything was quiet, and we greatly enjoyed seeing him and being with him. The weather, too, was fine, and he seemed to delight in our ride with him along the lines. I don't think I saw him but once more until everything was over and we met in Richmond. Some time before this, my mother, fearing for his health under the great amount of exposure and work he had to do, wrote to him and begged him to take better care of himself. In his reply, he says:

". . . But what care can a man give to himself in the time of war? It is from no desire for exposure or hazard that I live in a tent, but from necessity. I must be where I can, speedily, at all times, attend to the duties of my position, and be near or accessible to the officers with whom I have to act. I have been offered rooms in the houses of our citizens, but I could not turn the dwellings of my kind hosts into a barrack where officers, couriers, distressed women, etc., would be entering day and night. . . . "

General Fitz Lee, in his life of my father, says of him at this time:

"Self-possessed and calm, Lee struggled to solve the huge military problem, and make the sum of smaller numbers equal to that of greater numbers. . . . His thoughts ever turned upon the soldiers of his army, the ragged gallant fellows around him—whose pinched cheeks told hunger was their portion, and whose shivering forms denoted the absence of proper clothing."

His letters to my mother during the winter tell how much his men were in need. My mother was an invalid from rheumatism, confined to a rolling-chair. To help the cause with her own hands as far as she could, she was constantly occupied in knitting socks for the soldiers, and induced all around her to do the same. She sent them directly to my father, and he always acknowledged them. November 30th, he says:

". . . I received yesterday your letter on the 27th and am glad to learn your supply of socks is so large. If two or three hundred would send an equal number, we should have a sufficiency. I will endeavour to have them distributed to the most needy. . . . "

And on December 17th:

". . . I received day before yesterday the box with hat, gloves, and socks; also the barrel of apples. You had better have kept the latter, as it would have been more useful to you than to me, and I should have enjoyed its consumption by you and the girls more than by me. . . ."

His friends and admirers were constantly sending him presents; some, simple mementos of their love and affection; others, substantial and material comforts for the outer and inner man. The following letter, from its date, is evidently an acknowledgment of Christmas gifts sent him:

"December 30th. . . The Lyons furs and fur robe have also arrived safely, but I can learn nothing of the saddle of mutton. Bryan, of whom I inquired as to its arrival, is greatly alarmed lest it has been sent to the soldiers' dinner. If the soldiers get it, I shall be content. I can do very well without it. In fact, I should rather they should have it than I. . . ."

The soldiers' "dinner" here referred to was a Christmas dinner, sent by the entire country, as far as they could, to the poor starving men in the trenches and camps along the lines. It would not be considered much now, but when the conditions were such as my father describes when he wrote to the Secretary of War,

"The struggle now is to keep the army fed and clothed. Only fifty men in some regiments have shoes, and bacon is only issued once in a few days,"

anything besides the one-quarter of a pound of bacon and musty corn-bread was a treat of great service, and might be construed as "a Christmas dinner."

I have mentioned before my father's devotion to children. This sentiment pervaded his whole nature. At any time the presence of a little child would bring a brightness to his smile, a tender softness to his glance, and drive away gloom or care. Here is his account of a visit paid him, early in January, 1865, by three little women:

"... Yesterday afternoon three little girls walked into my room, each with a small basket. The eldest carried some fresh eggs, laid by her own hens; the second, some pickles made by her mother; the third, some popcorn grown in her garden. They were accompanied by a young maid with a block of soap made by her mother. They were the daughters of a Mrs. Nottingham, a refugee from Northampton County, who lived near Eastville, not far from 'old Arlington.' The eldest of the girls, whose age did not exceed eight years, had a small wheel on which she spun for her mother, who wove all the cloth for her two brothers—boys of twelve and fourteen years. I have not had so pleasant a visit for a long time. I fortunately was able to fill their baskets with apples, which distressed poor Bryan[3], and I begged them to bring me nothing but kisses and to keep the eggs, corn, etc., for themselves. I pray daily and almost hourly to our Heavenly Father to come to the relief of you and our afflicted country. I know He will order all things for our good, and we must be content."

CHAPTER VIII

THE SURRENDER

FORT FISHER CAPTURED—LEE MADE COMMANDER-IN-CHIEF—BATTLE OF FIVE FORKS—RETREAT OF THE ARMY OF NORTHERN VIRGINIA—FAREWELL TO HIS MEN—THE GENERAL'S RECEPTION IN RICHMOND AFTER THE SURRENDER—PRESIDENT DAVIS HEARS THE NEWS—LEE'S VISITORS—HIS SON ROBERT TURNS FARMER

THE year 1865 had now commenced. The strength of that thin gray line, drawn out to less than one thousand men to the mile, which had repulsed every attempt of the enemy to break through it, was daily becoming less. The capture of Fort Fisher, our last open port, January 15th, cut off all supplies and munitions from the outside world. Sherman had reached Savannah in December, from which point he was ready to unite with Grant at any time. From General Lee's letters, official and private, one gets a clear view of the desperateness of his position. He had been made commander-in-chief of all the military forces in the Confederate States on February 6th. In his order issued on accepting this command he says:

". . . Deeply impressed with the difficulties and responsibilities of the position, and humbly invoking the guidance of Almighty God, I rely for success upon the courage and fortitude of the army, sustained by the patriotism and firmness of the people, confident that their united efforts under the blessing of Heaven will secure peace and independence. . . ."

General Beauregard, who had so ably defended Petersburg when it was first attacked, and who had assisted so materially in its subsequent defense, had been sent to gather troops to try to check Sherman's advance through the Carolinas. But Beauregard's health was now very bad, and it was feared he would have to abandon the field. In a letter to the Secretary of War, dated February 21, 1865, my father says:

"... In the event of the necessity of abandoning our position on James River, I shall endeavour to unite the corps of the army about Burkeville[1], so as to retain communication with the North and South as long as practicable, and also with the West. I should think Lynchburg, or some point west, the most advantageous place to which to remove stores from Richmond. This, however, is a most difficult point at this time to decide, and the place may have to be changed by circumstances. It was my intention in my former letter to apply for General Joseph E. Johnston, that I might assign him to duty, should circumstances permit. I have had no official report of the condition of General Beauregard's health. It is stated from many sources to be bad. If he should break down entirely, it might be fatal. In that event, I should have no one with whom to supply his place. I therefore respectfully request General Johnston may be ordered to report to me, and that I may be informed where he is."

In a letter to the Secretary of War, written the next day:

"... But you may expect Sheridan to move up the Valley, and Stoneman from Knoxville, as Sherman draws near Roanoke. What then will become of those sections of the country? I know of no other troops that could be given to Beauregard. Bragg will be forced back by Schofield, I fear, and, until I abandon James River, nothing can be sent from this army. Grant, I think, is now preparing to draw out by his left with the intent of enveloping me. He may wait till his other columns approach nearer, or he may be preparing to anticipate my withdrawal. I cannot tell yet. . . . Everything of value should be removed from Richmond. It is of the first importance to save all powder. The cavalry and artillery of the army are still scattered for want of provender, and our supply and ammunition trains, which ought to be with the army in case of a sudden movement, are absent collecting provisions and forage—some in western Virginia and some in North Carolina. You will see to what straits we are reduced; but I trust to work out."

On the same day, in a letter to my mother, he writes:

". . . After sending my note this morning, I received from the express office a bag of socks. You will have to send down your offerings as soon as you can, and bring your work to a close, for I think General Grant will move against us soon—within a week, if nothing prevents—and no man can tell what may be the result; but trusting to a merciful God, who does not always give the battle to the strong, I pray we may not be overwhelmed. I shall, however, endeavour to do my duty and fight to the last. Should it be necessary to abandon our position to prevent being surrounded, what will you do? You must consider the question, and make up your mind. It is a fearful condition, and we must rely for guidance and protection upon a kind Providence. . . ."

About this time, I saw my father for the last time until after the surrender. We had been ordered up to the army from our camp nearly forty miles away, reaching the vicinity of Petersburg the morning of the attack of General Gordon on Fort Stedman, on March 25th. My brother and I had ridden ahead of the division to report its presence, when we met the General riding Traveller, almost alone, back from that part of the lines opposite the fort. Since then I have often recalled the sadness of his face, its careworn expression. When he caught sight of his two sons, a bright smile at once lit up his countenance, and he showed very plainly his pleasure at seeing us. He thanked my brother for responding so promptly to his call upon him, and regretted that events had so shaped themselves that the division would not then be needed, as he had hoped it would be.

No good results followed Gordon's gallant attack. His supports did not come up at the proper time, and our losses were very heavy, mostly prisoners. Two days after this, Sheridan, with ten thousand mounted men, joined Grant, having marched from the Valley of Virginia *via* Staunton and Charlottesville. On the 28th, everything being ready, General Grant commenced to turn our right, and having more than three men to our one, he had no difficult task. On that very day my father wrote to my mother:

". . . I have received your note with a bag of socks. I return the bag and receipt. The count is all right this time. I have put in the bag General Scott's autobiography, which I thought you might like to read. The General, of course, stands out prominently, and does not hide his light under a bushel, but he appears the bold, sagacious, truthful man that he is. I inclose a note from little Agnes. I shall be very glad to see her to-morrow, but cannot recommend pleasure trips now. . . ."

On April 1st the Battle of Five Forks was fought, where about fifty thousand infantry and cavalry—more men than were in our entire army—attacked our extreme right and turned it, so that, to save our communications, we had to abandon our lines at Petersburg, giving up that city and Richmond. From that time to April 9th the Army of Northern Virginia struggled to get back to some position where it could concentrate its forces and make a stand; but the whole world knows of that six-days' retreat. I shall not attempt to describe it in detail—indeed, I could not if I would, for I was not present all the time—but will quote from those who have made it a study and who are far better fitted to record it than I am. General Early, in his address at Lexington, Virginia, January 19, 1872—General Lee's birthday—eloquently and briefly describes these six days as follows:

". . . The retreat from the lines of Richmond and Petersburg began in the early days of April, and the remnant of the Army of Northern Virginia fell back, more than one hundred miles, before its overpowering antagonist, repeatedly presenting front to the latter and giving battle so as to check his progress. Finally, from mere exhaustion, less than eight thousand men with arms in their hands, of the noblest army that ever fought 'in the tide of time,' were surrendered at Appomattox to an army of 150,000 men; the sword of Robert E. Lee, without a blemish on it, was sheathed forever; and the flag, to which he had added such luster, was furled, to be, henceforth, embalmed in the affectionate remembrance of those who remained faithful during all our trials, and will do so to the end."

Colonel Archer Anderson, in his address at the unveiling of the Lee monument in Richmond, Virginia, May 29, 1890, speaking of the siege of Petersburg and of the surrender, utters these noble words:

". . . Of the siege of Petersburg, I have only time to say that in it for nine months the Confederate commander displayed every art by which genius and courage can make good the lack of numbers and resources. But the increasing misfortunes of the Confederate arms on other theatres of the war gradually cut off the supply of men and means. The Army of Northern Virginia ceased to be recruited, it ceased to be adequately fed. It lived for months on less than one-third rations. It was demoralised, not by the enemy in its front, but by the enemy in Georgia and the Carolinas. It dwindled to 35,000 men, holding a front of thirty-five miles; but over the enemy it still cast the shadow of its great name. Again and again, by a bold offensive, it arrested the Federal movement to fasten on its communications. At last, an irresistible concentration of forces broke through its long thin line of battle. Petersburg had to be abandoned. Richmond was evacuated. Trains bearing supplies were intercepted, and a starving army, harassed for seven days by incessant attacks on rear and flank, found itself completely hemmed in by overwhelming masses. Nothing remained to it but its stainless honour, its unbroken courage. In those last solemn scenes, when strong men, losing all self-control, broke down and sobbed like children, Lee stood forth as great as in the days of victory and triumph. No disaster crushed his spirit, no extremity of danger ruffled his bearing. In the agony of dissolution now invading that proud army, which for four years had wrested victory from every peril, in that blackness of utter darkness, he preserved the serene lucidity of his mind. He looked the stubborn facts calmly in the face, and when no military resource remained, when he recognised the impossibility of making another march or fighting another battle, he bowed his head in submission to that Power which makes and unmakes nations. The surrender of the fragments of the Army of Northern Virginia closed the imperishable record of his military life. . . ."

From the London *Standard,* at the time of his last illness, I quote these words relating to this retreat:

"When the Army of Northern Virginia marched out of the lines around Petersburg and Richmond, it still numbered some twenty-six thousand men. After a retreat of six days, in the face of an overwhelming enemy, with a crushing artillery—a retreat impeded by constant fighting and harassed by countless hordes of cavalry—eight thousand were given up by the capitulation at Appomattox Court House. Brilliant as were General Lee's earlier triumphs, we believe that he gave higher proofs of genius in his last campaign, and that hardly any of his victories were so honourable to himself and his army as that of his six-days' retreat."

Swinton, in his "History of the Army of the Potomac," after justly praising its deeds, thus speaks of its great opponent, the Army of Northern Virginia:

"Nor can there fail to arise the image of that other army that was the adversary of the Army of the Potomac, and—who that once looked upon it can ever forget it?—that array of tattered uniforms and bright muskets—that body of incomparable infantry, the Army of Northern Virginia, which, for four years, carried the revolt on its bayonets, opposing a constant front to the mighty concentration of power brought against it; which, receiving terrible blows, did not fail to give the like, and which, vital in all its parts, died only with its annihilation."

General Long, in speaking of its hardships and struggles during the retreat, thus describes how the army looked up to their commander and trusted him to bring them through all their troubles:

"General Lee had never appeared more grandly heroic than on this occasion. All eyes were raised to him for a deliverance which no human power seemed able to give. He alone was expected to provide food for the starving army and rescue it from the attacks of a powerful and eager enemy. Under the accumulation of difficulties, his courage seemed to expand, and wherever he appeared his presence inspired the weak and weary with renewed energy to continue the toilsome march. During these trying scenes his countenance wore its habitual calm, grave expression. Those who watched his face to catch a glimpse of what was passing in his mind could gather thence no trace of his inner sentiments."

No one can tell what he suffered. He did in all things what he considered right. Self he absolutely abandoned. As he said, so he believed, that "human virtue should equal human calamity." A day or two before the surrender, he said to General Pendleton:

". . . I have never believed we could, against the gigantic combination for our subjugation, make good in the long run our independence unless foreign powers should, directly or indirectly, assist us. . . . But such considerations really made with me no difference. We had, I was satisfied, sacred principles to maintain and rights to defend, for which we were in duty bound to do our best, even if we perished in the endeavour."

After his last attempt was made with Gordon and Fitz Lee to break through the lines of the enemy in the early morning of the 9th, and Colonel Venable informed him that it was not possible, he said:

"Then there is nothing left me but to go and see General Grant." When some one near him, hearing this, said:

"Oh, General, what will history say of the surrender of the army in the field?" he replied:

"Yes, I know they will say hard things of us; they will not understand how we were overwhelmed by numbers; but that is not the question, Colonel; the question is, is it right to surrender this army? If it is right, then I will take all the responsibility."

There had been some correspondence with Grant, just before the conversation with General Pendleton. After Gordon's attack failed, a flag of truce was sent out, and, about eleven o'clock, General Lee went to meet General Grant. The terms of surrender were agreed upon, and then General Lee called attention to the pressing needs of his men. He said:

"I have a thousand or more of your men and officers, whom we have required to march along with us for several days. I shall be glad to send them to your lines as soon as it can be arranged, for I have no provisions for them. My own men have been living for the last few days principally upon parched corn, and we are badly in need of both rations and forage."

Grant said he would at once send him 25,000 rations. General Lee told him that amount would be ample and would be a great relief. He then rode back to his troops. The rations issued then to our army were the supplies destined for us but captured at Amelia Court House. Had they reached us in time, they would have given the half-starved troops that were left strength enough to make a further struggle. General Long graphically pictures the last scenes:

"It is impossible to describe the anguish of the troops when it was known that the surrender of the army was inevitable. Of all their trials, this was the greatest and hardest to endure. There was no consciousness of shame; each heart could boast with honest pride that its duty had been done to the end, and that still unsullied remained its honour. When, after his interview with General Grant, General Lee again appeared, a shout of welcome instinctively went up from the army. But instantly recollecting the sad occasion that brought him before them, their shouts sank into silence, every hat was raised, and the bronzed faces of thousands of grim warriors were bathed in tears. As he rode slowly along the lines, hundreds of his devoted veterans pressed around the noble chief, trying to take his hand, touch his person, or even lay their hands upon his horse, thus exhibiting for him their great affection. The General then with head bare, and tears flowing freely down his manly cheeks, bade adieu to the army."

In a few words: "Men, we have fought through the war together; I have done my best for you; my heart is too full to say more," he bade them good-bye and told them to return to their homes and become good citizens. The next day he issued his farewell address, the last order published to the army:

"HEADQUARTERS, ARMY OF NORTHERN VIRGINIA,
April 10, 1865.

"After four years' of arduous service, marked by unsurpassed courage and fortitude, the Army of Northern Virginia has been compelled to yield to overwhelming numbers and resources. I need not tell the survivors of so many hard-fought battles, who have remained steadfast to the last, that I have consented to this result from no distrust of them; but, feeling that valour and devotion could accomplish nothing that could compensate for the loss that would have attended the continuation of the contest, I have determined to avoid the useless sacrifice of those whose past services have endeared them to their countrymen. By the terms of the agreement, officers and men can return to their homes and remain there until exchanged. You will take with you the satisfaction that proceeds from the consciousness of duty faithfully performed; and I earnestly pray that a merciful God will extend to you His blessing and protection.

With an increasing admiration of your constancy and devotion to your country, and a grateful remembrance of your kind and generous consideration of myself, I bid you an affectionate farewell.

"R. E. LEE, General."

General Long says that General Meade called on General Lee on the 10th, and in the course of conversation remarked:

"Now that the war may be considered over, I hope you will not deem it improper for me to ask, for my personal information, the strength of your army during the operations about Richmond and Petersburg." General Lee replied:

"At no time did my force exceed 35,000 men; often it was less." With a look of surprise, Meade answered:

"General, you amaze me; we always estimated your force at about seventy thousand men."

General de Chanal, a French officer, who was present, states that General Lee, who had been an associate of Meade's in the engineers in the "old army," said to him pleasantly:

"Meade, years are telling on you; your hair is getting quite gray."

"Ah, General Lee," was Meade's prompt reply, "it is not the work of years; *you* are responsible for my gray hairs!"

"Three days after the surrender," says Long, "the Army of Northern Virginia had dispersed in every direction, and three weeks later the veterans of a hundred battles had exchanged the musket and the sword for the implements of husbandry. It is worthy of remark that never before was there an army disbanded with less disorder. Thousands of soldiers were set adrift on the world without a penny in their pockets to enable them to reach their homes. Yet none of the scenes of riot that often follow the disbanding of armies marked their course."

A day or two after the surrender, General Lee started for Richmond, riding Traveller, who had carried him so well all through the war. He was accompanied by some of his staff. On the way, he stopped at the house of his eldest brother, Charles Carter Lee, who lived on the Upper James in Powhatan County. He spent the evening in talking with his brother, but when bedtime came, though begged by his host to take the room and bed prepared for him, he insisted on going to his old tent, pitched by the roadside, and passed the night in the quarters that he was accustomed to. On April 15th he arrived in Richmond. The people there soon recognised him; men, women, and children crowded around him, cheering and waving hats and handkerchiefs. It was more like the welcome to a conqueror than to a defeated prisoner on parole. He raised his hat in response to their greetings, and rode quietly to his home on Franklin Street, where my mother and sisters were anxiously awaiting him. Thus he returned to that private family life for which he had always longed, and became what he always desired to be—a peaceful citizen in a peaceful land.

In attempting to describe these last days of the Army of Northern Virginia, I have quoted largely from Long, Jones, Taylor, and Fitz Lee, all of whom have given more or less full accounts of the movements of both armies.

It so happened that shortly after we left our lines, April 2d or 3d, in one of the innumerable contests, my horse was shot, and in getting him and myself off the field, having no choice of routes, the pursuing Federal cavalry intervened between me and the rest of our command, so I had to make my way around the head of Sheridan's advance squadrons before I could rejoin our forces. This I did not succeed in accomplishing until April 9th, the day of the surrender, for my wounded horse had to be left with a farmer, who kindly gave me one of his own in exchange, saying I could send him back when I was able, or, if I was prevented, that I could keep him and he would replace him with mine when he got well.

As I was riding toward Appomattox on the 9th, I met a body of our cavalry with General T. H. Rosser at the head. He told me that General Lee and his army had surrendered, and that this force had made its way out, and was marching back to Lynchburg, expecting thence to reach General Johnston's army. To say that I was surprised does not express my feelings. I had never heard the word "surrender" mentioned, nor even suggested, in connection with our general or our army. I could not believe it, and did not until I was positively assured by all my friends who were with Rosser's column that it was absolutely so. Very sadly I turned back and went to Lynchburg along with them. There I found some wagons from our headquarters which had been sent back, and with them the horses and servants of the staff. These I got together, not believing for an instant that our struggle was over, and, with several officers from our command and others, we made our way to Greensboro, North Carolina. There I found Mr. Davis and his cabinet and representatives of the Confederate departments from Richmond. There was a great diversity of opinion amongst all present as to what we should do. After waiting a couple of days, looking over the situation from every point of view, consulting with my uncle, Commodore S. S. Lee, of the Confederate Navy, and with many others, old friends of my father and staunch adherents of the Southern cause, it was determined to go back to Virginia to get our paroles, go home, and go to work.

While at Greensboro I went to see President Davis, just before he proceeded on his way farther south. He was calm and dignified, and, in his conversation with several officers of rank who were there, seemed to think, and so expressed himself, that our cause was not lost, though sorely stricken, and that we could rally our forces west of the Mississippi and make good our fight. While I was in the room, Mr. Davis received the first official communication from General Lee of his surrender. Colonel John Taylor Wood, his aide-de-camp, had taken me in to see the President, and he and I were standing by him when the despatch from General Lee was brought to him. After reading it, he handed it without comment to us; then, turning away, he silently wept bitter tears. He seemed quite broken at the moment by this tangible evidence of the loss of his army and the misfortune of its general. All of us, respecting his great grief, silently withdrew, leaving him with Colonel Wood. I never saw him again.

I started for Richmond, accompanied by several companions, with the servants and horses belonging to our headquarters. These I had brought down with me from Lynchburg, where I had found them after the surrender. After two weeks of marching and resting, I arrived in Richmond and found my father there, in the house on Franklin Street, now the rooms of the "Virginia Historical Society," and also my mother, brother, and sisters. They were all much relieved at my reappearance.

As well as I can recall my father at this time, he appeared to be very well physically, though he looked older, grayer, more quiet and reserved. He seemed very tired, and was always glad to talk of any other subject than that of the war or anything pertaining thereto. We all tried to cheer and help him. And the people of Richmond and of the entire South were as kind and considerate as it was possible to be. Indeed, I think their great kindness tired him. He appreciated it all, was courteous, grateful, and polite, but he had been under such a terrible strain for several years that he needed the time and quiet to get back his strength of heart and mind. All sorts and conditions of people came to see him: officers and soldiers from both armies, statesmen, politicians, ministers of the Gospel, mothers and wives to ask about husbands and sons of whom they had heard nothing. To keep him from being overtaxed by this incessant stream of visitors, we formed a sort of guard of the young men in the house, some of whom took it by turns to keep the door and, if possible, turn strangers away. My father was gentle, kind, and polite to all, and never willingly, so far as I know, refused to see any one.

Dan Lee, late of the Confederate States Navy, my first cousin, and myself, one day had charge of the front door, when at it appeared a Federal soldier, accompanied by a darkey carrying a large willow basket filled to the brim with provisions of every kind. The man was Irish all over, and showed by his uniform and carriage that he was a "regular," and not a volunteer. On our asking him what he wanted, he replied that he wanted to see General Lee, that he had heard down the street the General and his family were suffering for lack of something to eat, that he had been with "the Colonel" when he commanded the Second Cavalry, and, as long as he had a cent, his old colonel should not suffer. My father, who had stepped into another room as he heard the bell ring, hearing something of the conversation, came out into the hall. The old Irishman, as soon as he saw him, drew himself up and saluted, and repeated to the General, with tears streaming down his cheeks, what he had just said to us. My father was very much touched, thanked him heartily for his kindness and generosity, but told him that he did not need the things he had brought and could not take them. This seemed to disappoint the old soldier greatly, and he pleaded so hard to be allowed to present the supplies to his old colonel, whom he believed to be in want of them, that at last my father said that he would accept the basket and send it to the hospital, for the sick and wounded, who were really in great need. Though he was not satisfied, he submitted to this compromise, and then to our surprise and dismay, in bidding the General good-bye, threw his arms around him and was attempting to kiss him, when "Dan" and I interfered. As he was leaving, he said:

"Good-bye, Colonel! God bless ye! If I could have got over in time I would have been with ye!"

A day or two after that, when "Dan" was doorkeeper, three Federal officers, a colonel, a major, and a doctor, called and asked to see General Lee. They were shown into the parlour, presented their cards, and said they desired to pay their respects as officers of the United States Army. When Dan went out with the three cards, he was told by some one that my father was up stairs engaged with some other visitor, so he returned and told them this and they departed. When my father came down, was shown the cards and told of the three visitors, he was quite put out at Dan's not having brought him the cards at the time, and that afternoon mounted him on one of his horses and sent him over to Manchester, where they were camped, to look up the three officers and to tell them he would be glad to see them at any time they might be pleased to call. However, Dan failed to find them.

He had another visit at this time which affected him deeply. Two Confederate soldiers in very dilapidated clothing, worn and emaciated in body, came to see him. They said they had been selected from about sixty other fellows, too ragged to come themselves, to offer him a home in the mountains of Virginia. The home was a good house and farm, and near by was a defile, in some rugged hills, from which they could defy the entire Federal Army. They made this offer of a home and their protection because there was a report that he was about to be indicted for treason. The General had to decline to go with them, but the tears came into his eyes at this hearty exhibition of loyalty.

After being in Richmond a few days, and by the advice of my father getting my parole from the United States Provost Marshal there, the question as to what I should do came up. My father told me that I could go back to college if I desired and prepare myself for some profession—that he had a little money which he would be willing and glad to devote to the completion of my education. I think he was strongly in favour of my going back to college. At the same time he told me that, if I preferred it, I could take possession of my farm land in King William County, which I had inherited from my grandfather, Mr. Custis, and make my home there. As there was little left of the farm but the land, he thought he could arrange to help me build a house and purchase stock and machinery.

My brother, General W. H. F. Lee, had already gone down to his place, "The White House" in New Kent County, with Major John Lee, our first cousin, had erected a shanty, and gone to work, breaking up land for a corn crop, putting their cavalry horses to the plow. As I thought my father had use for any means he might have in caring for my mother and sisters, and as I had this property, I determined to become a farmer. However, I did not decide positively, and in the meantime it was thought best that I should join my brother and cousin at the White House and help them make their crop of corn. In returning to Richmond, I had left at "Hickory Hill," General Wickham's place in Hanover County, our horses and servants, taken with me from Lynchburg to Greensboro and back. So bidding all my friends and family good-bye, I went by rail to "Hickory Hill" and started the next day with three servants and about eight horses for New Kent, stopping the first night at "Pampatike." The next day I reached the White House, where the reinforcements I brought with me were hailed with delight.

Though I have been a farmer from that day to this, I will say that the crop of corn which we planted that summer, with ourselves and army servants as laborers and our old cavalry horses as teams, and which we did not finish planting until the 9th of June, was the best I ever made.

CHAPTER IX

A PRIVATE CITIZEN

LEE'S CONCEPTION OF THE PART—HIS INFLUENCE EXERTED
TOWARD THE RESTORATION OF VIRGINIA—HE VISITS OLD
FRIENDS THROUGHOUT THE COUNTRY—RECEIVES OFFERS OF
POSITIONS—COMPARES NOTES WITH THE UNION GENERAL
HUNTER—LONGS FOR A COUNTRY HOME—FINDS ONE AT
"DERWENT," NEAR CARTERSVILLE

MY father remained quietly in Richmond with my mother and sisters. He was now a private citizen for the first time in his life. As he had always been a good soldier, so now he became a good citizen. My father's advice to all his old officers and men was to submit to the authority of the land and to stay at home, now that their native States needed them more than ever. His advice and example had great influence with all. In a letter to Colonel Walter Taylor,[1] he speaks on this point:

". . .I am sorry to hear that our returned soldiers cannot obtain employment. Tell them they must all set to work, and if they cannot do what they prefer, do what they can. Virginia wants all their aid, all their support, and the presence of all her sons to sustain and recuperate her. They must therefore put themselves in a position to take part in her government, and not be deterred by obstacles in their way. There is much to be done which they only can do. . . ."

And in a letter, a month later, to an officer asking his opinion about a decree of the Emperor of Mexico encouraging the emigration from the South to that country:

". . . I do not know how far their emigration to another land will conduce to their prosperity. Although prospects may not now be cheering, I have entertained the opinion that, unless prevented by circumstances or necessity, it would be better for them and the country if they remained at their homes and shared the fate of their respective States. . . ."

Again, in a letter to Governor Letcher[2]:

". . . The duty of its citizens, then, appears to me too plain to admit of doubt. All should unite in honest efforts to obliterate the effects of the war and to restore the blessings of peace. They should remain, if possible, in the country; promote harmony and good feeling, qualify themselves to vote and elect to the State and general legislatures wise and patriotic men, who will devote their abilities to the interests of the country and the healing of all dissensions. I have invariably recommended this course since the cessation of hostilities, and have endeavoured to practise it myself. . . ."

Also in a letter of still later date, to Captain Josiah Tatnall, of the Confederate States Navy, he thus emphasises the same sentiment:

". . . I believe it to be the duty of every one to unite in the restoration of the country and the re-establishment of peace and harmony. These considerations governed me in the counsels I gave to others, and induced me on the 13th of June to make application to be included in the terms of the amnesty proclamation. . . ."

These letters and many more show plainly his conception of what was right for all to do at this time. I have heard him repeatedly give similar advice to relatives and friends and to strangers who sought it. The following letters to General Grant and to President Johnson show how he gave to the people of the South an example of quiet submission to the government of the country:

"RICHMOND, Virginia, June 13, 1865.
"LIEUTENANT-GENERAL U. S. GRANT, Commanding the "Armies of the United States.

"*General:* Upon reading the President's proclamation of the 29th ult., I came to Richmond to ascertain what was proper or required of me to do, when I learned that, with others, I was to be indicted for treason by the grand jury at Norfolk. I had supposed that the officers and men of the Army of Northern Virginia were, by the terms of their surrender, protected by the United States Government from molestation so long as they conformed to its conditions. I am ready to meet any charges that may be preferred against me, and do not wish to avoid trial; but, if I am correct as to the protection granted by my parole, and am not to be prosecuted, I desire to comply with the provisions of the President's proclamation, and, therefore, inclose the required application, which I request, in that event, may be acted on. I am, with great respect,

"Your obedient servant,   R. E. LEE."

"RICHMOND, Virginia, June 13, 1865.
"HIS EXCELLENCY ANDREW JOHNSON,
"President of the United States.

"*Sir:* Being excluded from the provisions of the amnesty and pardon contained in the proclamation of the 29th ult., I hereby apply for the benefits and full restoration of all rights and privileges extended to those included in its terms. I graduated at the Military Academy at West Point in June, 1829; resigned from the United States Army, April, 1861; was a general in the Confederate Army, and included in the surrender of the Army of Northern Virginia, April 9, 1865. I have the honour to be, very respectfully,

"Your obedient servant,   R. E. LEE."

Of this latter letter, my brother, Custis Lee, writes me:

"When General Lee requested me to make a copy of this letter, he remarked it was but right for him to set an example of making formal submission to the civil authorities, and that he thought, by so doing, he might possibly be in a better position to be of use to the Confederates who were not protected by military paroles, especially Mr. Davis."

Colonel Charles Marshall[3] says:

". . . He (General Lee) set to work to use his great influence to reconcile the people of the South to the hard consequences of their defeat, to inspire them with hope, to lead them to accept, freely and frankly, the government that had been established by the result of the war, and thus relieve them from the military rule. . . . The advice and example of General Lee did more to incline the scale in favour of a frank and manly adoption of that course of conduct which tended to the restoration of peace and harmony than all the Federal garrisons in all the military districts."

My father was at this time anxious to secure for himself and family a house somewhere in the country. He had always had a desire to be the owner of a small farm, where he could end his days in peace and quiet. The life in Richmond was not suited to him. He wanted quiet and rest, but could not get it there, for people were too attentive to him. So in the first days of June he mounted old Traveller and, unattended, rode down to "Pampatike"—some twenty-five miles—to pay a visit of several days to his relations there. This is an old Carter property, belonging then and now to Colonel Thomas H. Carter, who, but lately returned from Appomattox Court House, was living there with his wife and children. Colonel Carter, whose father was a first cousin of General Lee's, entered the Army of Northern Virginia in the spring of 1861, as captain of the "King William Battery," rose grade by grade by his skill and gallantry, and surrendered in the spring of 1865, as Colonel and Chief of Artillery of his corps at that time. He was highly esteemed and much beloved by my father, and our families had been intimate for a long time.

"Pampatike" is a large, old-fashioned plantation, lying along the Pamunkey River, between the Piping Tree and New Castle ferries. Part of the house is very old, and, from time to time, as more rooms were needed, additions have been made, giving the whole a very quaint and picturesque appearance. At the old-fashioned dinner hour of three o'clock, my father, mounted on Traveller, unannounced, unexpected, and alone, rode up to the door. The horse and rider were at once recognised by Colonel Carter, and he was gladly welcomed by his kins-folk. I am sure the days passed here were the happiest he had spent for many years. He was very weary of town, of the incessant unrest incident to his position, of the crowds of persons of all sorts and conditions striving to see him; so one can imagine the joy of master and horse when, after a hot ride of over twenty miles, they reached this quiet resting-place. My father, Colonel Carter tells me, enjoyed every moment of his stay. There were three children in the house, the two youngest little girls of five and three years old. These were his special delight, and he fol-lowed them around, talking baby-talk to them and getting them to talk to him. Every morning before he was up they went into his room, at his special request, to pay him a visit. Another great pleasure was to watch Traveller enjoy himself. He had him turned out on the lawn, where the June grass was very fine, abun-dant, and at its prime, and would allow no corn to be fed to him, saying he had had plenty of that during the last four years, and that the grass and the liberty were what he needed. He talked to Colonel Carter much about Mexico, its people and climate; also about the old families living in that neighbourhood and else-where in the State, with whom both Colonel Carter and himself were connected; but he said very little about the recent war, and only in answer to some direct question.

About six miles from "Pampatike," on the same river and close to its banks, is "Chericoke," another old Virginia homestead, which had belonged to the Braxtons for generations, and, at that time, was the home of Corbin Braxton's widow. General Lee was invited to dine there, and to meet him my brother, cousin and I, from the White House, were asked, besides General Rosser, who was staying in the neighbourhood, and several others. This old Virginia house had long been noted for its lavish hospitality and bountiful table. Mrs. Braxton had never realised that the war should make any change in this respect, and her table was still spread in those days of desolation as it had been before the war, when there was plenty in the land. So we sat down to a repast composed of all the good things for which that country was famous. John and I did not seem to think there was too much in sight—at any rate, it did not daunt us, and we did our best to lessen the quantity, consuming, I think, our share and more! We had been for so many years in the habit of being hungry that it was not strange we continued to be so awhile yet. But my father took a different view of the abundance displayed, and, during his drive back, said to Colonel Carter:

"Thomas, there was enough dinner to-day for twenty people. All this will now have to be changed; you cannot afford it; we shall have to practise economy."

In talking with Colonel Carter about the situation of farmers at that time in the South, and of their prospects for the future, he urged him to get rid of the negroes left on the farm—some ninety-odd in number, principally women and children, with a few old men—saying the government would provide for them, and advised him to secure white labour. The Colonel told him he had to use, for immediate needs, such force as he had, being unable at that time to get the whites. Wereupon General Lee remarked:

"I have always observed that wherever you find the negro, everything is going down around him, and wherever you find the white man, you see everything around him improving."

He was thinking strongly of taking a house in the country for himself and family, and asked the Colonel whether he could not suggest some part of the State that might suit him. Colonel Carter mentioned Clarke County as representing the natural-grass section of Virginia, and Gloucester County the salt-water. My father unhesitatingly pronounced in favour of the grass-growing country. He told Mrs. Carter how pleased he was to hear that she had received her husband in tears when he returned from the surrender, as showing the true spirit, for, though glad to see him, she wept because he could fight no more for the cause. The day after this dinner he had to turn his back on these dear friends and their sweet home.

When Traveller was brought up to the door for him to mount, he walked all around him, looking carefully at the horse, saddle, and bridle. Apparently the blanket was not arranged to suit him, for he held the bridle while "Uncle Henry" took off the saddle. Then he took off the blanket himself, spread it out on the grass, and, folding it to suit his own ideas of fitness, carefully placed it on Traveller's back, and superintended closely the putting on and girthing of the saddle. This being done, he bade everybody good-bye, and, mounting his horse, rode away homeward—to Richmond. After crossing the Pamunkey at Newcastle ferry, he rode into "Ingleside," about a mile from the river, the lovely home of Mrs. Mary Braxton. Here he dismounted and paid his respects to the mistress of the house and her daughters, who were also cousins. That afternoon he reached Richmond, returning by the same road he had travelled coming out. After this visit, which he had enjoyed so much, he began looking about more than ever to find a country home.

The house he was occupying in Richmond belonged to Mr. John Stewart, of "Brook Hill," who was noted for his devotion to the cause of the South and his kindness to all those who had suffered in the conflict. My brother Custis had rented it at the time he was appointed on Mr. Davis's staff. A mess had been established there by my brother and several other officers on duty in Richmond. In time, my mother and sister had been made members of it, and it had been the headquarters of all of the family during the war, when in town. My father was desirous of making some settlement with his landlord for its long use, but before he could take the final steps my mother received the following note from Mr. Stewart:

". . . I am not presuming on your good opinion, when I feel that you will believe me, first, that you and yours are heartily welcome to the house as long as your convenience leads you to stay in Richmond; and, next, that you owe me nothing, but, if you insist on paying, that the payment must be in Confederate currency, for which alone it was rented to your son. You do not know how much gratification it is, and will afford me and my whole family during the remainder of our lives, to reflect that we have been brought into contact, and to know and to appreciate you and all that are dear to you."

My father had been offered, since the surrender, houses, lands, and money, as well as positions as president of business associations and chartered corporations.

"An English nobleman," Long says, "desired him to accept a mansion and an estate commensurate with his individual merits and the greatness of an historic family."

He replied: "I am deeply grateful; I cannot desert my native State in the hour of her adversity. I must abide her fortunes, and share her fate."

Until his death, he was constantly in receipt of such offers, all of which he thought proper to decline. He wrote to General Long:

"I am looking for some little, quiet home in the woods, where I can procure shelter and my daily bread, if permitted by the victor. I wish to get Mrs. Lee out of the city as soon as practical."

It so happened that nearly exactly what he was looking for was just then offered to him. Mrs. Elizabeth Randolph Cocke, of Cumberland County, a granddaughter of Edmund Randolph, had on her estate a small cottage which, with the land attached, she placed at his disposal. The retired situation of this little home, and the cordial way in which Mrs. Cocke insisted on his coming, induced my father to accept her invitation.

Captain Edmund Randolph Cocke[4] writes me the following:

"OAKLAND, Virginia, October 25, 1896.

"My mother, whose sympathies for everybody and everything connected with our cause were the greatest and most enlarged of any one I ever knew, thought it might be agreeable and acceptable to General Lee to have a retired place in which to rest. Having this little house unoccupied, she invited him to accept it as a home as long as he might find it pleasant to himself. The General came up with your mother and sisters about the last of June, General Custis Lee having preceded them a day or two on Traveller. At that time our mode of travel was on the canal by horse-packet: leaving Richmond at a little before sunset, the boat reached Pemberton, our landing, about sunrise. General Custis and I went down to meet them, and we all reached home in time for breakfast. That night on the boat the Captain had had the most comfortable bed put up that he could command, which was offered to your father. But he preferred to sleep on deck, which he did, with his military cloak thrown over him. No doubt that was the last night he ever spent under the open sky. After a week spent here, General Lee removed, with his family, to "Derwent." There he spent several months of quiet and rest, only interrupted by the calls of those who came in all honesty and sincerity to pay their respects to him. Old soldiers, citizens, men and women, all came without parade or ceremony. During this time he rode on Traveller daily, taking sometimes long trips—once, I recall, going to his brother's, Mr. Carter Lee's, about twenty miles, and at another time to Bremo, about thirty miles. During the month of August he was visited by Judge Brockenborough, of Lexington, who, as Rector of the Board of Trustees of Washington College, tendered him, on behalf of the Board, the presidency of the college. After considering the matter for several weeks, he decided to accept this position.

". . . During that summer he was a regular attendant at the various churches in our neighbourhood, whenever there was service. I never heard your father discuss public matters at all, nor did he express his opinion of public men. On one occasion, I did hear him condemn with great severity the Secretary of War, Stanton. This was at the time Mrs. Surratt was condemned and executed. At another time I heard him speak harshly of General Hunter, who had written to him to get his approval of his movements, during the Valley Campaign, against General Early. With these exceptions, I never heard him speak of public men or measures."

In this connection I quote the Rev. J. Wm. Jones in his "Personal Reminiscences of General Robert E. Lee":

"Not long after the close of the war, General Lee received a letter from General David Hunter, of the Federal Army, in which he begged information on two points:

"1. His (Hunter's) campaign in the summer of 1864 was undertaken on information received at the War Department in Washington that General Lee was about to detach forty thousand picked troops to send General Johnston. Did not his (Hunter's) movements prevent this, and relieve Sherman to that extent?

"2. When he (Hunter) found it necessary to retreat from before Lynchburg, did not he adopt the most feasible line of retreat?

"General Lee wrote a very courteous reply, in which he said:

"'The information upon which your campaign was undertaken was erroneous. I had *no troops* to spare General Johnston and no intention of sending him any—*certainly not forty thousand, as that would have taken about all I had.*

"'As to the second point—I would say that I am not advised as to the motives which induced you to adopt the line of retreat which you took, and am not, perhaps, competent to judge of the question, *but I certainly expected you to retreat by way of the*

Shenandoah Valley[5], and was gratified at the time that you preferred the route through the mountains to the Ohio—leaving the valley open for General Early's advance into Maryland.'"

Before leaving Richmond, my father wrote the following letter to Colonel Ordway, then Provost Marshal:

"RICHMOND, Virginia, June 21, 1865.

"LT.-COL. ALBERT ORDWAY,

"Provost Marshal, Department of Virginia.

"*Colonel:* I propose establishing my family next week in Cumberland County, Virginia, near Cartersville, on the James River canal. On announcing my intention to General Patrick, when he was on duty in Richmond, he stated that no passport for the purpose was necessary. Should there have been any change in the orders of the Department rendering passports necessary, I request that I may be furnished with them. My son, G. W. Custis Lee, a paroled prisoner with myself, will accompany me. Very respectfully your obedient servant,

"R. E. LEE."

The latter part of June, my father, mother, brother Custis, and sisters went to "Derwent," the name of the little place which was to be his home for that summer. They went by canal-boat from Richmond to Cartersville, and then had a drive of about six miles. Mrs. Cocke lived at "Oakland," two miles away, and her generous heart was made glad by the opportunity of supplying my father and his family with every comfort that it was possible to get at that time. In his letters to me, still at the White House busy with our corn, he gives a description of his surroundings:

". . . We are all well, and established in a comfortable but small house, in a grove of oaks, belonging to Mr. Thomas Cocke.[6] It contains four rooms, and there is a house in the yard which when fitted up will give us another. Only your mother, Agnes, and

Mildred are with me. Custis, who has had a return of his attack. . . is at Mrs. Cocke's house, about two miles off—is convalescent, I hope. I have been nowhere as yet. The weather has been excessively hot, but this morning there is an agreeable change, with some rain. The country here is poor but healthy, and we are at a long distance from you all. I can do nothing until I learn what decision in my case is made in Washington. All unite with me in much love.

> "Very truly, your father,
>
> "R. E. LEE."

The "case" referred to here was the indictment in June by a grand jury in Norfolk, Virginia, of Mr. Davis, General Lee, and others, for treason or something like it.

The Hon. Reverdy Johnson offered his professional services to my father in this case, but there was no trial, as a letter from General Grant to the authorities insisted that the parole given by him to the officers and soldiers of the Army of Northern Virginia should be respected. The following letter explains itself:

> "NEAR CARTERSVILLE, Virginia, July 27, 1865.
>
> "HON. REVERDY JOHNSON,
>
> "Baltimore, Md.
>
> "*My Dear Sir:* I very much regret that I did not see you on your recent visit to Richmond, that I might have thanked you for the interest you have shown in my behalf, and your great kindness in offering me your professional services in the indictment which I now understand is pending against me. I am very glad, however, that you had an opportunity of reading a copy of General Grant's letter of the 20th inst. to me, which I left with Mr. Macfarland for that purpose, and also that he might show it to other officers of the Army of Northern Virginia in my condition. I did not wish to give it greater publicity without the assent of General Grant, supposing that, if he desired it made public, he would take steps to have it done. Should he consent to your request to have it published,

I, of course, have no objection. But should he not, I request that you only use it in the manner I have above indicated. Again offering you my warmest thanks for your sympathy and consideration for my welfare, I am, with great respect,

"Your obedient servant,

"R. E. LEE."

In another letter to me he tells of his visit to his brother Charles Carter Lee, in Powhatan County, which was an easy ride from "Derwent." He was very fond of making these little excursions, and Traveller, that summer, was in constant use:

"NEAR CARTERSVILLE, July 22, 1865.

"*My Dear Rob:* I have just returned from a visit to your Uncle Carter, and, among my letters, find one from some of your comrades to you, which I inclose. I was happy to discover from the direction that it was intended for you and not for me. I find Agnes quite sick, and have sent for the doctor, as I do not know what to do for her. Poor little thing! she seems quite prostrated. Custis, I am told, is better. He is still at Mrs. Cocke's. The rest of us are well. I saw several of your comrades, Cockes, Kennons and Gilliams, who inquired after you all. Give my love to F. and Johnny, in which all here unite, and believe me most truly and affectionately

"Your father,   R. E. LEE.
"Robert E. Lee."

In another letter he gives an account of a trip that he and Traveller had taken across the river into Albemarle County:

"NEAR CARTERSVILLE, August 21, 1865.

"*My Dear Bertus:* I received only a few days ago your letter of the 12th. I am very sorry to hear of your afflictions, but hope you have shaken off all of them. You must keep your eyes open, you precious boy, and not run against noxious vines and fevers. I have just returned from a visit to Fluvanna. I rode up the gray and extended my peregrinations into Albemarle, but no further than the Green Mountain neighbourhood. I made short rides, stopping every evening with some friend, and had a very pleasant time. I commended you to all the young ladies on the road, but did not know I was extolling a poisoned beau! You must go up and see Miss Francis Galt. Tell Fitzhugh I wrote to him before I went away. I am glad to hear that your corn is so fine, and that you are making preparations to put in a good crop of wheat. I wish I had a little farm somewhere, to be at work too. Custis is paying a visit to his friend, Captain Watkins, in Powhatan. He came up for him last Saturday, and bore him off. He has got quite well now, and I hope will continue so. Agnes is also again well, though still feeble and thin. Your mother, Life, and myself as usual. We have not heard for some time from daughter. A report has reached us of her being at Mr. Burwell's. Miss Mary Cocke and her brother John paid us a short visit from Saturday to Monday, and several of our neighbors have been over to spend the day. We have a quiet time, which is delightful to me, but I fear not so exhilarating to the girls. I missed Uncle Carter's visit. He and his Robert rode up on a pair of colts while I was in Fluvanna, and spent several days. I wish we were nearer you boys. I want to see you very much, but do not know when that can be. I hope Johnny is well. I have heard nothing from his father since we parted in Richmond, but hear that Fitz has gone to see his mother. All here send their best love to you, and I pray that every happiness may attend you.

"Your devoted father,

"R. E. LEE.

"Robert E. Lee."

"Bertus" was a contraction of Robertus, my father's pet name for me as a child. My afflictions were "poison-oak," chills, and fever. The letter to my brother Fitzhugh, here referred to, I also give:

"NEAR CARTERSVILLE, Cumberland County, Virginia,

"July 29, 1865.

"My Dear Fitzhugh: I was very glad to receive, by the last packet from Richmond, your letter of the 22d. We had all been quite anxious to hear from you, and were much gratified to learn that you were all well, and doing well. It is very cheering to me to hear of your good prospects for corn and your cheerful prospects for the future. God grant they may be realised, which, I am sure, they will be, if you will unite sound judgment to your usual energy in your operations. As to the indictments, I hope you, at least, may not be prosecuted. I see no other reason for it than for prosecuting *all* who ever engaged in the war. I think, however, we may expect procrastination in measures of relief, denunciatory threats, etc. We must be patient, and let them take their course. As soon as I can ascertain their intention toward me, if not prevented, I shall endeavour to procure some humble, but quiet, abode for your mother and sisters, where I hope they can be happy. As I before said, I want to get in some grass country, where the natural product of the land will do much for my subsistence. . . . Our neighbours are very kind, and do everything in the world to promote our comfort. If Agnes is well enough, I propose to ride up to 'Bremo' next week. I wish I was near enough to see you. Give much love to Rob and Johnny, the Carters and Braxtons. All here unite in love and best wishes for you all.

"Most affectionately, your father,

"R. E. LEE."

CHAPTER X

PRESIDENT OF WASHINGTON COLLEGE

PATRIOTIC MOTIVES FOR ACCEPTANCE OF TRUST—CONDITION
OF COLLEGE—THE GENERAL'S ARRIVAL AT LEXINGTON—HE
PREPARES FOR THE REMOVAL OF HIS FAMILY TO THAT CITY—
ADVICE TO ROBERT, JUNIOR—TRIP TO "BREMO" ON PRIVATE
CANAL-BOAT—MRS. LEE'S INVALIDISM

ABOUT this time my father received from the Board of Trustees of
Washington College a notification of his election to the presidency of that institution, at a meeting of the board held in
Lexington, Virginia, on August 4, 1865. The letter apprising him
of the action was presented by Judge John W. Brockenbrough, rector of the college. This was a complete surprise to my father. He
had already been offered the vice-chancellorship of the
"University of the South," at Sewanee, Tennessee, but declined it
on the ground that it was denominational, and to some suggestions that he should connect himself with the University of
Virginia he objected because it was a State institution.

Washington College had started as an academy in 1749. It
was the first classical school opened in the Valley of Virginia.
After a struggle of many years, under a succession of principals
and with several changes of site, it at length acquired such a reputation as to attract the attention of General Washington. He
gave it a handsome endowment, and the institution changed its

name from "Liberty Hall Academy" to Washington College. In the summer of 1865, the college, through the calamities of civil war, had reached the lowest point of depression it had ever known. Its buildings, library, and apparatus had suffered from the sack and plunder of hostile soldiery. Its invested funds, owing to the general impoverishment throughout the land, were for the time being rendered unproductive and their ultimate value was most uncertain. Four professors still remained on duty, and there were about forty students, mainly from the country around Lexington. It was not a State institution, nor confined to any one religious denomination, so two objections which might have been made by my father were removed. But the college in later years had only a local reputation. It was very poor, indifferently equipped with buildings, and with no means in sight to improve its condition.

"There was a general expectation that he would decline the position as not sufficiently lucrative, if his purpose was to repair the ruins of his private fortune resulting from the war; as not lifting him conspicuously enough in the public gaze, if he was ambitious of office or further distinction; or as involving too great labour and anxiety, if he coveted repose after the terrible contest from which he had just emerged."[1]

He was very reluctant to accept this appointment, but for none of the above reasons, as the average man might have been. Why he was doubtful of undertaking the responsibilities of such a position his letter of acceptance clearly shows. He considered the matter carefully and then wrote the following letter to the committee:

"POWHATAN COUNTY, August 24, 1865.

"*Gentlemen:* I have delayed for some days replying to your letter of the 5th inst., informing me of my election by the board of trustees to the presidency of Washington College, from a desire to give the subject due consideration. Fully impressed with the responsibilities of the office, I have feared that I should be unable to discharge its duties to the satisfaction of the trustees or to the benefit of the country. The proper education of youth requires not only great ability, but I fear more strength than I now possess, for I do not feel able to undergo the labour of conducting classes in regular courses of instruction. I could not, therefore, undertake more than the general administration and supervision of the institution. There is another subject which has caused me serious reflection, and is, I think, worthy of the consideration of the board. Being excluded from the terms of amnesty in the proclamation of the President of the United States, of the 29th of May last, and an object of censure to a portion of the country, I have thought it probable that my occupation of the position of president might draw upon the college a feeling of hostility; and I should, therefore, cause injury to an institution which it would be my highest desire to advance. I think it the duty of every citizen, in the present condition of the country, to do all in his power to aid in the restoration of peace and harmony, and in no way to oppose the policy of the State or general government directed to that object. It is particularly incumbent on those charged with the instruction of the young to set them an example of submission to authority, and I could not consent to be the cause of animadversion upon the college. Should you, however, take a different view, and think that my services in the position tendered to me by the board will be advantageous to the college and country, I will yield to your judgment and accept it; otherwise, I must most respectfully decline the office. Begging you to express to the trustees of the college my heartfelt gratitude for the honour conferred upon me, and requesting you to accept my cordial thanks for the kind manner in which you have communicated their decision, I am, gentlemen, with great respect, your most obedient servant, R. E. LEE."

To present a clearer view of some of the motives influencing my father in accepting this trust—for such he considered it—I give an extract from an address on the occasion of his death, by Bishop Wilmer, of Louisiana, delivered at the University of the South, at Sewanee, Tennessee:

"I was seated," says Bishop Wilmer, "at the close of the day, in my Virginia home, when I beheld, through the thickening shades of evening, a horseman entering the yard, whom I soon recognised as General Lee. The next morning he placed in my hands the correspondence with the authorities of Washington College at Lexington. He had been invited to become president of that institution. I confess to a momentary feeling of chagrin at the proposed change (shall I say revulsion?) in his history. The institution was one of local interest, and comparatively unknown to our people. I named others more conspicuous which would welcome him with ardour as their presiding head. I soon discovered that his mind towered above these earthly distinctions; that, in his judgment, the *cause* gave dignity to the institution, and not the wealth of its endowment or the renown of its scholars; that this door and not another was opened to him by Providence, and he only wished to be assured of his competency to fulfil his trust and thus to make his few remaining years a comfort and blessing to his suffering country. I had spoken to his human feelings; he had now revealed himself to me as one 'whose life was hid with Christ in God.' My speech was no longer restrained. I congratulated him that his heart was inclined to this great cause, and that he was spared to give to the world this august testimony to the importance of Christian education. How he listened to my feeble words; how he beckoned me to his side, as the fulness of heart found utterance; how his whole countenance glowed with animation as I spoke of the Holy Ghost as the great Teacher, whose presence was required to make education a blessing, which otherwise might be the curse of mankind; how feelingly he responded, how *eloquently,* as I never heard him speak before—can never be effaced from memory; and nothing more sacred mingles with my reminiscences of the dead."

The board of trustees, on August 31st, adopted and sent to General Lee resolutions saying that, in spite of his objections, "his connection with the institution would greatly promote its prosperity and advance the general interest of education, and urged him to enter upon his duties as president at his earliest convenience."

My father had had nearly four years' experience in the charge of young men at West Point. The conditions at that place, to be sure, were very different from those at the one to which he was now going, but the work in the main was the same—to train, improve and elevate. I think he was influenced, in making up his mind to accept this position, by the great need of education in his State and in the South, and by the opportunity that he saw at Washington College for starting almost from the beginning, and for helping, by his experience and example, the youth of his country to become good and useful citizens.

In the latter part of September, he mounted Traveller and started alone for Lexington. He was four days on the journey, stopping with some friend each night. He rode into Lexington on the afternoon of the fourth day, no one knowing of his coming until he quietly drew up and dismounted at the village inn. Professor White, who had just turned into the main street as the General halted in front of the hotel, said he knew in a moment that this stately rider on the iron-gray charger must be General Lee. He, therefore, at once went forward, as two or three old soldiers gathered around to help the General down, and insisted on taking him to the home of Colonel Reid, the professor's father-in-law, where he had already been invited to stay. My father, with his usual consideration for others, as it was late in the afternoon, had determined to remain at the hotel that night and go to Mr. Reid's in the morning; but yielding to Captain White's (he always called him "Captain," his Confederate title) assurances that all was ready for him, he accompanied him to the home of his kind host.

The next morning, before breakfast, he wrote the following letter to my mother announcing his safe arrival. The "Captain Edmund" and "Mr. Preston" mentioned in it were the sons of our revered friend and benefactress, Mrs. E. R. Cocke. Colonel Preston and Captain Frank were her brother and nephew:

"Lexington, September 19, 1865.

"*My Dear Mary:* I reached here yesterday about one P.M., and on riding up to the hotel was met by Professor White, of Washington

College, who brought me up to his father-in-law's, Colonel Reid, the oldest member of the trustees of the college, where I am very comfortably quartered. To-day I will look out for accommodations elsewhere, as the Colonel has a large family and I fear I am intruding upon his hospitality. I have not yet visited the college grounds. They seem to be beautifully located, and the buildings are undergoing repairs. The house assigned to the president, I am told, has been rented to Dr. Madison (I believe), who has not been able to procure another residence, and I do not know when it will be vacated, nor can I tell you more about it. I saw Mrs. Cocke yesterday afternoon, who looks remarkably well, and will return to the Alum [Springs] to-morrow. Captain Edmund is with her and goes to-day to Kentucky. He and Mr. Preston are very well. The latter will accompany his mother to the Alum. I have not yet seen him. I saw Mrs. and Colonel Preston, Captain Frank, and his sister. All the family are well. I shall go after breakfast to inquire after my trunks. I had a very pleasant journey here. The first two days were very hot, but, reaching the mountain region the third day, the temperature was much cooler. I came up in four days' easy rides, getting to my stopping-place by one P.M. each day, except the third, when I slept on top of the Blue Ridge, which I reached at three P.M. The scenery was beautiful all the way. I am writing before breakfast, and must be short. Last night I found a blanket and coverlid rather light covering, and this morning I see a fire in the dining-room. I have thought much of you all since I left. Give much love to the girls and Custis and remember me to all at 'Oakland.'

"Most affectionately yours,   R. E. LEE.

"MRS. R. E. LEE."

When he first arrived, the family, very naturally, stood a little in awe of him. This feeling, however, was soon dispelled, for his simple and unaffected manners in a short while put them at ease. There were some little children in the house, and they and the General at once became great friends. With these kind and hospitable friends he stayed several days. After being present at a meeting of the board of trustees, he rode Traveller over to the Rockbridge Baths—eleven miles from Lexington—and from there writes to my mother, on September 25th:

". . . Am very glad to hear of Rob's arrival. I am sorry that I missed seeing the latter, but find it was necessary that I should have been present at the meeting of the board of trustees on the 20th. They adjourned on the eve of the 21st, and on the morning of the 22d I rode over here, where I found Annie and Miss Belle.[2] . . . The babies[3] are well and sweet. I have taken the baths every day since my arrival, and like them very much. In fact, they are delightful, and I wish you were all here to enjoy them. . . . Annie and Belle go in two, and sometimes three, times a day. Yesterday I procured some horses and took them up to the top of Jump Mountain, where we had one of the most beautiful views I ever saw. To-day I could get but one horse, and Miss Belle and I rode up Hays Creek Valley, which possessed beauties of a different kind. I shall return to Lexington on the 29th. I perceive, as yet, no change in my rheumatic affection. . . . Tell Custis I am much obliged to him for his attention to my baggage. All the articles enumerated by him arrived safely at Colonel Reid's Thursday morning early. I also received the package of letters he sent. . . . I hope he may receive the appointment at the V. M. I. Everyone interested has expressed a desire he should do so, and I am more desirous than all of them. If he comes by land, he will find the route I took very pleasant, and about 108 miles, namely: 'Bremo'—Dr. Wilmer's—Waynesboro'—Greenville. He will find me at the Lexington Hotel. . . . I wish you were all with me. I feel very solitary and miss you all dreadfully. Give much love to the girls and boys—kind remembrances to Mrs. P., Miss Louisa, and Mrs. Thos. Cocke. I have no news. Most affectionately,   R. E. LEE.

"P. S.—Annie and Belle send a great deal of love to all. R. E. L."

These little excursions and the meeting with old friends and dear cousins were sources of real enjoyment and grateful rest. The pains of the past, the worries of the present, and the cares for the future were, for the time being, banished. My father earnestly desired a quiet, informal inauguration, and his wish was gratified. On October 2, 1865, in the presence of the trustees, professors and students, after solemn and appropriate prayer by the Rev. W. S. White, D.D., the oldest Christian minister in the town,[4] he took the oath of office as required by the laws of the college, and was thus legally inaugurated as its president.

On October 3d he wrote my mother:

". . . I am glad to hear that Rob is improving, and hope you had the pleasure of seeing Mr. Dana.[5]. . . The college opened yesterday, and a fine set of youths, about fifty, made their appearance in a body. It is supposed that many more will be coming during the month. The scarcity of money everywhere embarrasses all proceedings. General Smith informs me that the Military Institute will commence its exercises on the 16th inst.; and that Custis was unanimously elected to the chair of Civil Engineering.[6] I am living at the Lexington Hotel, and he must come there if he comes up. . . . The ladies have furnished me a very nice room in the college for my office; new carpet from Baltimore, curtains, etc. They are always doing something kind. . . . I came up September 30th from the Baths. Annie and Miss Belle still there and very well. They expect to be here on the 10th. . . . You tell me nothing of the girls. I hope Agnes is getting strong and fat. I wished for them both at the Baths. Annie and Belle were my only companions. I could not trespass upon them always. The scenery is beautiful here, but I fear it will be locked up in winter by the time you come. Nothing could be more beautiful than the mountains now. . . .

"Most affectionately,   R. E. LEE."

In addition to his duties as college president, my father had to make all the arrangements for his new home. The house assigned him by the college was occupied by Dr. Madison, who was to move out as soon as he could. Carpenters, painters and glaziers had to be put to work to get it into condition; furniture, carpets, bedding to be provided, a cook procured, servants and provisions supplied. My mother was an invalid and absent, and as my sisters were with her, everything down to the minutest detail was done by my father's directions and under his superintendence. He had always been noted for his care and attention to little things, and that trait, apparent in him when a mere lad, practised all through his busy and eventful life, stood him in good stead now. The difficulties to be overcome were made greater by the scarcity and inaccessibility of supplies and workmen and the smallness of his means. In addition, he conducted a large correspondence, always answering every letter. To every member of his family he wrote continually, and was interested in all our pursuits, advising and helping us as no one else could have done. Some of his letters to my mother at this time show how he looked into every matter, great or small, which related to her comfort and welfare, and to the preparation of her new home. For example, on October 9th he writes:

". . . Life is indeed gliding away and I have nothing of good to show for mine that is past. I pray I may be spared to accomplish something for the benefit of mankind and the honour of God. . . . I hope I may be able to get the house prepared for you in time to reach here before the cold weather. Dr. Madison has sent me word that he will vacate the house on the 16th inst., this day week. I will commence to make some outside repairs this week, so as to get at the inside next, and hope by the 1st of November it will be ready for you. There is no furniture belonging to the house, but we shall require but little to commence with. Mr. Green, of Alexandria, to whom I had written, says that his manufacturing machinery, etc., has been so much injured that, although it has been returned to him, he cannot resume operations until next year, but that he will purchase for us anything we desire. I believe nothing is manufactured in Richmond—everything comes from the North, and we might as well write to

Baltimore at once for what we want. What do you think? I believe nothing of consequence is manufactured here. I will see this week what can be done. . . ."

And again, a few days later, he writes:

". . . I hope you are all well, and as comfortable as can be. I am very anxious to get you all here, but have made little progress in accomplishing it so far. Dr. M. expects to vacate the house this week, but I fear it is not certain he can do so. . . . I engaged some carpenters last week to repair the roof, fences, stable, etc., but for want of material they could not make a commencement. There is no lumber here at hand. Everything has to be prepared. I have not been in the house yet, but I hear there is much to be done. We shall have to be patient. As soon as it is vacated, I will set to work. I think it will be more expeditious and cheaper to write to Renwick [of Baltimore] to send what articles of furniture will be required, and also to order some carpets from Baltimore. . . ."

In a postscript, dated the 17th, he says:

"The carpenters made a beginning on the house yesterday. I hope it may be vacated this week. I will prepare your room first. The rest of us can bivouac. Love to all. Most affectionately,   R. E. LEE."

On October 19th:

". . . I have been over the house we are to occupy. It is in wretched condition. Mrs. M. has not yet vacated it, but I have some men at work, though this storm has interrupted their operations and I fear little will be done this week. I think I can make your room comfortable. The upstairs is very convenient and the rest of the house sufficiently so. I think you had better write at once to Brit[7] to send the curtains you speak of, and the carpets. It is better to use what we have than to buy others. Their use where originally intended[8] is very uncertain. They have been tossed about for four years, and may be lost or ruined. They can come by express to Lynchburg, and then up the canal, or by Richmond. The merchants say the former is the best way—much more expeditious and but little more expensive."

Spending the summer on the Pamunkey at the White House, exposed all day in the fields to the sun, and at night to the malaria from the river and marshes, I became by the last of September one continuous "chill," so it was decided that, as the corn was made, the fodder saved, the wheat land broken up, and hands not so greatly needed, I should get a furlough. Mounting my mare, I started on a visit to my mother and sisters, hoping that the change to the upper country would help me to get rid of the malaria. When I reached "Derwent" my father had gone to Lexington, but my mother and the rest were there to welcome me and dose me for my ailments. There was still some discussion among us all as to what was the best thing for me to do, and I wrote to my father, telling him of my preference for a farmer's life and my desire to work my own land. The following letter, which he wrote me in reply, is, like all I ever got from him, full of love, tenderness, and good, sensible advice:

"*My Dear Son:* I did not receive until yesterday your letter of the 8th inst. I regret very much having missed seeing you—still more to hear that you have been suffering from intermittent fever. I think the best thing you can do is to eradicate the disease from your system, and unless there is some necessity for your returning to the White House, you had better accompany your mother here. I have thought very earnestly as to your future. I do not know to what stage your education has been carried, or whether it would be advantageous for you to pursue it further. Of that you can judge. If you do, and will apply yourself so as to get the worth of your money, I can advance it to you for this year at least. If you do not, and wish to take possession of your farm, I can assist you a little in that. As matters now stand, you could raise money on your farm only by mortgaging it, which would put you in debt at the beginning of your life, and I fear in the end would swallow up all your property. As soon as I am restored to civil rights, if I ever am, I will settle up your grandfather's estate, and put you in possession of your share. The land may be responsible for some portion of his debts or legacies. If so, you will have to assume it. In the meantime, I think it would be better for you, if you determine to farm your land, to go down there as you propose and begin on a moderate scale. I can furnish you means to buy a team, wagon, implements, etc. What will it cost? If you cannot wait to accompany your mother here, come up to see me and we can talk it over. You could come up in the packet and return again. If you do come, ask Agnes for my box of private papers I left with her, and bring it with you; but do not lose it for your life, or we are all ruined. Wrap it up with your clothes and put it in a carpet-bag or valise, so that you can keep it with you or within your sight, and do not call attention to it. I am glad to hear that Fitzhugh keeps so well, and that he is prospering in his farming operations. Give him a great deal of love for me. The first thing you must do is to get well.

"Your affectionate father,

"R. E. Lee."

His letters to his daughters tell, in a playful way, much of his life, and are full of the quiet humour in which he so often indulged. We were still at "Derwent," awaiting the time when the house in Lexington should be ready. It had been decided that I should remain and accompany my mother and sisters to Lexington, and that some of us, or all, should go up the river to "Bremo," the beautiful seat of Dr. Charles Cocke, and pay a visit there before proceeding to Lexington. Here is a letter from my father to his daughter Mildred:

"Lexington, October 29, 1865.

"*My Precious Life:* Your nice letter gave me much pleasure and made me the more anxious to see you. I think you girls, after your mother is comfortable at 'Bremo,' will have to come up and arrange the house for her reception. You know I am a poor hand

and can do nothing without your advice. Your brother, too, is wild for the want of admonition. Col. Blair is now his 'fidus Achates,' and as he is almost as gray as your papa, and wears the same uniform, all gray, he is sometimes taken for him by the young girls, who consider your brother the most attentive of sons, and giving good promise of making a desirable husband. He will find himself married some of these days before he knows it. You had better be near him. I hope you give attention to Robert. Miss Sallie will thaw some of the ice from his heart. Tell her she must come up here, as I want to see her badly. I do not know what you will do with your chickens, unless you take them to 'Bremo,' and thus bring them here. I suppose Robert would not eat 'Laura Chilton' and 'Don Ella McKay.' Still less would he devour his sister 'Mildred.'[9] I have scarcely gotten acquainted with the young ladies. They look very nice in the walks, but I rarely get near them. Traveller is my only companion; I may also say my pleasure. He and I, whenever practicable, wander out in the mountains and enjoy sweet confidence. The boys are plucking out his tail, and he is presenting the appearance of a plucked chicken. Two of the belles of the neighbourhood have recently been married—Miss Mattie Jordan to Dr. Cameron, and Miss Rose Cameron to Dr. Sherod. The former couple go to Louisburg, West Virginia, and start to-morrow on horseback, the bride's trousseau in a baggage wagon; the latter to Winchester. Miss Sherod, one of the bridesmaids, said she knew you there. I did not attend the weddings, but have seen the pairs of doves. Both of the brides are remarkable in this county of equestrianism for their good riding and beauty. With true affection,   Your fond father,

"R. E. LEE."

To his daughter Agnes, about the same time, he writes:

"LEXINGTON, Virginia, October 26, 1865.
"My Dear Agnes: I will begin the correspondence of the day by thanking you for your letter of the 9th. It will, I am sure, be to me intellectually what my morning's feast is corporeally. It will

strengthen me for the day, and smoothe the rough points which constantly protrude in my epistles. I am glad Robert is with you. It will be a great comfort to him, and I hope, in addition, will dissipate his chills. He can also accompany you in your walks and rides and be that silent sympathy (for he is a man of few words) which is so soothing. Though marble to women, he is so only externally, and you will find him warm and cheering. Tell him I want him to go to see Miss Francis Galt (I think her smile will awake some sweet music in him), and be careful to take precautions against the return of the chills, on the 7th, 14th and 21st days. . . . I want very much to have you all with me again, and miss you dreadfully. I hope another month will accomplish it. In the meantime, you must get very well. This is a beautiful spot by nature—man has done but little for it. Love to all. Most affectionately,

"Your father,

"R. E. LEE."

About the first week of November we all went by canal-boat to "Bremo," some twenty-five miles up the James River, where we remained the guests of Doctor and Mrs. Charles Cocke until we went to Lexington. My sister Agnes, while there, was invited to Richmond to assist at the wedding of a very dear friend, Miss Sally Warwick. She wrote to my father asking his advice and approval, and received this reply, so characteristic of his playful, humorous mood:

"LEXINGTON, Virginia, November 16, 1865.

"*My Precious Little Agnes:* I have just received your letter of the 13th and hasten to reply. It is very hard for you to apply to me to advise you to go away from me. You know how much I want to see you, and how important you are to me. But in order to help you to make up your mind, if it will promote your pleasure and Sally's happiness, I will say go. You may inform Sally from me, however, that no preparations are necessary, and if they were no one could help her. She has just got to wade through it as if it was an attack of measles or anything else—naturally. As she would not marry

Custis, she may marry whom she chooses. I shall wish her every happiness, just the same, for she knows nobody loves her as much as I do. I do not think, upon reflection, she will consider it right to refuse my son and take away my daughter. She need not tell me whom she is going to marry. I suppose it is some cross old widower, with a dozen children. She will not be satisfied at her sacrifice with less, and I should think that would be cross sufficient. I hope 'Life' is not going to desert us too, and when are we to see you? . . . I have received your mother's letter announcing her arrival at 'Bremo.' . . . Tell your mother, however, to come when she chooses and when most to her comfort and convenience. She can come to the hotel where I am, and stay until the house is ready. There is no difficulty in that, and she can be very comfortable. My rooms are up on the 3d floor and her meals can be sent to her. Tell Rob the chills will soon leave him now. Mrs. Cocke will cure him. Give much love to your mamma, Mildred, Rob, and all at 'Bremo.'

"Your affectionate father,

"R. E. LEE.

"Miss Agnes Lee."

Colonel Ellis, President of the James River and Kanawha Canal Company, placed at my mother's disposal his private boat, which enabled her to reach "Bremo" with great ease and comfort, and when she was ready to go to Lexington the same boat was again given her. It was well fitted up with sleeping accommodations, carried a cook, and had a dining-room. It corresponded to the private car of the present, railroad magnate, and, though not so sumptuous, was more roomy and comfortable. When provisions became scarce we purchased fresh supplies from any farm-house near the canal-bank, tied up at night, and made about four miles an hour during the day. It was slow but sure, and no mode of travel, even at the present day, could have suited my mother better. She was a great invalid from rheumatism, and had to be lifted whenever she moved. When put in her wheel-chair, she could propel herself on a level floor, or could move about her room very slowly and with great difficulty on her crutches, but she was always bright, sunny-tempered, and uncomplaining, constantly occupied with her books, letters, knitting, and painting, for the last of which she had great talent.

On November 20th my father writes to her from Lexington:

"I was very glad to hear, by your letter of the 11th, of your safe arrival at 'Bremo.' I feel very grateful to Col. Ellis for his thoughtful consideration in sending you in his boat, as you made the journey in so much more comfort. It is indeed sad to be removed from our kind friends at 'Oakland,' who seemed never to tire of contributing to our convenience and pleasure, and who even continue their kindness at this distance. Just as the room which I had selected for you was finished, I received the accompanying note from Mrs. Cocke, to which I responded and thanked her in your name, placing the room at her disposal. The paint is hardly dry yet, but will be ready this week, to receive the furniture if completed. I know no more about it than is contained in her note. I was also informed, last night, that a very handsome piano had been set up in the house, brought from Baltimore by the maker as a present from his firm or some friends. I have not seen it or the maker. This is an article of furniture that we might well dispense with under present circumstances, though I am equally obliged to those whose generosity prompted its bestowal. Tell Mildred I shall now insist on her resuming her music, and, in addition to her other labours, she must practise *seven* hours a day on the piano, until she becomes sufficiently proficient to play agreeably to herself and others, and promptly and gracefully, whenever invited. I think we should enjoy all the amenities of life that are within our reach, and which have been provided for us by our Heavenly Father. . . . I am sorry Rob has a return of his chills, but he will soon lose them now. Ask Miss Mary to disperse them. She is very active and energetic; they cannot stand before her. . . . I hope Agnes has received my letter, and that she has made up her mind to come up to her papa. Tell her there are plenty of weddings here, if she likes those things. There is to be one Tuesday—Miss Mamie Williamson to Captain Eoff. Beverley Turner is to be married the same night, to Miss Rose Skinker, and sweet Margaret will also leave us. If they go at three a night, there will soon be none of our acquaintances left. I told Agnes to tell you to come up whenever most convenient to you. If the house is habitable I will take you there. If not, will bring you to the hotel. . . . I wish I could take advantage of this fine weather to perform the journey. . . ."

CHAPTER XI

THE IDOL OF THE SOUTH

PHOTOGRAPHS AND AUTOGRAPHS IN DEMAND—THE GEN-
ERAL'S INTEREST IN YOUNG PEOPLE—HIS HAPPY HOME LIFE—
LABOURS AT WASHINGTON COLLEGE—HE GAINS FINANCIAL
AID FOR IT—WORSLEY'S TRANSLATION OF HOMER DEDICATED
TO HIM—TRIBUTES FROM OTHER ENGLISH SCHOLARS

THE people of Virginia and of the entire South were continually giving evidence of their intense love for General Lee. From all nations, even from the Northern States, came to him marks of admiration and respect. Just at this time he received many applications for his photograph with autograph attached. I believe there were none of the little things in life so irksome to him as having his picture taken in any way, but, when able to comply, he could not refuse to do what was asked of him by those who were willing and anxious to do so much for him.

In the following letter the photographs referred to had been sent to him for his signature, from a supply that my mother generally kept on hand. She was often asked for them by those who very considerately desired to save my father the trouble:

"LEXINGTON, November 21, 1865.

"*My Dear Mary:* I have just received your letter of the 17th, and return the photographs with my signatures. I wrote to you by the boat of yesterday morning. I also sent you a packet of letters by

Captain Wilkinson,[1] which also ought to have reached you to-day. I have nothing to add to my former letters, and only write now that you may receive the photos before you leave. I answered Agnes' letter immediately, and inclosed her several letters. I was in hopes she had made up her mind to eschew weddings and stick to her papa. I do not think she can help little Sallie. Besides, she will not take the oath—how can she get married? The wedding party from this place go down in the boat to-night to Lynchburg—Miss Williamson and Captain Eoff. They are to be married in church at eight P. M. and embark at eleven. I wish them a pleasant passage and am glad I am not of the party. The scenery along the river will no doubt be cheering and agreeable. I think the repairs of the house will be completed this week; should the furniture arrive, it will be habitable next. The weather is still beautiful, which is in our favour. I am glad Caroline is so promising. I have engaged no servant here yet, nor have I found one to my liking. We can get some of some kind, and do better when we can. I have heard nothing of the wedding at 'Belmead,' and do not think Preston will go. Mrs. Cocke is very well, but the furniture she intends for your room is not yet completed. It will be more comfortable and agreeable to you to go at once to the house on your arrival. But if there is anything to make it more desirable for you to come before the house is ready, you must come to the hotel. If we could only get comfortable weather in December, it would be better not to go into the house until it is dry, the paint hard, etc. It will require all this week to get the wood done; then it must be scoured, etc., and the furniture properly arranged. Tell Rob he will soon be well. He must cheer up and come and see his papa. Give my love to Mrs. Cocke, Miss Mary, etc., etc. Tell Agnes, if she thinks Sallie is *in extremis,* to go to her. I do not want her to pass away, but it is a great disappointment to me not to have her with me. I am getting very old and infirm now, and she had better come to her papa and take care of him.

> "Most affectionately yours, R. E. LEE.
"MRS. M. C. LEE."

My father was always greatly interested in the love affairs of his relatives, friends, and acquaintances. His letters during the war show this in very many ways. One would suppose that the general commanding an army in active operations could not find the time even to think of such trifles, much less to write about them; but he knew of very many such affairs among his officers and even his men, and would on occasion refer to them before the parties themselves, very much to their surprise and discomfiture. Bishop Peterkin, of West Virginia, who served on the staff of General Pendleton, tells me of the following instances, in illustration of this characteristic:

"It was in the winter of 1863–4, when we were camped near Orange Court House, that, meeting the General after I had come back from a short visit to Richmond, he asked after my father, and then said, 'Did you see Miss———?' and I replied, 'No, sir; I did not.' Then again, 'Did you see Miss———?' and when I still replied 'No,' he added, with a smile, 'How exceedingly busy you must have been.'

"Again—at the cavalry review at Brandy Station, on June 8, 1863—we had galloped all around the lines, when the General took his post for the 'march past,' and all the staff in attendance grouped themselves about him. There being no special orders about our positions, I got pretty near the General. I noticed that several times he turned and looked toward an ambulance near us, filled with young girls. At last, after regiments and brigades had gone by, the Horse Artillery came up. The General turned and, finding me near him, said, 'Go and tell that young lady with the blue ribbon in her hat that such-and-such a battery is coming.'

"I rode up and saluted the young lady. There was great surprise shown by the entire party, as I was not known to any of them, and when I came out with my message there was a universal shout, while the General looked on with a merry twinkle in his eye. It was evidently the following up on his part of some joke which he had with the young lady about an officer in this battery."

My mother had arranged to start for Lexington on November 28th, via the canal, but for some reason was prevented on that day. In his next letter, my father, who was most anxious that she should make the journey before the bad weather set in, expresses his disappointment at not finding her on the packet on the expected morning.

"LEXINGTON, Virginia, November 30, 1865.

"*My Dear Mary:* I am much disappointed that you did not arrive on the boat last night, and as you had determined when you wrote Saturday, the 25th, to take the boat as it passed Tuesday, I fear you were prevented either by the indisposition of yourself or of Robert's. I shall, however, hope that it was owing to some less distressing cause. Our room is all ready and looks remarkably nice. Mrs. Cocke, in her great kindness, seems to have provided everything for it that you require, and you will have nothing to do but to take possession. The ladies have also arranged the other rooms as far as the furniture will allow. They have put down the carpets in the parlour, dining-room, and two chambers upstairs, and have put furniture in one room. They have also put up the curtains in the rooms downstairs, and put a table and chairs in the dining-room. We have, therefore, everything which is required for living, as soon as the crockery, etc., arrives from 'Derwent,' of which as yet I have heard nothing. Neither has the furniture from Baltimore arrived, and the season is so far advanced that we may be deprived of that all winter. But with what we now have, if we can get that from 'Derwent,' we shall do very well. There is some report of the packets between this place and Lynchburg being withdrawn from the line, which renders me more uneasy about your journey up. This is a bright and beautiful morning, and there is no indication of a change of weather, but the season is very uncertain, and snow and ice may be upon us any day. I think you had better come now the first opportunity. Do not take the boat which passes 'Bremo' Saturday. It reaches Lynchburg Sunday morning, arriving here Monday night. You would in that case have to lie at the wharf at Lynchburg all day Sunday. I have heard of

Agnes' arrival in Richmond, and shall be happy to have 'Precious Life' write me again. I have engaged a man for the balance of the year, who professes to know everything. He can at least make up fires, and go on errands, and attend to the yard and stable. I have heard nothing of Jimmy. Give my kind regards to all at 'Bremo.' Custis is well and went to the boat to meet you this morning. The boat stops one and one-quarter miles from town. Remain aboard until we come.

"Most affectionately yours,   R. E. LEE.

"P. S.—Since writing the foregoing I have received your letter of the 28th. I shall expect you Saturday morning.   R. E. L.

"MRS. M. C. LEE."

At this time the packet-boat from Lynchburg to Lexington, via the James River and Kanawha Canal, was the easiest way of reaching Lexington from the outside world. It was indeed the only way, except by stage from Goshen, twenty-one miles distant, a station of the Chesapeake & Ohio R. R. The canal ran from Lynchburg to Richmond, and just after the war did a large business. The boats were very uncertain in their schedules, and my father was therefore very particular in his directions to my mother, to insure her as far as he could a comfortable journey.[2]

We did get off at last, and after a very comfortable trip arrived at Lexington on the morning of December 2d. My father, on Traveller, was there to meet us, and, putting us all in a carriage, escorted us to our new home. On arriving, we found awaiting us a delicious breakfast sent by Mrs. Nelson, the wife of Professor Nelson. The house was in good order—thanks to the ladies of Lexington—but rather bare of furniture, except my mother's rooms. Mrs. Cocke had completely furnished them, and her loving thoughtfulness had not forgotten the smallest detail. Mrs. Margaret J. Preston, the talented and well-known poetess, had drawn the designs for the furniture, and a one-armed Confederate soldier had made it all. A handsomely carved grand piano, presented by Stieff, the famous maker of Baltimore, stood alone in the parlour. The floors were covered with the carpets rescued from Arlington—much too large and folded under to suit the reduced size of the rooms. Some of the bedrooms were partially furnished, and the dining-room had enough in it to make us very comfortable. We were all very grateful and happy—glad to get home—the only one we had had for four long years.

My father appeared bright and even gay. He was happy in seeing us all, and in knowing that my mother was comfortably established near to him. He showed us over the house, and pointed with evident satisfaction to the goodly array of pickles, preserves, and brandy-peaches which our kind neighbours had placed in the store-room. Indeed, for days and weeks afterward supplies came pouring in to my mother from the people in the town and country, even from the poor mountaineers, who, anxious to "do something to help General Lee," brought in hand-bags of walnuts, potatoes, and game. Such kindness—delicate and considerate always—as was shown to my father's family by the people, both of the town and the country around, not only then but to this day, has never been surpassed in any community. It was a tribute of love and sympathy from honest and tender hearts to the man who had done all that he could for them.

My father was much interested in all the arrangements of the house, even to the least thing. He would laugh merrily over the difficulties that appalled the rest of us. Our servants were few and unskilled, but his patience and self-control never failed. The silver of the family had been sent to Lexington for safe-keeping early in the war. When General Hunter raided the Valley of Virginia and advanced upon Lexington, to remove temptation out of his way, this silver, in two large chests, had been intrusted to the care of the old and faithful sergeant at the Virginia Military Institute, and he had buried it in some safe place known only to himself. I was sent out with him to dig it up and bring it in. We found it safe and sound, but black with mould and damp, useless for the time being, so my father opened his camp-chest and we used his forks, spoons, plates, etc., while his campstools supplied the deficiency in seats.

He often teased my sisters about their experiments in cookery and household arts, encouraging them to renewed efforts after lamentable failures. When they succeeded in a dish for the table, or completed any garment with their own hands, he was lavish with his praise. He would say:

"You are all very helpless; I don't know what you will do when I am gone," and

"If you want to be missed by your friends—be useful."

He at once set to work to improve all around him, laid out a vegetable garden, planted roses and shrubs, set out fruit and yard trees, made new walks and repaired the stables, so that in a short time we were quite comfortable and very happy. He at last had a home of his own, with his wife and daughters around him, and though it was not the little farm in the quiet country for which he had so longed, it was very near to it, and it gave rest to himself and those he loved most dearly.

His duties as president of Washington College were far from light. His time was fully occupied, and his new position did not relieve him from responsibility, care and anxiety. He took pains to become acquainted with each student personally, to be really his guide and friend. Their success gratified and pleased him, and their failures, in any degree, pained and grieved him. He felt that he was responsible for their well-doing and progress, and he worked very hard to make them good students and useful men.

The grounds and buildings of the college soon began to show his care, attention, and good taste. In all his life, wherever he happened to be, he immediately set to work to better his surroundings. The sites selected for his headquarter camps during the war, if occupied for more than a day, showed his tasteful touch. When superintendent at West Point, the improvements suggested and planned by him were going on for the three years he remained there. Very soon after he assumed charge of Arlington, the place showed, in its improved condition, the effects of his energetic industry. The college at Lexington was a splendid field for the exercise of his abilities in this line. The neighbouring Virginia Military Institute soon followed the example he had set, and after a year the municipal authorities of Lexington were aroused to the necessity of bettering their streets and sidewalks, and its inhabitants realised the need of improving and beautifying their homes. He managed a very large correspondence, answering every letter when possible, the greater proportion with his own hand. To the members of his own family who were away he wrote regularly, and was their best correspondent on home matters, telling in his charming way all the sayings and doings of the household and the neighbours.

My sister Agnes had gone to the wedding of Miss Warwick direct from "Bremo," and was in Richmond when my father sent her two of the first letters he wrote after the arrival of my mother in Lexington:

"LEXINGTON, Virginia, December 5, 1865.

"My Worrying Little Agnes: Your letter of the 1st received to-night. I have autographed the photographs and send a gross of the latter and a lock of hair. Present my love to the recipients and thank them for their favours. Sally is going to marry a widower. I think I ought to know, as she refused my son, and I do not wish to know his name. I wonder if she knows how many children he has. Tell Mr. Warwick I am sorry for him. I do not know what he will do without his sweet daughter. Nor do I know what I will do without her, either. Your mother has written—Mildred, too—and I presume has told you all domestic news. Custis is promenading the floor, Rob reading the papers, and Mildred packing her dress. Your mamma is up to her eyes in news, and I am crabbed as usual. I miss you very much and hope this is the last wedding you will attend. Good-bye. Love to everybody.

"Your affectionate father,   R. E. LEE.

"MISS AGNES LEE."

The other is dated nearly a month later, and from this it appears that the wedding so often referred to is about to take place:

"LEXINGTON, Virginia, January 3, 1866.

"*My Precious Little Agnes:* I sat down to give my dear little Sally—for she is dear to me in the broadest, highest sense of the word—the benefit of Jeremy Taylor's opinion on hasty marriages. But, on reflection, I fear it would be words lost, for your mother says her experience has taught her that when a young woman makes up her mind to get married, you might as well let her alone. You must, therefore, just thank her for the pretty inkstand, and say that I'll need no reminder of her, but I do not know when I shall make up my mind to stain it with ink. I was very glad to receive your letter of the 26th, and to think that you were mindful of us. I know you do not wish to be away, though you are striving to get as far away as possible. When you reach Norfolk, you will be so convenient to New York, whence steamers depart almost daily for Europe. Let us know when you sail. But I do not write to restrain your movements, though you know how solitary I am without you. I inclose . . . which, with what I gave Mildred, I hope will answer your purpose. Send me or bring me the photographs I asked for. I like them of the last edition; they seem to take with the little school-girls, and I have nothing else to give them. I hope you will have a safe and pleasant trip. Tell Mr. Warwick I shall sorrow with him to-night—though I believe Mrs. Lee is right. Remember me to all friends, and believe me,

"Your devoted father,   R. E. LEE.

"MISS AGNES LEE."

The latter part of January my father was sent by the board of trustees to Richmond to confer with the Committee on Education of the Virginia Legislature, then in session, as to some funds of the State held by Washington College. His mission was, I believe, successful, and great material aid was gained. He remained no longer than was absolutely necessary, and, returning to his duties at Lexington, encountered a severe snowstorm. The difficulties he had to overcome are described in the following letter to his daughter Agnes, whom he had met in Richmond, and who had gone from there to visit some friends in Norfolk:

"LEXINGTON, Virginia, January 29, 1866.

"*My Precious Little Agnes:* I have received your letter of the 17th, transmitting the photographs, for which I am very much obliged. I returned the one for Miss Laura Lippett, whom I wish I could see once again. It would be more agreeable to me than any photograph. I had quite a successful journey up, notwithstanding the storm. The snow increased as we approached the mountains, and night had set in before we reached Staunton. The next morning, before sunrise, in spite of the predictions of the wise ones, I took passage on the single car which was attached to the locomotive, and arrived at Goshen about 10 A. M., where, after some little encouragement, the stage-driver attached his horses to the stage, and we started slowly through the mountains, breaking the track. On reaching the Baths, the North River was unfordable, but I was ferried across in a skiff, with all my bundles (I picked up two more in Staunton and one at Goshen) and packages, and took a stage detained on the opposite bank for Lexington, where I arrived in good time. I found all as well as usual, and disappointed at not seeing you with me, though I was not expected. I told them how anxious you were to come with me, and how you wanted to see them, but that you looked so wretchedly I could not encourage you. I hope you are now in Norfolk, and that the fish and oysters will fatten you and cure your feet! . . . But get strong and keep well, and do not wear yourself out in the pursuit of pleasure. I hope you will soon join us, and that Lexington may prove to you a happy home. Your mother is a great sufferer, but is as quiet and uncomplaining as ever. Mildred is active and cheerful, and Custis and I as silent as our wont. Major Campbell Brown is here on a visit. I am surprised to find him such a talker. I am very sorry to find that Preston Cocke has been obliged to leave on account of his health. I have one comfort: my dear nephew will never injure himself by studying. Do not be alarmed about him. . . . Remember me to Colonel Taylor, all his mother's family, his wife, the Bakers, Seldens, etc. I know none of the latter but the

Doctor, for whom I have always had a great esteem. Your mother, brother, and Mildred send their best love and kindest wishes. I am always,

"Your devoted father,   R. E. LEE.
"MISS AGNES LEE."

It was at Dr. Selden's house that my sister was visiting. He had been very kind in offering assistance to my father and mother. I remember well the supper given me and several of my comrades when we were coming back from the surrender, and while the Doctor and his family were refugees at Liberty, now Bedford City, Va. Stopping there one night, weary and hungry, while looking for quarters for man and beast, I got a note asking me and my friends to come to their house. An invitation of that kind was never refused in those days. We went and were treated as if we had been sons of the house, the young ladies themselves waiting on us. In the morning, when we were about to start, they filled our haversacks with rations, and Mrs. Selden, taking me aside, offered me a handful of gold pieces, saying that she had more and that she could not bear to think of my father's son being without as long as she possessed any.

The love and devotion shown my father by all the people of the South was deeply appreciated by him. He longed to help them, but was almost powerless. I think he felt that something could be done in that direction by teaching and training their youth, and I am sure this idea greatly influenced him in deciding to accept the presidency of Washington College. The advantages to the South of a proper education of her youth were very evident to him. He strongly urged it wherever and whenever he could. In a letter written at this time to the Reverend G. W. Leybum, he speaks very forcibly on the subject:

"So greatly have those interests [educational] been disturbed at the South, and so much does its future condition depend upon the rising generation, that I consider the proper education of its youth one of the most important objects now to be attained, and one from which the greatest benefits may be expected. Nothing will compensate us for the depression of the standard of our moral and intellectual culture, and each State should take the most energetic measures to revive the schools and colleges, and, if possible, to increase the facilities for instruction, and to elevate the standard of learning. . . . "

Again, in a letter to General John B. Gordon, written December, 1867, he says:

"The thorough education of all classes of the people is the most efficacious means, in my opinion, of promoting the prosperity of the South. The material interests of its citizens, as well as their moral and intellectual culture, depend upon its accomplishment. The text-books of our schools, therefore, should not only be clear, systematic, and scientific, but they should be acceptable to parents and pupils in order to enlist the minds of all in the subjects."

In a letter to a friend in Baltimore he is equally earnest:

"I agree with you fully as to the importance of a more practical course of instruction in our schools and colleges, which, calling forth the genius and energies of our people, will tend to develop the resources and promote the interests of the country."

In many other letters at this time and later on, especially in one to Professor Minor, who had been appointed with him upon a board by the Educational Society of Virginia, did he urge the importance of education for the present and future safety, welfare, and prosperity of the country. Among the many tokens of respect and admiration, love, and sympathy which my father received from all over the world, there was one that touched him deeply. It was a "Translation of Homer's Iliad by Philip Stanhope Worsley, Fellow of Corpus Christi College, Oxford, England," which the talented young poet and author sent him, through the General's nephew, Mr. Edward Lee Childe, of Paris, a special friend of Mr. Worsley. I copy the latter's letter to Mr. Childe, as it shows some of the motives influencing him in the dedication of his work:

"*My Dear Friend:* You will allow me, in dedicating this work to you, to offer it at the same time as a poor yet not altogether unmeaning tribute of my reverence for your brave and illustrious uncle, General Lee. He is the hero, like Hector in the Iliad, of the most glorious cause for which men can fight, and some of the grandest passages in the poem come to me with yet more affecting power when I remember his lofty character and undeserved misfortunes. The great names that your country has bequeathed from its four lurid years of national life as examples to mankind can never be forgotten, and among these none will be more honoured, while history endures, by all true hearts, than that of your noble relative. I need not say more, for I know you must be aware how much I feel the honour of associating my work, however indirectly, with one whose goodness and genius are alike so admirable. Accept this token of my deepest sympathy and regard, and believe me,

"Ever most sincerely yours,

"P. S. WORSLEY."

On the fly-leaf of the volume he sent my father was written the following beautiful inscription:

"To GENERAL LEE,
THE MOST STAINLESS OF LIVING COMMANDERS
AND, EXCEPT IN FORTUNE, THE GREATEST,
THIS VOLUME IS PRESENTED
WITH THE WRITER'S EARNEST SYMPATHY
AND RESPECTFUL ADMIRATION
'. . . οἶος γὰρ ἐρύετο Ἰλιου Ἕκτωρ'

Iliad VI—403,"

and just beneath, by the same hand, the following beautiful verses:

"The grand old bard that never dies,
Receive him in our English tongue!
I send thee, but with weeping eyes,
The story that he sung.

"Thy Troy is fallen,—thy dear land
Is marred beneath the spoiler's heel—
I cannot trust my trembling hand
To write the things I feel.

"Ah, realm of tears!—but let her bear
This blazon to the end of time:
No nation rose so white and fair,
None fell so pure of crime.

"The widow's moan, the orphan's wail,
Come round thee; but in truth be strong!
Eternal Right, though all else fail,
Can never be made Wrong.

"An angel's heart, an angel's mouth,
Not Homer's, could alone for me
Hymn well the great Confederate South—
Virginia first, and *Lee*.
                                         "P. S. W."

His letter of thanks, and the one which he wrote later, when he heard of the ill health of Mr. Worsley—both of which I give here—show very plainly how much he was pleased:

"LEXINGTON, Virginia, February 10, 1866.
"MR. P. S. WORSLEY.
"*My Dear Sir:* I have received the copy of your translation of the Iliad which you so kindly presented to me. Its perusal has been my evening's recreation, and I have never more enjoyed the beauty and

grandeur of the poem than as recited by you. The translation is as truthful as powerful, and faithfully represents the imagery and rhythm of the bold original. The undeserved compliment in prose and verse, on the first leaves of the volume, I received as your tribute to the merit of my countrymen, who struggled for constitutional government.

"With great respect,

"Your obedient servant,

"R. E. LEE."

"LEXINGTON, Virginia, March 14, 1866.

"*My Dear Mr. Worsley:* In a letter just received from my nephew, Mr. Childe, I regret to learn that, at his last accounts from you, you were greatly indisposed. So great is my interest in your welfare that I cannot refrain, even at the risk of intruding upon your sickroom, from expressing my sincere sympathy in your affliction. I trust, however, that ere this you have recovered and are again in perfect health. Like many of your tastes and pursuits, I fear you may confine youself too closely to your reading. Less mental labour and more of the fresh air of Heaven might bring to you more comfort, and to your friends more enjoyment, even in the way in which you now delight them. Should a visit to this distracted country promise you any recreation, I hope I need not assure you how happy I should be to see you at Lexington. I can give you a quiet room, and careful nursing, and a horse that would delight to carry you over our beautiful mountains. I hope my letter informing you of the pleasure I derived from the perusal of your translation of the Iliad, in which I endeavoured to express my thanks for the great compliment you paid me in its dedication, has informed you of my high appreciation of the work.

"Wishing you every happiness in this world, and praying that eternal peace may be your portion in that to come, I am most truly,   Your friend and servant,

"R. E. LEE."

That winter, my father was accustomed to read aloud in the long evenings to my mother and sisters "The Grand Old Bard," equally to his own and his listeners' enjoyment.

Two or three years after this, Professor George Long, of England, a distinguished scholar, sent my father a copy of the second edition of his "Thoughts of the Emperor Marcus Aurelius." The first edition of this translation was pirated by a Northern publisher, who dedicated the book to Emerson. This made Long very indignant, and he immediately brought out a second edition with the following prefatory note:

"... I have never dedicated a book to any man, and if I dedicated this, I should choose the man whose name seemed to me most worthy to be joined to that of the Roman soldier and philosopher. I might dedicate the book to the successful general who is now President of the United States, with the hope that his integrity and justice will restore peace and happiness, so far as he can, to those unhappy States which have suffered so much from war and the unrelenting hostility of wicked men. But as the Roman poet says,

"'*Victrix causa deis placuit, sed victa Catoni;*'

"And if I dedicated this little book to any man, I would dedicate it to him who led the Confederate armies against the powerful invader, and retired from an unequal contest defeated, but not dishonoured; to the noble Virginian soldier whose talents and virtues place him by the side of the best and wisest man who sat on the throne of the imperial Cæsars."

These two nearly similar tributes came from the best-cultured thought of England, and the London *Standard*, speaking more for the nation at large, says:

"A country which has given birth to men like him, and those who followed him, may look the chivalry of Europe in the face without shame; for the *fatherlands of Sidney and Bayard never produced a nobler soldier, gentleman, and Christian than General Robert E. Lee.*"

In a letter to his old friend, Mr. H. Tutweiler, of Virginia, Professor Long sent the following message to my father, which, however, was never received by him, it having been sent to my mother only after his death:

"I did not answer General Lee's letter [one of thanks for the book, sent by Professor Long through Mr. Tutweiler], because I thought that he is probably troubled with many letters. If you should have occasion to write to him, I beg you will present to him my most respectful regards, and my hope that he will leave behind him some commentary to be placed on the same shelf with Cæsar's. I am afraid he is too modest to do this. I shall always keep General Lee's letter, and will leave it to somebody who will cherish the remembrance of a great soldier and a good man. If I were not detained here by circumstances, I would cross the Atlantic to see the first and noblest man of our days."

Another noble English gentleman, who had shown great kindness to the South and who was a warm admirer of General Lee, was the Honourable A. W. Beresford Hope. He, I think, was at the head of a number of English gentlemen who presented the superb statue of "Stonewall" Jackson by Foley to the State of Virginia. It now stands in the Capitol Square at Richmond, and is a treasure of which the whole Commonwealth may justly be proud. Through Mr. Hope, my father received a handsome copy of the Bible, and, in acknowledgment of Mr. Hope's letter, he wrote the following:

"LEXINGTON, Virginia, April 16, 1866.
"HONOURABLE A. W. BERESFORD HOPE,
"Bedgebury Park,
"Kent, England
"*Sir:* I have received within a few days your letter of November 14, 1865, and had hoped that by this time it would have been followed by the copy of the Holy Scriptures to which you refer, that I might have known the generous donors, whose names, you state, are inscribed on its pages. Its failure to reach me will, I fear, deprive me of that pleasure, and I must ask the favour of you to thank them most heartily for their kindness in providing me with a book in comparison with which all others in my eyes are of

minor importance, and which in all my perplexities has never failed to give me light and strength. Your assurance of the esteem in which I am held by a large portion of the British nation, as well as by those for whom you speak, is most grateful to my feelings, though I am aware that I am indebted to their generous natures, and not to my own merit, for their good opinion. I beg, sir, that you will accept my sincere thanks for the kind sentiments which you have expressed toward me, and my unfeigned admiration of your exalted character. I am, with great respect,

"Your most obedient servant,

"R. E. Lee."

CHAPTER XII

LEE'S OPINION UPON THE LATE WAR

HIS INTENTION TO WRITE THE HISTORY OF HIS VIRGINIA
CAMPAIGNS — CALLED BEFORE A COMMITTEE OF CONGRESS —
PREACHES PATIENCE AND SILENCE TO THE SOUTH — SHUNS
CONTROVERSY AND PUBLICITY — CORRESPONDENCE WITH
AN ENGLISHMAN, HERBERT C. SAUNDERS

MY father had a strong desire at this time to write a history of his
campaigns. I think, however, he gradually gave it up when he saw
the great difficulties to be overcome and the labour required to
produce anything worthy of the subject, especially as he began to
realise that his strength was slowly failing—a fact which his letters
indicate. Just after the cessation of hostilities, he had taken some
preliminary steps toward acquiring the necessary material. In a
circular letter which he sent out to a great many of his general
officers, he wrote:

"I am desirous that the bravery and devotion of the Army of
Northern Virginia be correctly transmitted to posterity. This is
the only tribute that can now be paid to the worth of its noble
officers and soldiers, and I am anxious to collect the necessary
information for the history of its campaigns, including the operations in the Valley and in Western Virginia, from its organisation to its final surrender. . . ."

In a letter to the Honourable W. B. Reid, of Philadelphia, he writes on the same subject:

". . . I concur with you entirely as to the importance of a true history of the war, and it is my purpose, unless prevented, to write the history of the campaigns in Virginia. With this view, I have been engaged since the cessation of hostilities in endeavouring to procure the necessary official information. All my records, reports, returns, etc., etc., with the headquarters of the army, were needlessly destroyed by the clerks having them in charge on the retreat from Petersburg, and such as had been forwarded to the War Department in Richmond were either destroyed in the conflagration or captured at the South in the attempt to save them. I desire to obtain some vouchers in support of my memory, or I should otherwise have made some progress in the narrative. I have not even my letter- or order-books to which to refer. I have thought it possible that some of my official correspondence, which would be of value to me, might be found among the captured records in Washington, and that General Grant, who possesses magnanimity as well as ability, might cause me to be furnished with copies. I have, however, hesitated to approach him on the subject, as it is one in which he would naturally feel no interest."

In a letter to General Early, written in November, 1865, on the same subject, he says:

". . . I desire, if not prevented, to write a history of the campaigns in Virginia. . . . Your reports of your operations in '64 and '65 were among those destroyed. Can not you repeat them, and send me copies of such letters, orders, etc., of mine (including that last letter, to which you refer), and particularly give me your recollections of our effective strength at the principal battles? My only object is to transmit, if possible, the truth to posterity, and do justice to our brave soldiers."

Here is another letter to General Early, written March 16th, containing references to the same subject, and to two letters of General Early which had been published in the papers. It is interesting, also, as showing his moderation in speaking of those who had misrepresented his words and acts:

"*My Dear General:* I am very much obliged to you for the copies of my letters, forwarded with yours of January 25th. I hope you will be able to send me reports of the operations of your commands in the campaign, from the Wilderness to Richmond, at Lynchburg, in the Valley, Maryland, etc.; all statistics as regards numbers, destruction of private property by the Federal troops, etc., I should like to have, as I wish my memory strengthened on these points. It will be difficult to get the world to understand the odds against which we fought, and the destruction or loss of all returns of the army embarrass me very much. I read your letter from Havana to the New York *Times,* and was pleased with the temper in which it was written. I have since received the paper containing it, published in the City of Mexico, and also your letter in reference to Mr. Davis. I understand and appreciate the motives which prompted both letters, and think they will be of service in the way you intended. I have been much pained to see the attempts made to cast odium upon Mr. Davis, but do not think they will be successful with the reflecting or informed portion of the country. The accusations against myself I have not thought proper to notice, or even to correct misrepresentations of my words and acts. *We shall have to be patient* and suffer for awhile at least; and all controversy, I think, will only serve to prolong angry and bitter feeling, and postpone the period when reason and charity may resume their sway. At present, the public mind is not prepared to receive the truth. The feelings which influenced you to leave the country were natural, and, I presume, were uppermost in the breasts of many. It was a matter which each one had to decide for himself, as he only could know the reasons which governed him. I was particularly anxious on your account, as I had the same apprehensions to which you refer. I am truly glad that you are beyond the reach of annoyance, and hope you may be able to employ yourself profitably and usefully. Mexico is a beautiful country, fertile, of vast resources; and, with a stable government and virtuous population, will rise to greatness. I do not think that your letters can be construed by your former associates as reflecting upon them, and I have never heard the least blame cast by those who have remained upon those who thought it best to leave the country. I think I stated in a former letter the reasons which governed me, and will not therefore repeat them. I hope, in time, peace will be restored to the country, and that the South may enjoy some measure of prosperity. I fear, however, much suffering is still in store for her, and that her people must be prepared to exercise fortitude and forbearance. I must beg you to present my kind regards to the gentlemen with you, and, with my best wishes for yourself and undiminished esteem, I am,

> "Most truly yours,
>
> "R. E. LEE."

That his purpose had been heard of in the outside world is evident from this reply to a publisher in Cincinnati:

> "NEAR CARTERSVILLE, Virginia, August 26, 1865.
> "MR. JOSEPH TOPHAM,
> "Cincinnati, Ohio.

"*My Dear Sir:* I have just received your letter of the 17th inst., in reference to a history of the late war to be written by myself. I cannot, at present, undertake such a work, but am endeavouring to collect certain material to enable me to write a history of the campaigns in Virginia. Its completion is uncertain, and dependent upon so many contingencies that I think it useless to speak of arrangements for its publication at present. Thanking you for your kind proposition, I am,

> "Very respectfully yours,
>
> "R. E. LEE."

There were a great many letters of this kind from Northern publishing houses, and his replies were all of the same character. His failure to carry out this much-cherished wish is greatly to be deplored. How much we and our children have missed, those who know his truth and honesty of purpose, his manliness, simplicity, and charity, can best tell.

During the last days of February he was summoned to Washington to appear before a committee of Congress which was inquiring into the conditions of things in the Southern States, with a view to passing some of the so-called reconstruction measures. His testimony was simple, direct, and dignified, and is well worth reading by all who wish to hear the plain truth. It was his first appearance in any city save Richmond since the war, and being at a time of such political excitement, his visit was an occasion of absorbing interest to the crowds then in the capital.

When in Washington, Amanda, one of the house-servants at Arlington, called on him but failed to see him. In answer to a letter from her, my father replies as follows:

"LEXINGTON, Virginia, March 9, 1866.

"AMANDA PARKS.

"*Amanda:* I have received your letter of the 27th ult., and regret very much that I did not see you when I was in Washington. I heard on returning to my room, Sunday night, that you had been to see me; and I was sorry to have missed you, for I wished to learn how you were, and how all the people from Arlington were getting on in the world. My interest in them is as great now as it ever was, and I sincerely wish for their happiness and prosperity. At the period specified in Mr. Custis's will—five years from the time of his death—I caused the liberation of all the people at Arlington, as well as those at the White House and Romancoke, to be recorded in the Hustings Court at Richmond; and letters of manumission to be given to those with whom I could communicate who desired them. In consequence of the war which then existed, I could do nothing more for them. I do not know why you should ask if I am angry with you. I am not aware of your having done anything to give me offense, and I hope you would not say or do what was wrong. While you lived at Arlington you behaved very well, and were attentive and faithful to your duties. I hope you will always conduct yourself in the same manner. Wishing you health, happiness, and success in life,   I am truly,

"R. E. LEE."

Shortly after his return to Lexington, he writes to Mrs. Jefferson Davis. In this letter he expresses such noble sentiments, and is so moderate and sensible in his views of those who were harassing him and the South, that all who read it must profit thereby:

"LEXINGTON, Virginia, February 23, 1866.

"*My Dear Mrs. Davis:* Your letter of the 12th inst. reached Lexington during my absence at Washington. I have never seen Mr. Colfax's speech, and am, therefore, ignorant of the statements it contained. Had it, however, come under my notice, I doubt whether I should have thought it proper to reply. *I have thought, from the time of the cessation of hostilities, that silence and patience on the part of the South was the true course;* and I think so still. *Controversy of all kinds* will, in my opinion, only serve to continue excitement and passion, and will prevent the public mind from the acknowledgment and acceptance of the truth. These considerations have kept me from replying to accusations made against myself, and induced me to recommend the same to others. As regards the treatment of the Andersonville prisoners, to which you allude, I know nothing and can say nothing of my own knowledge. I never had anything to do with any prisoners, except to send those taken on the fields, where I was engaged, to the Provost Marshal General at Richmond. I have felt most keenly the sufferings and imprisonment of your husband, and have earnestly consulted with friends as to any possible mode of affording him relief and consolation. He enjoys the sympathy and respect of all good men; and if, as you state, his trial is now near, the exhibition of the whole truth in his case will, I trust, prove his defense and justification. With sincere prayers for his health and speedy restoration to liberty, and earnest supplications to God that He may take you and yours under His guidance and protection, I am, with great respect,

"Your obedient servant,

"R. E. LEE."

In further illustration of these views, held so strongly by him and practised so faithfully throughout his life, the following, written to a gentleman in Baltimore, is given:

"LEXINGTON, Virginia, April 13, 1866.

"*My Dear Sir:* Your letter of the 5th inst., inclosing a slip from the Baltimore *American,* has been received. The same statement has been published at the North for several years. The statement is not true; but I have not thought proper to publish a contradiction, being unwilling to be drawn into a newspaper discussion, believing that those who know me would not credit it and those who do not would care nothing about it. I cannot now depart from the rule I have followed. It is so easy to make accusations against the people at the South upon similar testimony, that those so disposed, should one be refuted, will immediately create another; and thus you would be led into endless controversy. I think it better to leave their correction to the return of reason and good feeling.

"Thanking you for your interest in my behalf, and begging you to consider my letter as intended only for yourself, I am,

"Most respectfully your obedient servant,

"R. E. LEE."

In this connection I give the following letter thanking Mr. Burr for a copy of the "Old Guard" which he had sent him, and showing also what, in his opinion, the South had fought for, and of what true republicanism consists:

"LEXINGTON, Virginia, January 5, 1866.

"MR. C. CHAUNCEY BURR.

"*My Dear Sir:* I am very much obliged to you for your letter of the 27th ult., and for the number of the 'Old Guard' which you kindly sent me. I am glad to know that the intelligent and respectable people at the North are true and conservative in their opinions, for I believe by no other course can the right interests of the country be maintained. All that the South has ever desired was that the Union, as established by our forefathers, should be preserved, and that the government as originally organised should be administered in purity and truth. If such is the desire of the North, there can be no contention between the two sections, and all true patriots will unite in advocating that policy which will soonest restore the country to tranquillity and order, and serve to perpetuate true republicanism. Please accept my thanks for your advocacy of right and liberty and the kind sentiments which you express toward myself, and believe me to be, with great respect,

"Your obedient servant,

"R. E. LEE."

An interesting view of my father's desire to keep himself from public attention is shown by his correspondence with an English gentleman, Mr. Herbert C. Saunders. The connected interview states his opinions on several points which are valuable. The copy of these papers was kindly furnished me by Mr. John Lyle Campbell, the Proctor of Washington and Lee University:

"WASHINGTON and LEE UNIVERSITY,

"LEXINGTON, Virginia, January 19, 1900.

"CAPT. ROBERT E. LEE,

"West Point, Virginia.

"*Dear Capt. Lee:* I inclose the copy promised you of the papers found in General Lee's desk. The paper seems to have had his careful revision, as there are a good many passages stricken out and a good many insertions in what seems to me undoubtedly to be his handwriting; and I was very much interested in the

changes that he made, as they were most characteristic of him—toning everything down, striking out adjectives, turning phrases from a personal to a general character, and always adding simplicity and force to the original. It seems to me most likely that he was at first disposed to allow the publication, but declined at last, on August 22d, the full limit of time indicated in Mr. Saunders's letter. I am   Yours truly,
    "(Dict.)   JNO. L. CAMPBELL."

The papers of which the following are copies were found in General Robert E. Lee's desk in the President's Office at Washington and Lee University. On the envelope in which they were inclosed was the following indorsement in General Lee's handwriting:

    "LONDON, July 31, 1866.
"Herbert C. Saunders asks permission to publish his conversation with me. August 22d—Refused."

    "3 BOLTON GARDENS, SOUTH KENSINGTON,
        "LONDON, July 31, 1866.
"My Dear General Lee: Presuming on the acquaintance with you which I had the honour and pleasure of making last November at Lexington, while travelling in Virginia, I venture now to write to you under these circumstances. You may remember that, at the time I presented to you my letter of introduction, I told you that two other Englishmen, friends of mine, who had come with me to America, were then making a tour through Georgia, the Carolinas, and some other Southern States. One of them, Mr. Kennaway, was so much interested with all he saw, and the people at home have appreciated his letters descriptive of it so well, that he is intending to publish a short account of his visit. Not having, however, had an introduction to yourself, he is anxious to avail himself of the somewhat full accounts I wrote home at the time, descriptive of my most interesting interview with you, and, with this view, he has asked me to put into the shape of a letter all those more prominent points which occur to

me as gathered from my letters and my recollection, and which are likely to interest and instruct the English public. I have, after some hesitation, acceded to the request—a hesitation caused mainly by the fact that at the time I saw you I neither prepared my notes with a view to publication nor did I inform you that there was any chance of what you told me being repeated. I may add that I never until a month or two ago had the slightest thought of publishing anything, and, in fact, have constantly resisted the many applications by my friends that I should let my letters see the light. My object in now writing to you is to know whether you have any objection to my giving my friend the inclosed short account of our interview, as it would, I am convinced, add greatly to the interest of the narrative. If you have no objection to this, perhaps you would kindly correct any statements put into your mouth which are not quite accurate, or expunge anything which might prejudice you with the public either of the North or the South, if unluckily anything of this nature should have crept in. My letters were written a day or two after the conversation, but you had so much of interest and new to tell me that I do not feel sure that I may not have confused names of battles, etc., in some instances. It will be necessary for me to deliver my part of the performance early in September to the publishers, and, therefore, I should feel much obliged by your sending me an answer at your earliest convenience. There will be a mail due here about the first of that month, leaving the United States on Wednesday, the 22d, and I shall, therefore, wait till its arrival before sending my letter to Mr. Kennaway; but should I not hear from you then I shall consider you have no objections to make or alterations to suggest, and act accordingly. If you have any new facts which you think it desirable should be known by the public, it will give me much pleasure to be the medium of their communication.

"I am sure I need scarcely tell you with what keen interest I have read all the accounts from your continent of the proceedings in Congress and elsewhere in connection with the reconstruction of the South. I do sincerely trust it may be eventually effected in a way satisfactory to the South, and I most deeply deplore the steps taken by the Radical side of the House to set the two (North and South) by the ears again. President Johnson's policy seems to me to be that which, if pursued, would be most likely to contribute to the consolidation of the country; but I am both surprised and pained to find how little power the Executive has against so strong a faction as the Radicals, who, while they claim to represent the North, do, in fact, but misrepresent the country. I am sure you will believe that I say with sincerity that I always take great interest in anything I hear said or that I read of yourself, and I am happy to say that, even with all the rancour of the Northern Radicals against the South, it is little they find of ill to say of you.

"Hoping you will not think I am doing wrong in the course I propose to take, and that your answer may be satisfactory, I remain, my dear General Lee,

"Yours very sincerely,   HERBERT C. SAUNDERS.

"GENERAL ROBERT E. LEE."

"LEXINGTON, Virginia, August 22, 1866.

"MR. HERBERT C. SAUNDERS,

"3 Bolton Gardens,

"South Kensington, London, England.

"*My Dear Mr. Saunders:* I received to-day your letter of the 31st ult. What I stated to you in conversation, during the visit which you did me the honour to pay me in November last, was entirely for your own information, and was in no way intended for publication. My only object was to gratify the interest which you apparently evinced on the several topics which were introduced, and to point to facts which you might investigate, if you so desired, in your own way. I have an objection to the publication of my private conversations, which are never intended but for those to whom they are addressed. I cannot, therefore, without an entire disregard of the rule which I have followed in other cases, and in violation of my own sense of propriety, assent to what you propose. I hope, therefore, you will excuse me. What you may think proper to publish I hope will be the result of your own observations and convictions, and not on my authority. In the hasty perusal which I have been obliged to give the manuscript inclosed to me, I perceive many inaccuracies, resulting as much, perhaps, from my imperfect narration as from misapprehension on your part. Though fully appreciating your kind wish to correct certain erroneous statements as regards myself, I prefer remaining silent to doing anything that might excite angry discussion at this time, when strong efforts are being made by conservative men, North and South, to sustain President Johnson in his policy, which, I think, offers the only means of healing the lamentable divisions of the country, and which the result of the late convention at Philadelphia gives great promise of doing. Thanking you for the opportunity afforded me of expressing my opinion before executing your purpose, I am, etc.,

"R. E. LEE."

The following is Mr. Saunders' account of the interview:

"On only one subject would he talk at any length about his own conduct, and that was with reference to the treatment of the Federal prisoners who had fallen into his hands. He seemed to feel deeply the backhanded stigma cast upon him by his having been included by name in the first indictment framed against Wirz, though he was afterward omitted from the new charges. He explained to me the circumstances under which he had arranged with McClellan for the exchange of prisoners; how he had, after the battles of Manassas, Fredericksburg, and (I think) Chancellorsville, sent all the wounded over to the enemy on the engagement of their generals to parole them. He also told me that on several occasions his commissary generals had come to him after a battle and represented that he had not rations enough both for prisoners and the army when the former had to be sent several days' march to their place of confinement, and he had always given orders that the wants of the prisoners should be first attended to, as from their position they could not save themselves from starvation by foraging or otherwise, as the army could when in straits for provisions. The General also explained how every effort had always been made by the Confederates to do away with the necessity of retaining prisoners by offering every facility for exchange, till at last, when all exchange was refused, they found themselves with 30,000 prisoners for whom they were quite unable to do as much as they wished in the way of food. He stated, furthermore, that many of their hardships arose from the necessity of constantly changing the prisons to prevent recapture. With the management of the prisons he assured me he had no more to do than I had, and did not even know that Wirz was in charge of Andersonville prison (at least, I think he asserted this) till after the war was over. I could quite sympathise with him in his feeling of pain under which his generous nature evidently suffered that the authorities at Washington should have included him and others similarly circumstanced in this charge of cruelty at the time that letters written by himself (General Lee), taken in Richmond when captured, complaining that the troops in his army had actually been for days together on several occasions without an ounce of meat, were in possession of the military authorities.

"When discussing the state of feeling in England with regard to the war, he assured me that it had all along given him the greatest pleasure to feel that the Southern cause had the sympathies of so many in the 'old country,' to which he looked as a second home; but, in answer to my questions, he replied that he had never expected us to give them material aid, and added that he thought all governments were right in studying only the interests of their own people and in not going to war for an 'idea' when they had no distinct cause of quarrel.

"On the subject of slavery, he assured me that he had always been in favour of the emancipation of the negroes, and that in Virginia the feeling had been strongly inclining in the same direction, till the ill-judged enthusiasm (amounting to rancour) of the abolitionists in the North had turned the Southern tide of feeling in the other direction. In Virginia, about thirty years ago, an ordinance for the emancipation of the slaves had been rejected by only a small majority, and every one fully expected at the next convention it would have been carried, but for the above cause. He went on to say that there was scarcely a Virginian now who was not glad that the subject had been definitely settled, though nearly all regretted that they had not been wise enough to do it themselves the first year of the war. Allusion was made by him to a conversation he had with a distinguished countryman of mine. He had been visiting a large slave plantation (Shirley) on the James River. The Englishman had told him that the working population were better cared for there than in any country he had ever visited, but that he must never expect an approval of the institution of slavery by England, or aid from her in any cause in which that question was involved. Taking these facts and the well-known antipathy of the mass of the English to the institution into consideration, he said he had never expected help from England. The people 'at the South' (as the expression is), in the main, though scarcely unanimously, seem to hold much the same language as General Lee with reference to our neutrality, and to be much less bitter than Northerners generally—who, I must confess, in my own opinion, have much less cause to complain of our interpretation of the laws of neutrality than the South. I may mention here, by way of parenthesis, that *I* was, on two separate occasions (once in Washington and once in Lexington), told that there were many people in the country who wished that General Washington had never lived and that they were still subjects of Queen Victoria; but I should certainly say as a rule the Americans are much too well satisfied with themselves for this feeling to be at all common. General Lee, in the course of this to me most interesting evening's *séance*, gave me many details of the war too long to put on paper, but, with reference to the small result of their numerous victories, accounted for it in this way: the force which the Confederates brought to bear was so often inferior in numbers to that of the Yankees that the more they followed up the victory against one portion of the enemy's line the more did they lay themselves open to being surrounded by the remainder of the enemy. He likened the operation to a man breasting a wave of the sea, who, as rapidly as he clears a way before him, is enveloped by the very water he has displaced. He spoke of the final surrender as inevitable owing to the superiority in numbers of the enemy. His own army had, during the last few weeks, suffered materially from defection in its ranks, and, discouraged by failures and worn out by hardships, had at the time of the surrender only 7,892 men under arms, and this little army was almost surrounded by one of 100,000. They might, the General said with an air piteous to behold, have cut their way out as they had done before, but, looking upon the struggle as hopeless, I was not surprised to hear him say that he thought it cruel to prolong it. In two other battles he named (Sharpsburg and Chancellorsville, I think he said), the Confederates were to the Federals in point of numbers as 35,000 to 120,000 and as 45,000 to 155,000 respectively, so that the mere disparity of numbers was not sufficient to convince him of the necessity of surrender; but feeling that his own army was persuaded of the ultimate hopelessness of the contest as evidenced by their defection, he took the course of surrendering his army in lieu of reserving it for utter annihilation.

"Turning to the political bearing of the important question at issue, the great Southern general gave me, at some length, his feelings with regard to the abstract right of secession. This right, he told me, was held as a constitutional maxim at the South. As to its exercise at the time on the part of the South, he was distinctly opposed, and it was not until Lincoln issued a proclamation for 75,000 men to invade the South, which was deemed clearly unconstitutional, that Virginia withdrew from the United States.

"We discussed a variety of other topics, and, at eleven o'clock when I rose to go, he begged me to stay on, as he found the nights full long. His son, General Custis Lee, who had distinguished himself much during the war, but whom I had not the good fortune of meeting, is the only one of his family at present with him at Lexington, where he occupies the position of a professor in the Military Institute of Virginia. This college had 250 cadets in it when the war broke out, General 'Stonewall' Jackson being one of the professors. At one moment in the war, when the Federals were advancing steadily up the Shenandoah Valley, these youths (from 16 to 22 years of age) were marched to join the Confederate Army, and did good service. In one battle at Newmarket, of which I shall have occasion to speak later in my letters, they distinguished themselves in a conspicuous way under the leadership of Colonel Shipp, who is still their commandant. By a brilliant charge, they contributed, in a great measure, to turn the tide of affairs, losing nine of their number killed and more than forty wounded. General Hunter, on a subsequent occasion, when occupying Lexington with a body of Federal troops, quartered his men in the Military Institute for several days, and, on leaving, had the building—a very handsome and extensive one—fired in numerous places, completely destroying all but the external walls, which now stand. The professors' houses stood in detached positions, and these, too, with the house of Mr. Letcher, a former governor of the State, he also burnt to the ground. The Washington College, the presidency of which General Lee now holds, they also ransacked, destroying everything it contained, and were preparing it for the flames, to which they were with difficulty restrained from devoting it by earnest representations of its strictly educational nature."

CHAPTER XIII

FAMILY AFFAIRS

I had before this time gone to my farm in King William County
and started out in life as a farmer. As there was nothing but the
land and a few old buildings left, for several years I had a very
up-hill time. My father encouraged, advised me, and gave me
material aid. His letters to me at this time will show the interest
he took in my welfare. In one written March 16, 1866, after
advising me as to steps to be taken in repairing an old mill on
the place, he writes:

"I am clear for your doing everything to improve your property
and make it remunerative as far as you can. You know my objection to incurring debt. I cannot overcome it. . . . I hope you will
overcome your chills, and by next winter you must patch up your
house, and get a sweet wife. You will be more comfortable, and not
so lonesome. Let her bring a cow and a churn. That will be all you
will want. . . . Give my love to Fitzhugh. I wish he were regularly
established. He cannot afford to be idle. He will be miserable."

My brother Fitzhugh, here referred to, was negotiating to rent his farm, the White House, to some so-called English capitalists, and had not as yet established himself. In another letter to me, of May 26, 1866, my father says:

". . . I will state, at the outset, that I desire you to consider Romancoke with its appurtenances your own; to do with as you consider most to your interest; to sell, farm, or let; subject, however, to the conditions imposed by your grandfather's will, as construed by the decree of the Court of Appeals of Virginia, which declares, 'If the legacies are not paid off by the personal property, hires of slaves, rents, and sale of the real estate, charged with their payment, at the end of five years, the portion unpaid remains a charge upon the White House and Romancoke until paid. The devisees take their estates *cum onere.*'

"The result of the war having deprived the estates of the benefit of the hire of the slaves and the sale of Smith's Island, and the personal property having all been swept off by the Federal armies, there is nothing left but the land of the two estates named. A court might make some deduction from the amount of the legacies to be paid in consideration of these circumstances, and I should think it would be fair to do so. But of that I cannot say. Now, with this understanding, make your own arrangements to suit yourself, and as you may determine most conducive to your interests. In confirming your action, as the executor of your grandfather, I must, however, take such measures as may be necessary to carry out the purpose of his will. . . . If you are determined to hold the estate, I think you ought to make it profitable. As to the means of doing so, you must decide for yourself. I am unable to do it for you, and might lead you astray. Therefore, while always willing to give you any advice in my power, in whatever you do you must feel that the whole responsibility rests with you. . . . I wish, my dear son, I could be of some advantage to you, but I can only give you my love and earnest prayers, and commit you to the keeping of that God who never forgets those who serve Him. May He watch over and preserve you.

"Your affectionate father,

"R. E. LEE."

In another letter, of June 13th, after telling me of the visit of a cousin of my mother's and how much gratification it was to have her with them, he regrets that her son, who brought his mother up to Lexington, had to hurry home on account of having left his wife and little son:

". . . When you have such pleasing spurs in your flanks, I hope you may be on the fair road to prosperity. All unite in love to you and Fitzhugh. Ask the latter if George has yet found a horse to trade with the gray. We miss him very much,[1] and want to see you as badly. You may judge how poorly we are off. The examination has commenced at Washington College. Three days are over successfully, and I hope to finish in twelve more. ——— has been up in two subjects, and not got thrown. He has two more. But, in the meantime, I am much occupied, and will be confined all day. I have no time for letters of affection, so must tell you good-bye.

"Most affectionately,

"R. E. LEE."

This was the first final examination at Washington College since my father became its president. He worked very hard, and was kept busy attending to all the details and the putting into practice of several new methods and systems he had introduced.

That summer he took my mother to the Rockbridge Baths, about eleven miles from Lexington, to give her the benefit of the waters, which, he hoped, might give her some relief from the continual pain she suffered. She did derive benefit, but, unfortunately, had a fall which seriously impeded the improvement.

In reply to a note from my mother telling him of her misfortune and asking him to send her some medicines, he writes the following note:

"LEXINGTON, Virginia, August 10, 1866.

"*My Dear Mary:* On receiving your note, yesterday, I had only time to get the arnica and send it by the stage. I am very sorry that you received such a fall, and fear it must have been a heavy shock to you. I am, however, very thankful that you escaped greater injury, and hope it is no worse than you describe. I will endeavour to get down to see you to-morrow evening, and trust I may find you somewhat relieved from its effects. We are pretty well here. Many people are out of town, and I have not seen those who are in. Love to the girls.

"Truly and affectionately yours,

"R. E. LEE.

"MRS. M. C. LEE."

My father was still very busy with his college work, and, after establishing her there, spent most of the time in Lexington, riding Traveller over to see her whenever he could get a spare day. Among the few letters preserved of those written to her at this time, I have a note of July 16th:

"*My Dear Mary:* I am glad to see by your letter of yesterday that you are recovering so well from your fall. I hope you may soon be well again. . . . Caroline² got back this morning. Left her daughter better. Says there is a very good girl in Lynchburg, from General Cocke's estate, anxious to live with us. I shall have more conversation with her [Caroline], and, if satisfied, will write for her, by the boat to-night. Her father is in Lynchburg, and anxious for her to come. . . . Tell Mrs. Cabell I am sorry to have missed seeing her. Where is Katie? I wish she would send her to see me. I will endeavour to find some one to carry this to you. Love to all.

"Very affectionately and truly yours,

"R. E. LEE."

The mails in those days were not very direct, and private messenger was often the surest and speediest method of letter-carriage. In the absence of my mother, my father was trying to better the staff of servants. Their inefficiency was the drawback to our comfort then, as it is now. Often the recommendation of some was only the name of the estate from which they came. A few days later, my father writes again:

"LEXINGTON, Virginia, July 20, 1866.

"*My Dear Mary:* I was glad to receive your note this morning, and wish it could have reported a marked improvement in your health. But that, I trust, will come in time. It has been impossible for me to return to you this week, and, indeed, I do not see how I can absent myself at all. I shall endeavour to go to the Baths Monday, and hope during the week you may be able to determine whether it would be more advantageous for you to remain there or go further, as I shall have to return here as soon as I can. I can accomplish nothing while absent. Custis has determined to accompany Mr. Harris to the White Sulphur Monday, and the girls seem indifferent about leaving home. They ask, properly, what is to become of it? Mr. Pierre Chouteau, son of Julia Gratiot and Charles Chouteau, will hand you this. He will remain over Sunday at the Baths, and can tell you all about St. Louis. I send such letters as have come for you. I have no news. The heat seems to extend everywhere, but it will be cool enough after a time. We are as usual, except that 'Aunt' Caroline[3] seems more overcome, and Harriet[4] indulges in lighter attire. I fear Mrs. Myers had an awful time. The Elliotts do not seem in haste to leave town. They are waiting for a cool day to go to the Natural Bridge, and do not seem to have decided whether to go to the Baths or Alum Springs. We had an arrival last night from the latter place—General Colquit and daughters. They return to-morrow. The girls will write of domestic matters. I received a letter from Rob at Romancoke. He is still taking cholagogue, but well. Nothing of interest has occurred.

"Affectionately yours,

"R. E. LEE."

Cholagogue was a fever-and-ague remedy of which I partook largely at that time. After this letter, my sisters joined my mother at the Baths, my father still spending most of his time in Lexington, but riding over to see them whenever he could. He was very busy repairing some of the old buildings of the college and arranging his work for the next session. Here is another short note to my mother:

"LEXINGTON, Virginia, August 2, 1866.

"*My Dear Mary:* Mr. Campbell has just informed me that Cousins George and Eleanor Goldsborough are with you. Tell them they must not go till I can get to the Baths. I think the waters of the latter will do them as much good as anything they can try, and the sight of them will do me great benefit. I find here much to do, but will endeavour to be with you to-morrow evening or Saturday morning. Custis has just come, but finding me occupied with builders, shook hands, got his dinner, and left for the Institute. So I do not know where he is from or where he will go next. Our neighbours are generally well, and inquire for you. Colonel Reid better. Tell the girls, if I find them improving, I will bring them something. Remember me to Cousins George and Eleanor and all the ladies. I have about a bushel of letters to answer and other things to do.

"Very affectionately,

"R. E. LEE."

On one of his visits to my mother, he took advantage of the comparative quiet and rest there and wrote me a long letter, which I give here in full:

"ROCKBRIDGE BATHS, July 28, 1866.

"*My Dear Robert:* I was very glad to see from your letter of the 2d the progress you are making in your farm. I hope things may move prosperously with you, but you must not expect this result without corresponding attention and labour. I should like very much to visit you, but it will be impossible. I have little time for anything but my business. I am here with your mother, waiting to see the effects of these waters upon her disease, before proceeding to the Warm Springs. She is pleased with the bath, which she finds very agreeable, and it has reduced the swelling in her feet and ankles, from which she has been suffering for a long time, and, in fact, from her account, entirely removed it. This is a great relief in itself, and, I hope, may be followed by greater. I do not think she moves with more facility, though I think she walks [on her crutches] oftener and longer than heretofore, and probably with more confidence. She has been here too short a time to pronounce positively as to the effects of the water, and will have to remain three or four weeks before we determine whether she will go further. I am unwilling for her to lose the whole summer here unless it promises some advantage, and, after the middle of next week, unless some marked change takes place, shall take her to the Warm Springs. Custis has gone to the White Sulphur, but expects to be in Richmond on August 6th to meet Fitzhugh, with the view of going to the Warrenton White Sulphur Springs in North Carolina, to witness the erection of a monument over dear Annie, which the kind people of that country have prepared for the purpose. My attendance on your mother, which is necessary, prevents my being present. Agnes and Mildred are here. I think the baths have been beneficial to them already, though they have not been here a week. I will leave them to describe the place and visitors. I applied the dressing of salt to the old meadow at Arlington with the view of renovating the grass. I believe it is equally good for corn. It was refuse salt—Liverpool—which I bought cheaply in Alexandria from the sacks having decayed and broken, but I cannot recollect exactly how much I applied to the acre. I think it was about two or three bushels to the acre. You had better consult some work on farming as to the quantity. I would advise you to apply manure of some kind to all your land. I believe there is nothing better or cheaper for you to begin with than shell lime. I would prefer cultivating less land manured in some way than a large amount unassisted. We are always delighted to hear from you, and I trust with care you may escape the chills. The incentives I spoke of were a sweet wife and child. God bless you, my dear son.

"Most affectionately,

"R. E. LEE."

My mother continued to improve so much that she did not go that summer to the Warm Springs. My father spent most of his time in Lexington, but rode over to the Baths about once a week. There was nothing he enjoyed more than a good long ride on Traveller. It rested him from the cares and worries incident to his duties, and gave him renewed energy for his work. He was often seen that summer along the eleven miles of mountain road between Lexington and the Baths. He made himself acquainted with the people living near it, talked to them about their affairs, encouraged and advised them, and always had a cheery greeting and a pleasant word for them. The little children along his route soon became acquainted with the gray horse and his stately rider. College reopened the last of September, and by October he had his wife and daughters with him again. He writes to me on October 18th, trying to help me in my agricultural perplexities:

"...Am glad to hear that you are well and progressing favourably. Your Uncle Smith says, in a letter just received in which he writes of his difficulties and drawbacks, 'I must tell you that if you desire to succeed in any matter relating to agriculture you must personally superintend and see to everything.' Perhaps your experience coincides with his.

"I hope your wheat will reimburse you for your labour and guano. I think you are right in improving your land. You will gain by cultivating less and cultivating that well, and I would endeavour to manure every crop—as to the kind of manure which will be the most profitable, you must experiment. Lime acts finely on your land, and is more lasting than guano. If you can, get shells to burn

217

on your land, or, if not, shell lime from Baltimore. I think you would thereby more certainly and more cheaply restore your fields. I hope your sale of ship-timber may place you in funds to make your experiments. You will have to attend to your contractors. They will generally bear great attention, and then circumvent you. . . . I hope I shall see you this winter, when we can talk over the matter. We are pretty well. Your mother is better by her visit to the Baths. Mildred talks of going to the Eastern Shore of Maryland next month, and I fear will be absent from us all winter. I must refer you to your sisters for all news. They are great letter-writers, and their correspondence extends over the globe. Miss Etta Seldon is with us. All our summer visitors have gone, and some who, I hoped, would have visited us have not come. . . . Good-bye, my dear son. God bless you. . . .

"Your affectionate father,

"R. E. LEE."

"ROBERT E. LEE, JR."

My uncle, Smith Lee, was farming on the Potomac, and was constantly sending me messages of condolence through my father. Our experiences were the same as all others starting to farm under the new order of things. My father was very hospitable, and it delighted him to have his relatives and friends come to see him. So many kindnesses had been shown to himself and family for the last five years that he greatly enjoyed this, his first opportunity of greeting in his own home those who had so often offered my mother and sisters the shelter of theirs. The country around Lexington was most beautiful, and the climate in the summer and autumn all that could be desired. So, at those seasons, whenever he was at home, there was generally some one visiting him, nearly always relatives or old and dear friends. He entertained very simply, made every one feel at home, and was always considerate and careful of the amusement and welfare of his guests.

People came from all over the world to Lexington to see him. Amongst the visitors from afar were the Marquis of Lorne and the Hon. Mr. Cooper, who were on a tour through the United States.

They came to Lexington to see General Lee. When they called at the house there happened to be no servant at hand, and my father, meeting them at the door, received their cards. Not having on his glasses, he could not read the names, but ushered the strangers into the parlour, and presented them to Mrs. Lee, without calling their names. My mother thought the tall, slender youth was a new student, and entered into conversation with him as such. Struck by his delicate appearance, she cautioned him against the harsh winter climate of the mountains, and urged him to be careful of his health. On this, Mr. Cooper explained who his compainon was, and there was much amusement over the mistake.

The professors and students of the two institutions of learning were constant visitors, especially in the evenings, when young men came to see the girls. If his daughters had guests, my father usually sat with my mother in the dining-room adjoining the drawing-room. When the clock struck ten he would rise and close the shutters carefully and slowly, and, if that hint was not taken, he would simply say "Good night, young gentlemen." The effect was immediate and lasting, and his wishes in that matter, finally becoming generally known, were always respected. Captain W., who had very soon found out the General's views as to the time of leaving, was told on one occasion that General Lee had praised him very much.

"Do you know why?" said the Captain. "It is because I have never been caught in the parlour at ten o'clock. I came very near it last night, but got out into the porch before the General shut the first blind. That's the reason he calls me 'a fine young man.'"

A young friend who was a cadet at the Virginia Military Institute called on my sisters one evening, and remarked, just for something to say:

"Do you know this is the first civilian's house I have entered in Lexington."

My father was in the room in his gray Confederate coat, shorn of the buttons; also my two brothers, Custis and Fitzhugh, both of whom had been generals in the Confederate Army; so there was quite a laugh over the term *civilian*. I have already mentioned how particular my father was about answering all letters. It was a great tax on his time, and some of them must have been a trial to his temper. The following will explain itself:

"Lexington, Virginia, September 5, 1866.
"A. J. Requier,
  "81 Cedar St., New York.

"*My Dear Sir:* I am very much obliged to you for your kind letter of the 22d ult. So many articles formerly belonging to me are scattered over the country that I fear I have not time to devote to their recovery. I know no one in Buffalo whom I could ask to reclaim the Bible in question. If the lady who has it will use it, as I hope she will, she will herself seek to restore it to the rightful owner. I will, therefore, leave the decision of the question to her and her conscience. I have read with great pleasure the poem you sent me, and thank you sincerely for your interest in my behalf. With great respect,

"Your obedient servant,
"R. E. Lee."

Here is another one of many of a similar character:

"Lexington, Virginia, September 26, 1866.
"Mr. E. A. Pollard,
  "104 West Baltimore St.,
    "Baltimore, Md.

"*Dear Sir:* I return you my thanks for the compliment paid me by your proposition to write a history of my life. It is a hazardous undertaking to publish the life of any one while living, and there are but few who would desire to read a true history of themselves. Independently of the few national events with which mine has been connected, it presents little to interest the general reader, nor do I know where to refer you for the necessary materials. All my private, as well as public, records have been destroyed or lost, except what is to be found in published documents, and I know of nothing available for the purpose. Should you, therefore, determine to undertake the work, you must rely upon yourself, as my time is so fully occupied that I am unable to promise you any assistance.

"Very respectfully,

"R. E. LEE."

This autumn my sister Mildred paid a visit to our cousins, Mr. and Mrs. George Goldsborough, living at "Ashby," near Easton, on the Eastern Shore of Maryland. She remained away there and elsewhere for several months. My father's letters to her, many of which have been preserved, are most interesting. They show very plainly many beautiful phases of his noble character and disposition:

"LEXINGTON, Virginia, December 21, 1866.

"*My Precious Life:* I was very glad to receive your letter of the 15th inst., and to learn that you were well and happy. May you be always as much so as is consistent with your welfare here and hereafter, is my daily prayer. I was much pleased, too, that, while enjoying the kindness of your friends, we were not forgotten. Experience will teach you that, notwithstanding all appearances to the contrary, you will never receive such a love as is felt for you by your father and mother. That lives through absence, difficulties, and time,. Your own feelings will teach you how it should be returned and appreciated. I want to see you very much, and miss you at every turn, yet am glad of this opportunity for you to be with those who, I know, will do all in their power to give you pleasure. I hope you will also find time to read and improve your mind. Read history, works of truth, not novels and romances. Get correct views of life, and learn to see the world in its true light. It will enable you to live pleasantly, to do good, and, when summoned away, to leave without regret. Your friends here inquire constantly after you, and wish for your return. Mrs. White and Mrs. McElwee particularly regret your absence, and the former sends especial thanks for your letter of remembrance. We get on in our usual way. Agnes takes good care of us, and is very thoughtful and attentive. She has not great velocity, but is systematic and quiet. After to-day, the mornings will begin to lengthen a little, and her trials to lessen. It is very cold, the ground is covered with six inches of snow, and the mountains, as far as the eye can reach in every direction, elevate their white crests as monuments of winter. This is the night for the supper for the repairs to the Episcopal church. Your mother and sisters are busy with their contributions. It is to take place at the hotel, and your brother, cousins, and father are to attend. On Monday night (24th), the supper for the Presbyterian church is to be held at their lecture-room. They are to have music and every attraction. I hope both may be productive of good. But you know the Episcopalians are few in numbers and light in purse, and must be resigned to small returns. . . . I must leave to your sisters a description of these feasts, and also an account of the operation of the Reading Club. As far as I can judge, it is a great institution for the discussion of apples and chestnuts, but is quite innocent of the pleasures of literature. It, however, brings the young people together, and promotes sociability and conversation. Our feline companions are flourishing. Young Baxter is growing in gracefulness and favour, and gives cat-like evidences of future worth. He possesses the fashionable colour of 'moonlight on the water,' apparently a dingy hue of the kitchen, and is strictly aristocratic in appearance and conduct. Tom, surnamed 'The Nipper,' from the manner in which he slaughters our enemies, the rats and the mice, is admired for his gravity and sobriety, as well as for his strict attention to the pursuits of his race. They both feel your absence sorely. Traveller and Custis are both well, and pursue their usual dignified gait and habits, and are not led away by the frivolous entertainments of lectures and concerts. All send united love, and all wish for your return. Remember me most kindly to Cousins Eleanor and George, John, Mary, Ida, and all at 'Myrtle Grove,' and to other kind friends when you meet them. Mrs. Grady carried yesterday to Mr. Charles Kerr, in Baltimore, a small package for you. Be careful of your health, and do not eat more than half the plum-puddings Cousin Eleanor has prepared for Xmas. I am glad to hear that you are fattening, and I hope you will reach 125 lbs. Think always of your father, who loves you dearly.

"R. E. LEE.

"P. S., 22d.—Rob arrived last night with 'Lucy Long.' He thinks it too bad you are away. He has not seen you for two years.

"R. E. LEE."

"Baxter" and "Tom, the Nipper" were Mildred's pets. All of us had a fondness for cats, inherited from my mother and her father, Mr. Custis. My father was very fond of them in his way and in their place, and was kind to them and considerate of their feelings. My mother told of his hearing one of the house-pets, possibly Baxter or the Nipper, crying and lamenting under his window one stormy night. The General got out of bed, opened the window, and called pussy to come in. The window was so high that the animal could not jump up to it. My father then stepped softly across the room, took one of my mother's crutches, and held it so far out of the window that he became wet from the falling rain; but he persuaded the cat to climb up along the crutch, and into the window, before he thought of dry clothing for himself. "Lucy Long" was my father's mare, which had been lost or stolen at the end of the war, and which I had just brought back to him. I will give in the following letter his account of her:

"LEXINGTON, Virginia, September 4, 1866.
"DR. C. S. GARNETT.

"*Dear Sir:* I am much obliged to you for your letter of the 23d ult. and the information it contained. The mare about which my son wrote you was bred by Mr. Stephen Dandridge, of 'The Bower,' Berkeley County, Virginia, and was purchased from him for me by General J. E. B. Stuart in the fall of 1862—after the return of the army from Maryland. She is nine or ten years old, about fifteen hands high, square built, sorrel (not chestnut) colour, has a fast walk, easy pace, and short canter. When I parted with her she had a full long mane and tail. I rode her in conjunction with my gray horse from the fall of '62 to the spring of '64, when she was sent back for refreshment; and it was in recalling her in the spring of '65 from Mr. Hairston's, in Henry County, that she got into Major Paxton's stables of public horses and went to Danville with them. I think she might be recognised by any member of the Army of Northern Virginia, in Essex, unless much changed. I now recollect no distinctive marks about her except a blaze in her forehead and white hind-legs. My son, General W. H. F. Lee, residing at the White House, in New Kent, might recognise her, and also my son Robert, who resides near West Point, in King William. Captain Hopkins, to whom you refer in your letter, is dead, but Major Paxton, who had general charge of the public stables, and to whom I referred your letter, has sent me the accompanying affidavits of two of the men employed by him. Should their evidence not be satisfactory, he will procure statements from some of the officers, which probably may be more definite. I should be obliged to you, if the mare in question is the one I am seeking for, that you would take steps to recover her, as I am desirous of reclaiming her in consideration of the donor, General Stuart.

"Your obedient servant,   R. E. LEE."

It was proved to the satisfaction of all parties that the mare in question was "Lucy Long," and my father reimbursed the man who had bought her from some one who had no right to her. She was brought to my place and I recognised her at once. She stayed with me until I was ready to pay my Christmas visit to Lexington. She then was put on the train and sent to Staunton, where I met her. I found there Colonel William Allan, a professor of Washington College, who had a buggy and no horse, and as I had a horse and no buggy, we joined forces and I drove him over to Lexington, "Lucy Long" carrying us with great ease to herself and comfort to us. My father was glad to get her, as he was very fond of her. When he heard how she came over, he was really shocked, as he thought she had never been broken to harness. She lived to be thirty-three years old, and was then chloroformed, because my brother thought she had ceased to enjoy life. For the last ten years of her life she was boarded out in the country, where she did nothing but rest, and until about a year before her death she seemed in good health and spirits.

CHAPTER XIV

AN IDEAL FATHER

LETTERS TO MILDRED LEE—TO ROBERT—TO FITZHUGH—
INTERVIEWED BY SWINTON, HISTORIAN OF THE ARMY OF THE
POTOMAC—IMPROVEMENT IN GROUNDS AND BUILDINGS OF
WASHINGTON COLLEGE—PUNCTUALITY A PROMINENT TRAIT
OF ITS PRESIDENT—A STRONG SUPPORTER OF THE Y. M. C. A.

MY sister, after the Christmas holidays, went from "Ashby" to Baltimore, Cousins George and Eleanor Goldsborough taking her with them to their town house. I think my father always wanted his daughters with him. When they were away he missed them, their love, care, and attention. The next letter I find is to Mildred, in Baltimore:

"LEXINGTON, Virginia, January 27, 1867.

"*My Precious Daughter:* Your letter to your mother gave us the satisfactory information of your continued good health, for I feared that your long silence had been caused by indisposition of body, rather than that due to writing. I hope you will not let so long an interval between your letters occur again, for you know I am always longing to hear from you, when I cannot see you, and a few lines, if only to say you are well, will prevent unpleasant apprehensions. I am delighted at your increased bodily dimensions, and your diminished drapery. One hundred and twenty-eight avoirdupois is approximately a proper standard.

Seven more pounds will make you all right. But I fear before I see you the unnatural life, which I fear you will lead in Baltimore, will reduce you to skin and bone. Do not go out to many parties, preserve your simple tastes and manners, and you will enjoy more pleasure. Plainness and simplicity of dress, early hours, and rational amusements, I wish you to practise. You must thank Cousins Eleanor and George for all their kindness to you, and remember me to all friends. If you see your uncle Marshall, present my kind regards to him, and my best wishes for his health and happiness. I hope you will see Robert. I heard that he stayed at Mr. Edward Dallam's when in Baltimore, but do not know whether he will return there from Lynwood. I was sorry to hear that you lost your purse. Perhaps the finder was more in want than you are, and it may be of service to him, and you can do without it. A little money is sometimes useful. You must bear in mind that it will not be becoming in a Virginia girl now to be fine or fashionable, and that gentility as well as self-respect requires moderation in dress and gaiety. While her people are suffering, she should practise self-denial and show her sympathy in their affliction. We are all pretty well. Your poor mother suffers more pain than usual during this inclement weather. Your sister is devoted to the snow and ice, and Agnes is becoming a very good housekeeper. She has received a letter from a gentleman, whose judgment she respects, recommending her to acquire that useful knowledge, and assuring her that it will not only promote domestic happiness, but will add greatly to connubial bliss. This is a great encouragement to her. Our young friends, the law students and cadets, all inquire after you and wish for your return. Mrs. McElwee and Mrs. White also send their particular regards, and Colonel Reid, who seems to be failing fast, sends his love, and hopes that you will soon return. You know that is my wish and hope, so whenever you are ready to return you will know that I am waiting to receive you. I will leave your mother and sisters to give you all domestic news. Tell Annette I have been looking for her in every stage since her letter last fall, and that I hope for her arrival daily. Nipper is well, and endeavours, by stern gravity, to repress the frivolity of Baxter. All unite in much love, and I am, as ever,

"Your father,   R. E. LEE.

"MISS MILDRED LEE."

Just after the intermediate examinations, he writes to Mildred again:

"LEXINGTON, Virginia, February 16, 1867.

"*My Precious Daughter:* I have wished to answer your letter of the 2d for some days, but have not been able. The intermediate examinations which were in progress when it arrived continued ten entire days, and since their termination the necessary arrangements for the resumption of studies, and the reorganisation of the classes, have occupied all my time not devoted to other pressing matters. The students generally passed very creditable examinations. Many of your friends were distinguished. The ordeal through which the higher classes passed was as severe as any I ever witnessed. Colonel Johnston[1] has arrived and entered upon his duties. He is living at the hotel with his wife and six sweet little children, being unable to procure a house, and the college being too poor to build one for him. We have other professors also houseless. Robert has returned to his 'broken-back cottage,' though he confesses to having enjoyed great pleasure during his visit to Baltimore. He dwells with delight upon his intercourse with the Misses—, whom he considers angels upon earth, without wings. His account of them increases my desire to get them to Virginia. Miss—once promised me to have Fitzhugh. Tell her I will release her from her engagement if she will take Rob. He was also much gratified at being able to spend a week with you, and I am getting very anxious for your return. The winter has passed, the snow and ice have disappeared, and the birds have returned to their favourite resorts in the yard. We have, however, a sea of mud around us, through which we have to plunge, but I hope the pleasant air and sun now visiting us will soon dissipate it. I am glad you are enjoying yourself among such kind friends, but do not remain too long, as you may detain Cousins Eleanor and George from the Eastern Shore. Markie has sent me a likeness of you on porcelain, from the negative taken by the celebrated Plecker, which she carried with her to Philadelphia. It is very good, but I prefer the original. . . . Everybody seems anxious for your return, and is surprised you can stay so long from your papa. May God bless and keep you, my dear child, is the constant prayer of

"Your devoted father, R. E. LEE."

Before Mildred returned to Lexington she received one more letter from my father, in which he advises her of the two routes to Lexington, and tells her some college news:

"LEXINGTON, Virginia, February 23, 1867.

"*My Precious Daughter:* Agnes wishes you to purchase some articles for her, and your mother and sister may have some commissions, which I fear will reduce your purse to an inconvenient collapse. I therefore send a check for—dollars, which I hope will enable you to gratify their wishes and serve as a reserve for your own wants. I hope you are well and passing your time profitably as well as pleasantly. The cadets are under the impression that you are at the Patapsco Institute, and will expect to find you, on your return, more agreeable than ever. They are labouring so industriously in mental culture that they believe every one is similarly engaged. I went last evening to the celebration of the anniversary of the Washington Society, and was much pleased with the speeches. It was held in the Methodist church, which was filled to overflowing. The Institute and Ann Smith [Female Academy] were represented. Your sisters were present, and as they were both absent from breakfast this morning I fear so much learning made them sleepy. They were also at a cadet hop on the 21st, and did not get home till between two and three A. M. on the 22d. I suppose, therefore, they had 'splendid times' and very fresh society.

We were somewhat surprised the other morning at Mrs. Grady's committing matrimony. I missed, at our chapel exercises, Captain Grady and our acting chaplain, but did not know at the time what prevented their attendance. I heard afterwards that they had put the happy pair in the stage and sent them on their way rejoicing. She is now Mrs. Richard Norris, and has gone to Baltimore. It will be but fair now that Captain Grady should go to Baltimore and bring us a young lady from there in return for his mother. If you see Miss Armistead, ask her to be ready on short notice, as we are a people of few words in this region, and proceed in all matters in a businesslike way. Agnes, I suppose, has told you of all matters of gaiety and fashion. She has, no doubt, too, kept you advised of the progress of young Baxter and of the deeds of 'Thomas, the Nipper.' They are both flourishing, and are much admired. . . . The roads are so muddy that my evening rides have been suspended, and I see nobody. . . . You must write me when to expect you. The stage from Staunton now crosses during the night, and, when the roads are favourable, arrives about two A. M. When the roads are unfavourable, it gets in generally in time for an early breakfast. The canal-boats have resumed their trips now, so you will have a choice of routes from Richmond, if you conclude to go there. All unite with me in much love, and I am, always,

"Your father,   R. E. LEE."

From Lexington I had gone to Baltimore for a short visit, and had spent a week with Mildred at the home of our cousin, Mr. George Washington Peter, near Ellicott City. Soon after getting back to my farm, I received the following letter from my father, still trying to help me along in my work:

"LEXINGTON, Virginia, February 8, 1867.

"*My Dear Son:* I was very glad to learn from your letter of the 31st ult. that you had enjoyed your visit to Baltimore, for I feared when you left us that you might have a visit from your shaking enemy. I trust, however, that he has now left you never to return.

Still be prudent and watch his approach closely. I hope you may be able to procure some good mules in Richmond, as it is a matter of importance to your operations. If you can get the lime delivered at ten cents, I do not know a more economical application to your land. I believe you will be repaid by the first crop, provided it acts as I think it will. Of this you must judge, and I can only say that if you can accomplish it, and wish to try, I can send you $300, and will send it by draft to you, or to any one in Baltimore that you will designate, as soon as I hear from you. I commend you for not wishing to go in debt, or to proceed faster in your operations than prudence dictates. I think it economy to improve your land, and to begin upon the system you prefer as soon as possible. It is your only chance of success, so let me know. I have to write in haste, as the examination is in progress, and I have to be present. George and Robert both came up to-day in the subjects in which they are respectively weakest, so give them your good wishes. I received yesterday a letter from Mildred regretting your departure from Baltimore, and expressing the pleasure she derived from having been with you even a short week. I hope she will continue well and return to us soon. We are all about as you left us. The weather has moderated and the ice disappeared from the river, though the boats have not yet resumed their trips. Mud predominates now instead of snow. . . . Wishing you all happiness, I am,   Your affectionate father,   R. E. LEE.
"ROBERT E. LEE, JR."

The Robert and George mentioned here were two of his nephews whom he was educating at the college, the sons, respectively, of his brothers, Sydney Smith Lee and Charles Carter Lee. They were members of his household and were treated as his own family.

To my brother Fitzhugh he writes at this time the following, chiding him for his extravagance in a Christmas gift, and asking him for some data of the movements of his command. It is full of good advice, encouragement, and affection:

"LEXINGTON, Virginia, February 26, 1867.

"*My Dear Fitzhugh:* You must not think because I write so seldom that you are absent from my thoughts. I think of you constantly, and am ever revolving in my mind all that concerns you. I have an ardent desire to see you re-established at your home and enjoying the pleasure of prosperity around you. I know this cannot be accomplished at once, but must come from continuous labour, economy, and industry, and be the result of years of good management. We have now nothing to do but to attend to our material interests which collectively will advance the interests of the State, and to await events. The dominant party cannot reign forever, and truth and justice will at last prevail. I hope I shall be able to get down to see you and Rob during the next vacation. I shall then have a more correct apprehension of existing circumstances, and can follow your progress more satisfactorily. I was very much obliged to you for the nice eye-glasses you sent me Xmas, and asked your mother and the girls to thank you for them, which I hope they did. I fear they are too nice for my present circumstances, and do not think you ought to spend anything, except on your farm, until you get that in a prosperous condition. We have all, now, to confine ourselves strictly to our necessities. . . . While you are your own manager you can carry on cultivation on a large scale with comparatively less expense than on a small scale, and your profits will of course be greater. I would commence a system of progressive improvement which would improve your land and add steadily to your income. I have received, lately, from Fitz Lee a narrative of the operations of his division of cavalry. I requested Custis to write to you for a report of your operations during the winter of 1863–4 down to April 18, 1865. How are you progressing with it? I know the difficulties of making such a narrative at this time; still, by correspondence with your officers, and by exerting your own memory, much can be done, and it will help me greatly in my undertaking. Make it as full as you can, embracing all circumstances bearing on the campaigns affecting your operations and illustrating the conduct of your division. I hope you will be able to get up to see us this spring or summer. Select the time when you can best absent yourself, that you may feel the freer and enjoy yourself the more. . . . I wish I were nearer to you all. . . . Your mother is about the same, busy with her needle and her pen, and as cheerful as ever. . . .

"Affectionately your father,   R. E. LEE.
"GENERAL WM. H. F. LEE."

His desire for accounts from his officers of the movements of their commands shows he still intended to attempt to write his campaigns with the Army of Northern Virginia. Some months later he writes again to my brother, and in it he alludes to the dark cloud of the "reconstruction" days, hanging then over the South:

"LEXINGTON, Virginia, June 8, 1867.

"*My Dear Son:* Your letter written on your birthday has been welcomed by the whole family, and I assure you that we reciprocate your regrets at the distance which separates us. Although the future is still dark, and the prospects gloomy, I am confident that, if we all unite in doing our duty, and earnestly work to extract what good we can out of the evil that now hangs over our dear land, the time is not distant when the angry cloud will be lifted from our horizon and the sun in his pristine brightness again shine forth. I, therefore, can anticipate for you many years of happiness and prosperity, and in my daily prayers to the God of mercy and truth I invoke His choicest blessings upon you. May He gather you under the shadow of His almighty wing, direct you in all your ways, and give you peace and everlasting life. It would be most pleasant to my feelings could I again, as you propose, gather you all around me, but I fear that will not be in this world. Let us all so live that we may be united in that world where there is no more separation, and where sorrow and pain never come. I think after next year I will have done all the good I can for the college, and I should then like, if peace is restored to the country, to retire to some quiet spot, east of the mountains, where I might prepare a home for your mother and sisters after my death, and where I could earn my daily bread. We will talk of it when we meet. This summer I wish to carry your mother to some of the mineral springs where she might obtain some relief, but it is hard to know where that can be found. She seems now to prefer White Sulphur, merely on the ground, I believe, that she has never tried those waters, and, therefore, they might be of service to her. If she makes up her mind to go, I will endeavour to get her there with one of the girls, at least. Mildred has returned to us, looking very well, and says she has had a very pleasant tour among her friends, and has received a great deal of kindness wherever she has been. She seems to be very contented now at home. I think you did right to defer your visit to us until you had more leisure. I am glad your prospects for a harvest are so good. Every one must look to his material interests now, as labour is our only resource. The completion of the railroad to the Pamunkey will be a great advantage to you in getting to market what you make, and I hope you will put everything to account. I hope Robert is doing well. Mary is in Staunton, where she went a week since to attend Miss Stribling's wedding. . . . Miss Mary Stewart is staying with us, and I believe is to remain until July, when her sister Belle is to join her. The examination of the students has been progressing a week and will continue until the 20th. The young men have, so far, done very well on the whole. . . . Mr. Swinton has paid his visit. He seemed to be gentlemanly, but I derive no pleasure from my interviews with book-makers. I have either to appear uncivil, or run the risk of being dragged before the public. . . . I am,

"Always as ever, your father,   R. E. LEE.

"GENERAL WM. H. FITZHUGH LEE."

The Pamunkey was the name of the river on which the White House, my brother's estate, was situated. The railroad from Richmond, torn up during the war, had just been rebuilt to that point. Swinton was the historian of the Federal Army of the

Potomac. He spent some days in Lexington, and, I suppose, sought from my father information on points connected with his history of the movements of General Grant's army.

My father, as I have said before, commenced almost as soon as he became the president of the college to improve the grounds, roads, walks, fences, etc., and systematically kept up this work up to the time of his death. The walks about the college grounds were in a very bad condition, and, in wet weather, often ankle-deep in mud. As a first step toward improving them the president had a quantity of limestone broken up and spread upon the roads and walks. The rough, jagged surface was most uninviting, and horsemen and footmen naturally took to the grass. Seeing Colonel T. L. Preston riding one day across the campus on his way to his classes at the Virginia Military Institute, my father remarked:

"Ah, Colonel, I have depended upon you and your big sorrel to help smooth down my walks!"

Another day, a student who was walking on the grass saw the General not far away, and immediately stepped into the middle of the rocks, upon which he manfully trudged along. A strange lady, going in the same direction, followed in the student's footsteps, and when the youth came within speaking distance, my father, with a twinkle in his eye, thanked him for setting so good an example, and added, "The ladies do not generally take kindly to my walks."

The buildings also were altered and renovated, so far as funds for the purpose permitted. He urged the erection as soon as possible of a chapel, which should be of dimensions suitable for the demands of the college. There were other objects calling for a far greater outlay of money than the resources of the college afforded, but he deemed this of great importance, and succeeded in getting appropriations for it first. He hastened the selection of the site and the drawing of the plans. The completion of the work was much retarded owing to the want of funds, but his interest in its erection never flagged. He gave it his personal superintendence from first to last, visiting it often two or three times a day.

After it was dedicated, he always attended morning prayers and all other religious exercises held there, unless prevented by sickness. Whenever I was there on a visit I always went with him every morning to chapel. He had a certain seat which he occupied, and you could have kept your watch regulated by the time he entered the doors. As he thought well of the young men who left his drawing-room by ten o'clock, so he placed in a higher estimate those who attended chapel regularly, especially if they got there in proper time. There was no regular chaplain, but the ministers of the different denominations who had churches in the village undertook, by turns, to perform a month's service. The hour was forty-five minutes past seven o'clock every morning, except Sunday, during the session, save in the three winter months, December, January, and February, when it was one hour later. He was the earnest friend and strong supporter of the Young Men's Christian Association, and an annual contributor to its funds. Upon one occasion, at least, he placed in its library a collection of suitable books, which he had purchased with that intention. In his annual reports to the trustees, he always made mention of the association, giving an account of its operations and progress.

CHAPTER XV

MOUNTAIN RIDES

AN INCIDENT ABOUT "TRAVELLER"—THE GENERAL'S LOVE FOR
CHILDREN—HIS FRIENDSHIP FOR EX-PRESIDENT DAVIS—A
RIDE WITH HIS DAUGHTER TO THE PEAKS OF OTTER—
MILDRED LEE'S NARRATIVE—MRS. LEE AT THE WHITE
SULPHUR SPRINGS—THE GREAT ATTENTION PAID HER
HUSBAND THERE—HIS IDEA OF LIFE

SINCE the arrival of "Lucy Long" my father was generally accompanied by one of my sisters in his rides, whenever the weather and the condition of the roads admitted of their going. It took very severe weather to keep him in, though often he could not spare the time, for during the winter months the days were very short. Every Monday afternoon there was a faculty meeting, and the vestry meetings of his church were held two or three times a month. Whenever I was in Lexington I rode with him, and when he was prevented by any of the above-mentioned causes he would ask me to take Traveller out and give him a gallop, which I was delighted to do, and I think I had my revenge for his treatment of me on that ride from Orange to Fredericksburg in the winter of 1862. My father's affection for his horses was very deep and strong. In a letter written from the Springs one summer, to his clerk in Lexington, he says:

"How is Traveller? Tell him I miss him dreadfully, and have repented of our separation but once—and that is the whole time since we parted."

I think Traveller appreciated his love and sympathy, and returned it as much as was in a horse's nature to do. As illustrative of this bond between them, a very pretty story was told me by Mrs. S. P. Lee[1]:

"One afternoon in July of this year, the General rode down to the canal-boat landing to put on board a young lady who had been visiting his daughters and was returning home. He dismounted, tied Traveller to a post, and was standing on the boat making his adieux, when some one called out that Traveller was loose. Sure enough, the gallant gray was making his way up the road, increasing his speed as a number of boys and men tried to stop him. My father immediately stepped ashore, called to the crowd to stand still, and advancing a few steps gave a peculiar low whistle. At the first sound, Traveller stopped and pricked up his ears. The General whistled a second time, and the horse with a glad whinny turned and trotted quietly back to his master, who patted and coaxed him before tying him up again. To a bystander expressing surprise at the creature's docility the General observed that he did not see how any man could ride a horse for any length of time without a perfect understanding being established between them. My sister Mildred, who rode with him constantly this summer, tells me of his enjoyment of their long rides out into the beautiful, restful country. Nothing seemed to delight him so much.

"I have often known him to give rein to Traveller and go at full speed to the top of some long hill, then turn and wait for me jogging along on Lucy, calling out with merry voice, 'Come along, Miss Lucy, Miss Lucy, Lucy Long!' He would question the country people about the roads, where they came from, where they led to, and soon knew every farmer's name and every homestead in the county. He often said:

"'I wish I had a little farm of my own, where we could live in peace to the end of our days. You girls could attend to the dairy and the cows and the sheep and wait on your mother and me, for it is time now for us old people to rest and for the young people to work.'"

All the children in the country around were devoted to him, and felt no hesitation in approaching him, after they once knew him. He used to meet his favourites among the little ones on the street, and would sometimes lift them up in front of him to give them a ride on Traveller. That was the greatest treat he could provide. There is a very pretty story told of Virginia Lee Letcher, his goddaughter, and her baby sister, Fannie, which is yet remembered among the Lexington people. Jennie had been followed by her persistent sister, and all the coaxing and the commanding of the six-year-old failed to make the younger return home. Fannie had sat down by the roadside to pout, when General Lee came riding by. Jennie at once appealed to him:

"General Lee, won't you please make this child go home to her mother?"

The General immediately rode over to where Fannie sat, leaned over from his saddle and drew her up into his lap. There she sat in royal contentment, and was thus grandly escorted home. When Mrs. Letcher inquired of Jennie why she had given General Lee so much trouble, she received the naive reply:

"I couldn't make Fan go home, and I thought *he* could do anything."[2]

There was a little boy living with his mother, who had come from New York. His father had been killed in our army. The little fellow, now Colonel Grier Monroe, of New York city, was much teased at his playmates calling him "Yankee" when he knew he was not one. One day he marched into my father's office in the college, stated his case, and asked for redress.

"The next boy that calls you 'Yankee' send him to me," said the General, which, when reported, struck such terror into the hearts of his small comrades that the offense was never repeated.

There was another little boy who was accustomed to clamber up by the side of my father at the morning chapel exercises, and was so kindly treated that, whenever he saw his distinguished friend, he straightway assumed a position beside him. At the college commencement, which was held in the chapel, the little fellow glided from his mother's side and quietly stole up to the platform. Soon he was nestled at the feet of the dignified president, and, resting his head upon his knees, dropped asleep. General Lee tenderly remained without moving, preferring to suffer from the constrained position rather than disturb the innocent slumberer. This boy is now the Reverend Carter Jones of the Baptist Church.

About this time Ex-President Davis was freed from the confinement of his prison at Fortress Monroe, where he had been for about two years. There was a warm personal friendship between these two men, dating from the time they were cadets at West Point together, and as his unjust and unnecessary imprisonment had pained and distressed none more than my father, so his release gave him corresponding joy. He at once wrote to him the following letter, full of feeling and sympathy:

"LEXINGTON, Virginia, June 1, 1867.
"HONOURABLE JEFFERSON DAVIS.

"*My Dear Mr. Davis:* You can conceive better than I can express the misery which your friends have suffered from your long imprisonment, and the other afflictions incident thereto. To no one has this been more painful than to me, and the impossibility of affording relief has added to my distress. Your release has lifted a load from my heart which I have not words to tell. My daily prayer to the great Ruler of the world is that He may shield you from all future harm, guard you from all evil, and give you that peace which the world cannot take away. That the rest of your days may be triumphantly happy is the sincere and earnest wish of

"Your most obedient, faithful friend and servant,
"R. E. LEE."

Though my father would take no part in the politics of the country, and rarely expressed his views on questions of that nature then occupying the minds of all, nevertheless, when he deemed it necessary, and to the proper person, he very plainly said what he thought. The following letter to General Longstreet, in answer to one from him written about this time, illustrates what I have said in this connection, and explains itself:

"LEXINGTON, Virginia, October 29, 1867.
"GENERAL J. LONGSTREET,
"21 Carondelet Street, New Orleans, La.

"*My Dear General:* When I received your letter of the 8th of June, I had just returned from a short trip to Bedford County, and was preparing for a more extended visit to the White Sulphur Springs for the benefit of Mrs. Lee's health. As I could not write such a letter as you desired, and as you stated that you would leave New Orleans for Mexico in a week from the time you wrote, to be absent some months, I determined to delay my reply till my return. Although I have been here more than a month, I have been so occupied by necessary business, and so incommoded by the effects of an attack of illness, from which I have not yet recovered, that this is the first day that I have been able to write to you. I have avoided all discussion of political questions since the cessation of hostilities, and have, in my own conduct, and in my recommendations to others, endeavoured to conform to existing circumstances. I consider this the part of wisdom, as well as of duty; but, while I think we should act under the law and according to the law imposed upon us, I cannot think the course pursued by the dominant political party the best for the interests of the country, and therefore cannot say so or give it my approval. This is the reason why I could not comply with the request in your letter. I am of the opinion that all who can should vote for the most intelligent, honest, and conscientious men eligible to office, irrespective of former party opinions, who will endeavour to make the new constitutions and the laws passed under them as beneficial as possible to the true interests, prosperity, and liberty of all classes and conditions of the people. With my best wishes for your health and happpiness, and my kindest regards to Mrs. Longstreet and your children, I am, with great regard, and very truly and sincerely yours,

"R. E. LEE."

This summer my father paid a visit to the Peaks of Otter, a famous group of mountains in the Blue Ridge range, situated in Bedford County, Virginia. He rode Traveller, and my sister Mildred accompanied him on "Lucy Long." After visiting the Peaks and ascending the summit, which is 4,000 feet in height, he rode on to Liberty, now Bedford City, ten miles distant, and spent the night at "Avenel," the home of the Burwells, who were friends and connections of his.

From there the riding party went to Captain Buford's, about twelve miles distant, where they spent the night and the next day. The Captain was a farmer, a great admirer and a staunch upholder of his native State, Virginia, in her fight for constitutional liberty, from '61 to '65. He had sent his sons into the army, and had given of his substance freely to support the troops, as well as the poor and needy, the widow and orphan, who had been left in want by the death in battle of their natural protectors and by the ravages of war. In the early years of the struggle, my mother and sisters, when "refugeeing," had boarded, as they thought and intended at the time, at his home. But when they tried to induce him to accept pay for the shelter and food he had given them for a month or more, he sternly refused. His was a patriotism that hesitated at no sacrifice, and was of a kind and character that admitted of no self-consideration. This trait, so strongly developed in him, attracted the admiration and respect of my father. The visit he paid him was to thank him in person for the kindness extended to his wife and daughters, and also for a very large and handsome horse which he had sent my father the last year, I think, of the war. My sister Mildred tells me what she can recollect of this ride. It is a source of endless regret to us that we cannot recall more. His companionship was at all times delightful to his children, and on an occasion of this kind, invigorated by the exercise, inspired by the bright skies and relieved of all harassing cares, he became almost a boy again.

My sister Mildred says:

"We started at daybreak one perfect June day, papa on Traveller, I on Lucy Long, our saddle-bags being our only luggage. He was in the gayest humour, laughing and joking with me as I paced along by his side on quiet 'Miss Lucy.' Traveller seemed to sympathise with his master, his springy step, high head, and bright eye clearly showing how happy he was and how much interest he took in this journey. He had to be constantly chided for his restlessness, and was told that it would be well for him to reserve some of his too abundant energy for the latter part of his trip. At midday we dismounted, and, tying our horses while resting on the soft grass under a wild-plum hedge by the roadside, ate our lunch. We then rode on, and soon came to the James River, which was crossed by a ferry-boat. The ferry-man was an old soldier, who of course recognised papa, and refused payment; nor could he be induced to take any. Further on the road, as our horses were climbing a steep rocky ascent, we met some little children, with very dirty faces, playing on the roadside. He spoke to them in his gentle, playful way, alluding to their faces and the desirability of using a little water. They stared at us with open-eyed astonishment, and then scampered off up the hill; a few minutes later, in rounding this hill, we passed a little cabin, when out they all ran with clean faces, fresh aprons, and their hair nicely brushed, one little girl exclaiming, 'We know you are General Lee! we have got your picture!'

"That night about nine o'clock we reached the little mountain inn at the foot of the Peaks, ate a hearty supper, and soon went to bed, tired out by our thirty-mile ride. Our bedrooms seemed to be a loft, and the beds were of feathers, but I, at least, slept without turning. Next morning, at dawn of day, we set out, accompanied by the master of the house, and rode for a long time up the mountain-side, Lucy following closely behind Traveller. Finally it became impossible to proceed further on horseback, so the horses were fastened to some trees and we climbed the rest of the way to the summit on foot. When the top was reached, we sat for a long time on a great rock, gazing down on the glorious prospect beneath. Papa spoke but a few words, and seemed very sad. I have heard there is now a mark on that rock showing where he sat. The inn-keeper, who accompanied us all the way, told us that we had ridden nearer the top than any other persons up to that time. Regaining our horses, we proceeded on our second day's journey, which was to end at Liberty, some ten miles distant.

"We had not ridden far, when suddenly a black thunder-cloud arose and in a few minutes a heavy shower broke over us. We galloped back to a log cabin we had just passed. Papa lifted me off of Lucy and, dripping with water, I rushed in, while he led the horse under an adjacent shed. The woman of the house looked dark and glum on seeing the pools of water forming from my dress on her freshly scoured floor, and when papa came in with his muddy boots her expression was more forbidding and gloomy. He asked her permission to wait there until the shower was over, and praised her nice white floor, regretting that we had marred its beauty. At this praise, so becomingly bestowed, she was slightly appeased, and asked us into the best room, which was adorned with colored prints of Lee, Jackson, Davis, and Johnston. When the shower ceased and papa went out for the horses I told her who he was. Poor woman! She seemed stunned, and kept on saying: 'What will Joe say? What will Joe say!' Joe was her husband, and had been, like every other man in the country, a soldier in the 'Army of Northern Virginia.'

"The shower over and the sun shining brightly, we rode along joyously through the refreshed hills and dustlaid roads, arriving at Liberty in good time, and went to 'Avenel,' the pretty home of the Burwells. The comforts of this sweet old place seemed very delicious to me after my short experience of roughing it. Papa was much amused when I appeared in crinoline, my 'hoops' having been squeezed into the saddle-bags and brought with me. We remained here the next day, Sunday, and the day after rode on some twelve miles to Captain Buford's. The Captain, in his shirt-sleeves, received us with open arms, seemed much surprised at my full growth, and said, 'Why, General, you called her your 'little girl,' and she is a real chunk of a gal!' He showed us his fine Jersey cattle, his rich fields and well-filled barns, and delighted in talking of the time during the war when mama, Mary, and Agnes paid him a visit.

He overflowed with kindness and hospitality, and his table fairly groaned with the good things. Papa afterwards constantly quoted his original sayings, especially one on early rising, which was made on the eve of our arrival, when he told us good-night. Papa asked him what time he must be ready for breakfast next morning.

"'Well, General,' said the Captain, 'as you have been riding hard, and as you are company, we will not have breakfast to-morrow until sun-up,' which meant in those June days somewhere before five o'clock.

"After a day spent pleasantly here, we started next morning early on our return. Halting for a short time in Buchanan, we stopped at Colonel Edmund Pendleton's, who then lived there in an imposing white pillared edifice, formerly a bank. Mrs. Pendleton gave us some delicious apricots from her garden, which my father enjoyed greatly. We then proceeded on the road to Lexington, going by the Natural Bridge, where we had another short rest, and reached home the same night, about ten o'clock, after a forty-mile ride.

"Shortly after this visit Captain Buford sent me a fine Jersey cow, on condition that I would get up early every morning and milk her, and also send him a part of the butter I made."

After my father returned from this trip, he began his arrangements for taking my mother to the Greenbrier White Sulphur Springs. He hoped that the waters and the change might be of service to her general health, even if they should not alleviate the severity of her rheumatic pains.

About the first of July, my mother, sister Agnes and Miss Mary Pendleton, with my brother Custis in charge, set out for the White Sulphur Springs. My father, with Professor J. J. White, decided to make the journey to the same place on horseback. They started a day in advance, and were at Covington when the ladies, travelling by stage-coach to Goshen, thence by rail, arrived there. After spending the night at Covington, the passengers were put into as many stage-coaches as were necessary, and the long, rough drive over the mountains by "Callahan's" commenced.

General Lee on Traveller was at once recognised, and when it was found out by his fellow-travellers that Mrs. Lee was with him, attentions and services of all kinds were pressed on her party, and a most enjoyable lunch was sent to the stage reserved for her. Seeing that the other stages were much crowded, while the one reserved for his wife had vacant seats, my father insisted that some of the others should join his party, which they very gladly did. He and Professor White went ahead of the stages on their horses.

At the White Sulphur Springs the "Harrison Cottage," in "Baltimore Row," had been put at my father's disposal, and the entire party was soon most pleasantly established there. Mr. W. W. Corcoran, of Washington, Professor White, Miss Mary Pendleton, Agnes, and my father and brother had a table together. Almost every day some special dainty was sent to this table. My mother, of course, had her meals served in her cottage. Her faithful and capable servant, Milly Howard, was always most eager for her to appear at her best, and took great pride in dressing her up, so far as she was allowed, in becoming caps, etc., to receive her numerous visitors. My father's usual custom while there was to spend some time in the morning in the large parlour of the hotel, before taking his ride on Traveller. After dinner he went again to the parlour, and also after tea.

Among the company were many old friends and acquaintances from Baltimore, who could not sufficiently testify their pleasure in this renewal of intercourse. Whenever he appeared in parlour or ballroom he was the centre of attraction, and in vain the young men tried to engage the attention of the young ladies when General Lee was present.

During his visit, a circus came to "Dry Creek," a neighbouring settlement, and gave an exhibition. The manager rode over to the Springs, came to my father's cottage, and insisted on leaving several tickets, begging that General Lee would permit him to send carriages for him and any friends he might like to take to his show. These offers my father courteously declined, but bought many tickets, which he presented to his little friends at the Springs.

During the morning he rode over to "Dry Creek," where the crowds of country people, many of them his old soldiers, feasted their eyes on him to the neglect of the circus. That night a special exhibition was given by the manager to General Lee's friends, who were taken to seats draped with Confederate colors, red, and white. After the return from the circus, my father invited a large party to his cottage to partake of a huge watermelon sent him by express from Mobile. It weighed about sixty pounds, and its producer thought the only fitting way he could dispose of it was to present it to General Lee.

Every possible attention that love, admiration, and respect could prompt was paid my father by the guests at the Springs, each one seeming anxious to do him homage. My mother and sister shared it all with him, for any attention and kindness shown them went straight to his heart.

After spending three weeks at "the White," my father's party went to the Old Sweet Springs, where they were all made very comfortable, one of the parlours being turned into a bedroom for my mother, so that in her wheeled chair she could go out on the verandas and into the ballroom.

He was taken quite sick there, and, though he rode over from the White Sulphur Springs, was unable to continue his early rides for some time. His room was on the first floor, with a window opening on the end of the building. One morning, when he was very unwell and it was important that he should not be disturbed, Miss Pendleton found a countryman cautiously opening the shutters from the outside. She quickly interfered, saying:

"Go away; that is General Lee's room."

The man dropped back, saying mournfully:

"I only wanted to see him."

On another occasion some country people came to the Springs with plums and berries for sale. Catching sight of him on the piazza, they put down their baskets, took off their hats, and hurrahed most lustily for "Marse Bob." They were his old soldiers. When he acknowledged their loyalty by shaking hands with them, they insisted on presenting him with their fruit.

About the first week in September my father rode back to Lexington on Traveller, Custis taking my mother and Agnes back over the same tedious journey by stage and rail.

There have been preserved very few letters from him at this time. I find one to me, full of kindness, wholesome advice, and offers of aid, in which he sends his thanks to the President of the York River Railroad for a courtesy tendered him:

"WHITE SULPHUR SPRINGS,
"GREENBRIER COUNTY, WEST VIRGINIA,
"August 5, 1867.

"*My Dear Son:* I received to-day your letter of the 28th ult., inclosing a free ticket over the Richmond & York River Railroad, from its president, Mr. Dudley. Please present him my grateful thanks for this mark of his esteem. I am very glad to hear that the road is completed to the White House, and that a boat connects it with Norfolk. The convenience of the community and the interests of the road will be promoted thereby. It is a difficult undertaking in these times to build a road, and I hope the company will soon be able to finish it to West Point. I suppose you have received before this the letter from your mother and Agnes, announcing our arrival at this place and informing you of the company. The latter has been much increased, and among the arrivals are the Daingerfields, Haxalls, Capertons, Miss Belle Harrison, etc., etc. I told Agnes to tell you how much we wished you were with us, and as an inducement for you to join us, if you could leave home, if you would come, I would pay your expenses. I feel very sensibly, in my old age, the absence of my children, though I recognise the necessity of every one's attending to his business, and admire him the more for so doing. I am very glad that you and Fitzhugh have, so far, escaped the fever, and hope you may avoid it altogether. Be prudent. I am very sorry that your harvest promises a poor yield. It will be better next year, but you must continue systematically the improvement of the land. I know of no better method than by liming, and if you wish to prosecute it, and are in need of help, I will

aid you to the extent of last year or more. So make your arrangements, and let me know your wishes. A farmer's life is one of labour, but it is also one of pleasure, and the consciousness of steady improvement, though it may be slow, is very encouraging. I think you had better also begin to make arrangements to build yourself a house. If you can do nothing more than prepare a site, lay out a garden, orchard, etc., and get a small house partly finished, so as to inhabit it, it will add to your comfort and health. I can help you in that too. Think about it. Then, too, you must get a nice wife. I do not like you being so lonely. I fear you will fall in love with celibacy. I have heard some very pleasing reports of Fitzhugh. I hope that his desires, if beneficial to his happiness, may be crowned with success. I saw the lady when I was in Petersburg, and was much pleased with her. I will get Agnes or your mother to tell you what occurs at the Springs. There are some 500 people here, very pleasant and kind, but most of my time is passed alone with Traveller in the mountains. I hope your mother may derive some benefit from the waters, but I see none now. It will, at least, afford her some variety, and give her some pleasure, of which there is a dearth with us now. Give much love to Fitzhugh. All unite in love to you. God bless you, my son, prays
"Your affectionate father,
"R. E. LEE."

Early in September my father sent my mother and sister home to Lexington, while he mounted Traveller and rode back by way of the Hot Springs, Healing, and Rockbridge Alum. He was detained by indisposition a day or two at the Healing, and writes to my mother a little note from that place:

"HEALING SPRINGS, September 12, 1867.
"*My Dear Mary:* I arrived here on the 10th, and had expected to resume my journey this morning, but did not feel able. Should nothing prevent, I will leave here to-morrow, but I fear I shall not be able to reach the Rockbridge Alum, which I am told is twenty-nine

miles distant. In that event, I will halt on the road, and arrive there on Saturday, lie over Sunday, and reach Lexington on Monday. I am very anxious to get to Lexington, and think nothing on the route will benefit me, as I feel much concerned about the resumption of the college exercises. Mr. John Stewart, Misses Mary and Marian, Mr. Price and his daughters came over from the Hot yesterday to see me. The Stewarts are there on Miss Belle's account. Give much love to everybody. I hope you reached Lexington safely and comfortably and that all are well. I hope to see you Monday. Till then, farewell.

"Very truly and affectionately,

"R. E. LEE."

It is to be regretted that we have no accounts of these rides, the people he met, and what he said to them, where he stayed, and who were his hosts. He was very fond of horseback journeys, enjoyed the quiet and rest, the freedom of mind and body, the close sympathy of his old war-horse, and the beauties of Nature which are to be seen at every turn in the mountains of Virginia. Ah, if we could only obtain some records of his thoughts as he rode all alone along the mountain roads, how much it would help us all in our trials and troubles! He was a man of few words, very loath to talk about himself, nor do I believe any one ever knew what that great heart suffered. His idea of life was to do his duty, at whatever cost, and to try to help others do theirs.

CHAPTER XVI

AN ADVISER OF YOUNG MEN

LEE'S POLICY AS COLLEGE PRESIDENT—HIS ADVICE ON AGRI-
CULTURAL MATTERS—HIS AFFECTION FOR HIS PROSPECTIVE
DAUGHTER-IN-LAW—FITZHUGH'S WEDDING—THE GENERAL'S
OVATION AT PETERSBURG—HIS PERSONAL INTEREST IN THE
STUDENTS UNDER HIS CARE

THE college exercises were resumed in the last weeks of September. My mother and sisters were all back at home. The President's work, now more in hand, began to show results. The number of students this session was largely increased and the outlook of the college was very much brighter.

"He had from the beginning of his presidency a distinct policy and plan which he had fully conceived and to which he steadily adhered, so that all his particular measures of progress were but consistent steps in its development. His object was nothing less than to establish and perfect an institution which should meet the highest needs of education in every department. At once, and without waiting for the means to be provided in advance, he proceeded to develop this object. Under his advice, new chairs were created, and professors called to fill them, so that before the end of the first year the faculty was doubled in numbers. Still additional chairs were created, and finally a complete system of 'schools' was established and brought into full operation. So admirably was the plan conceived and administered by General Lee, that, heterogeneous as were the students, especially in the early years, each one found his proper place, and all were kept in line of complete and systematic study. Under this organisation, and especially under the inspiration of his central influence, the utmost harmony and utmost energy pervaded all the departments of the college. The highest powers of both professors and students were called forth, under the fullest responsibility. The standards of scholarship were rapidly advanced; and soon the graduates of Washington College were the acknowledged equals of those from the best institutions elsewhere, and were eagerly sought after for the highest positions as teachers in the best schools. The results . . . were due directly and immediately, more than to all other causes, to the personal ability and influence of General Lee as president of the college."

So wrote Professor Edward S. Joynes in an article published soon after General Lee's death, in the *University Monthly*. All of this had not been accomplished as yet, but the work was well advanced, and the results began to be evident. His health had not been strong since the middle of the summer, but he never ceased in his endeavour to better the condition of the college, and to improve the minds, morals, and bodies of the young men committed to his charge. He writes to me about this time, encouraging me to renewed efforts, telling me how to better my condition, and advising me not to be cast down by difficulties:

"LEXINGTON, Virginia, October 26, 1867.

"*My Dear Rob:* Your letter of the 10th did not give me a very favourable account of yourself or your prospects, but I have no doubt it was true and therefore commendable. We must not, however, yield to difficulties, but strive the harder to overcome them. I am sorry for the failure of your crops, your loneliness and uncomfortableness, and wish it were in my power to visit you and advise with you. But you must come up this winter, when convenient, and we will discuss the whole matter. Fitzhugh, I hope, will be married soon, and then he will have more time to counsel with you. I hope, between you two, you will devise some mode of relief. The only way to improve your crop is to improve your land, which requires time, patience, and good cultivation. Lime, I think, is one of the chief instruments, and I advise you to apply that systematically and judiciously. I think, too, you had better purchase another pair of mules. I can help you in these items, and, if you need, can advance you $500. Then, as regards a house, I can help you in that too, but you must first select a site and a plan. The first can only be found on the land, and the latter might be adopted on the progressive principle, commencing with the minor members, and finishing with the principal ones as convenience or necessity might authorise. If no better can be found, how would the present site answer? If you are going to cultivate the lower part of the farm, it would at least have the advantage of convenience, or if you thought it better to divide and sell your farm it would answer for one of the divisions. I am clear for your marrying, if you select a good wife; otherwise you had better remain as you are for a time. An imprudent or uncongenial woman is worse than *the minks*[1]. I think, upon the whole, you are progressing very well and have accomplished the worst part. A failure in crops will occur occasionally to every farmer, even the best, with favourable surroundings. It serves a good purpose, inculcates prudence and economy, and excites energy and perseverance. These qualities will overcome everything. You are very young still, and if you are virtuous and laborious you will accomplish all the good you propose to yourself. Let me know if you want the money. We are pretty well. I am better and your poor mother more comfortable, I think, than she was last year. The girls are as usual, and Custis is in far better health than he was before his visit to the Springs. He seems, however, not happy, and I presume other people have their troubles as well as farmers. God bless you, my son, and may He guard, guide, and direct you in all you do. All would unite in love did they know I was writing.

"Truly and affectionately, your father,

"R. E. LEE.

"ROBERT E. LEE, JR."

My brother Fitzhugh was to be married that autumn. This event, so soon to take place, gave my father great pleasure. He was an earnest advocate of matrimony, and was constantly urging his sons to take to themselves wives. With his daughters he was less pressing. Though apparently always willing to have another daughter, he did not seem to long for any more sons. He thus writes to my brother when his engagement was formally announced to him:

"LEXINGTON, Virginia, September 20, 1867.

"*My Dear Fitzhugh:* I have been anxious for some time to write to you, to express the pleasure I have felt at the prospects of your marriage with Miss Bolling; but sickness has prevented, and I am still so feeble that I cannot attend to the pressing business connected with the college. As you know how deeply I feel all that concerns you, you may feel assured of the pleasure I derived from your letter to your mother informing her of your engagement. I have the most pleasing recollection of 'Miss Tabb,' and of her kindness to me, and now that she has consented to be my daughter the measure of my gratitude is filled to overflowing. I hope she will not delay the consummation, for I want to see her very much, and I fear she will not come to see me until then. You must present her my warm love, and you both must accept my earnest prayers and most fervent wishes for your future happiness and prosperity. I am glad that your house is progressing and that your crops promise well. I hope that you soon will be able to come and see us. Your mother, I hope, has derived some benefit from her visit to the Springs. Her general health is improved, but I see no relaxation in her rheumatic complaint. The girls are quite well, and all send love. . . .

"Your affectionate father,

"R. E. LEE.

"GENERAL WILLIAM H. F. LEE."

The young lady who was so soon to become a member of his family was Miss Mary Tabb Bolling, the daughter of Mr. G. W. Bolling, of Petersburg, Virginia. Her father had been very kind to General Lee during the eventful months of the siege of that town, and his daughter had been often to see him and was a great favourite of his. My brother was especially anxious that his father should be present at his wedding, and had been urging him to make his arrangements to come. The sickness to which he frequently alludes in his recent letters had been annoying him since his return from the White Sulphur Springs up to this time, and he now writes proposing that my brother and bride should come to him instead of his going down to the wedding:

"LEXINGTON, Virginia, October 25, 1867.

"*My Dear Fitzhugh:* I have been wishing to write to you every day since the reception of your letter of the 6th inst., but have been prevented by business and sickness. I am delighted that your marriage is so near at hand, and it would give me great pleasure to attend, but I do not think that I could add to the enjoyment of any one. I suppose it will take place in church, according to the present fashion, and I should see very little of you. I therefore propose that, instead of going directly to the White House, you both come up here, and spend as much time with us as you can. It will give your house more time for completion, and I suppose the pretty bride will want to see her old father and mother and what kind of people her sisters are. At any rate, I want to see her very much, and I should be unable to do so in Petersburg, as she would be surrounded by her old beaux and companions. . . . We shall all be delighted to see you, and you may go back as soon as you are tired. Tell me what you think of this plan. There is another thing I wish you to aid me in—to tell me what agreeable present I can make to my daughter to remind her, hereafter, of her papa, or if I send you $100 will you get for me something she would like? I have been quite sick lately, but am better now. The rest of the family are as usual, and your mother, I hope, is more comfortable than she was last year. . . . I am very glad you have enjoyed good health all the summer, and hope that nothing will occur to mar the happiness of your wedding or to postpone it. . . .   Your devoted father,

"R. E. LEE."

My brother, after receiving this, ran up to Lexington and paid him a short visit. His next letter shows that he had yielded to his wishes and had determined to be present at his wedding:

"LEXINGTON, Virginia, November 15, 1867.

"*My Dear Fitzhugh:* I received this morning your letter of the 13th, and am glad to hear of your safe arrival and of the favourable condition of things at your home. I was afraid your house would not be ready at the time supposed, but I would not delay the wedding on that account—you can exist without it. We have one here at your service, though a poor one. I am obliged to you for having arranged about my clothes. Upon reflection, I think it better not to go to the White House and Romancoke before the wedding. You and Robert could hardly pay the necessary attention to business matters with your hands filled with love and matrimony. I think of catching up Rob and marrying him to some of my sweethearts, while I am down, so as to prevent the necessity of going down again. Custis says it will be inconvenient for him to leave here before the time necessary for him to reach Petersburg by the 28th, and we have arranged to commence our journey on Monday night, 25th inst., at 12 M., so as to reach Richmond Tuesday evening, remain there the 27th and go to Petersburg the 28th. I do not think I shall be able to go to the White House at all. I should not be able to aid you or Rob, my only object, and would put you to much trouble. . . . We are all as you left us, and miss you and Mildred very much.

"Very affectionately, your father,

"R. E. LEE.

"GENERAL WILLIAM H. F. LEE."

So it was all settled satisfactorily; my brother gained his point, and my father arranged his affairs so that he could absent himself without detriment to his work at the college. He left on the appointed day and hour, and the morning after arriving in Richmond, writes my mother:

"EXCHANGE HOTEL, RICHMOND, November 26, 1867.

"*My Dear Mary:* We reached here yesterday about 4 P. M., after a not uncomfortable journey, and found Fitzhugh waiting for the important event. I doubt whether his house will be finished, from his account, till January, though he thinks it will. His plans, I believe, as far as he can form them, are to leave Petersburg the morning after the wedding for Baltimore, where they will probably spend a week gathering up their furniture, etc., and after that all is undetermined. I renewed the invitation for their visit to us, but he could not decide. Robert is expected to-morrow. Mildred is well and seems to be perfectly happy, as she had on, last evening, a dress about two yards longer than Norvell's. I saw Mr. Davis, who looks astonishingly well, and is quite cheerful. He inquired particularly after you all. He is at Judge Ould's. No one seems to know what is to be done. Judge Chase had not arrived yesterday, but it was thought probable he would reach here in the ten o'clock train last night. I have not heard this morning. I will present myself to the court this morning, and learn, I hope, what they wish of me. Williams Wickham is here, and will attend the wedding. Annie will also go. Fitzhugh is to go out to Hickory Hill this morning, and return this afternoon, to pay his adieux. Mrs. Caskie was not well last evening. The rest as usual, and send much love. Custis is well, and I have my clothes. I left my sleeve-buttons in my shirt hanging up in my dressing-room. Ask Cornelia to to take care of them. Mr. Alexander said he would send you up some turkeys, and Colonel Johnston, that he would help you revise the manuscript. It is time I should get my breakfast, as I wish to transact some business before going to court. Give much love to the girls and everybody. I hope you are well and will want for nothing while I am away.

Most truly yours,

"MRS. M. C. LEE.   R. E. LEE."

General Lee was summoned this time as a witness in the trial of Mr. Davis, but after some delay a *nolle prosequi* was filed.

General Lee after the war was asked by a lady his opinion of the position and part Mr. Davis had taken and acted during the war. He replied:

"If my opinion is worth anything, you can *always* say that few people could have done better than Mr. Davis. I knew of none that could have done as well."

On the morning after the wedding he writes to my mother:

"PETERSBURG, November 29, 1867.

"*My Dear Mary:* Our son was married last night and shone in his happiness. The bride looked lovely and was, in every way, captivating. The church was crowded to its utmost capacity, and the streets thronged. Everything went off well, and I will enter into details when I see you. Mr. Wickham and Annie, Mr. Fry, John Wood, and others were present. Mr. Davis was prevented from attending by the death of Mrs. Howell. The Misses Haxall, Miss Enders, Miss Giles, etc., came down from Richmond. Fitzhugh Lee was one of the groomsmen, Custis very composed, and Rob suffering from chills. Many of my acquaintances were present, and everybody was very kind. Regrets were often expressed that you, Mary, and Agnes were not present. I believe the plan was for the bride and groom to start on their travels this morning, but I doubt whether it will be carried out, as I thought I saw indications of a change of purpose before I left, which I had no doubt would be strengthened by the reflections of this morning. I shall remain to-day and return to Richmond to-morrow. I wish to go to Brandon Monday, but do not know that I can accomplish it. Until leaving Richmond, my whole time was taken up by the august court, so that I could do nothing nor see anybody there. Mildred was all life, in white and curls. I am staying at General Mahone's and have got hold of one of his needle-pens, with which I can do nothing. Excuse illegibility. No one has descended to breakfast yet. I received, on arriving here yesterday, at 3 P. M., a kind note from our new daughter asking me to come and see her as soon after my arrival as convenient, which I did and carried over the necklace, which she pronounced very pretty. Give my love to all. Most truly yours,

"R. E. LEE.

"MRS. M. C. LEE."

A special car carried General Lee and the other wedding guests from Richmond to Petersburg. He did not enter into the gay conversation of the young people, but appeared sad and depressed, and seemed to dread seeing the town of Petersburg and meeting its people. This feeling was dispelled by the enthusiastic welcome given him by every one there. General Mahone, whose guest he was to be, met him at the depot with a carriage and four white horses. Many of the citizens tried to take out the horses and pull the carriage into the town, but the General protested, declaring, if they did so, he would have to get out and help them. The morning after the wedding he drove out to "Turnbull's" to see an old woman who had been very kind to him, sending him eggs, butter, etc., when he had had his headquarters near by during the siege. On his return he took lunch at Mr. Boiling's, and held an impromptu reception, everybody coming in to speak to him.

That night he went to an entertainment given to the bride at Mr. Johnson's. He enjoyed the evening very much and expressed his feeling of relief at seeing every one so bright and cheerful. He was delighted to find the people so prosperous, and to observe that they had it in their hearts to be gay and happy. The next morning he returned to Richmond. He was escorted to the train in the same way in which he had been received. All the people turned out to see him leave, and he departed amid tremendous cheering.

My father enjoyed this visit. It had been a success in every way. His old friends and soldiers called on him in great numbers, all eager to look on his face and clasp his hand again. The night of the wedding, the streets were filled with crowds anxious to see him once more, and many to look on him for the first time. Wherever he was seen, he was treated with the greatest love, admiration, and respect. It was with devotion, deep, sincere, and true, mixed with awe and sadness, that they beheld their old commander, on foot, in citizen's dress, grayer than three years ago, but still the same, passing along the ways where he had so often ridden on Traveller, with the noise of battle all around. What a change for him; what a difference to them! But their trust and faith in him was as unshaken as ever. A glimpse of his feelings at this time is shown in one of his letters written a few weeks later, which I will give in its proper place. The day after his return to Richmond he writes to my mother:

"RICHMOND, December 1, 1867.

"*My Dear Mary:* I returned here yesterday with Custis, Robert, and Fitz. Lee. We left Fitzhugh and his bride in Petersburg. Mildred is with them. In consequence of being told that the new couple were to leave Petersburg the morning after the wedding, I had made my arrangements to return here Saturday. If I had known that they would remain till Monday, as it is now their intention, I should have made my arrangements to stay. Mildred will come up with them on Monday and go to Mrs. Caskie's. I proposed to Custis, Rob, and Fitz to remain in Petersburg till that time, but they preferred coming with me. I shall go to Brandon to-morrow morning, and will take Custis and Robert with me. I propose to return here Tuesday, finish my business Wednesday, spend Thursday at Hickory Hill, take passage for Lexington Friday, where I hope to arrive Saturday. As far as I could judge, our new daughter will go to Baltimore December 2d and probably return here the following Monday. Fitzhugh will go down to the White House during the week and make arrangements for their sojourn there. He can go down in the morning and return in the evening. I repeated our invitation to her to visit us on their return from Baltimore, but she said Fitzhugh thought it better for them to defer it till the spring, but she would write to let us know. I do not think she will come at this time, for she is in that happy state which causes her to take pleasure in doing what she thinks he prefers, and he, I think, would like to go to the White House and arrange for the winter. I went up to Caskie's last evening. Saw Norvell, but Mr. and Mrs. Caskie were both sick upstairs. The latter is better than when I last wrote, and free from pain. I paid several visits yesterday evening, and took Rob with me. Mrs. Triplett's, Mrs. Peebles', Mrs. Brander's, Mrs. J. R. Anderson's. At the latter place I met Mrs. Robert Stannard, who looked, I thought, remarkably well. She is living with Hugh (her son), on his farm. I also went to Mrs. Dunlop's and saw there General and Miss Jennie Cooper. The latter looked remarkably well, but the former is very thin. They will remain here some weeks. I have not seen Colonel Allan since my return from Petersburg, but am told that he is better. You must give a great deal of love to all with you. I am very anxious to get back, and I hope that you are all well. It is very cold here this morning, and ice is abundant. Good-bye.

"Truly and affectionately,

"R. E. Lee."

The people mentioned here as those he called on were all friends living in Richmond, with whom my mother had become well acquainted during her stay there, in war times. There were many others he went to see, for I remember going with him. He sat only a few minutes at each place— "called just to shake hands," he would say. All were delighted to see him. From some places where he had been well known he could hardly get away. He had a kind word for all, and his excuse for hurrying on was that he must try to see so and so, as Mrs. Lee had told him to be sure to do so. He was bright and cheerful, and was pleased with the great affection shown him on all sides.

On the day he had appointed—Monday, the 2d of December— we started in the morning for "Brandon." We took the steamer down James River, passing through much of the country where he had opposed McClellan in '62 and Grant in '64. Custis and I were with him. He said very little, as I remember—nothing about the war—but was interested in all the old homesteads along the route, many of which he had visited in the days long ago and whose owners had been his relatives and friends. He expressed great regret at not being able to stop at "Shirley," which was the birthplace and home of his mother before she married. He stayed at "Brandon" one night only, taking the same boat as it returned next day to Richmond. They were all glad to see him and sorry to let him go, but his plans had been formed beforehand, according to his invariable custom, and he carried them out without any change. Spending one day in Richmond, he went from there to "Hickory Hill," thence to Lexington, arriving there the Saturday he had fixed on. I bade him and my brother Custis good-bye in Richmond, and returned to my home. To my brother, Fitzhugh, after his return from his wedding trip, he writes:

"LEXINGTON, Virginia, December 21, 1867.

"*My Dear Fitzhugh:* I was very glad last night to receive your letter of the 18th announcing your return to Richmond. I did not like my daughter to be so far away. I am glad, however, that you had so pleasant a visit, which has no doubt prepared you for the enjoyments of home, and will make the repose of Xmas week in Petersburg doubly agreeable. I had a very pleasant visit to Brandon after parting with you, which Custis and Robert seemed equally to enjoy, and I regretted that I could only spend one night. I passed Shirley both going and returning with regret, from my inability to stop; but Custis and I spent a day at Hickory Hill on our way up very agreeably. My visit to Petersburg was extremely pleasant. Besides the pleasure of seeing my daughter and being with you, which was very great, I was gratified in seeing many friends. In addition, when our armies were in front of Petersburg I suffered so much in body and mind on account of the good townspeople, especially on that gloomy night when I was forced to abandon them, that I have always reverted to them in sadness and sorrow. My old feelings returned to me, as I passed well-remembered spots and recalled the ravages of the hostile shells. But when I saw the cheerfulness with which the people were working to restore their condition, and witnessed the comforts with which they were sur-rounded, a load of sorrow which had been pressing upon me for years was lifted from my heart. This is bad weather for completing your house, but it will soon pass away, and your sweet helpmate will make everything go smoothly. When the spring opens and the mocking-birds resume their song you will have much to do. So you must prepare in time. You must give a great deal of love for me to all at Mr. Bolling's, to General and Mrs. Mahone, and other friends. We shall be very glad when you can bring our daughter to see us. Select the time most convenient to you, and do not let it be long distant. Tell her I wish to see her very much, as do also her mama and sisters. Your mother regrets that you did not receive her letter in answer to yours from Baltimore. She wrote the day of its reception, and addressed it to New York, as you directed. The box about which you inquired arrived safely and was much enjoyed. Mary is in Baltimore, where she will probably spend the winter. As I am so far from Mildred, it will be difficult for her to make up her mind when to return, so that the whole care of the household devolves upon Agnes, who is occupied all the morning, teaching our niece, Mildred. . . . God bless you all is the prayer of

Your devoted father,   R. E. LEE.

"GENERAL WM. H. F. LEE."

The Christmas of 1867 I spent, as usual, in Lexington with my father. He had been president of the college now a little more than two years. The number of professors and students had largely increased. The chapel had been built, many improvements made to the lecture-rooms and halls, the grounds improved by the lay-ing out of new roads and walks, the inclosures renewed, the grass restored to the campus, and new shade trees set out over the col-lege grounds. The increase in the number of professors demanded more houses for them. As a move in this direction, the trustees decided to build a new house for the president, so that the one he now occupied could be used for one of the faculty. Accordingly, the appropriation of a sum was made, and my father was authorised to build according to a plan of his own selection. He took a keen interest in this matter, and at once commenced designing a new "President's House" on the lot which had previously been occupied by an old building devoted to the same purpose. This house was completed in the summer of 1869.

The endowment fund of the college had been increased by liberal contributions from several philanthropic persons, and also by a better investment of the resources already belonging to the institution. The fees from the greater number of students also added much to its prosperity. His interest in the students individually and collectively was untiring. By the system of reports made weekly to the president, and monthly to the parent or guardian, he knew well how each one of his charges was getting on, whether or not he was progressing, or even holding his own. If the report was unsatisfactory, the student was sent for and remonstrated with. If that had no effect, the parents were advised, and requested to urge the son to try to do better. If the student still persisted in wasting his time and money, his parents were asked to call him home.

As illustrating how well the president was acquainted with the students, and how accurate was his remembrance of their individuality, it is related that on one occasion a name was read out in faculty meeting which was unfamiliar to him. He asked that it be read out again, and repeated the name to himself, adding in a tone of self-reproach:

"I have no recollection of a student of that name. It is very strange that I have forgotten him. I thought I knew every one in college. How long has he been here?"

An investigation proved that the student had recently entered during his absence, and that he had never seen him. He won the confidence of the students, and very soon their affections. He regarded a mass of petty regulations as being only vexatious, and yet by his tact and firmness his discipline became most effective. Very seldom was there any breaking of the laws. He was so honoured and loved that they tried to please him in all things. Of course, there were exceptions. I give here some letters written to parents and guardians which will show how he tried to induce these triflers to become men:

"LEXINGTON, Virginia, March 25, 1866.
"*My Dear Sir:* I am very glad to learn from your letter of the 13th inst. that you have written your son in reference to his neglect of his studies. I am sure your letter and the kind admonition of his mother will have a beneficial effect upon him. I have myself told him as plainly but as kindly as I could that it was necessary for him to change his course, or that he would be obliged to return home. He has promised me that he would henceforth be diligent and attentive, and endeavour in all things to perform his duty. I hope that he may succeed, for I think he is able to do well if he really makes the effort. Will you be so kind as to inform Mrs. W. that I have received her letter of the 19th? It will give me pleasure at all times to aid her son in every way I can, but if he desires no benefit from his connection with the college it will be to his interest to return home.

"Very truly your obedient servant,　　　R. E. LEE."

Here is another letter showing the patience and forbearance of the president and his earnest desire to help on in life the young men committed to his charge:

"WASHINGTON COLLEGE,
"LEXINGTON, Virginia, April 20, 1868.
"*My Dear Sir:* I regret to see, from your letter of the 29th ult., to the clerk of the faculty, that you have misunderstood their action in reference to your son. He was not dismissed, as you suppose, from college, but every means having been tried by the faculty to induce him to attend faithfully and regularly to his studies, without effect, and great forbearance having been practised, it was thought best for him, and just to you, that he should return home. The action of the faculty was purposely designed, not to prevent his being received into any other college, or to return to this, should you so desire. The monthly reports are intended to advise parents of the progress of their sons, and it was supposed you would have seen the little advancement made by yours in his studies, and that

no further notice was required. The action of the faculty was caused by no immorality on his part, but by a systematic neglect of his duties, which no counsel on the part of his professors, or my own, could correct. In compliance, however, with your wishes, and on the positive promise of amendment on the part of your son, he has been received into college, and I sincerely hope that he will apply himself diligently to his studies, and make an earnest effort to retrieve the time he has lost. With great respect,

"Your obedient servant,   R. E. LEE."

This letter, too, shows his fatherly interest:

"WASHINGTON COLLEGE,
"LEXINGTON, Virginia, March 19, 1868.

"*My Dear Sir:* Before this you have learned the affecting death of your son. I can say nothing to mitigate your grief or to relieve your sorrow; but if the sincere sympathy of his comrades and friends and of the entire community can bring you any consolation, I can assure you that you possess it in its fullest extent. When one, in the pureness and freshness of youth, before having been contaminated by sin or afflicted by misery, is called to the presence of his Merciful Creator, it must be solely for his good. As difficult as this may be for you now to recognise, I hope you will keep it constantly in your memory and take it to your comfort; and I pray that He who in His wise Providence has permitted this crushing sorrow may sanctify it to the happiness of all. Your son and his friend, Mr. Birely, often passed their leisure hours in rowing on the river, and, on last Saturday afternoon, the 4th inst., attempted what they had more than once been cautioned against—to approach the foot of the dam, at the public bridge. Unfortunately, their boat was caught by the return-current, struck by the falling water, and was immediately upset. Their perilous position was at once seen from the shore, and aid was hurried to their relief, but before it could reach them both had perished. Efforts to restore your son's life, though long continued, were unavailing. Mr.

Birely's body was not found until next morning. Their remains were, yesterday, Sunday, conveyed to the Episcopal church in this city, where the sacred ceremonies for the dead were performed, by the Reverend Dr. Pendleton, who nineteen years ago, at the far-off home of their infancy, placed upon them their baptismal vows. After the service a long procession of the professors and students of the college, the officers and cadets of the Virginia Military Academy, and the citizens of Lexington accompanied their bodies to the packet-boat for Lynchburg, where they were placed in charge of Messrs. Wheeler & Baker to convey them to Frederick City.

"With great regard and sincere sympathy, I am,
"Most respectfully,   R. E. LEE."

CHAPTER XVII

THE RECONSTRUCTION PERIOD

THE GENERAL BELIEVES IN THE ENFORCEMENT OF LAW AND
ORDER—HIS MORAL INFLUENCE IN THE COLLEGE—PLAYFUL
HUMOUR SHOWN IN HIS LETTERS—HIS OPINION OF NEGRO
LABOUR—MR. DAVIS'S TRIAL—LETTER TO MRS. FITZHUGH
LEE—INTERCOURSE WITH FACULTY

VIRGINIA was at this time still under military rule. The "recon-struction" days were not over. My father had himself accepted the political situation after the war, and had advised every one who had sought his advice to do the same. The following incident and letters will show his acquiescence in the law of the land, and ready submission to the authorities. In a street disturbance that spring a student had been shot by a negro, and it was reported that, in case of the young man's death, the murderer would be summarily dealt with by his collegemates. Captain Wagner, the military commis-sioner, wrote to General Lee informing him of these reports. He received the following reply:

"WASHINGTON COLLEGE,
"LEXINGTON, Virginia, May 4, 1868.
"CAPTAIN WAGNER, Commissioner District,
"LEXINGTON, Virginia.
"*Sir:* Upon investigation of the reports which you communi-cated to me yesterday afternoon, I can find no foundation for the

apprehension that the students of Washington College contemplate any attack upon the man confined in jail for shooting Mr.— Friday night. On the contrary, I have been assured by members of the faculty and individual students that they have heard no suggestion of the kind, and they believe that no such intention has been entertained or now exists. I think, therefore, the reports made to you are groundless.

"Very respectfully, your obedient servant,

"R. E. LEE."

However, in order to take all precautions and provide against any disturbance, he wrote as follows to the president of the Young Men's Christian Association, whom he knew and trusted, and who was a man of much influence with his fellow-students:

"MR. G. B. STRICKLER,

"President Young Men's Christian Association,
"Washington College.

"I have just been informed by Captain Wagner, Military Commissioner of this district, that from information received by him, he had reason to apprehend that, should the wound received by Mr.—Friday night prove fatal, the students of Washington College contemplate taking from the jail the man who shot him and inflicting upon him summary punishment. I cannot believe that any such act is intended or would be allowed by the students of Washington College, though it is possible that such an intention may have been spoken of amongst them. I think it only necessary to call the attention of the students to the report to prevent such an occurrence. I feel convinced that none would countenance such outrage against law and order, but that all will cheerfully submit to the administration of justice by the legal authorities As the readiest way of communicating with the students, at this hour, on Sunday, I have concluded to address you this letter that through the members of the Young Men's Christian Association the students generally may be informed of the apprehension entertained by the military authorities; and I earnestly invoke the students to abstain from any violation of law, and to unite in preserving quiet and order on this and every occasion.

"Very respectfully, your obedient servant,

"R. E. LEE."

The young man recovered, there was no disturbance of any kind, nor was it believed that there would have been, after this appeal from the president, even if the wound had proved fatal.

"Nor was it a moral influence alone that he exerted in the college. He was equally careful of the intellectual interests. He watched the progress of every class, attended all the examinations, and strove constantly to stimulate both professors and students to the highest attainments. The whole college, in a word, felt his influence as an ever-present motive, and his character was quietly but irresistibly impressed upon it, not only in the general working of all its departments, but in all the details of each. Of this influence General Lee, modest as he was, was perfectly aware, and, like a prudent ruler, he husbanded it with wise economy. He preferred to conconfine his direct interposition to purely personal acts, and rarely—and then only on critical occasions—did he step forward to present himself before the whole body of students in the full dignity of his presidential office. On these occasions, which in the latter years hardly ever occurred, he would quietly post an address to the students, in which, appealing only to the highest principles of conduct, he sought to dissuade them from threatened evil. The addresses, which the boys designated as his 'general orders,' were always of immediate efficacy. No single case ever occurred in which they failed of instant and complete effect; and no student would have been tolerated by his fellow-students who would have dared to disregard such an appeal from General Lee."[1]

My father had recovered from the spell of sickness of the previous summer at the Old Sweet Springs, which had weakened and depressed him until about the time he attended my brother's wedding. That marriage had been a great joy to him. His trip there and back, and his visits to "Brandon" and "Hickory Hill," the change of climate and scene, seeing old friends and new places, had all contributed to benefit his health and spirits. I remember this Christmas of 1867 he seemed particularly bright and cheerful. I give a letter he wrote me after I had left for my home which reflects his playful humour and good spirits:

"LEXINGTON, Virginia, January 23, 1868.

"*My Dear Robert:* I inclose a letter which has just arrived in the mail. It seems to be from a nice young lady, judging from the style and address. I hope she is the right one and that her response is favourable. Put in a good crop, and recollect you may have two to feed after harvest. We are doing what we can in this region to supply the springs and streams that form the lowland rivers. It is still raining, though the snow and ice have not left us. After your departure, Mr. Gordon brought to me a letter from Fitzhugh to your mother which had come in the Sunday mail and was overlooked among the papers. I am sorry it had not been found before you left, as you would have known their plans. Tell them I am sorry not to have seen them. We miss you very much. 'Life' has it all her own way now, and expends her energy in regulating her brother and putting your mother's drawers and presses to rights. It's her only vent, and furnishes exercise for body and mind. There is to be a great *fete* in your mother's room to-day. The Grace Church Sewing Society is to meet there at 10 A. M.—that is, if the members are impervious to water. I charged the two Mildreds to be seated with their white aprons on and with scissors and thimbles in hand. I hope they may have a refreshing time. Good-bye.

"Your father,

"R. E. LEE.

"ROBERT E. LEE."

The second Mildred mentioned here was my father's niece, daughter of Charles Carter Lee. She was living with my father at this time, going to school, and was, like her cousin the other Mildred, not very fond of her needle. His nickname for her was "Powhattie," derived, I presume, from her native County of Powhatan. He was very fond of teasing her in his playful way. Indeed, we all enjoyed that attention from him. He never teased any one whom he did not specially like.

To his new daughter I find the following letter, written at this time, in which he shows his affection and admiration for her:

"LEXINGTON, Virginia, March 10, 1868.

"*My Beautiful Daughter:* I have been wishing to write to you for a long time, but have supposed that you would be so engrossed with my sons, with their plans and their projects, that you could not lend an ear to your papa. But now I must tell you how much I have thought of you, how much I want to see you, and how greatly I was disappointed at your not getting to see us at the time you proposed. You must not postpone your visit too long, or you may not find us here. Our winter, which has been long and cold, I hope now is over. The gardeners are busy, the grass is growing green, and the atmosphere warm and inspiring. I presume under its genial influence you and Fitzhugh are busy improving your new home. I hope everything is agreeable, and that you are becoming more and more interested in making those around you happy. That is the true way to secure your own happiness, for which my poor prayers are daily offered to the throne of the Most High. I have been summoned to Richmond the third Thursday in this month, as a witness in the trial against Mr. Davis; and though that will be a painful errand for me, I hope that it will give me the pleasure of seeing you. I will endeavour to get down some day to the White House, if it is only to spend Sunday with you. I hope that you will be able to pay some attention to your poor brother Robert. Do not let his elder brother monopolise you altogether. You will have to take care of both till you can find some one like yourself to take Romancoke in hand. Do you think Miss Anne Banister will consent? Mildred, you know, is the only one of the girls who has been with us this winter. She has consequently had her hands full, and considers herself now a great character. She rules her brother and my nephews with an iron rod, and scatters her advice broadcast among the young men of the college. I hope that it may yield an abundant harvest. The young mothers of Lexington ought to be extremely grateful to her for her suggestions to them as to the proper mode of rearing their children, and though she finds many unable to appreciate her system, she is nothing daunted by their obtuseness of vision, but takes advantage of every opportunity to enlighten them as to its benefits. Mary and Agnes are still in Baltimore, and are now at the house of Mrs. Charles Howard. Agnes expects, I believe, to return to the Peters near Ellicott City, and then go over to the Eastern Shore of Maryland to visit the Goldsboroughs and other friends. I hardly think either of them will get back before June. I have recently received a very pretty picture from a young lady of Baltimore, Miss Mary Jones, whom I met last summer at the White Sulphur Springs. In one of my morning rides to the Beaver-dam Falls, near the Sweet Springs, I found her at the foot of the Falls making a sketch of the scene, and on her return home she finished it and has sent it to me. It is beautifully painted and is a faithful representation of the Falls. I think you will be pleased with it when you come up, and agree with me in the opinion that it is the principal ornament of our parlour. I am sorry to inform you that your poor mama has been suffering more than usual lately from her rheumatic pains. She took cold in some way, which produced a recurrence of her former pangs, though she is in a measure now relieved. We often wish for you and Fitzhugh. My only pleasure is in my solitary evening rides, which give me abundant opportunity for quiet thought. With a great deal of love to your husband, I am your sincerely attached father,

"R. E. LEE.

"MRS. WILLIAM H. FITZHUGH LEE."

The next letter I find is a reply to one of mine, in which I evidently had been confiding to him my agricultural woes:

"LEXINGTON, Virginia, March 12, 1868.

"*My Dear Rob:* I am sorry to learn from your letter of the 1st that the winter has been so hard on your wheat. I hope, however, the present good weather is shedding its influence upon it, and that it will turn out better than it promises. You must, however, take a lesson from the last season. What you do cultivate, do well. Improve and prepare the land in the best manner; your labour will be less, and your profits more. Your flat lands were always uncertain in wet winters. The uplands were more sure. Is it not possible that some unbidden guest may have been feasting on your corn? Six hundred bushels are a large deficit in casting up your account for the year. But you must make it up by economy and good management. A farmer's motto should be *toil and trust*. I am glad that you have got your lime and sown your oats and clover. Do you use the drill or sow broadcast? I shall try to get down to see you if I go to Richmond, for I am anxious to know how you are progressing and to see if in any way I can aid you. Whenever I can, you must let me know. You must still think about your house and make up your mind as to the site and kind, and collect the material. I can help you to any kind of plan, and with some ready money to pay the mechanics. I have recently had a visit from Dr. Oliver, of Scotland, who is examining lands for immigrants from his country. He seems to be a sensible and judicious man. From his account, I do not think the Scotch and English would suit your part of the country. It would require time for them to become acclimated, and they would probably get dissatisfied, especially as there is so much mountainous region where they could be accommodated. I think you will have to look to the Germans; perhaps the Hollanders, as a class, would be the most useful. When the railroad shall have been completed to West Point, I think there will be no difficulty in getting the whites among you. I would try to get some of our own young men in your employ. I rode out the other day to Mr.

Andrew Cameron's and went into the field where he was plowing. I took great pleasure in following the plows around the circuit. He had four in operation. Three of them were held by his former comrades in the army, who are regularly employed by him, and, he says, much to his satisfaction and profit. People have got to work now. It is creditable to them to do so; their bodies and their minds are benefited by it, and those who can and will work will be advanced by it. You will never prosper with the blacks, and it is abhorrent to a reflecting mind to be supporting and cherishing those who are plotting and working for your injury, and all of whose sympathies and associations are antagonistic to yours. I wish them no evil in the world—on the contrary, will do them every good in my power, and know that they are misled by those to whom they have given their confidence; but our material, social, and political interests are naturally with the whites. Mr. Davis's trial was fixed for the last of this month. If Judge Chase's presence is essential, I do not see how it can take place, unless that of Mr. Johnson is to be postponed. I suppose that will be decided to-day or to-morrow, and then I shall know what to expect. I shall not go to Richmond unless necessary, as it is always inconvenient for me to leave home, and I am not at all well. Your poor mother is also more ailing than she is ordinarily, in conse-quence of a cold she has taken. But it is passing away, I trust. I must leave you to her and Mildred for all local and domestic news. Custis and the boys are well, and 'Powhattie,' I hope, has got rid of the chills. We hear regularly from Mary and Agnes, who seem to be enjoying themselves, and I do not think from their programme that they will get back to us till summer. All unite in much love, and I am always,   Your father,

"R. E. LEE."

This same month he writes a long letter to his daughter Agnes, who was visiting friends in Baltimore. The Annette, Mildred, and Mary he mentions in this letter were the daughters of Charles Henry Carter, of "Goodwood," Maryland, a first cousin of my father:

"LEXINGTON, Virginia, March 28, 1868.

"*My Precious Agnes:* I was so glad to receive your letter, to learn that you were well and enjoying yourself among pleasant friends. I hope that you will soon get through all your visits and come home. Your uncle Smith says you girls ought to marry his sons, as you both find it so agreeable to be from home, and you could then live a true Bohemian life and have a happy time generally. But I do not agree with him; I shall not give my consent, so you must choose elsewhere. I have written to Annette telling her of my alarm for her. Now that Mildred is engaged, and she sees how much Mary is in love, I fear she will pick up an Adonis next, so that she had better run away to the mountains at once. I am glad that you saw Mr. Davis. It is a terrible thing to have this prosecution hanging over him, and to be unable to fix his thoughts on a course of life or apply his hands to the support of his family. But I hope a kind Providence will shield and guide him. You must remember me to all my friends, the Taggarts, Glenns, McKims, Marshalls, etc. . . . As to the young ladies you mention, you must tell them that I want to see them very much, and hope that they will all come to the mountains this summer, and not pass us by in Lexington. When you go to 'Goodwood' and the Eastern Shore, do the same there for me, and present me to all by name. Tell sweet Sallie Warwick I think she ought to come to Lexington, if only to show those babies; but in truth I want to see her more than them, so she may leave them with Major Poor², if she chooses. You must see everybody you wish and enjoy yourself as much as you can, and then come home. I told Mildred to tell you if you wanted any funds you must let me know and where to send them. I do not know whether she delivered my message. She has become very imperious, and may not think you require any. She has been much exercised of late on the score of servants, but hopes to get some relief on the 1st proximo from the promised change of Miss Mary Dixon to Miss Eliza Cyrus. I hope her expectations may be realised. Little Mildred has had a return of her chills. It has been a sharp attack, and though it has been arrested, when I left her this morning I feared she might have a relapse, as this is her regular day. She was looking remarkably well before it came on, better than she had ever done, but every cold terminates in this way, however slight it may be. Colds have been quite prevalent, and there have been two deaths among the cadets from pneumonia. Fortunately so far the students have escaped. I am relieved of mine I hope, and your poor mother is, I hope, better. The storm seems to have subsided, and I trust the bright weather may ameliorate her pains. Custis, Mildred, and the boys are well, as are most of our friends in Lexington. . . . Fitzhugh writes that everything is blooming at the 'White House,' and that his wheat is splendid. I am in hopes that it is all due to the presence of my fair daughter. Rob says that things at Romancoke are not so prosperous—you see, there is no Mrs. R. E. Lee, Jr., there, and that may make the difference. Cannot you persuade some of those pretty girls in Baltimore to take compassion on a poor bachelor? I will give them a plan for a house, if they will build it. . . . All would unite with me in love if they knew I was writing. You ought to be here to enjoy the birds Captain O. C. H. sends us. With much love for yourself, and my poor prayers for your happiness, I am,   Your devoted father,

"R. E. LEE."

A few days afterward he writes to his son Fitzhugh, who was now established very happily in his new house, and warns him not to depend entirely on sentiment, but to arrange for something material. He also speaks of Mr. Davis and his trial, which was continually being postponed, and in the end was dismissed, and gives him some good advice about importing cattle:

LEXINGTON, Virginia, March 30, 1868.
"*My Dear Fitzhugh:* I was very glad to receive your letter of the 19th, and as you are aware of the order of the court postponing Mr. Davis's trial till the 14th proximo, I presume that you have not been expecting me down. I see it stated in the Washington *Star*

that the trial is again postponed till May 4th, but I have seen as yet no order from the court. Mr. and Mrs. Davis went from Baltimore to New York on Tuesday last, and were to go on to Canada. He said that he did not know what he should do or what he could turn his hands to for a support. As long as this trial is hanging over him, of course, he can do nothing. He can apply his mind to nothing, nor could he acquire the confidence of the business community in anything he might undertake, from the apprehension of his being interrupted in the midst of it. Agnes and Mary saw them as they passed through Baltimore. They say Mr. Davis was well, though he had changed a great deal since they saw him last. I am very glad that you are so pleased with your house. I think it must be my daughter that gives it such a charm. I am sure that she will make everything look bright to me. It is a good thing that the wheat is doing so well, for I am not sure 'that the flame you are so rich in will light a fire in the kitchen, nor the little god turn the spit, spit, spit.' Some material element is necessary to make it burn brightly and furnish some good dishes for the table. Shad are good in their way, but they do not run up the Pamunkey all the year. I am glad that you are making arrangements for some cows, and think you are right in getting those of the best breed. It used to be thought that cows from the North would not prosper in that lower country, and indeed cows from the upper part of Virginia did not succeed well, but were apt to become sick and die; and that the surest process to improve the stock was to purchase calves of good breed and cross on the native stock. You must, therefore, be careful and not invest too much. We have had a cold winter, and March has been particularly harsh. Still, vegetation is progressing and the wheat around Lexington looks beautiful. My garden is advancing in a small way. Pease, spinach, and onions look promising, but my hot-bed plants are poor. The new house, about which you inquire, is *in statu quo* before winter. I believe the money is wanting and the workmen cannot proceed. We require some of that latter article here, as elsewhere, and have but little. . . . I heard of you in Richmond the other day, but did not learn whether my daughter was with you. I wish you would send her up to her papa when you go away. With much love,

"Your devoted father, R. E. LEE."

A month later he writes me, telling me that he expects to be in Richmond the following week, and will try to get down to see us; also telling of his garden, and horse, and, as he always did, encouraging, cheering me, and offering help:

"LEXINGTON, Virginia, April 25, 1868.

"*My Dear Rob:* Your letter of the 21st is just received. I am very glad that your wheat is improving in appearance, and hope that at harvest it will yield a fair return for your care and labour. Your corn I am sure will be more remunerative than the crop of last year, and I trust that at the end of the year you will find you have advanced in the field of agriculture. Your mule and provender was a heavy loss. You must make it up. Replace the first by a good one and I will pay for it. I hope the warm sun will bring forward the grass to supply the latter. Should I go to Richmond, next week, as I now expect, I will be prepared to pay for the mule, and if I do not I will send you a check for the amount. I am sorry to hear that you have not been well. You must get out of that too. . . . You must refresh yourself when you can by going up to the White House to see your brother and sister. Take a good look at the latter for me. . . . In our garden nothing is up but the hardy plants, pease, potatoes, spinach, onions, etc. . . . Beets, carrots, salsify, etc., have been sown a long time, but are not up, and I cannot put in the beans, squash, etc., or set out the hot-bed plants. But we can wait. I have not been as well this winter as usual, and have been confined of late. I have taken up Traveller, however, who is as rough as a bear, and have had two or three rides on him, in the mud, which I think has benefited me. Mildred sometimes accompanies me. Your mother, I am glad to say, is better. She has less pain than when I last wrote, and is more active on her crutches. . . . Good-bye, my dear son. If I go to Richmond I will try to get to see you.

"Affectionately your father,

"R. E. LEE.

"R. E. LEE, JR."

My father came to Richmond, summoned to attend the trial of Mr. Davis, but when he arrived he found that it was again postponed. So he went to the White House and spent several days. I came up from Romancoke and stayed with him till he left. It was a great pleasure to him to meet his sons and to see his new daughter in her new home. After his return to Lexington he wrote to her this letter:

"LEXINGTON, Virginia, May 29, 1868.

"*My Dear Daughter:* I have been enjoying in memory, ever since my return, my visit to the Pamunkey, and whenever I have thought of writing to you the pleasure I experienced in your company and in that of Fitzhugh and Robert absorbed the moment I could devote to a letter, and other calls made me postpone it. But I have thought of you often, and always with renewed pleasure; and I rejoice at your having around you more comforts and within your reach more pleasures than I had anticipated. I pray that both may be increased and be long continued. There is one thing I regret— that you are so far from us. I know the difficulty of farmers and their wives leaving home. Their success, and in a measure their pleasure, depend upon their daily attention to their affairs, and it is almost an impossibility for us old people to get to you. Yet I trust we may meet this summer some time, and whenever you can you must come and see us. Our small house will never be so full that there will not be room for you, or so empty that you will not be most cordially welcome. Letters received from Mary and Agnes report them still on the Eastern Shore of Maryland, where they were detained by the sickness of Agnes. They expected, however, to be able to return to Baltimore last Tuesday, 26th, where, after a few days' sojourn, they were to go to Mrs. Washington Peter's. I fear, however, that Agnes might not have been well enough, as she had had an attack of bilious fever and was much prostrated. Should you find yourself in danger of becoming sick, you must come right up to your papa. I know you will pine, but I would rather you should suffer in that way than burn with fever, and while on that subject I will tell you something that may be of comfort: you may reasonably expect Fitzhugh soon to follow, so you will not suffer long. I wish to take your mama to the Warm Springs, and to the Hot or Healing, if she will go, to try to obtain for her some relief; but we will not leave home till the last of June or first of July. I am so much occupied that I feel that I ought never to go away, and every absence accumulates my work. I had a pleasant visit of three days, to Lynchburg, attending the Episcopal Convention, and I have not yet brought up my correspondence, etc. I fear, too, I shall have to go to Richmond next week, as everything seems to portend the certainty of Mr. Davis's trial. God grant that, like the impeachment of Mr. Johnson, it may be dismissed. If I do go, I fear I shall have no time to visit you. The examinations of the senior classes of the college are now in progress, and after their completion the examination of the undergraduates will commence, and will not terminate till the 15th of June, and the commencement exercises then begin and end on the 18th. So you see how necessary it is for me to be here and that I shall be obliged to hasten back as soon as permitted. I wanted, if possible, to pass one day at 'Shirley'—I have not been there for ten years. It was the loved home of my mother, and a spot where I have passed many happy days in early life, and one that probably I may never visit again. But I do not know that I shall be able. We are all as usual, and all would send much love if they knew I was writing. Mildred is very happy in the company of Miss Charlotte Haxall, and Custis retains his serenity of character. Our young members of the family are looking forward to their return to Powhatan as soon as the college exercises close, which I hope will bring some relief to me also. I see that you have been much visited of late, but you know that no one wants to see you as much as I do. Tell Fitzhugh that his old friend, Miss Helen Peters, has come to Lexington, from New York, to pass the summer. See what an attractive place it is becoming. She is now Mrs. Taylor and has brought with her two babies. She is as cordial and as affectionate as ever. Give much love to Fitzhugh and Rob, and believe me always your devoted father,

"R. E. Lee.

"Mrs. Wm. H. Fitzhugh Lee."

My father was back at the college in full time for the "final examinations." He always made it a point to be present, and took his full share of sitting in the rooms while the students were working out their papers. When occasion offered, somewhat to the surprise of the learned faculty, he showed himself thoroughly conversant with each and every department. Even with Greek he seemed somewhat familiar, and would question the students as to their knowledge of this language, much to their astonishment.

The commencement exercises of the college began about June 1st and lasted a week. At this time, the town was crowded with visitors, and my father had his house full, generally of young girls, friends of my sisters who came to assist at the "final ball," the great social event connected with this college exercise. He seemed to enjoy their society as much as the young men did, though he could not devote so much time to them as the boys did, and I know that the girls enjoyed his society more than they did that of their college adorers. On the occasion of an entertainment at his house, in going amongst his guests saying to each group something bright and pleasant, he approached a young lady, a great belle, completely surrounded by her admirers—students, cadets, and some old "Confeds." He stopped and began to rally her on her conquests, saying:

"You can do as you please to these other young gentlemen, but you must not treat any of my *old soldiers* badly."

Those who have never known him cannot imagine the charm of his manner, the brightness of his smile, and the pleasant way he had of speaking, especially to young people and little children. His rebukes to the young were administered in the kindest, gentlest way, almost persuasively, but he could be stern when the occasion demanded. Colonel William Preston Johnston, a member of his faculty and a very dear and trusted friend, says:

"In his intercourse with his faculty he was courteous, kind, and often rather playful in manner. We all thought he deferred entirely too much to the expression of opinion on the part of the faculty, when we would have preferred that he should simply indicate his own views or desire. One characteristic of General Lee I noted then and have often recalled: I never saw him take an ungraceful posture. No matter how long or fatiguing a faculty meeting might be, he always preserved an attitude in which dignity, decorum, and grace were united. He was a very well built man, with rounded body and limbs, and seemed without the slightest affectation of effort to sit or stand or walk just as a gentleman should. He was never in a hurry, and all his gestures were easy and significant. He was always an agreeable companion. There was a good deal of bonhomie and pleasantry in his conversation. He was not exactly witty, nor was he very humorous, though he gave a light turn to table-talk and enjoyed exceedingly any pleasantry or fun, even. He often made a quaint or slightly caustic remark, but he took care that it should not be too trenchant. On reading his letters one discovers this playful spirit in many of them, as, for instance, in his letter to the spiritualist who asked his opinion of Von Moltke and the French war. He wrote in reply a most courteous letter in which he said that 'the question was one about which military critics would differ, that his own judgment about such matters was poor at best, and that inasmuch as they had the power to consult (through their mediums) Cæsar, Alexander, Napoleon, Wellington, and all of the other great captains who had ever lived, he could not think of obtruding his opinion in such company.'

General Lee did not talk politics, but he felt very deeply the condition of the country, and expressed to me several times in strong terms his disapproval of the course of the dominant party."

There is a story told of my father which points to his playful manner here alluded to. At a certain faculty meeting they were joking Mr. Harris, who so long and so ably filled the chair of Latin, about his walking up the aisle of the Presbyterian church with the stem of his pipe protruding from his pocket. Mr. Harris took out the offending stem and began cutting it shorter. My father, who had been enjoying the incident, said:

"No, Mr. Harris, don't do that; next time leave it at home."

Sometimes he deemed it advisable to be a little stern. One of the young professors went off for a few days without asking the president's permission. On his return the General met him very stiffly, saying:

"Mr.—, I congratulate you on your return to your friends and your duties. I was not aware of your absence until I heard it by chance."

Mr.—told this on himself, and added that it was the last time he ever went away without a formal leave of absence. His particularity in little things has often been commented on. He applied it to all his affairs. Dr. Kirkpatrick, Professor of Moral Philosophy, came into the president's office and asked for a certain paper. My father told him where it could be found. After a while, turning to the doctor he said:

"Did you find the paper?"

"Yes, General," replied the Doctor.

"Did you return it to the place where you found it?"

"Yes, General."

At another time he asked Professor Harris to look at a catalogue on the table. The Professor took up a new one, wrapped ready for the mail, and was about to tear the cover off, when my father, hastily handing him one already opened, said:

"Take this, if you please."

My mother used to say that he could go, in the dark, and lay his hand on any article of his clothing, or upon any particular paper, after he had once arranged them, provided they had not been disturbed. One of his "quaint or slightly caustic remarks," alluded to by Colonel Johnston, I recall as told to me. He met a lady friend down in the town, who bitterly complained that she could get nothing to eat in Lexington suitable for Lent—no fish, no oysters, etc.

"Mrs.—," the General replied, "I would not trouble myself so much about special dishes; I suppose if we try to abstain from *special sins* that is all that will be expected of us."

CHAPTER XVIII

MRS. R. E. LEE

GOES TO WARM SPRINGS FOR RHEUMATISM—HER DAUGHTER
MILDRED TAKES TYPHOID THERE—REMOVES TO HOT SPRINGS—
HER HUSBAND'S DEVOTION—VISIT OF FITZHUGH AND BRIDE
TO LEXINGTON—MISS JONES, A WOULD-BE BENEFACTOR OF
WASHINGTON COLLEGE—FATE OF WASHINGTON RELICS
BELONGING TO MRS. LEE'S FAMILY

THAT summer my father determined to take my mother to the Warm Springs, in Bath County, Virginia, hoping that the baths there might be of service to her, and purposing, if she was not benefited, to go to the Hot Springs, five miles distant. He was most anxious that his new daughter should join her there and go with him to any place she might select, and come back with them to Lexington. In the following letter to his son he tells of his plans for the summer:

"LEXINGTON, Virginia, July 1, 1868.

"*My Dear Fitzhugh:* I received yesterday your letter of the 28th ultimo, and regret very much to learn of Tabb's indisposition. I hope that she will soon be well, and I wish very much she would join us in the mountains and return here with us. In my letter to her about the time when she went to her sister's wedding, which I hope she got, I told her of my wishes on this subject, and believe gave her our general plans. I can now say with more distinctness that, unless something now unforeseen should prevent, I will take your mother to the Warm Springs, from the 10th to the 15th inst., and after trying the water there about two weeks, if not favourable, will take her over to the Hot. After seeing her comfortably established, I will then go anywhere Tabb desires—to the Healing or the White Sulphur or Sweet. I intend to go myself to the White Sulphur for about a fortnight, to drink the water, and will take Mildred with me. Agnes, having gone last summer, will not care to go, I presume, and can remain with her mother. Mildred has been quite sick for the past week, but is now much better, and in a week will be strong enough for the journey, I think. If not, we shall have to delay our departure a little. Agnes was also sick on the Eastern Shore of Maryland about three weeks, and, I am told, looks badly. She is now at the University of Virginia, and will be home in a few days and go with us to the Springs. You must arrange your plans to suit your interests and convenience, coming to us when you can and staying as long as you can. You know the interest I take in your prosperity and advancement, which cannot be assured without earnest attention to your business on your part, and therefore I never urge you to act contrary to your own judgment in reference to them. As to my daughter, Tabb, tell her if she will trust herself to her papa she shall never want anything he can do for her, and I think she will find the prediction in my letter to her verified. She might join us at Goshen and go with us, or come here. Why did she not come up with her father? I went to see him last evening, but he was out. Your mother, I presume, has told you of home affairs. She has become nervous of late, and broods over her troubles so much that I fear it increases her sufferings. I am therefore the more anxious to give her new scenes and new thoughts. It is the principal good I anticipate. Love to Rob. Custis still talks of visiting you, but I have not heard of his having fixed the day of his departure. He is quite well. With my best love to my daughter T—and the same to yourself, I am,

"Most affectionately your father,

"R. E. LEE."

The morning he left Lexington he, while waiting for the stage, writes as follows to a great favourite of his, a friend of Mildred's, who had been on a visit to her that summer:

"LEXINGTON, Virginia, July 14, 1868.

". . . The stage is at the door to carry us to Goshen, and if Mrs. Lee's strength permits, we hope to reach the Warm Springs to-night. After two or three weeks' trial of its waters we shall go to the Hot, where, leaving Agnes to take care of her mother, I shall take Mildred to the White Sulphur, and hope to meet you at Covington and carry you along. Will you not come? . . . Mildred is quite well again and is flying about this morning with great activity. Agnes is following with slower steps, Mrs. Lee is giving her last injunctions to Sam and Eliza. Letitia[1] is looking on with wonder at the preparations, and trying to get a right conception of the place to which she is going, which she seems to think is something between a steel-trap and a spring-gun. Custis is waiting to help his mother into the stage, and you see how patient I am. To add interest to the scene, Dr. Barton has arrived to bid adieu and to give Mildred an opportunity of looking her best. I believe he is the last rose of summer. The others, with their fragrance and thorns, have all departed. . . ."

A few days after their arrival at the Warm Springs, Mildred was taken ill with typhoid fever, and during many anxious weeks my father and Agnes were her only nurses. My mother's room was on the first floor of the "Brockenborough Cottage," my sister's in the second, so she could not get upstairs to her room. Mildred was very fanciful—would have no one but my father to nurse her, and could not sleep unless she had his hand in hers. Night after night he sat by her side, watching over her and attending to every want with gentleness and patience. He writes to the same young lady, at Mildred's request:

"WARM SPRINGS, Virginia, July 30, 1868.

". . . She [Mildred] has been so anxious to write to you, and so uneasy at her inability to do so, that I hope you will permit me to tell you the reason. She has been quite sick and is so still—confined to her bed with low fever, which retains its hold very pertinaciously. She took cold a few days after our arrival, from some imprudence, and is now very much enfeebled. She has been more comfortable the last day or two, and I hope is better, but I presume her recovery will necessarily be slow. You know she is very fanciful, and as she seems to be more accessible to reason from me, I have come be her chief nurse, and am now writing in her room, while she is sleeping. . . . This is a beautiful valley, and we have quite a pleasant company—Mr. and Mrs. Chapman and their three daughters from Alabama; Mrs. Coleman and her two daughters from Baltimore; some ladies from Richmond, Washington, Kentucky, Iowa, etc., and an ever-changing scene of faces. As soon as Mildred is strong enough, we will go to the Hot, after which, if she desires it, I will take her to the White. Mrs. Lee and Agnes are improving slightly, I am glad to say. We hear of many friends at the Hot, Healing, and White, and hope we shall reach these respective waters before they depart. . . . The Harrisons have written me that they will be here on the 14th proximo, but unless Mildred's recovery is much retarded it will be too late for me to see them. The Caskies will be at the Hot about the same time. . . . I am,

"Yours most sincerely,   R. E. LEE."

On August 3d, from the same place, he writes to my brother Fitzhugh:

". . . this was the day I had appointed to go to the Hot, but Mildred is too sick to move. She was taken more than a fortnight since, . . . and her attack seems to have partaken of a typhoid character. She has had since a low and persistent fever, which retains its hold. She is very feeble, but, in the doctor's opinion, somewhat better. I myself see little change, except that she is now free from pain. I cannot speak of our future movements. I fear I shall have to abandon my visit to the White. Your mother and Agnes are better than when they arrived. The former bathes freely, eats generously, and sleeps sweetly. Agnes, though feeble, is stronger. I am the same, and can see no effects of the waters upon myself. Give much love to my sweet daughter and dear sons. All unite with me in this message. . . . I am, as ever and always,

"Your father,

"R. E. LEE."

Another letter to my brother, Fitzhugh, from the Warm Springs, tells of his daughter's convalescence. Smith's Island, of which he writes, belonged to my grandfather's estate, of which my father was executor. He was trying to make some disposition of it, so that it might yield a revenue. It is situated on the Atlantic, just east of Cape Charles, in Northampton County, Virginia.

"WARM SPRINGS, Virginia, August 14, 1868.

"*My Dear Fitzhugh:* I received, yesterday, your letter of the 9th, and, as your mother informed you of Mildred's condition, I deferred replying to it until to-day. I am glad to inform you that she is better, and that the doctor pronounces her convalescent this morning. He says her progress must necessarily be slow, but with care and prudence he sees nothing to prevent her recovery, unless something unforeseen occurs. I hope, therefore, we may dismiss our anxiety. As regards Smith's Island, I should be very glad if you could go over and see it, and, if you think proper, make such disposition of it as you and Robert think most advantageous. See Mr. Hamilton S. Neale (Eastville, Northampton County, Virginia) and consult with him on the subject and let me know your determination. I think you will find him kind and intelligent. I have visited the island twice in my life, a long while ago, and thought that, if a person lived on it, he might, by grazing, planting, and fishing, make a comfortable living. You and Robert might, if you choose, buy the island from the estate. I fear the timber, etc., has been cut from it. I never thought it as valuable as your grandfather did. You will have to go to Norfolk, take the steamer to Cherrystone, where, I suppose, you can find a conveyance to Eastville. You know Cobb's Island has been a fashionable bathing-place. John Lewis wrote that the beach was delightful and fare excellent, and that they had sail-vessels there at the disposal of visitors. But Mr. Neale and Mr. John Simpkins, the present agent, can put you in the way of visiting the island, and you might carry my sweet daughter, Tabb, over and give her a surf bath. But do not let the mosquitoes annoy her. Give her much love from me. I am writing in Mildred's room, who is very grateful for your interest in her behalf. She is too weak to speak. I hope Rob had a pleasant trip. Tell me Custis's plans. I have not heard from him. Your mother and Agnes unite in love to you, Rob, and Tabb. I have a fan in one hand, while I wield the pen with the other, so excuse brevity. Most affectionately yours, R. E. Lee.

"P.S.—George and Eleanor Goldsborough and Miss Mary G— express themselves as much pleased with Cobb's Island. I do not know how far it is east of Smith's Island. R. E. Lee."

His daughter being convalescent, he carried out his plan, and went over to the White Sulphur Springs, after he had placed my mother and sisters at the Hot Springs. In a letter from there, on August 28th, he writes:

". . . The place looks beautiful—the belles very handsome, and the beaux very happy. All are gay, and only I solitary. I am all alone. There was a grand fancy masked ball last night. The room was overflowing, the music good, as much spring in the boards as in the conversation, and the german continued till two o'clock this morning. I return to the Hot next week, and the following to

Lexington. Mildred is much better, but says she has forgotten how to write. I hope that she will be strong enough to return with me. . . . I am, Truly and affectionately yours, R. E. LEE."

They all returned to Lexington early in September, in time for the opening of the college. Mildred was still weak and nervous, nor did she recover her normal strength for several months. She was always my father's pet as a little girl, and during this illness and convalescence he had been very tender with her, humouring as far as he could all of her fancies. Not long before that Christmas, she enumerated, just in fun, all the presents she wished—a long list. To her great surprise, when Christmas morning came she found each article at her place at the breakfast-table—not one omitted.

His sympathy with all who were suffering, ill, and afflicted was warm and sincere. Colonel Shipp, now superintendent of the Virginia Military Institute, was the commandant of cadets when my father came to Lexington. He tells me that he was ill for some weeks, laid up in his room, which was next to that of my brother Custis. He hardly knew General Lee, and had spoken to him only a few times, but my father went to see him quite often, would sit by him, talk to him, and seemed much interested in his getting well. He said that he would consult Mrs. Lee ("who is a great doctor"), and he finally brought a bottle of something in which sudor-berries were the chief ingredient. Colonel Shipp found out afterward that the sudor-berries had been sent from the White House, and that my mother had concocted the medicine.

On one occasion, calling at Colonel Preston's, he missed two little boys in the family circle, who were great favourites of his, and on asking for them he was told that they were confined to the nursery by croup. The next day, though the weather was of the worst description, he went trudging in great storm-boots back to their house, carrying in one hand a basket of pecan nuts and in the other a toy, which he left for his little sick friends.

To my mother, who was a great invalid from rheumatism for more than ten years, he was the most faithful attendant and tender nurse. Every want of hers that he could supply he anticipated. His considerate forethought saved her from much pain and trouble. During the war he constantly wrote to her, even when on the march and amidst the most pressing duties. Every summer of their life in Lexington he arranged that she should spend several months at one of the many medicinal springs in the neighbouring mountains, as much that she might be surrounded by new scenes and faces, as for the benefit of the waters. Whenever he was in the room, the privilege of pushing her wheeled chair into the dining-room and out on the verandas or elsewhere about the house was yielded to him. He sat with her daily, entertaining her with accounts of what was doing in the college, and the news of the village, and would often read to her in the evening. For her his love and care never ceased, his gentleness and patience never ended.

This tenderness for the sick and helpless was developed in him when he was a mere lad. His mother was an invalid, and he was her constant nurse. In her last illness he mixed every dose of medicine she took, and was with her night and day. If he left the room, she kept her eyes on the door till he returned. He never left her but for a short time. After her death the health of their faithful servant, Nat, became very bad. My father, then just graduated from West Point, took him to the South, had the best medical advice, a comfortable room, and everything that could be done to restore him, and attended to him himself.

I can find very few family letters written by my father at this time. Those which have been preserved are to my brother Fitzhugh, and are mostly about Smith's Island and the settling up of my grandfather's estate. The last of September he writes:

"LEXINGTON, Virginia, September 28, 1868.

"*My Dear Fitzhugh:* Your report of the condition of Smith's Island corresponds with my own impressions, based upon my knowledge of the island and the reports of others. I think it would be advantageous, under present circumstances, to make sale of the island as soon as a fair price can be obtained, and I have so instructed Mr. Hamilton S. Neale, who has consented to act as my agent. . . . I should like this whole matter arranged as soon as possible, for my life is very uncertain, and its settlement now may avoid future difficulties. I am very glad to hear that you and Rob have continued well, and that my daughter is improving. Give my love to them both. The loss of your fine cows is a serious one, and I believe you will have to procure them in your vicinity and improve them. Get some calves this fall of a good breed. We hope that we shall see you this fall. Your mother is as comfortable as usual, and Mildred is improving. Custis, Mary, and Agnes are well, and all would send love, did they know I was writing.

"Very affectionately your father,   R. E. LEE."

This autumn he had a visit from his nephew, Edward Lee Childe. Edward lived in Paris, and had crossed over in the summer to see my father and mother. He made a very pleasant impression on everybody, and was much pleased with his visit. Here is a letter written by my father to my brother just after Edward left:

"LEXINGTON, Virginia, October 14, 1868.

"*My Dear Fitzhugh:* I have returned to Mr. Hamilton S. Neale the advertisement of the sale of Smith's Island, with my approval, and have requested him to advertise in the Northern and Richmond papers, etc., and to send out such other notices as he deems best calculated to attract attention to the property, and to take every measure to enhance the value of the island and to procure for your grandfather's estate the full benefit of the sale. . . . I have heard from Mr. Compton that my daughter Tabb has returned to the White House in improved health, which I am very glad of. I hope that you will soon be able to bring her up to see us. Do not wait until the weather becomes too cold. Our mountain atmosphere in winter is very harsh. So far, the weather has been delightful. Your cousin Edward left us last Thursday evening on his way to see you. We enjoyed his visit greatly. Agnes and I rode down to the Baths last Saturday to see the Harrisons, and returned Sunday evening. They were well, and somewhat benefited by their visit. Mr. George Ritchie's death no doubt threw a shade of sadness over the whole party on Mrs. Harrison's account, though all were charming and Miss Belle very sweet. We are about the same— your poor mother comfortable, Mildred improving. All would unite in love to you and yours, did they know I was writing. Give much love to my dear daughter, Tabb, and tell her that I want to see her very much.

"Truly and affectionately your father,

"GENERAL W. H. FITZHUGH LEE.   R. E. LEE."

In a few days, he writes again, still about Smith's Island, but adds much about the family and friends:

"LEXINGTON, Virginia, October 19, 1868.

"*My Dear Fitzhugh:* I received your letter of the 12th the day I last wrote to you. I am glad we agree that $—should be the minimum limit for the price of Smith's Island. You will see by my letter referred to that it has been so fixed. December 22d is the day proposed by Mr. Neale as the time of public sale, which was approved by me, though I feared the notice might be too short. Still there are good reasons for the sale being made without unnecessary delay. I think November, which you suggest, would not afford sufficient notice. I would recommend that you and Robert attend the sale, and be governed by circumstances in what you do. I would go myself, but it would be a long, hard journey for me at that season of the year, and I do not see any material good that I can do. Mr. Neale kindly offered to meet me at Cherrystone landing and take me to his house, but I shall decline in your favour. I am sorry that Edward did not get down to see you, for I wanted him to see my daughter, Tabb. I am sure he has seen none like her in Paris. He left here with the purpose of visiting you and his uncle Smith, and I do not know what made him change his mind. I hope that you will get in a good crop of wheat, and get it in well. The latter is very important and unless accomplished may deprive you of the whole benefit of your labour and expense. We shall look anxiously for your visit. Do not put it off too late or the weather may be unfavourable. Our mountain country is not the most pleasant in cold weather, but we will try and make you warm. Give my love to Tabb, and tell her I am wanting to see her all the time. All unite in love to her and you. Your mother is about the same, very busy, and full of work. Mildred is steadily improving, and is able to ride on horseback, which she is beginning to enjoy. Mary and Agnes very well. We see but little of Custis. He has joined the mess at the institute, which he finds very comfortable, so that he rarely comes to our table to breakfast now. The rest of the time he seems to be occupied with his classes and studies. Remember me to Rob. I hear of a great many weddings, but his has not been announced yet. He must not forget his house. I have not, and am going to take up the plan very soon. Mildred says a good house is an effective card in the matrimonial game. She is building a castle in the air. The Harrisons propose leaving the Baths to-morrow. George arrived a week ago. I did not get down Saturday to see them as I wished. I hope the health of the whole party has been improved. I wish I could spend this month with you. That lower country is delightful to me at this season, and I long to be on the water again, but it cannot be. With much love,

"R. E. Lee.

"General Wm. H. Fitzhugh Lee."

The last of October he went to Staunton on some business. He rode Traveller, and Colonel Wm. Allan rode with him. It was the time of the Augusta Agricultural Fair, and while there he visited the exhibition and was received by the people with great demonstrations of delight. A student standing by remarked dryly:

"I don't see why the Staunton people make all this to do over General Lee; why, in Lexington, he *sends* for me to come to see him!"

In a letter of November 2d he mentions this little journey:

". . . I have recently paid a visit to Staunton and saw the young people there. They seemed very happy in their fair, and the beaux with their belles. I rode over on Traveller and was accompanied by Colonel Allan. The former was delighted at the length of the road, and the latter relieved from an obstinate cold from which he was suffering. On the second morning, just as the knights were being marshalled to prove their prowess and devotion, we commenced our journey back to Lexington, which we reached before nine P. M., under the light of a beautiful moon."

At this time his son Fitzhugh and his new daughter paid their long-promised visit, which he enjoyed immensely. My mother and sisters were charmed with her, and the entire community vied in paying her attention. My father was proud of his daughter-in-law and much gratified at his son's marriage. He was delighted with the manner in which she adapted herself to the ways of all her new relations, with her sweet attention to my mother, and, above all, with her punctuality. She had been warned beforehand by her husband that, to please his father, she must be always ready for family prayers, which were read every morning by him just before breakfast. This she succeeded in doing, never failing once to be on time. As breakfast was at seven o'clock, it was no small feat for one not accustomed to such early hours. She said afterward that she did not believe that General Lee would have an entirely high opinion of any person, even General Washington, if he could return to earth, if he were not ready for prayers! After a delightful visit of three weeks my brother and his wife returned home. Just as the latter was packing, my father came into her room and filled all the space in the top of her trunk with pecan nuts, which some friend had sent him from the South.

The hour fixed for the service in the college chapel was, as I have said, a quarter to eight o'clock every morning except Sunday. In the three winter months, December, January, and February, it was one hour later. As the president never failed to attend, when not prevented by sickness or absence, it was necessary to have an early breakfast. After chapel he went to his office and was seated at his desk by eight o'clock, where he remained, unless called out by public business, till two P. M. This room was open to all in the college who had business with him. The new students were required to report to him here in person, and from their first interviews he obtained a knowledge of the young men of which he availed himself in their future career in the college. As president, he was always disposed to be lenient with students who were reported for disorderly conduct or for failure in their studies or duties. He would say to the faculty, when they seemed to think it necessary to send a student home:

"Don't you think it would be better to bear with him a little longer? Perhaps we may do him some good."

Being sent for to this office was anything but pleasant to the students. Lewis, one of the janitors, went around with the names of those the president wanted to see, written by his own hand on a long slip of paper. He carried the paper in one hand, a pencil in the other, and when he could find the one he wanted in a crowd of his comrades, he took special pleasure in serving his notice, and would say in his solemn, sepulchral voice:

"Mr.—, the president wants to see you at the office."

Then Mr.—took the pencil and made a cross-mark opposite his name, which was evidence of his having received his summons. What transpired at these interviews was seldom known, except as the student himself might reveal it; for unless it became necessary to summon the delinquent a second time, the president never alluded to the subject. An old student writes me the following account of his experience in the president's office:

"I was a frolicsome chap at college, and, having been absent from class an unreasonable number of times, was finally summoned to the General's office. Abject terror took possession of me in the presence of such wise and quiet dignity; the reasons I had carefully prepared to give for my absence stood on their heads, or toppled over. In reply to General Lee's grave but perfectly polite question, I stammered out a story about a violent illness, and then, conscious that I was at that moment the picture of health, I hastened on with something about leaving my boots at the cobbler's, when General Lee interrupted me: 'Stop, Mr.M—,' he said; 'stop, sir! *One good reason is enough.'* But I could not be mistaken about the twinkle in the old hero's eyes!"

Only a few cases required more than one summons to appear at the office. No instance is known where a student complained of injustice or harshness, and the effect on his mind was that of greater respect and admiration for the president.

The new house was approaching completion, and my father was much interested in the work, going there very often and discussing with the workmen their methods. That Christmas I spent two weeks in Lexington, and many times my father took me all over the new building, explaining all the details of his plan. All of his family were here together this Christmas except Fitzhugh and his wife, an occurrence rather rare of late years. My father's health was unusually good, and he was bright and almost gay. He rode out often, taking me with him, as it was too cold for the girls. He also took me around with him visiting, and in the mild festivities of the neighbours he joined with evident pleasure. My visit ended all too soon, and the first week of January I started back to the "low country." Soon after my departure, he forwarded a letter to me with the accompanying one of his own:

"LEXINGTON, Virginia, January 14, 1869.

"*My Dear Rob:* The accompanying letter was inclosed to me by Lawrence Butler[2] with the request that I would forward it, as he did not know your address, and urge you to be present at his wedding. I do not know that I can say more, except to inform you that he says he has the very girl for you if you will come on. You must therefore decide the question according to your best judgment. General Hoke, from North Carolina, has also sent you his wedding-cards. We have missed you very much since your departure, and wished you back. I hope you got home comfortably and found all well. Drive all your work with judgment and energy, and when you have decided about the house, let me know. Tell Fitzhugh I have signed the insurance policy and sent it to Mr. Wickham for his signature, with the request that he forward it to Grubb & Williams. The weather still continues pleasant, and I fear we shall suffer for it by the late spring. There has so far been a great lack of snow, and consequently the wheat is exposed to the great changes of temperature. We are all as you left us. Custis, I think, looks better. No news. Mail heavy this morning. Love to F— and T—. With great affection,

"Your father,

"R. E. LEE.

"R. E. LEE, JR."

Some one wrote to General Lee suggesting that General Grant, then the president of the United States, should be invited to Washington College. His reply was as follows:

"LEXINGTON, Virginia, January 8, 1869.

"*My Dear Sir:* I am much obliged to you for your letter of the 29th ult., which I am sure has been prompted by the best motives. I should be glad if General Grant would visit Washington College, and I should endeavour to treat him with the courtesy and respect due the President of the United States; but if I were to invite him to do so, it might not be agreeable to him, and I fear my motives might be misunderstood at this time, both by himself and others, and that evil would result instead of good. I will, however, bear your suggestion in mind, and should a favourable opportunity offer I shall be glad to take advantage of it. Wishing you happiness and prosperity, I am, Very respectfully,

"Your obedient servant,

"R. E. LEE."

A lady living in New York wrote to General Lee in 1867, asking for a catalogue of Washington College and a copy of its charter and laws. She wished also to know whether or not the college was sectarian, and, if so, of what denomination. She intimated that she desired to make a donation to some institution of learning, and was rather inclined to select the Episcopal Theological Seminary, near Alexandria, Virginia. The president sent her the following reply to her letter:

"LEXINGTON, Virginia, June 24, 1867.
"MISS ANN UPSHUR JONES,
"No. 156 Lafayette Avenue, Brooklyn, N. Y.

"*My Dear Madam:* I have had the honour to receive your letter of the 17th inst., and I send to your address a catalogue of Washington College and a copy of its charter and laws. On the thirty-seventh page of the former, and the eleventh of the latter, you will find what is prescribed on the subject of religion. I do not know that it ever has been sectarian in its character since it was chartered as a college; but it certainly is not so now. Located in a Presbyterian community, it is natural that most of its trustees and faculty should be of that denomination, though the rector, president, and several of the professors are members of the Episcopal Church. It is furthest from my wish to divert any donation from the Theological Seminary at Alexandria, for I am well acquainted with the merits of that institution, have a high respect for its professors, and am an earnest advocate of its object. I only give you the information you desire, and wish you to follow your own preferences in the matter. With great respect,
"Your obedient servant,
"R. E. LEE."

In 1869 she wrote again, stating that she proposed breaking up housekeeping, that she had no family to whom to give her books, furniture, and silver, that she did not wish to sell them nor store them away, and had therefore determined to present them to the "greatest living man," and she begged him to accept them, or, if his house was already furnished, to make use of them in his college. To this letter he replied:

"LEXINGTON, Virginia, February 13, 1869.

"*My Dear Miss Jones:* After long and diligent inquiry I only this moment learned your address, and have been during this time greatly mortified at my inability to acknowledge the receipt and disposition of your valuable and interesting donation to Washington College. The books were arranged in the library on their arrival, the globes in the philosophical department, while the furniture, carpets, sofas, chairs, etc., have been applied to the furnishing of the dais of the audience-room of the new chapel, to the comfort and ornament of which they are a great addition. I have yet made no disposition of the plate and tableware, and they are still in the boxes in which they came. I inclose the resolution of thanks passed by the Board of Trustees of the College at their annual meeting, to which I beg to add my personal acknowledgments and grateful sense of your favour and kindness to this institution. It would give me great pleasure if you would visit Lexington at the commencement in June next, the third Thursday, that I might then show you the successful operation of the college. Mrs. Lee joins me in sentiments of esteem and regard, praying that the great and merciful God may throw around you His protecting care and love. I am, with great respect,

"Your obedient servant,

"R. E. LEE.

"MISS ANN UPSHUR JONES,
    "No. 38 Union Square, New York."

The plate, tableware, and a curious old work-table, for which no place could be found in the college, valuable only on account of their antiquity and quaintness, he finally allowed to be called his own.

When my mother hurriedly left her home in the spring of 1861, she found it impossible to carry away the valuable relics of General Washington which her father had inherited from Mount Vernon, and which had been objects of great interest at Arlington for more than fifty years. After the Federal authorities took possession of the place, the most valuable of these Mount Vernon relics were conveyed to Washington City and placed in the Patent Office, where they remained on exhibition for many years labelled "Captured from Arlington." They were then removed to the "National Museum," where they are now, but the card has been taken off. In 1869, a member of Congress suggested to my mother that she should apply to President Johnson to have them restored to her. In a letter from my father to this same gentleman, this bit of quiet humour occurs:

"LEXINGTON, Virginia, February 12, 1869.

". . . Mrs. Lee has determined to act upon your suggestion and apply to President Johnson for such of the relics from Arlington as are in the Patent Office. From what I have learned, a great many things formerly belonging to General Washington, bequeathed to her by her father, in the shape of books, furniture, camp equipage, etc., were carried away by individuals and are now scattered over the land. I hope the possessors appreciate them and may imitate the example of their original owners, whose conduct must at times be brought to their recollection by these silent monitors. In this way they will accomplish good to the country. . . ."

He refers to this same subject in a letter to the Honourable George W. Jones, Dubuque, Iowa:

". . . In reference to certain articles which were taken from Arlington, about which you inquire, Mrs. Lee is indebted to our old friend Captain James May for the order from the present administration for their restoration to her. Congress, however, passed a resolution forbidding their return. They were valuable to her as having belonged to her great-grandmother (Mrs. General Washington), and having been bequeathed to her by her father. But as the country desires them, she must give them up. I hope their presence at the capital will keep in the remembrance of all Americans the principles and virtues of Washington. . . ."

To the Honourable Thomas Lawrence Jones, who endeavoured to have the order to restore the relics to Mrs. Lee executed, the following letter of thanks was written:

"LEXINGTON, Virginia, March 29, 1869.
"HONOURABLE THOMAS LAWRENCE JONES,
"Washington City, District of Columbia.
"*My Dear Sir:* I beg to be allowed to tender you my sincere thanks for your efforts to have restored to Mrs. Lee certain family relics in the Patent Office in Washington. The facts related in your speech in the House of Representatives on the 3d inst., so far as known to me, are correct, and had I conceived the view taken of the matter by Congress I should have endeavoured to dissuade Mrs. Lee from applying for them. It may be a question with some whether the retention of these articles is more 'an insult,' in the language of the Committee on Public Buildings, 'to the loyal people of the United States,' than their restoration; but of this I am willing that they should be the judge, and since Congress has decided to keep them, she must submit. However, her thanks to you, sir, are not the less fervent for your kind intercession in her behalf, and with highest regards, I am, with great respect,
"Your obedient servant,
"R. E. LEE."

Washington's opinion of this transaction, if it could be obtained, would be of interest to many Americans![3]

CHAPTER XIX

LEE'S LETTERS TO HIS SONS

THE BUILDING OF ROBERT'S HOUSE—THE GENERAL AS A
RAILROAD DELEGATE—LIONISED IN BALTIMORE—CALLS
ON PRESIDENT GRANT—VISITS ALEXANDRIA—DECLINES
TO BE INTERVIEWED—INTERESTED IN HIS GRANDSON—
THE WASHINGTON PORTRAITS

My father, being very anxious that I should build a good house on
my farm, had agreed to supply the necessary means, and was interested in my plans and estimates. In a letter of February 18th, after
a long and full explanation of the arrangements for the purchase
of Smith's Island by Fitzhugh and myself, he writes:

"... I am glad that you are considering the construction of
your house and taking steps in the matter. Let me know how you
advance, the amount of its cost, etc., and when I can help you
.... The fine weather we have had this winter must have enabled
you to advance in your farm work and put you ahead in that, so
you will come out square, I hope. We are as usual, your poor
mother about the same, the girls well, and I tolerable. All unite
in much love.

"Truly and affectionately,

"R. E. Lee."

A week later he writes to me on the same subject:

"LEXINGTON, Virginia, February 27, 1869.

"*My Dear Son:* I am glad you have obtained a good pair of oxen. Try to get another pair to work with them. I will make good the deficit in my contribution. Your fences will be a great advantage to you, and I am delighted at the good appearance of your wheat. I hope it will continue to maturity. It is very probable, as you say, however, that it may fail in the grain. Should you find it so, would it not be well next year to experiment with phosphates? That must be the quality the land lacks. Have you yet heard from Mr. West about your house? What are the estimates? Let me know. The difficulty I fear now will be that the burning of the bricks may draw you away from your crops. You must try not to neglect them. What would the bricks cost if purchased? Ask F— to cut the lumber for you. I will furnish the funds to pay for it. I hope the break in the mill may not prove serious, and that you may be able to make up your delay in plowing occasioned by the necessary hauling. I am very glad to hear that you and F— can visit each other so easily. It will be advantageous to communicate with each other, as well as a pleasure. I suppose Tabb has not returned to the White House yet. I am delighted to hear that she and her boy are so well. They will make everything on the Pamunkey shine. We are all as usual.

"General Breckenridge[1] is on a visit to his sons and has been with us to-day. He will return to Baltimore Monday. He looks well, seems cheerful, and talks hopefully. All unite in love to you, and your acquaintances inquire regularly after you. I think of you very often, and wish I were nearer and could assist you. Custis is in better health this winter than he has been, and seems content, though his sisters look after him very closely. I have no news and never have. General B— saw Fitzhugh Lee in Alexandria. He told him he was a great farmer now, and when he was away, his father, who had now taken to the land, showed uncommon signs of management. Good-bye, my dear son. May you enjoy every happiness prays   Your affectionate father,

"R. E. LEE.

"ROBERT E. LEE, JR."

The completion of the railroad from the "White House" to "West Point" made communication between Fitzhugh and myself very easy. On February 11th, my father had become the proud and happy possessor of a grandson, which event gave him great joy. Mr. West, an architect of Richmond, had drawn me up plans and estimates for a house. My father had also sent me a plan drawn by himself. These plans I had submitted to several builders and sent their bids to him to examine and consider. In the following letter, he gives me his opinion:

"LEXINGTON, Virginia, March 21, 1869.

"*My Dear Rob:* I have received your two letters of the 3d and 9th insts., and would have answered the former before, but had written a few days before its date, and as our letters had been crossing each other, I determined to let them get right.

"First, as to Smith's Island, I merely want to fulfil the conditions of the sale as prescribed in the published notice. I should have required them of any other purchasers, and must require them of you. . . .

"Now as for the house: The estimates of your bidders are higher than I anticipated, and I think too high by at least $1,000. You see, there is about $1,000 difference between the highest and lowest of their offers you sent me. What does F— say about it? I am confident that I could build that house here for but little over $2,000, including materials, and I could do it there, if I could get two good workmen. But you are unaccustomed to building, and I would not advise you to undertake it, unless you could engage a proper foreman. If, therefore, I were in your place, I should reject all the offers, unless the one you had not received when you wrote suited better. I would not, however, give up my house, but procure the bricks either by purchase or by making them on the ground, as was most advantageous, and the shingles in the same way, and get all the lumber and flooring prepared. While preparing the necessary materials, I would see the builder that made the lowest offer, or any other that I preferred, and get him to revise his estimate and cut it down, leaving him a margin for profit; and when satisfied with his offer, accept it and set him to work.

"Now as for the means: I understood when you were here that you could manage the materials—that is, make arrangements for procuring the bricks, lumber, shingles, and flooring. Indeed, you might also get the lime and sand cheaper, perhaps, than the builder, and make a deduction on his bill. I can let you have funds to pay your contractor. If I did not understand you rightly—that is, if you cannot procure the materials, I can help you in them too. In fact, if you desire so much, I can let you have the whole amount, $3,500. You can have the use of it without interest, and return it to me when I require it, or sooner if you are able, as I take it from the fund I was saving for a homestead for your mother. At present, I cannot use it, and it is of no advantage to me, except its possession. Will that suit you? If it does not, let me know what will, and you shall have that, too. You must feel that it gives me pleasure to do anything I can for you, and if I had only myself to consider, you should have it unconditionally, but I must consider one person above all. I want you to do, therefore, just as you prefer. I want you to have the comfort of a house, but I do not wish to force one upon you, against your will or against your judgment. I merely wish you to feel that you can procure one without inconveniencing me. The only hesitation I have on the subject is that I think you ought to get a better house for $3,500 than I fear you will get. The house according to the first plan, in my opinion, ought not to cost more than that sum. But if you think the estimate is a fair one, and are satisfied, accept it and set to work. But consult Fitzhugh, and let me know when you want the money, and in what sums. Now that is plain, I hope, so keep this letter for reference, as I have not time to take a copy.

"We are all pretty well. Your mother has been troubled by a cold, but is over it I hope. The girls are well, and have as many opinions with as few acts as ever; and Custis so-so. We have had accounts of Lawrence Butler's wedding, and all were as gay as a flock of snowbirds. They regretted your absence. I will ask your mother to send you reports. I am tolerable and wish I could get down to see you. I had hoped to go down this spring, but I fear the dilatoriness of the workmen in finishing the house, and the necessity of my attending to it, getting the grounds inclosed and preparing the garden, will prevent me. I shall also have to superintend the moving. In fact, it never seems convenient for me to go away. Give much love to F—, my daughter Tabb, and grandson. I wonder what he will think of his grandpa. All unite in love, and I am, as always,

"Your affectionate father,   R. E. LEE.
"ROBERT E. LEE, JR."

In April, there are two letters written on the same day, to each of his sons, Fitzhugh and myself. I had determined for many reasons to postpone building my house for the present, which decision my father regrets. In the matter of Smith's Island, the arrangement proposed by my brother and myself for its purchase was agreed to by him:

"LEXINGTON, Virginia, April 17, 1869.

"*My Dear Rob:* I have written to Fitzhugh, informing him of my agreement to all the propositions in your joint letter, which I hope will be satisfactory to you. You can read my letter to him, so I will not repeat. I am sorry that you have concluded not to build, but if, in your judgment, that is the best course, I must be content. I do not wish you to hamper yourself with obligations, but to my mind building in the way proposed would not be onerous to you and would have given you the use of a house some years prior to the time that you may be able to erect one, and thus have added to your comfort, health, and probable ability to increase your resources from your farm. But I hope you have decided wisely, and should circumstances occur to cause you to change your views, you must not fail to let me know; for I shall at all times stand ready to help you to the extent of my ability, which I am now obliged to husband, lest I may become a burden to others. I am very glad to learn that your farm is promising better in the second cultivation of the fields, and feel assured that if treated judiciously it will recover its fertility and be remunerative. If you can perceive that you are progressing, though with a slow and regular step, you have cause for congratulation and encouragement; for there are many, I am sorry to say, that are worse off now than when they commenced at the end of the war, and have to begin again. Industry with economy must prevail in the end. There seems to be a necessity for my going to Baltimore next Tuesday, but I feel so poorly now that I do not know that I shall be able. If I do go, it will interfere materially with my proposed visit to you and Fitzhugh this spring, and I fear will put an end to it. I shall be obliged to spend some days in Alexandria on my return, and could not then delay my return here. I hope to see you both some time this summer, and, if I cannot get to you, you must come to me. I have been confined to the house for more than a week with a bad cold, the effects of which still cling to me, and, though I am better this morning, I am suffering. Your mother, too, I am sorry to say, has been suffering from the same cause, and has had to resort to medicine, as well as myself. You know that is bad for old people. Agnes has not been well, but Mildred is herself, and surrounded by her two fresh broods of kittens she would not call the king her uncle . . . God bless you, my dear son, prays

"Your affectionate father,   R. E. LEE.

"R.E. LEE, JR."

The letter to his son Fitzhugh is mostly upon business, but some of it relates to more interesting matters:

"LEXINGTON, Virginia, April 17, 1869.

"*My Dear Fitzhugh:* I expect to go to Baltimore next Tuesday, if well enough. The Valley Railroad Company are very anxious for me to accompany their delegation to that city with a view of obtaining from the mayor or council a subscription for their road, and, though I believe I can be of no service to them, they have made such a point of it that it would look ill-mannered and unkind to refuse. I wish I could promise myself the pleasure of returning by the 'White House,' but I cannot. If I go to Baltimore, I must take time to pay certain visits and must stop a while in Alexandria. I shall, therefore, from there be obliged to return here. If I could stop there on my way to Baltimore, which I cannot for want of time, I would then return by the 'White House.' I shall hope, however, to see you and Rob during the summer, if I have to go down immediately after commencement. But it is so inconvenient for me to leave home now that I cannot say. . . . Poor little Agnes also has been visited by Doctor Barton of late, but she is on the mend. 'Life' holds her own. Both of her cats have fresh broods of kittens, and the world wags cheerily with her. Custis is well, and Mary is still in New York, and all unite with me in much love to you and my daughter Tabb and my grandson. I hope the latter has not formed the acquaintance of his father in the same manner as Warrington Carter's child.

"Your affectionate father,   R. E. Lee.
"General Wm. H. Fitzhugh Lee."

In order to induce the city of Baltimore to aid them in building their railroad from Staunton to Salem, the Valley Railroad Company got together a large delegation from the counties through which it was proposed the line should pass, and sent it to that city to lay the plans before the mayor and council and request assistance. Among those selected from Rockbridge County was General Lee. Lexington at this time was one of the most inaccessible points in Virginia. Fifty miles of canal, or twenty-three of staging over a rough mountain road, were the only routes in existence. The one from Lynchburg consumed twelve hours, the other, from Goshen (a station on the Chesapeake & Ohio Railroad), from seven to eleven. On one occasion, a gentleman during his first visit to Lexington called on General Lee and on bidding him good-bye asked him the best way to get back to Washington.

"It makes but little difference," replied the General, "for whichever route you select, you will wish you had taken the other."

It was, therefore, the desire of all interested in the welfare of the two institutions of learning located in Lexington that this road should be built. My father's previous habits of life, his nature and his tastes made him averse to engaging in affairs of this character; but because of the great advantage to the college, should it be carried through, and at the earnest request of many friends of his and of the road, he consented to act. General John Echols, from Staunton, Colonel Pendleton, from Buchanan, Judge McLaughlin, from Lexington, were amongst those who went with him. While in Baltimore he stayed at the house of Mr. and Mrs. Samuel Tagart, whom he had met several summers at the White Sulphur Springs.

The delegation was invited to the floor of the Corn and Flour Exchange, to meet the business men of the city. My father, for the same reasons given above, earnestly desired to be excused from this part of the programme, and asked some of his friends to see Mr. John W. Garrett, the president of the Baltimore & Ohio Railroad, who had the delegation in charge, and try to have it so arranged. Mr. Garrett, however, was very positive.

"General Lee is a most interesting man; I think he had better come," was the message brought back to him.

As he appeared on the floor, which was filled with a great crowd, he was greeted with deafening cheers, and was soon surrounded by the thousands who had assembled there to see him. Everywhere that he appeared in the city he received an ovation. Sunday intervening, he attended service in the morning at St. Paul's church on Charles Street. When it became known that General Lee was there, large numbers collected to see him come out, waiting patiently and quietly until the congregation was dismissed. As he appeared at the door, all heads were uncovered and kept so until he had passed through the long lines extending down the street.

A reception was given by Mr. Tagart in his honour. There his friends crowded to see him, and the greatest affection and deference were shown him. He had lived in Baltimore about twenty years before this time, and many of his old friends were still there; besides, Baltimore had sent to the Army of Northern Virginia a large body of her noble sons, who were only too glad to greet once more their former commander. That he was still "a prisoner on parole," disfranchised from all civil rights, made their love for him stronger and their welcome the more hearty. On his return to Lexington, he was asked how he enjoyed his visit. With a sad smile, he said:

"Very much; but they would make too much fuss over the old rebel."

A few days after he came home, when one of his daughters remonstrated with him about the hat he was wearing, he replied:

"You don't like this hat? Why, I have seen a whole cityful come out to admire it!"

There is only a short note to my mother that I can find written during this trip:

"BALTIMORE, April 27, 1869.

"My Dear Mary: I am still at Mr. Tagart's, but propose going to-morrow to Ella's, and thence to Washington's, which will consume Wednesday and Thursday. If not obliged to return here, which I cannot tell till this evening or to-morrow morning, I will then go to Washington, where I shall be obliged to spend a day or two, and thence to Alexandria, so I shall not be able to return to Lexington till the last of next week. What has become of little Agnes? I have seen many of our old friends, of whom I will tell you on my return. I have bought you a little carriage, the best I could find, which I hope will enable you to take some pleasant rides. All send love. Give mine to Mildred, and Custis, and all friends. I am just about starting to Mrs. Baker's.

"Truly and affectionately,   R. E. LEE.

"MRS. M. C. LEE."

The "Ella" mentioned was Mrs. Sam George, of Baltimore, who as a girl had always been a pet and favourite of my father. She was a daughter of his first cousin, Mr. Charles Henry Carter, of "Goodwood," Prince George County, Maryland, and a schoolmate of my sister Mary. Their country place was near Ellicott City. He went there to see her, and from there to "Lynwood," near by, the seat of Washington Peter, my mother's first cousin and an intimate friend of us all.

On Saturday, my father, accompanied by Mr. and Mrs. Tagart, went to Washington on an early train. They drove immediately to the Executive Mansion and called on the President. This meeting was of no political significance whatever, but simply a call of courtesy. It had been intimated to General Lee that it would be most agreeable to General Grant to receive him. Mr. and Mrs. Tagart went with him, and they met there Mr. Motley, the newly appointed Minister to England. The interview lasted about fifteen minutes, and neither General Lee nor the President spoke a word on political matters. While in Washington my father was the guest of Mrs. Kennon, of Tudor Place, Georgetown Heights. On Sunday he dined with Mrs. Podestad and her husband, the Secretary of the Spanish Legation, who were old friends and relatives.

After leaving Washington, he stopped in Alexandria for several days, as the guest of Mrs. A. M. Fitzhugh. It was at her country place, "Ravensworth," about ten miles from town, that his mother had died, and there, in the old ivy-covered graveyard, she was buried. Mrs. Fitzhugh was the wife of my mother's uncle, Mr. William Henry Fitzhugh, who, having no children, had made my mother his heir. The intimacy between "Arlington" and "Ravensworth" was very close. Since Mr. Fitzhugh's death, which occurred some thirty years prior to this time, my father and mother and their children had been thrown a great deal with his widow, and "Aunt Maria," as we called her, became almost a member of the family. She had the greatest love and admiration for "Robert," sought his advice in the management of her estate, and trusted him implicitly. His brother, Admiral Sidney Smith Lee, came up from "Richland," his home on the Potomac near Acquia Creek, to meet him, and he found at Mrs. Fitzhugh's "Aunt Nannie"² and her son Fitz. Lee. This was the first time they had met each other since their parting in Richmond just after the war.

On his arrival in Alexandria my father had walked up from the wharf to "Aunt Maria's." He was recognised by a number of citizens, who showed him the greatest deference and respect. So many of his friends called upon him at Mrs. Fitzhugh's that it was arranged to have a reception for him at the Mansion House. For three hours a constant stream of visitors poured into the parlours. The reception was the greatest ovation that any individual had received from the people of Alexandria since the days of Washington. The next day, in Bishop Johns' carriage, he drove out to Seminary Hill to the home of Mr. Cassius F. Lee, his first cousin, where he spent the night. In the afternoon he went to see the bishop and his family—General Cooper and the Reverend Dr. Packard. The next morning, with Uncle Smith, he attended Ascension-Day services at Christ church, and was afterward entertained at a dinner-party given by Mr. John B. Daingerfield. Before he left Alexandria he called on Mr. John Janney, who was president of the Virginia Convention in 1861, when, as Colonel Lee, he appeared before it and accepted the command of the Virginia forces, organised and to be organised.

One evening a correspondent of the New York *Herald* paid him a visit for the purpose of securing an interview. The General was courteous and polite, but very firm. He stood during the interview, and finally dismissed the reporter, saying:

"I shall be glad to see you as a friend, but request that the visit may not be made in your professional capacity."

The same correspondent had tried to interview him, for his paper, while he was in Baltimore, but had failed.

My father was much amused at an occurrence that took place during this visit. Late one afternoon a visitor was announced. As the General was very tired, Uncle Smith Lee volunteered to relieve him. The visitor was found to be an Irishwoman, very stout and unprepossessing, who asked if she could see the General. The Admiral bowed, intimating that he was the desired person, when she said:

"My boy was with you in the war, honey, and I must kiss you for his sake." And with that she gave the Admiral an embrace and a kiss. Mr. Cassius Lee, to whom he told this, suggested that he should take General Fitz. Lee along to put forward in such emergencies.

My father's first letter after his return to Lexington was the following:

"LEXINGTON, Virginia, May 11, 1869.

"*My Dear Fitzhugh:* I reached here last Saturday, bringing Agnes and Miss Peyton with me from Staunton. Found everybody well and Custis better. I had, upon the whole, a pleasant visit, and was particularly glad to see again our old friends and neighbours in Alexandria and vicinity; though should have preferred to enjoy their company in a more quiet way. Your Uncle Smith came up to meet me, and your Aunt Nannie and Fitz. were there. I had not seen them since I parted from them in Richmond after the war. I wish I could have visited you and Rob and have seen my daughter and grandson; but that pleasure, I trust, is preserved for a future day. How is the little fellow? I was much relieved after parting from you to hear from the doctors that it was the best time for him to have the whooping-cough, in which opinion the 'Mim' concurs. I hope that he is doing well. Bishop Whittle will be here Friday next and is invited to stay with us. There are to be a great many preparatory religious exercises this week. A great feeling of religion pervades the young in the community, especially at the Virginia Military Institute. All send love.

"Your affectionate father,

"R. E. LEE."

Since his establishment in Lexington, General Lee had been a member of the vestry of Grace (Episcopal) church. At the council of 1868, which met at Lynchburg, he had been sent as a delegate, and spent three days there. This year the council was to meet in Fredericksburg, and he was again elected to represent his church. This was a busy time with him. The examinations were commencing, his new home was about ready to move into, and the preparations for the commencement exercises had to be made; yet he accepted the trust imposed upon him by his church and took a week out of his valuable time to perform it. In his next letter to his son, after writing on some Smith's Island business, he tells him of his proposed journey to Fredericksburg and of his regret at not being able to visit him as he had intended:

"LEXINGTON, Virginia, May 22, 1869.

"*My Dear Fitzhugh:* The weather here has been very hard on the corn-fields, and I hear of many having to be replanted. The wheat, so far, is very promising, and I am glad to hear that yours and Rob's is equally so. I have been elected by our little church to represent it at the coming convention, and have concluded to go. I shall leave for Fredericksburg Tuesday, June 1st, and shall endeavour while there to spend a night with your Uncle Smith, the only visit I shall be able to make him. It is very inconvenient for me to be absent at this time. The examination of the senior classes is in progress, and I must hasten back to attend as many as I can. The new house is about finished. The contractors say they will deliver the keys on Monday, the 31st inst. I will make arrangements to have it cleaned out during the week, so as to be able to move in on my return. The commencement, a busy time with me, is approaching, and we must try to be prepared. I shall not, therefore, be able to pay you a visit at this time, but hope Custis and I will be able to do so after the close of the session. I met Bishop Whittle at Lynchburg last convention, and was much pleased with him. My favourable impressions were much strengthened and increased by this visit here.

"I am so glad to learn that my little grandson is getting on so well with his whooping-cough. You must kiss him and his mother for me. We are all about the same. Your mother is becoming interested in her painting again, and is employing her brush for the benefit of our little church, which is very poor. She yet awhile confines herself to colouring photographs, and principally to those of General and Mrs. Washington, which are sold very readily. The girls are well, and have Miss Peyton with them still. Custis, I hope, is better. He is getting over some of his confinement with his classes now, which I hope will be of benefit to him. Give my love to Robert and tell my daughter Tabb I long to see her. All unite with me in affectionate love. I am,

"Truly your father,

"R. E. LEE."

These photographs that were being coloured by my mother were from the original portraits of General Washington by Peale and of Mrs. Washington by W—. These paintings hung at Mt. Vernon until the death of Mrs. Washington, and were then inherited by my grandfather, Mr. Custis. They were at "Arlington" till '61, when they were removed to "Ravensworth," where they remained until the end of the war. When they were being sent to Lexington, the boat carrying them on the canal between Lynchburg and Lexington sank. These pictures, with many others belonging to my mother, were very much injured and had to be sent to a restorer in Baltimore, who made them as good as ever, and they were finally safely hung in the president's house in Lexington, and are now in the library of the university. My mother coloured the photographs like these originals, and sold a great many, on account of their association rather than their merit.

There must have been some change of date in my father's plans, for though he said he would start on June 1st for Fredericksburg, his first and only letter from there was written on May 28th:

"FREDERICKSBURG, May 28, 1869.

"*My Dear Mary:* I reached here Tuesday night, the night after the morning I left you, about twelve o'clock, and found Major Barton at the depot, who conducted me to his house. The town seems very full of strangers, and I have met many acquaintances. I have seen no one yet from 'Cedar Grove,' and cannot learn whether any of them are coming. They are no doubt in distress there, for you may have heard of the death of Charles Stuart, on his way from Arkansas. He died at Lynchburg of congestive chills. Harriott Cazenove (his sister) went on to see him, but he died before her arrival. Rosalie, I heard, was at 'Cedar Grove,' Turbeville in Essex. I have delivered all your packages but Margaret's. Cassius Lee and all from the seminary are here. Sally came up from Gloucester, and also Mrs. Taliaferro. But I must tell you of all occurrences upon my return, and of all whom I have met. All friends inquire very particularly and affectionately after you, particularly your cousin, Mrs.—, who turns up ever day at all assemblies, corners, and places, with some anxious question on her mind upon which some mighty—though to me hidden—importance depends. Fitz. Lee arrived to-day, though I have not seen him yet. If I can accomplish it, I will go to 'Richland' to-morrow, Saturday, and spend Sunday, and take up my line of march Monday, in which event I hope to reach Lexington Wednesday morning, or rather Tuesday night, in the stage from Goshen. I may not be able to get away from the council before Monday. In that case, I shall not arrive before Wednesday night. Tell the girls there are quantities of young girls here and people of all kinds. I hope that you are all well, and that everything will be ready to move into our new house upon my arrival. I am obliged to stop. I am so much interrupted and occupied that, though I have tried to write ever since my arrival, I have been unable. Love to all.

> "Very affectionately,
>
> "R. E. LEE.

"MRS. R. E. LEE."

"Cedar Grove" was the plantation of Dr. Richard Stuart, in King George County, some fifty miles from Fredericksburg. His wife, a Miss Calvert, of "Riversdale," Maryland, was a near cousin of my mother, had been her bridesmaid, and the two families had been intimate all their lives. All the persons mentioned by my father were cousins and friends, several of them old neighbours from Alexandria and the Theological Seminary near by.

From Fredericksburg, after the completion of his duties at the council, he went to "Richland" on the Potomac, near Acquia Creek, where his brother Smith was then living. This meeting was a great pleasure to them both, for two brothers were never more devoted. This was the last time they saw one another alive, as Smith died two months afterward.

CHAPTER XX

THE NEW HOME IN LEXINGTON

NUMEROUS GUESTS—FURTHER SOJOURNS AT DIFFERENT
BATHS—DEATH OF THE GENERAL'S BROTHER, SMITH
LEE—VISITS TO "RAVENSWORTH" AND "THE WHITE
HOUSE"—MEETINGS WITH INTERESTING PEOPLE AT WHITE
SULPHUR SPRINGS—DEATH OF PROFESSOR PRESTON

ON my father's return to Lexington the new house was ready. It adjoined the one he had been occupying, so the distance was not great and the transfer was easily accomplished. It was much larger and more comfortable than the one given up. My mother's room was on the first floor and opened out on the veranda, extending three sides of the house, where she could be rolled in her chair. This she enjoyed intensely, for she was very fond of the open air, and one could see her there every bright day, with Mrs. "Ruffner," a much petted cat, sitting on her shoulder or cradled in her lap. My father's favourite seat was in a deep window of the dining-room, from which his eyes could rest on rolling fields of grass and grain, bounded by the ever-changing mountains. After his early and simple dinner, he usually took a nap of a few minutes, sitting upright in his chair, his hand held and rubbed by one of his daughters. There was a new stable, warm and sunny, for Traveller and his companion, "Lucy Long," a cow-house, wood-shed, garden, and yard, all planned, laid out, and built by my father. The increased room enabled him to invite a greater number to visit him, and this summer the house was full.

In answer to a letter from me on business, which reached him during commencement week, he writes:

"LEXINGTON, Virginia, June 19, 1869.

"*My Dear Son:* I have just received your letter of the 10th, and have only time for a word. . . . I hope all things are going well with you both. With the improvement of your farm, proceeds will increase, and, with experience, judgment, and economy, will augment greatly. You will have to get married if you wish to prosper, and must therefore make arrangements to build your house this fall. If I live through this coming week, I wish to pay you and F— a visit the week following, about July 1st. I am trying to persuade Custis to accompany me, but he has not yet responded. I am very much occupied with examinations, visitors, arrangements, etc.

"All are well, and would send love if accessible. Mildred is full of housekeeping and dresses, and the house is full of young ladies—Misses Jones, Albert, Burwell, Fairfax, and Wickham; others in expectation. Good-bye,

"Affectionately your father,

"R. E. LEE.

"ROBERT E. LEE, JR."

Ten days later, he writes to his son, Fitzhugh, giving up his proposed visit to him at this time, expressing his regrets at the necessity, and telling his reasons for so doing:

"LEXINGTON, Virginia, June 30, 1869.

"*My Dear Fitzhugh:* This is the day that I had proposed to visit you, but I find it impossible to get away. I find a great deal to do in closing up the past session and in preparing for the new. In addition, our college officers have all been changed—proctor, clerk, treasurer, librarian—and the new incumbents enter upon their duties to-morrow. I shall have to be with them some days to initiate and install them. That would only delay me, but then on the 15th proximo the Educational Association of Virginia will meet here, and I should not be able to return in time. As I have never attended any of their meetings when elsewhere, if I were to go away when appointed here it would look as if I wished to avoid them, which is not the case. After that is over, I must locate your poor mother at the Baths,[1] which she has made up her mind to visit, and prepare to go myself to the White Sulphur, the waters of which I want to drink for three or four weeks. So I do not see how I could get to the Pamunkey before the fall. I want to get there very much to see you all, and, as far as my personal predilections are concerned, would rather go there than to the White; but the doctors think it would not be so beneficial to me, and I am obliged now to consider my health. I propose, therefore, that you bring Tabb and the baby up to the mountains and leave them either at the Baths with 'the Mim' or with me, if you cannot remain. Tell Rob, if he can, he must also come and see us. If he were here, now, he would find very pleasant company, Misses Jones, Albert, Kirkland, Burwell, Fairfax, and Wickham, all in the house, with others out of it. They are so much engaged with the collegiates that Custis and I see but little of them, but he could compete with the *yearlings,* which we cannot. Tell my daughter Tabb, her father is here, very well, and dined with us yesterday. Give my much love to grandson. He must not forget me. I have a puppy and a kitten for him to play with. All send love.

"Truly your father,

"R. E. LEE.

"GENERAL WILLIAM H. FITZHUGH LEE."

In a letter dated Lexington, Virginia, July 9th, he gives a further account of his plans for the summer:

". . . I have delivered your letter to Mildred, who has just returned from a visit to the University of Virginia, where she saw a great many persons and met with a great deal of pleasure. She ought to be, and I believe is, satisfied with commencements for this year, having participated in three. I am sorry to tell you that I cannot go down to the Pamunkey this summer as I had intended; . . . I had hoped to be able, after the conclusion of the commencement exercises of Washington College, to visit the Pamunkey, and to return by the 15th inst. so as to be present at the Convention of the Teachers of Virginia, which assembles here on that day; but I was detained here so long that I found I would be unable to accomplish what I desired. Custis, who was to have accompanied me, will go down in a day or two. . . .

"About the 20th of this month I shall go to the Rockbridge Baths with Mrs. Lee, who wishes to try the waters again, and after seeing her comfortably located, if nothing prevents, I shall go with Mildred and Agnes to the White Sulphur for a few weeks. . . . It is delightfully quiet here now. Both institutions have closed, and all are off enjoying their holiday. I should like to remain, if I could. Colonels Shipp and Harding have gone to get married, report says. Colonel Lyle and Captain Henderson, it is said, will not return. Captain Preston having been appointed professor at William and Mary, we shall necessarily lose him, but Colonel Allan will be back, and all the rest. We are as well as you left us. The girls had several of their friends at commencement. All have departed except Miss Fairfax and Miss Wickham. The election is over and the town is tranquil."

The quiet and rest which he so much desired, and which he was enjoying when he wrote, did not long remain his. He had just gotten my mother comfortably settled at the Baths, when he received the news of the sudden death of his brother Smith. He went at once to Alexandria, hoping to be in time for the burial. From there he writes my mother:

"ALEXANDRIA, July 25, 1869.

"*My Dear Mary:* I arrived here last evening, too late to attend the burial of my dear brother, an account of which I have clipped from the Alexandria *Gazette* and inclose to you. I wish you would preserve it. Fitz. and Mary went up to 'Ravensworth' the evening of the funeral services, Friday, 23d, so that I have not seen them, but my nephew Smith is here, and from him I have learned all particulars. The attack of his father was short, and his death apparently unexpected until a short time before it occurred. Mary[2] was present, and I hope of some comfort to her uncle and assistance to her aunt. Fitz. came here the afternoon of his father's death, Thursday, 22d, made all arrangements for the funeral, went out to 'Ravensworth' to announce the intelligence to our aunt. He carried down, Friday morning, on the steamer, Mrs. Cooper and Jennie, to stay with his mother, and returned that afternoon with his father's remains, which were committed to earth as you will see described.

"John returned the next morning, yesterday, in the mail-boat, to his mother, with whom Dan stayed. Robert arrived this morning and has gone to 'Ravensworth' to announce my arrival. I shall remain here until I see or hear from Fitz., for, as you will see by the *Gazette's* account, the last resting-place of the body has not been determined upon. Fitz., I understand, wishes it interred at Hollywood, Richmond; Nannie at the cemetery here, where her father, mother, and daughter are buried; and Mrs. Fitzhugh at 'Ravensworth.' I think Nannie's wishes should be consulted. I shall probably leave to-day or to-morrow, and, after seeing all that remains to us of our dear brother deposited in its last earthly home, and mingling my sorrow for a brief season with that of his dear wife and children, I shall return to you. Please send this letter after perusal to Agnes and Mildred, as I shall be unable to write to them. I am staying at the Mansion House. Our Aunt Maria did not come down to the funeral services, prevented, I fear, by her rheumatic attack. May God bless us all and preserve us for the time when we, too, must part, the one from the other, which is now close at hand, and may we all meet again at the footstool of our merciful God, to be joined by His eternal love never more to separate.

"Most truly and affectionately,

"R. E. LEE.

"MRS. M. C. LEE."

The loss of his brother was a great sorrow to him. They were devoted to each other, having always kept warm their boyish love. Smith's admiration for and trust in my father were unbounded, and it was delightful to see them together and listen to the stories of the happy long ago they would tell about each other. No one could be near my Uncle Smith without feeling his joyful influence. My sister Mary, who knew him long and well, and who was much attached to him, thus writes:

"No one who ever saw him can forget his beautiful face, charming personality, and grace of manner which, joined to a nobility of character and goodness of heart, attracted all who came in contact with him, and made him the most generally beloved and popular of men. This was especially so with women, to whom his conduct was that of a *preux chevalier,* the most chivalric and courteous; and, having no daughters of his own, he turned with the tenderest affection to the daughters of his brother Robert."

After all the arrangements connected with this sad event had been completed, my father went up to "Ravensworth" to see "Aunt Maria," who had always been a second mother to his brother. There, amid the cool shades of this lovely old home, he rested for a day or two from the fatigues of travel and the intense heat. During this visit, as he passed the room in which his mother had died, he lingered near the door and said to one present:

"Forty years ago, I stood in this room by my mother's death-bed! It seems now but yesterday!"

While here he determined to go back to Lexington *via* Richmond, and to run down thence to the "White House" to see his grandson. He arrived there on Friday, July 30th. On Sunday he wrote to my mother:

"WHITE HOUSE, NEW KENT, August 1, 1869.

"*My Dear Mary:* I arrived here on Friday last and found them all well. Our daughter Tabb has not been altogether well, and shows its effects. Her baby, I think, would also be improved by mountain air. I have therefore persuaded her to accompany me and join you at the Baths. We shall leave Richmond, if nothing prevents, on Tuesday morning, 3d inst., and hope to reach the Baths that evening in the stage from Goshen. I have written to Mr. Peyton, requesting him to prepare a good room for Tabb and her little family as near you as convenient, and trust we may reach there in health and comfort at the time appointed. I hope I shall find you well and comfortable, and Markie in the enjoyment of every good. How are the poor little children? My previous letters will have informed you of everything important. I will supply all omissions when I see you. Custis is here, much improved. I have not yet seen Rob. Farmers here are threshing out their wheat, which occupies them closely. Fitzhugh's is turning out well, and he hopes to gather a fair crop. Robert came up last Wednesday with his friend Mr. Dallam, and went down Thursday. He was very well. Custis arrived Saturday week. Mr. Kepler is here and will preach at St. Peter's this morning. I hope to attend. Mr. Kepler says his health is much improved. Fitzhugh doses him with cholagogue. Goodbye.

Affectionately yours,
"R. E. LEE."

St. Peter's was the old Colonial church a few miles away, in which General Washington and Mrs. Custis were married about one hundred years prior to this time. Mr. Kepler, the pastor, preached there twice a month. He lived in Richmond, and, to keep him free from fever-and-ague, my brother dosed him freely with cholagogue whenever he came down into the malarial country. I came up from Romancoke Sunday morning, arriving in time to be present at the christening of my nephew, which ceremony was decided on rather hurriedly in order that the grandfather might stand as godfather. After returning from the morning service at St. Peter's, where we all went, it was decided that the mother and child should go to the mountains with my father. As there were some preparations for the summer to be made, his daughter and her baby went to Petersburg that afternoon, agreeing to meet the General in Richmond Monday night and start for the Rockbridge Baths Tuesday morning. On Monday, he writes to a friend, with whom he had intended to stop for a day on his way back to Lexington:

"WHITE HOUSE, NEW KENT COUNTY,
"August 1, 1869.

". . . I had promised myself the pleasure of seeing you on my way to Lexington, of spending with you one short day to cheer and refresh me; but I shall travel up in a capacity that I have not undertaken for many years—as escort to a young mother and her infant, and it will require the concentration of all my faculties to perform my duties even with tolerable comfort to my charge. . . . I go up with my daughter, I may say this time, too, my youngest daughter[3], to place her with her mama at the Rockbridge Baths, the waters of which I hope will invigorate both mother and child, who have been wearied and weakened by the long attack of whooping-cough from which the latter has suffered. I came down from Richmond to spend Sunday and was fortunate enough to find here my three sons, but I am sorry to say but one daughter. . . . Most truly yours,

"R. E. LEE."

Monday night was spent in Richmond. It was soon known that General Lee was at the Exchange Hotel, and great numbers came to call upon him, so that he was compelled to hold an informal reception in the large parlours. The next day, with his "new daughter" and her baby, he started for the Baths, where they arrived safely the same night. Then he proceeded to carry out his original plan for the summer, and went with his two daughters to the White Sulphur Springs. From there he writes to his wife:

"WHITE SULPHUR SPRINGS,
"GREENBRIER COUNTY, West Virginia, August 10, 1869.
"*My Dear Mary:* I received this morning your *addenda* to Annie Wickham's letter inclosing Custis's. I also received by same mail a letter from Mr. Richardson, reiterating his request to insert my

portrait in my father's Memoirs, saying that it was by the desire 'of many mutual friends' on the ground of its 'giving additional interest to the work, and increasing its sale.' That may or may not be so; at any rate, I differ from them. Besides, there is no good portrait accessible to him, and the engraving in the 'Lee Family' I think would be an injury to any book. His recent proposition of inserting my portrait where the family history is given takes from it a part of my obligation, and if it were believed that such an addition would add to the interest of the book, I should assent. I have so told him, and that I would write to you for your suggestions, and to ask whether you could send him a portrait worth inserting. What do you think?

"There is to be a grand concert here to-night for the benefit of our church at Lexington. It is gotten up by Miss Mary Jones and other kind people here, and the proposition is so favourably received that I hope a handsome sum will be realised.

"The girls are well. I do not know how long they will continue so. They seem to be foot-free. A great many visitors were turned off last night—no room for them! A grand ball in honour of Mr. Peabody is to come off to-morrow, after which it is supposed there will be more breathing-space. I have seen Mr. and Mrs. Charles Ridgely of 'Hampton' since I wrote, also numerous other acquaintances. I should prefer more quiet. How is my daughter Tabb? Mother and son are improving, I trust. I hope you and Markie are also doing well. No change in myself as yet. The girls would send love if I could find them.   Affectionately yours,

"Mrs. R. E. Lee.   R. E. Lee."

A few days later he writes:

"White Sulphur Springs, August 14, 1869.

"*My Dear Mary:* I received last night your letter of the 13th—very prompt delivery—and am very glad to learn of the well-doing of all with you. I am particularly pleased to hear that our daughter and grandson are improving, and should you find them not benefiting I wish you would urge them to try some other springs, for I have it greatly to heart that they should receive all possible advantage from their summer trip. I hope Markie will be benefited by the Red Sweet. The water is considered a great tonic, but I fear none will be warm enough for her but the *Hot*. If I cannot get over to see her, I will notify her of our departure from here, which will be in about two weeks. I have received a letter from Fitz. Lee, saying that Mary would leave 'Richlands' last Tuesday, 10th inst., for 'Ravensworth,' which I presume she did, as his letter was postmarked that day at Acquia Creek, and was probably mailed by him, or one of the boys, on putting her aboard the mail-boat. You will be glad to learn that the proceeds of the concert for our church at Lexington netted $605, which has been subsequently increased to $805 by Messrs. Corcoran and Peabody with a donation of $100 from each. For all of this I am extremely grateful.

"As regards the portrait for Mr. Richardson, you must do as you please. I shall not write to him any more on the subject. Unless the portrait is good and pleasing, I think it will be an injury to the book. I have had a visit since commencing this letter from a Mrs. William *Bath*, of New Orleans, who showed me a wreath, made in part, she says, of my, your and Mildred's hair, sent her by you more than two years ago. She says she sent you a similar one at the time, but of this I could tell her nothing, for I recollect nothing about it. She says her necessities now compel her to put her wreath up to raffle, and she desired to know whether I had any objection to her scheme, and whether I would head the list. All this, as you may imagine, is extremely agreeable to me, but I had to decline her offer of taking a chance in her raffle.

"Miss Mary Jones has gone to the Sweet. Tell Miss Belle I wish she were coming here. I shall be glad to see Mrs. Caskie. Mildred has her picture. The girls are always busy at something, but never ready. The Stuarts have arrived. Mrs. Julia is improving very perceptibly. Love to all.

"R. E. LEE."

The "Markie" referred to in each of the above letters was Martha Custis Williams, a great-niece of my grandfather, Mr. Custis, who had for many years lived at Arlington with her uncle. The "little children" were her motherless nieces, whom she had brought that summer to the mountains for their health. General Lee had been engaged for some time in bringing out a third edition of his father's "Memoirs of the War of '76 in the Southern States." It was now in the hands of his publisher, Mr. Richardson, of New York. To this edition he had added a sketch of the famous "Light Horse Harry," written by himself. It was to his publisher's proposition of placing his portrait in the "Introduction" to the new work that he at first objected, and then agreed, as stated in the two letters just given. The season of '69 is still noted in the annals of the White Sulphur as having had in its unusually large company so many noted and distinguished men. Mr. George Peabody and Mr. W. W. Corcoran, the two great philanthropists, were among them and helped to enlarge the receipts of the concert for the benefit of the little Episcopal church in Lexington, of which General Lee was a member and a vestryman.

By the last of August he was back again in Lexington, making arrangements for the home-coming of his wife and her party from the Baths. Here is part of another letter written soon after his arrival home, some lines of which (apparently relating to the servants) have been partially obliterated by time:

"LEXINGTON, Virginia, August 31, 1869.

"*My Dear Mary:* I received this evening your note by Miss Mays. You had better come up whenever agreeable to your party. . . we can only try them and make the best of them. Alice, when she gets well, will return if wanted. If Cousin Julia[4] will return with you, you can see her here as well as there, and we can all have that pleasure. If she will not, you had better remain with her as long as she will stay. Mrs. Pratt died to-day at 12:30 P. M.

"I received a letter to-day from Edward Childe, saying that he and Blanche would leave Liverpool in the *Java* on September 4th, and after spending a few days in the North, would come to Lexington. He will probably reach Boston about September 15th, so that they may be expected here from the 20th to the 30th of September. I am anxious for them to see our daughter and grandson and all our sons. Give my best love to all with you. The girls would send love, but a 'yearling' and a 'leader of the herd'[5] occupy them. Affectionately yours,

"R. E. LEE.

"MRS. M. C. LEE."

This session of Washington College opened with very favourable prospects. The number of students was larger than ever before, every southern, and some northern States being represented. The new chairs of instruction which had been instituted were now in good working order, their professors were comfortably established, and the entire machinery of the institution was running well and smoothly. The president commenced to see some of the results of his untiring energy and steady work. He had many plans which lack of funds prevented him from carrying out. One of them was a School of Commerce in which a student, while following the branches which would discipline and cultivate the mind, might also receive special instruction and systematic training in whatever pertained to business in the largest sense of the term. Another was a School of Medicine, the plan for which, with full details, was drawn up under his eye, and kept in readiness until the funds of the institution should permit of its being carried into effect.

His meeting with Mr. Peabody at the White Sulphur Springs attracted that gentleman's attention to the college and to his work as its president. To a request for his photograph to be placed in the Peabody Institute among the friends of its founder, he sends with the likeness the following note:

"WASHINGTON COLLEGE, Virginia, September 25, 1869.
"F. POOLE, Secretary Peabody Institute,
"Peabody, Massachusetts.

"*Dear Sir:* In compliance with your request, I send a photograph of myself, the last that has been taken, and shall feel honoured in its being placed among the 'friends' of Mr. Peabody, for, though they can be numbered by millions, yet all can appreciate the man who has illustrated his age by his munificent charities during his life, and by his wise provisions for promoting the happiness of his fellow-creatures.

"Very respectfully, your obedient servant,

"R. E. LEE."

My father's family was now comfortably established in their new home, and had the usual number of friends visiting them this autumn. In due time Edward Childe, Blanche, and "Duckie," their little dog, arrived and remained a week or two. The last-named member of the party was of great interest. He was very minute, very helpless, and received more attention than the average baby. He had crossed the Atlantic in fear and trembling, and did not apparently enjoy the new world. His utter helplessness and the great care taken of him by his mistress, his ill-health and the unutterable woe of his countenance greatly excited my father's pity. After he went away, he often spoke of him, and referred to him, I find, in one of his letters. During this trip to America, Edward and his wife, carrying the wretched "Duckie" with them, paid their visit to the "White House."

This autumn the "little carriage" my father mentioned having purchased for my mother in Baltimore was put into use. He frequently drove out in it with my mother, his new daughter, and grandson. "Lucy Long," under his guidance, carefully carried them over the beautiful hills around Lexington. One afternoon, while paying a visit with his daughter, Tabb, to Colonel William Preston Johnston, who lived two miles down the river, in pulling up a steep ascent to the front door, "Lucy" fell, choked into unconsciousness by too tight a collar. My father jumped out, hastily got off the harness, and on perceiving the cause of the accident reproached himself vehemently for his carelessness and thoughtlessness. He was very much distressed at this accident, petted his mare, saying to her in soothing tones that he was ashamed of himself for having caused her all this pain after she had been so faithful to him.

His rides on Traveller in which he delighted so much were not so frequent now. He was not so strong as he had been through the spring and summer, and, indeed, during November he had a very severe attack of cold, from which he did not recover for several weeks. However, during the beautiful days of October he was often seen out in the afternoons on his old gray. His favourite route was the road leading to the Rockbridge Baths. A year previous to this time, he would sometimes go as far as the Baths and return in an afternoon, a trip of twenty miles. A part of this road led through a dense forest. One afternoon, as he told the story himself, he met a plain old soldier in the midst of these woods, who, recognising the General, reined in his horse and said:

"General Lee, I am powerful glad to see you, and I feel like cheering you."

The General replied that this would not do, as they were all alone, only two of them, and there would be no object whatever in cheering. But the old soldier insisted that he must, and, waving his hat about his head, cried out:

"Hurrah for General Lee!" and kept repeating it. As the General rode away he continued to hear the cheers until he was out of sight.

On another afternoon, as Professors White and Nelson, taking a horseback ride, approached the summit of a long hill, they heard behind them the sound of a horse's feet running rapidly. In a few moments General Lee appeared on Traveller at full speed. On joining his friends he reined up and said:

"I thought a little run would be good for Traveller."

He often gave his horse a "breather," as he called it. The animal was so strong and powerful that he chafed at restraint, and, unless ridden regularly and hard, had a very disagreeable, fretful trot. After a good gallop up one of the long Rockbridge hills he would proceed at a quiet walk.

The tenderness in my father's heart for children I have already often remarked upon. One afternoon two little girls, the daughters of two of his professors, were riding on a gentle old horse up and down one of the back streets of the town, fearing to go far from home. The General, starting out on his afternoon ride, came up with them, and knowing them well, said gaily:

"Come with me, little girls, and I will show you a beautiful ride."

Only too delighted, they consented to go. He took them out beyond the fair-grounds, from which point there is one of the grandest stretches of mountain scenery in the world. One of the little maidens had her face tied up, as she was just recovering from the mumps. He pretended that he was much alarmed lest his horse should catch them from her, and kept saying:

"I hope you won't give Traveller the mumps!" and "What shall I do if Traveller gets the mumps?"

An hour later, this party was seen returning, the two little girls in sun-bonnets on the one old, sleepy horse, and General Lee by their side on Traveller, who was stepping very proudly, as if in scorn of his lowly companion. My father took the children to their homes, helped them to dismount, took a kiss from each, and, waving a parting salute, rode away. It was such simple acts of kindness and consideration that made all children confide in him and love him.

Soon after the attack of cold mentioned above, he writes to his son Fitzhugh, then at the "White House" with his family:

"LEXINGTON, Virginia, December 2, 1869.

"*My Dear Fitzhugh:* . . . Your letters to Custis told us of your well-doing. I want to see you all very much, and think the sight of my daughter and grandson would do me good. I have had a wretched cold, the effects of which have not left me, but I am better. The doctors still have me in hand, but I fear can do no good. The present mild weather I hope will be beneficial, enabling me to ride and be in the open air. But Traveller's trot is harder to me than it used to be and fatigues me. We are all as usual—the women of the family very fierce and the men very mild. Custis has been a little unwell, but is well regulated by his sisters. Neither gaiety nor extravagance prevails amongst us, and the town is quiet. Our community has been greatly grieved at the death of Mr. Frank Preston, to whom I was much attached and for whom I had a high esteem. Give my love to Bertus. Tell him I hope Mrs. Taylor will retain one of her little daughters for him. She always reserves the youngest of the flock for Custis, as he is not particular as to an early date.

"Your affectionate father,

"R. E. LEE.

"GENERAL WILLIAM H. F. LEE."

Frank Preston, at the time of his death, was professor of Greek at William and Mary College. He had been, prior to his appointment to that position, an assistant professor at Washington College. He was a native of Lexington, a son of Colonel Thomas L. Preston, who was for so long a time professor at the Virginia Military Institute. A brilliant scholar, trained in the best German universities, and a gentleman in the highest sense of the word, Frank had served his State in the late war, and had left an arm on the heights of Winchester. On hearing of his death, President Lee issued the following announcement:

"WASHINGTON COLLEGE, November 23, 1869.

"The death of Professor Frank Preston, a distinguished graduate, and late Associate Professor of Greek in this college, has caused the deepest sorrow in the hearts of the institution.

"Endowed with a mind of rare capacity, which had been enriched by diligent study and careful cultivation, he stood among the first in the State in his pursuit in life.

"We who so long and so intimately possessed his acquaintance, and so fully enjoyed the privilege of his companionship, feel especially his loss, and grieve profoundly at his death; and we heartily sympathise with his parents and relations in their great affliction, and truly participate in the deep sorrow that has befallen them.

"With the view of testifying the esteem felt for his character and the respect due to his memory, all academic exercises will be suspended for the day, and the faculty and students are requested to attend in their respective bodies his funeral services at the Presbyterian church, at eleven o'clock, to pay the last sad tribute of respect to his earthly remains, while cherishing in their hearts his many virtues.

"R. E. LEE, President."

CHAPTER XXI

FAILING HEALTH

THE GENERAL DECLINES LUCRATIVE POSITIONS IN NEW YORK
AND ATLANTA—HE SUFFERS FROM AN OBSTINATE COLD—
LOCAL GOSSIP—HE IS ADVISED TO GO SOUTH IN THE SPRING
OF 1870—DESIRES TO VISIT HIS DAUGHTER ANNIE'S GRAVE

AFTER General Lee had accepted the presidency of Washington College, he determined to devote himself entirely to the interest and improvement of that institution. From this resolution he never wavered. An offer that he should be at the head of a large house to represent southern commerce, that he should reside in New York, and have placed at his disposal an immense sum of money, he declined, saying:

"I am grateful, but I have a self-imposed task which I must accomplish. I have led the young men of the South in battle; I have seen many of them die on the field; I shall devote my remaining energies to training young men to do their duty in life."

To a request from some of his old officers that he should associate himself with a business enterprise in the South, as its president, he replied with the following letter:

"LEXINGTON, Virginia, December 14, 1869.
"GENERAL J. B. GORDON, President,
"Southern Life Insurance Company,
"Atlanta, Georgia.
"*My Dear General:* I have received your letter of the 3d inst., and am duly sensible of the kind feelings which prompted your pro-

posal. It would be a great pleasure to me to be associated with you, Hampton, B. H. Hill, and the other good men whose names I see on your list of directors, but I feel that I ought not to abandon the position I hold at Washington College at this time, or as long as I can be of service to it. Thanking you for your kind consideration, for which I know I am alone indebted for your proposition to become president of the Southern Life Insurance Company, and with kindest regards to Mrs. Gordon and my best wishes for yourself, I am,

"Very truly yours,

"R. E. LEE."

His correspondence shows that many like propositions were made to him.

The Christmas of '69, neither my brother nor myself was with him. Knowing of our plans in that respect, he wrote before the holidays to Fitzhugh, wishing us both the compliments of the season and a pleasant time in the visits we were going to make:

"LEXINGTON, Virginia, December 18, 1869.

"*My Dear Fitzhugh:* I must begin by wishing you a pleasant Christmas and many, many Happy New Years, and may each succeeding year bring to you and yours increasing happiness. I shall think of you and my daughter and my grandson very often during the season when families are generally united, and though absent from you in person, you will always be present in mind, and my poor prayers and best wishes will accompany you all wherever you are. Bertus will also be remembered, and I hope that the festivities of 'Brandon' will not drive from his memory the homely board at Lexington. I trust that he will enjoy himself and find some one to fill that void in his heart as completely as he will the one in his— system. Tell Tabb that no one in Petersburg wants to see her half as much as her papa, and now that her little boy has his mouth full of teeth, he would not appear so *lonesome* as he did in the summer. If she should find in the 'Burg' a 'Duckie' to take his place, I beg that she will send him up to me.

"I duly received your letter previous to the 12th inst., and requested some of the family who were writing about that time to inform you. When I last wrote, I could not find it on my table and did not refer to it. 'The Mim' says you excel her in counting, if you do not in writing, but she does not think she is in your debt. I agree with you in your views about Smith's Island, and see no advantage in leasing it, but wish you could sell it to advantage. I hope the prospects may be better in the spring. Political affairs will be better, I think, and people will be more sanguine and hopeful. You must be on the alert. I wish I could go down to see you, but think it better for me to remain here. To leave home now and return during the winter would be worse for me. It is too cold for your mother to travel now. She says she will go down in the spring, but you know what an exertion it is for her to leave home, and the inconvenience, if not the suffering, is great. The anticipation, however, is pleasing to her and encourages hope, and I like her to enjoy it, though am not sanguine that she will realise it. Mildred is probably with you, and can tell you all about us. I am somewhat reconciled to her absence by the knowledge of the benefit that she will be to Tabb. Tell the latter that she [Mildred] is modest and backward in giving advice, but that she has mines of wealth on that subject, and that she [Tabb] must endeavour to extract from her her views on the management of a household, children, etc., and the proper conduct to be observed toward husbands and the world in general. I am sure my little son will receive many wise admonitions which he will take open-mouthed. I have received a letter from your Uncle Carter telling me of his pleasant visit to you and of his agreeable impressions of his nephew and new niece. He was taken very sick in Richmond and delayed there so long that he could not be present at Wm. Kennon's wedding, and missed the festivities at his neighbour Gilliam's and at Norwood. Indeed, he had not recoverd his strength when Lucy wrote a few days ago, and her account makes me very uneasy about him. I am glad Rob has so agreeable a neighbour as General Cooke, and I presume it is the North Carolina brigadier.[1] When you go to Petersburg, present my kind regards to Mr. and Mrs. Bolling, 'Miss Melville,' and all friends. All here unite with me in love to you, Tabb, and the boy, in which Mildred is included.

"Your affectionate father,

"R. E. LEE.

"GENERAL WILLIAM H. F. LEE."

In a note, written the day after, acknowledging a paper sent to him to sign, he says:

". . . I wrote to you yesterday, Saturday, in reply to your former letter, and stated the reasons why I could not visit you. Your mother has received Mildred's letter announcing her arrival in Richmond and will write to her there. I can only repeat my love and prayers that every blessing may attend you and yours. We are as usual.

"Truly and affectionately,

"R. E. LEE.

"GENERAL WILLIAM H. F. LEE."

The attack of cold from which my father suffered in October had been very severe. Rapid exercise on horseback or on foot produced pain and difficulty in breathing. After he was considered by most of his friends to have gotten well over it, it was very evident to his doctors and himself that there was a serious trouble about the heart, and he often had great weariness and depression. He complained but little, was often very bright and cheerful, and still kept up his old-time fun and humour in his conversation and letters, but his letters written during this year to his immediate family show that he was constantly in pain and had begun to look upon himself as an invalid. To Mildred, who was in Richmond on a visit to friends, he writes jokingly about the difficulty experienced by the family in finding out what she meant in a letter to him:

"LEXINGTON, Virginia, January 8, 1870.

"*My Precious Life:* I received your letter of the 4th. We held a family council over it. It was passed from eager hand to hand and attracted wondering eyes and mysterious looks. It produced few words but a deal of thinking, and the conclusion arrived at, I believe unanimously, was that there was a great fund of amusement and information in it if it could be extracted. I have therefore determined to put it carefully away till your return, seize a leisure day, and get you to interpret it. Your mother's commentary, in a suppressed soliloquy, was that you had succeeded in writing a wretched hand. Agnes thought that it would keep this cold weather—her thoughts running on jellies and oysters in the store-room; but I, indignant at such aspersions upon your accomplishments, retained your epistle and read in an elevated tone an interesting narrative of travels in sundry countries, describing gorgeous scenery, hairbreadth escapes, and a series of remarkable events by flood and field, not a word of which they declared was in your letter. Your return, I hope, will prove the correctness of my version of your annals. . . . I have little to tell. Gaiety continues. Last night there was a cadet hop. Night before, a party at Colonel Johnston's. The night preceding, a college *conversazione* at your mother's. It was given in honour of Miss Maggie Johnston's visit of a few days to us. You know how agreeable I am on such occasions, but on this, I am told, I surpassed myself.

"On New Year's Day the usual receptions. Many of our friends called. Many of my ancients as well as juniors were present, and all enjoyed some good Norfolk oysters. I refer you to Agnes for details. We are pretty well. I think I am better. Your mother and sisters as usual. Custis busy with the examination of the cadets, the students preparing for theirs. Cadet Cook, who was so dangerously injured by a fall from his window on the 1st, it is hoped now will recover. The Misses Pendleton were to have arrived this morning, and Miss Ella Heninberger is on a visit to Miss Campbell. Miss Lizzie Letcher still absent. Messrs. Anderson, Baker, W. Graves, Moorman, Strickler, and Webb have all been on visits to their sweethearts, and have left without them. 'Mrs. Smith' is as usual. 'Gus' is as wild as ever[2]. We catch our own rats and mice now, and are independent of cats. All unite in love to you.

"Your affectionate father,

"R. E. LEE.

"MISS MILDRED LEE."

A month later he writes again to this daughter in the same playful strain, and sends his remembrances to many friends in Richmond:

"LEXINGTON, Virginia, February 2, 1870.

"*My Precious Life:* Your letter of the 29th ultimo, which has been four days on the road, reached me this morning, and my reply, unless our mails whip up, will not get to you before Sunday or Monday. There is no danger, therefore, of our correspondence becoming too brisk. What do the young girls do whose lovers are at Washington College or the Institute? Their tender hearts must always be in a lacerated and bleeding condition! I hope you are not now in that category, for I see no pining swains among them, whose thoughts and wishes are stretching eagerly toward Richmond. I am glad you have had so pleasant a visit to the Andersons. You must present my regards to them all, and I hope that Misses Ellen and Mary will come to see you in the summer. I am sure you will have an agreeable time at Brook Hill. Remember me to all the family, and tell Miss Belle to spare my friend Wilkins. He is not in a condition to enjoy the sufferings which she imposes on her Richmond beaux. Besides, his position entitles him to tender treatment.

"I think it time that you should be thinking of returning home. I want to see you very much, and as you have been receiving instruction from the learned pig, I shall expect to see you much improved. We are not reduced to apply to such instructors at Lexington. Here we have learned professors to teach us what we wish to know, and the Franklin Institute to furnish us lectures on science and literature. You had better come back, if you are in search of information on any subject. I am glad that Miss 'Nannie' Wise found one occasion on which her ready tongue failed her. She will have to hold it in subjection now. I should like to see Miss Belle under similar circumstances, provided she did not die from suppressed ideas. What an awful feeling she must experience, if the occasion should ever come for her to restrain that active member! Although my friend Wilkins would be very indulgent, I think he would want her to listen sometimes. Miss Pendleton has just been over to give us some pleasing news. Her niece, Miss Susan Meade, Philip's daughter, is to be married next month to a Mr. Brown, of Kentucky, who visited her two years ago upon the recommendation of the Reverend Charles Page, found her a school-girl, and has waited until she became a woman. He is rich, forty-nine, and has six children. There is a fair start in the world for a young woman! I recommend her example to you. We are all as usual, and 'Mrs. Smith' is just the same. Miss Maggie Johnston, who has been staying with us occasionally for a few days at a time, is now on a visit to us. There is to be an anniversary celebration of the societies of the Institute on Friday, and a students' party on Monday night, and a dance at the College Hotel. To-morrow night your mother has an evening for some young students. Gaiety will never cease in Lexington so long as the ladies are so attractive and the men so agreeable. Surprise parties are the fashion now. Miss Lucy Campbell has her cousin, Miss Ella Heninberger, staying with her, who assists her to surprise and capture too unwary youths. I am sorry to hear of Mrs. Ould's illness. If you see her, present me most kindly to her; also to Mrs. George Randolph. Do beware of vanilla cream. Recollect how far you are from home, and do not tamper with yourself. Our semi-annual examination has been in progress for a fortnight. We shall conclude on Saturday, which will be a great relief to me, for, in addition to other things, I have to be six hours daily in the examination rooms. I was sorry that I could not attend Mr. Peabody's funeral, but I did not feel able to undertake the journey, especially at this season. I am getting better, I hope, and feel stronger than I did, but I cannot walk much farther than to the college, though when I get on my horse I can ride with comfort. Agnes accompanies me very often. I must refer you to her and your mother for all local news. Give my love to Fitzhugh, and Tabb, and Robert when you see them, and for yourself keep an abundance. I have received letters from Edward and Blanche. They are very anxious about the condition of political affairs in France. Blanche sent you some receipts for creams, etc. You had better come and try them.

"Your affectionate father,   R. E. LEE.

"MISS MILDRED LEE."

The following letter to his son, Fitzhugh, further shows his tender interest in his children and grandson:

"Lexington, Virginia, February 14, 1870.

"*My Dear Fitzhugh:* . . . I hope that you are all well and that you will not let any one spoil my grandson. Your mother has written all the family and Lexington news. She gathers much more than I do. I go nowhere but to the college, and when the weather permits I ride in the mountains. I am better, I think, but still troubled. Mildred, I hope, is with you. When she gets away from her papa, she does not know what she wants to do, tell her. You have had a fine winter for work, and later you will have a profitable season. Custis is well and very retired; I see no alarming exhibition of attention to the ladies. I have great hopes of Robert. Give much love to my daughter Tabb and to poor little 'Life.' I wish I could see you all; it would do my pains good. Poor little Agnes is not at all well, and I am urging her to go away for a while. Mary as usual.

"Affectionately your father,   R. E. Lee.

"General W. H. F. Lee."

After waiting all winter for the improvement in his health, my father, yielding at last to the wishes of his family, physician, and friends, determined to try the effect of a southern climate. It was thought it might do him good, at any rate, to escape the rigours of a Lexington March, and could do no harm. In the following letters to his children he outlines his plans and touchingly alludes to the memory of his daughter Annie, who died in 1862 and was buried at Warrenton Springs, North Carolina:

"Lexington, Virginia, March 21, 1870.

"*My Dear Daughter:* The doctors and others think I had better go to the South in the hope of relieving the effects of the cold, under which I have been labouring all the winter. I think I should do better here, and am very reluctant to leave home in my present condition; but they seem so interested in my recovery and so persuasive in their uneasiness that I should appear obstinate, if not perverse, if I resisted longer. I therefore consented to go, and will take Agnes to Savannah, as she seems anxious to visit that city, or, perhaps, she will take me. I wish also to visit my dear Annie's grave before I die. I have always desired to do so since the cessation of active hostilities, but have never been able. I wish to see how calmly she sleeps away from us all, with her dear hands folded over her breast as if in mute prayer, while her pure spirit is traversing the land of the blessed. I shall diverge from the main route of travel for this purpose, and it will depend somewhat upon my feelings and somewhat upon my procuring an escort for Agnes, whether I go further south.

"I am sorry not to be able to see you before I go, but if I return, I hope to find you here well and happy. You must take good care of your mother and do everything she wants. You must not shorten your trip on account of our departure. Custis will be with her every day, and Mary is with her still. The servants seem attentive. Good-bye, my dear child. Remember me to all friends, and believe me,

"Your affectionate father,   R. E. LEE.

"MISS MILDRED LEE."

"LEXINGTON, Virginia, March 22, 1870.

"*My Dear Fitzhugh:* Your letter of the 17th inst. has been received. Lest I should appear obstinate, if not perverse, I have yielded to the kind importunities of my physicians and of the faculty to take a trip toward the South. In pursuance of my resolution, I shall leave here Thursday next in the packet-boat, and hope to arrive in Richmond on Friday afternoon. I shall take with me, as my companion, Agnes, who has been my kind and uncomplaining nurse, and if we could only get down to you that evening we would do so, for I want to see you, my sweet daughter, and dear grandson, But as the doctors think it important that I should reach a southern climate as soon as practicable, I fear I shall have to leave my visit to you till my return. I shall go first to

Warrenton Springs, North Carolina, to visit the grave of my dear Annie, where I have always promised myself to go, and I think, if I am to accomplish it, I have no time to lose. I wish to witness her quiet sleep, with her dear hands crossed over her breast, as it were in mute prayer, undisturbed by her distance from us, and to feel that her pure spirit is waiting in bliss in the land of the blessed. From there, according to my feelings, I shall either go down to Norfolk or to Savannah, and take you if practicable on my return. I would ask you to come up to Richmond, but my movements are unknown to myself, as I cannot know the routes, schedules, etc., till I arrive there, but I have promised not to linger there longer than necessary; so I must avoid temptation. We are all as usual. Your mother still talks of visiting you, and when I urge her to make preparations for the journey, she replies rather disdainfully she has none to make; they have been made years ago. Custis and Mary are well, and Mildred writes that she will be back by April 1st. We are having beautiful weather now, which I hope may continue. From

"Your affectionate father,   R. E. LEE."

To his daughter Mildred he writes again, giving her the minutest details as to the routes home. This is very characteristic of him. We were always fully instructed as to the best way to get to Lexington and, indeed, all the roads of life were carefully marked out for us by him:

"LEXINGTON, Virginia, March 23, 1870.

"*My Dear Daughter:* I wrote to you the other day, telling you of my intention of going South and of my general plan as far as formed. This morning your letter of the 21st arrived. . . . I hope you will get back comfortably and safely, and if you can fall in with no escort, you had better go as far as Alexandria, the first stage of your journey. Aunt Maria, Cassius Lee, the Smiths, etc., would receive you. If you wish to come by Goshen, you must take the train from Alexandria on Tuesday, Thursday, or Saturday, so as to reach us on any of those evenings, when you will arrive here about twelve o'clock at night. By taking the train from Alexandria on the alternate days, Monday, Wednesday, or Friday, you will reach Staunton that evening by four P. M., remain all night, and come over by daylight the following day in the stage. By taking the train from Alexandria to Lynchburg, Mondays, Wednesdays, or Fridays, you will reach there the same afternoon, about four P. M., then go *immediately* to the packet-boat, and you will arrive here next morning. This last is the *easiest* route, and the best if you find no escort. Tell all the conductors and captains that you are my runaway daughter, and they will take care of you. I leave to-morrow evening on the packet-boat. I told you that Agnes would accompany me. Tell my cousins Washington, Jane, and Mary that I wish I were going to see them. I should then anticipate some pleasure. But the doctors say I must turn my face the other way. I know they do not know everything, and yet I have often had to do what I was told, without benefit to myself, and I shall have to do it again. Good-bye, my dear daughter. All unite in love.

"Your affectionate father, R. E. LEE.

"MISS MILDRED LEE."

CHAPTER XXII

THE SOUTHERN TRIP

LETTERS TO MRS. LEE FROM RICHMOND AND SAVANNAH—
FROM BRANDON—AGNES LEE'S ACCOUNT OF HER FATHER'S
GREETINGS FROM OLD FRIENDS AND OLD SOLDIERS—
WILMINGTON AND NORFOLK DO HIM HONOUR—VISITS TO
FITZHUGH AND ROBERT IN THEIR HOMES

IT is to be regretted that so little was written by my father while on this trip. In the letters extant he scarcely refers to his reception by the people at different points visited. His daughter Agnes tells more, and we can imagine how tenderly and joyfully he was greeted by his old soldiers, their wives, children, and friends. He was very unwilling to be made a hero anywhere, and most reluctant to show himself to the crowds assembled at every station along his route, pressing to catch sight of him.

"Why should they care to see me?" he would say, when urged to appear on the platform of the train; "I am only a poor old Confederate!"

This feeling, natural to him, was probably intensified at that time by the state of his health. On Sunday he writes to my mother of his trip to Richmond and of his stay there:

"RICHMOND, Virginia, March 29, 1870.

"*My Dear Mary:* I reached here Friday afternoon, and had a more comfortable journey than I expected. The night aboard the packet was very trying, but I survived it, and the dust of the railroad the following day. Yesterday the doctors, Huston, McCaw, and Cunningham, examined me for two hours, and, I believe, contemplate returning to-day. They say they will make up their opinion and communicate it to Doctor Barton, who will write me what to do. In the meantime they desire me to continue his prescriptions. I think I feel better than when I left Lexington, certainly stronger, but am a little feverish. Whether it is produced by the journey, or the toddies that Agnes administers, I do not know. I have not been able to see anybody, nor was I able to get the groceries yesterday. Agnes thinks you will have enough to last till I get back here, when I will select them and send them up. Should you want any particular article, write to Messrs. Bacon & Lewis for it. I saw, yesterday morning, Mr. John Stewart and Miss Mary,[1] who had called to see Agnes but found she was out. Miss Mary looked very sweet, and inquired about you all. Agnes rode out there yesterday afternoon and saw all the family. I am told all our friends here are well. Many of my northern friends have done me the honour to call on me. Among them 'Brick Pomeroy.' They like to see all that is going on. Agnes has gone to church with Colonel Corley. I was afraid to go. The day is unfavourable, and I should see so many of my old friends, to whom I would like to speak, that it might be injurious to me. I was in hopes that Fitzhugh might make his appearance yesterday, when we should have learned all about those below, but he did not. I hear that they are all well, however. I expect to continue our journey to-morrow, if nothing prevents, though I have not yet got the information I desire about the routes. Still, I will get on. I will leave to Agnes to tell about herself. Love to all, Truly, R. E. LEE."

The next letter that I find is written from Savannah:

"SAVANNAH, Georgia, April 2, 1870.

"*My Dear Mary:* I reached here yesterday evening and have borne the journey much better than I expected. I think I am stronger than when I left Lexington, but otherwise can discover no difference. I have had a tedious journey upon the whole, and have more than ever regretted that I undertook it. However, I have enjoyed meeting many friends, and the old soldiers have greeted me very cordially. My visit to dear Annie's grave was mournful, yet soothing to my feelings, and I was glad to have the opportunity of thanking the kind friends for their care of her while living and their attention to her since her death. I saw most of the ladies of the committee who undertook the preparation of the monument and the inclosure of the cemetery, and was very kindly received by all the citizens of Warrenton, and, indeed, at all the towns through which we passed. Yesterday, several gentlemen from Savannah met the train in which we came from Augusta—General Lawton, Mr. Andrew Lowe, Mr. Hodgson, etc., etc. I found they had arranged among themselves about my sojourn, so I yielded at once, and, after depositing Agnes at General Lawton's, I came off to Mr. Lowe's, where I am now domiciled. His house is partially dismantled and he is keeping house alone, so I have a very quiet time. This morning I took a short drive around the city with Agnes and Miss Lawton, and on returning called on Mrs. Elliot, who has her two widowed daughters living with her, Mrs. Elliot and Mrs. Habersham. I also went to see Mrs. Gordon, Mrs. Gilmer, and Mrs. Owen, and then returned to the Lowes', where I find he has invited some gentlemen to meet me at dinner—General Joe Johnston, General Lawton, General Gilmer, Colonel Corley, etc. Colonel Corley has stuck to me all the journey, and now talks of going to New Orleans. The weather to-day is rather cool and raw, with an easterly wind, and if it continues I will go on to Florida next week. The woods are filled with flowers, yellow jasmine covering all the trees, etc., and fresh vegetables everywhere. I must leave Agnes to give you all details. The writing-desk is placed in a dark corner in this handsome house, prepared for younger eyes than mine, and I can hardly see what I write. All friends inquire after you, Custis, Mary, and Mildred. Give my love to all, and believe me,

"Most truly,   R. E. LEE.

"MRS. R. E. LEE."

The Colonel Corley mentioned in the above letters had been on General Lee's staff, as chief quartermaster, from the time he assumed command of the Army of Northern Virginia until the surrender. His voluntary service as escort on this trip, so delicately offered and performed, was highly appreciated by his old commander. A letter from his daughter to her mother, written the next day, tells many particulars of their journey, but still leaves much to be desired:

"SAVANNAH, Georgia, April 3, 1870.

". . . I hardly know where to commence, I have so little time to write. We left Richmond Monday, 2 P. M. We reached Warrenton at ten o'clock and were taken to their house by Mr. and Mrs. White, who met us at the depot. The next morning papa and I drove with Captain White's horses to the cemetery. Mrs. White gave me a quantity of beautiful white hyacinths, which she said were for you, too, and I had brought some gray moss that Kitty Stiles had given me. This I twined on the base of the monument. The flowers looked very pure and beautiful. The place is just as it is in Mr. Hope's picture (which I have). It was a great satisfaction to be there again. We did not go to the springs, a mile off. Returning, we stopped at Mr. Joe Jones's (old Mr. J——'s son). They insisted on our taking dinner. He has eleven children, I think, and there were numberless others there. They loaded me with flowers, the garden full of hyacinths and early spring flowers. Mrs. Jones is a very nice lady, one of those who were foremost in erecting the monument. We then stopped at the farm of the Jones's, who were at the springs when we were there in the autumn of 1862, and Mrs. J—— knew me at once, and asked affectionately after you. Saw Patty and

352

Emma—all the daughters married except Patty and the youngest. Mr. J— is very infirm—eighty-three years old. That evening a number of persons came to see us, Mrs. Alston and Miss Brownlow, two others of the committee of ladies. Every one was very kind. Indeed, I wish you could travel with papa, to see the affection and feeling shown toward him everywhere. We spent that night in the sleeping-car, very handsome and comfortable, but the novelty, I suppose, made us wakeful. At Raleigh and another place the people crowded to the depot and called 'Lee! Lee!' and cheered vociferously, but we were locked up and 'mum.' Everywhere along the road where meals were provided the landlords invited us in, and when we would not get out, sent coffee and lunches. Even soldiers on the train sent in fruit, and I think we were expected to die of eating. At Charlotte and Salisbury there were other crowds and bands. Colonel Corley joined us at C., having asked to go to Savannah with us. The train stopped fifteen minutes at Columbia. Colonel Alexander Haskell took charge of the crowd, which, in spite of the pouring rain, stood there till we left. General E. Porter Alexander was there, and was very hearty in his inquiries after all of us. His little girl was lifted into the car. Namesakes appeared on the way, of all sizes. Old ladies stretched their heads into the windows at way-stations, and then drew back and said 'He is mightily like his pictures.' We reached Augusta Wednesday night. The mayor and council met us, having heard a few minutes before that papa was on the train. We were whirled off to the hotel, and papa decided to spend Thursday there. They had a reception the whole of the morning. Crowds came. Wounded soldiers, servants, and working-men even. The sweetest little children—namesakes—dressed to their eyes, with bouquets of japonica—or tiny cards in their little fat hands—with their names. Robert Burwell, of Clarke, who married Miss Clayton there; Randell, author of 'My Maryland'; General McLaws, Wright, Gardner, and many others. Saw the Misses Boggs, General B—'s sisters. Miss Rebecca knew Mrs. Kirkpatrick very well, and asked after her. Miss Russell, with whose father and sisters we had been at the White Sulphur, helped us to receive. She is very tall and handsome, and was superb in a white lace shawl, a moire-antique with a train. The Branch brothers rather took possession of me. Melville, who was at the Institute [Virginia Military Institute, Lexington, Virginia] and knew the Letchers very well, drove me in and around the town—at the rate of a mile a minute. Another brother took me to the 'Skating Rink' at night. . . . a serenade that night. At some point on the way here Generals Lawton and Gilmer, Mr. Andrew Lowe, and others, got on the cars with us. Flowers were given us at various places. I so much enjoyed the evidences of spring all along our route—more and more advanced as we proceeded. The jasmine, though passing away, was still in sufficient abundance, in some places, to perfume the air. The dark marshes were rich in tall magnolia trees, beautiful red buds, and other red blossoms I did not know. The jasmine and the trees hanging with gray moss—perfectly weird-looking—have been the least luxuriant places in the interim. Savannah is green with live-oaks—and filled with trees and shrubbery. I wish you could see a large marble table in the parlour, where I am writing, with a pyramid of jasmine in the centre and four large plates full at the corners, almost covering the square, all sent me Saturday. The Lawtons are as kind as possible, wanted papa to stay here, but Mr. Andrew Lowe had arranged to take him to his house at bed-time. So he lost the benefit of a serenade from two bands, alternating, which we enjoyed—General Lawton telling the crowd General Lee had retired from fatigue. Papa has borne the journey and the crowds far better than I thought he would and seems stronger. (*Monday.*) It seems impossible to finish this—I inclose some scraps which will tell our story. Crowds of persons have been coming to see me ever since I came. Saw Mrs. General Johnston—Nannie Hutchenson—of course, and Reverend and Mrs. Moore yesterday. They left to-day. . . . Colonel Corley has taken Corinne[2] and me on a beautiful drive this morning to 'Bonaventure,' which is to be a cemetery, and to several places in its vicinity. I never saw anything more impressive and beautiful than the avenues of live-oaks, literally covered with long gray moss, arching over the roads. Tell Messrs. Owens and Minis I have seen their families, who are very kind to us. General and Mrs. Gilmer asked especially after Custis. . . . We think of going to Florida in a few days. Haven't heard from you.

"AGNES."

This is the only letter from his daughter Agnes, written at this time, that can be found. My father, in his letters to his family, left "details" and "particulars" for her to describe, and doubtless she did so. Unfortunately, there is but this single letter.

On April 17th, he writes again from Savannah to my mother:

"*My Dear Mary:* I have received your letter of the Wednesday after our departure and am glad to hear that you are well and getting on so comfortably. The destruction of the bridge is really a loss to the community, and I fear will inconvenience Mildred in her return. However, the spring is now advancing and they ought to be able to get up the new bridge. I hope I am a little better. I seem to be stronger and to walk with less difficulty, but it may be owing to the better streets of Savannah. I presume if any change takes place it will be gradual and slow. Please say to Doctor Barton that I have received his letter and am obliged to him for his kind advice. I shall begin to-day with his new prescriptions and will follow them strictly. To-morrow I expect to go to Florida, and will stop first at Amelia Island. The visitors to that region are coming out, saying the weather is uncomfortably hot. If I find it so, I shall return. Savannah has become very pleasant within the last few days, and I dare say I shall do as well here as elsewhere. The spring, however, is backward. I believe I told you that I was staying with Mr. Andrew Lowe, who is very kind, and where I am very comfortable. I am going to be separated from Agnes, and have received invitations from several of the inhabitants where we could be united. But it is awkward to change. Agnes has been sick, too, since her arrival, which has made me the more anxious to be with her. You know she is like her papa—always wanting something. She is, however, better to-day, as I learn, though I have not seen her yet. I saw her twice yesterday. She was better then and came down to Mrs. Lawton's room, so I hope she will be well enough to go with me to Amelia Island. The Messrs. Mackay got down from Etowa last evening, both looking very well, and have reopened their old house in Broughton Street, which I am glad of. I have seen Mrs. Doctor Elliot and family, the Andersons, Gordons, etc., etc., and all my former acquaintances and many new ones. I do not think travelling in this way procures me much quiet and repose. I wish I were back. . . . Give my love to her [his daughter Mary] and to Custis, and tell the latter I hope that he will be able to keep Sam in the seeds he may require. Praying a merciful God to guard and direct you all, I am,

"Most affectionately,   R. E. LEE.

"P. S.—I received a letter from F—: all well.

"R. E. L."

Sam was the gardener and man-of-all-work at Lexington. My father took great interest in his garden and always had a fine one. Still, in Savannah, he again writes to his wife acknowledging the letters forwarded to him and commenting on the steps being taken:

"SAVANNAH, Georgia, April 11, 1870.

"*My Dear Mary:* I received yesterday your letters of the 3d and 6th, inclosing Reverend Mr. Brantley's and daughter's and Cassius Lee's. I forwarded the petition to the President, accompanying the latter, to Cassius, and asked him to give it to Mr. Smith. Hearing, while passing through Richmond, of the decision of the Supreme Court referred to, I sent word to Mr. Smith that if he thought the time and occasion propitious for taking steps for the recovery of Arlington, the Mill, etc., to do so, but to act quietly and discreetly. I presume the petition sent you for signature was the consequence. I do not know whether this is a propitious time or not, and should rather have had an opportunity to consult friends, but am unable to do so. Tell Custis that I wish that he would act for me, through you or others, for it is mainly on his account that I desire the restitution of the property. I see that a resolution has been introduced into Congress 'to perfect the title of the Government to Arlington and other National Cemeteries,' which I have been apprehensive of stirring, so I suppose the matter will come up anyhow. I did not sign the petition, for I did not think it necessary, and believed the more I was kept out of sight the better. We must hope for the best, speak as little and act as discreetly as possible.

"The Reverend Dr. Brantley was invited by the faculty of the college to deliver the baccalaureate sermon next June, and I invited him and his daughter, in the event of his accepting, to stay with us. Do you know whether he has accepted? I should have gone to Florida last Friday, as proposed, but Agnes was not well enough. She took cold on the journey or on her first arrival, and has been quite sick, but is better now. I have not seen her this morning, but if she is sufficiently recovered we will leave here to-morrow. I have received a message saying that she was much better. As regards myself, my general health is pretty good. I feel stronger than when I came. The warm weather has also dispelled some of the rheumatic pains in my back, but I perceive no change in the stricture in my chest. If I attempt to walk beyond a very slow gait, the pain is always there. It is all true what the doctors say about its being aggravated by any fresh cold, but how to avoid taking cold is the question. It seems with me to be impossible. Everything and anything seems to give me one. I meet with much kindness and consideration, but fear that nothing will relieve my complaint, which is fixed and old. I must bear it. I hope that you will not give over your trip to the 'White House,' if you still desire to make it. I shall commence my return about the last of April, stopping at some points, and will be a few days in Richmond, and the 'White House' if able. I must leave to Agnes all details. Give much love to Custis, Mary, and Mildred. Tell the latter I have received her letters. Remember me to all friends.

"Most sincerely yours, R. E. LEE.

"MRS. R. E. LEE."

After visiting Cumberland Island and going up the St. John's River as far as Palatka, and spending the night at Colonel Cole's place near there, they returned to Savannah. Colonel Cole was on General Lee's staff as chief commissary during the time he commanded the Army of Northern Virginia, and was a very dear friend of us all:

"SAVANNAH, Georgia, April 18, 1870.

"*My Dear Mary:* I have received your letter of the 13th, and am glad to learn that you propose visiting the 'White House,' as I feared my journey might prevent you. I am, however, very anxious on the subject, as I apprehend the trip will be irksome and may produce great inconvenience and pain. I hope you received my letter of the 11th, written just before my departure for Florida. In case you did not, I will state that I forwarded your petition to Cassius Lee as received, not thinking my signature necessary or advantageous. I will send the money received from the 'University Publishing Company' to Carter, for whom I intend it.[3] I returned from Florida Saturday, 16th, having had a very pleasant trip as far as Palatka on the St. John's. We visited Cumberland Island, and Agnes decorated my father's grave with beautiful fresh flowers. I presume it is the last time I shall be able to pay to it my tribute of respect. The cemetery is unharmed and the grave is in good order, though the house of Dungeness has been burned and the island devastated. Mr. Nightingale, the present proprietor, accompanied me from Brunswick. Mr. Andrew Lowe was so kind as to go with us the whole way, thinking Agnes and I were unable to take care of ourselves. Agnes seemed to enjoy the trip very much, and has improved in health. I shall leave to her all details. We spent a night at Colonel Cole's, a beautiful place near Palatka, and ate oranges from the trees. We passed some other beautiful places on the river, but could not stop at any but Jacksonville, where we remained from 4 P. M. to 3 A. M. next morning, rode over the town, etc., and were hospitably entertained by Colonel Sanderson. The climate was delightful, the fish inviting and abundant. We have returned to our old quarters, Agnes to the Lawtons' and I to Lowe's. We shall remain here this week, and will probably spend a few days in Charleston and Norfolk, if we go that way, and at 'Brandon' and 'Shirley' before going to the 'White House,' where we shall hope to meet you. I know of no certain place where a letter will catch me before I reach Richmond, where the doctors desire me to spend a few days that they may again examine me. Write me there whether Fitzhugh is too full to receive us. It will depend upon my feelings, weather, etc., whether I make the digression by Norfolk. Poor little Agnes has had, I fear, but little enjoyment so far, and I wish her to have all the pleasure she can gather on the route. She is still weak and seems to suffer constantly from the neuralgia. I hope I am better, I know that I am stronger, but I still have the pain in my chest whenever I walk. I have felt it also occasionally of late when quiescent, but not badly, which is new. To-day Doctors Arnold and Reed, of this city, examined me for about an hour. They concur in the opinion of the other physicians, and think it pretty certain that my trouble arises from some adhesion of the parts, not from any injury of the lungs and heart, but that the pericardium may not be implicated, and the adhesion may be between the pleura and———, I have forgotten the name. Their visit was at the urgent entreaty of friends, which I could not well resist, and perhaps their opinion is not fully matured. I am continuing the prescriptions of Doctors Barton and Madison. My rheumatic pains, either from the effects of the medicine or the climate, or both, have diminished, but the pain along the breast bone ever returns on my making any exertion. I am glad Mildred has returned so well. I hope that she will continue so. After perusal, send this letter to one of the children to whom you may be writing, that Doctors Barton, etc., may be informed how I am getting along, as I have been unable to write to them or to any one at Lexington. I have so many letters to write in answer to kind invitations, etc., and so many interruptions, that my time is consumed. Besides, writing is irksome to me. Give my love to Fitzhugh, Tabb, and

Robert and to Custis, Mary, and Mildred when you write. Agnes said she was going out to return some of her numerous visits to-day, and I presume will not be able to write. She has had but little comfort in her clothes. Her silk dress was spoiled on the way, and she returned it to Baltimore, but has learned that they can do nothing with it, so she will have to do without it, which I presume she can do. I hope you may reach the 'White House' comfortably. I will apprise you of my movements from time to time. I hope my godson will know you. Tell him I have numbers of his namesakes since I left Virginia, of whom I was not aware. I hope they will come to good.

"With great affection,

"R. E. LEE.

"MRS. R. E. LEE."

From the following letters—all that I can find relating to this part of the journey—it appears that the travellers started for Virginia, stopping at Charleston, Wilmington, and Norfolk. Of their visit to Charleston I can find no record. He and Agnes stayed at the beautiful home of Mr. Bennet, who had two sons at the college, and a lovely daughter, Mary Bennet. I remember Agnes' telling me of the beautiful flowers and other attentions lavished upon them.

At Wilmington they spent a day with Mr. and Mrs. Davis. His coming there was known only to a few persons, as its announcement was by a private telegram from Savannah, but quite a number of ladies and gentlemen secured a small train and went out on the Southern Road to meet him. When they met the regular passenger-train from Savannah, General Lee was taken from it to the private one and welcomed by his many friends. He seemed bright and cheerful and conversed with all. He spoke of his health not being good, and on this account begged that there would be no public demonstration on his arrival, nor during his stay at Wilmington.

On reaching that place, he accompanied Mr. George Davis[4] to his house and was his guest during his sojourn in the city.

Mrs. Davis was a Miss Fairfax, daughter of Dr. O. Fairfax, of Alexandria, Virginia. They had been and were very old and dear friends and neighbours. The next morning my father walked out and called on Bishop Atkinson, with whom he had been well acquainted when they both lived in Baltimore, some twelve years before, the one as rector of St. Peter's (Episcopal) church, the other as Captain of United States Engineers, in charge of the harbour defenses of the city.

There was a dinner given to my father that day at Mr. Davis's home, and a number of gentlemen were present. He was looking very well, but in conversation said that he realised there was some trouble with his heart, which he was satisfied was incurable.

The next day, May 1st, he left for Norfolk, Virginia, where Dr. and Mrs. Selden were the kind entertainers of his daughter and himself. Agnes told me that in going and returning from church the street was lined with people who stood, hats off, in silent deference. From Norfolk they visited "Lower" and "Upper Brandon" on the James River, the homes of the Harrisons; then " Shirley," higher up the river. Then they proceeded by way of Richmond to the "White House," my mother having arrived there from Lexington a short time previously. The General wrote from "Brandon" to his wife:

"'BRANDON,' May 7, 1870.

"*My Dear Mary:* We have reached this point on our journey. Mrs. Harrison and Miss Belle are well and very kind, and I have been up to see Mr. William Harrison and Mr. George and their families. The former is much better than I expected to find him, and I hope will recover his health as the spring advances. The ladies are all well, and Miss Gulie is very handsome. Agnes and I went over to see Warrenton Carter and his wife this morning. They are both very well, and everything around them looks comfortable and flourishing. They have a nice home, and, as far as I could see, everything is prospering. Their little boy was asleep, but we were invited in to see him. He is a true Carter. Mrs. Page, the daughter of General Richardson, is here on a visit, and Mrs. Murdock, wife of their former pastor, arrived this morning. We are to go up to Mr. George Harrison's this evening, where the children are to have some tableaux, and where we are expected to spend the evening. In Norfolk we saw all our friends, but I did not succeed in getting out to Richard Page's as I desired, on account of the heavy rain on the appointed day and engagements that interfered on others. Agnes and Mrs. Selden rode out, however, and saw all the family. Everybody inquired kindly after you, down to Bryan, and all sent their love. 'Brandon' is looking very beautiful, and it is refreshing to look at the river. The garden is filled with flowers and abounds in roses. The yellow jasmine is still in bloom and perfumes the atmosphere. I have not heard from you or from Lexington since I left Savannah. I hope all are well. I am better, I trust; am getting fat and big, but am still rigid and painful in my back. On Tuesday night I expect to go to 'Shirley,' and on Thursday, 12th inst., to Richmond, and on Friday to the 'White House,' unless I hear that you are crowded, in which case I will submit myself to the doctors for two or three days, as they desire, and then go down. Agnes now says she will accompany me to the 'White House,' so that I shall necessarily pass through Richmond, as our baggage renders that route necessary. Therefore, unless something unforeseen prevents, I shall be with you on Friday next. All unite in love. Agnes, I hope, is better than when she left Lexington, but is not strong. You must give a great deal of love to Fitzhugh, Tabb, my grandson Robert, and all with you.

"Most truly and affectionately,

"R. E. LEE.

"P. S.—Monday. Your note of the 6th with Colonel Allan's letter has just been received. I am very sorry to hear of Tabb's sickness. I hope that she will be well by the time of my arrival. I shall be glad to see Markie.

"R. E. LEE.

"MRS. R. E. LEE."

On the same date, he writes to his daughter Mildred at Lexington:

"'BRANDON,' May 7, 1870.

"*My Dear Daughter:* Miss Jennie is putting up her mail and says that my letter must go with it, so I have but a few minutes to inform you that we have reached this point on our way home. We stayed a day in Wilmington with the Davises after leaving Charleston, and several with the Seldens in Norfolk, and shall on Tuesday next go up to 'Shirley,' and then to the 'White House.' Agnes threatens to abandon me at 'Shirley,' and I wish that you were there to take her place. I am better, I hope, certainly am stronger and have less pain, but am far from comfortable, and have little ability to move or do anything, though am growing large and fat. Perhaps that is the cause. All here are well and send love. Miss Belle very sweet; all very kind. I rode yesterday to the other 'Brandons,' and saw all the inhabitants. Captain Shirley spent the day here. Mr. Wm. Harrison much better, and Miss Gulie very pretty. They have some visitors. It is quiet and delightful here, the river beautiful. Agnes will write when she finds 'time,' which is a scarce commodity with her. I had intended to write before breakfast, the longest portion of the day, but walked out and forgot it. We have little time after breakfast. Give much love to Mary and Custis. I hope that you are all well and comfortable. I was very glad to receive your letter the morning I left Savannah, and I hope that 'Mrs. Smith' and Traveller are enjoying themselves. I hope to get back to Lexington about the 24th, but will write. After paying my visit to the 'White House' I will have to spend some days in Richmond at the doctors' request, as they wish to examine me again and more thoroughly. I hope all are well at the college. Remember me to all there and in Lexington.

"With affectionate love,   Your father,

"R. E. LEE.

"MISS MILDRED LEE."

The "White House," my brother's home at that time, is on the Pamunkey River, about twenty-five miles north of "Shirley." From my father's letter it is evident he had thought of driving over, instead of going by boat and rail through Richmond. This plan was abandoned when his daughter determined to accompany him, as a lady's baggage, even in those days, was too voluminous for private conveyance. Mr. Wm. Harrison lived at "Upper Brandon" and Mr. George Harrison at "Middle Brandon." The mistress of "Lower Brandon," the old historic home, was Mrs. Isabella Ritchie Harrison, widow of the late George Harrison. Miss Jennie, referred to in the above letter, was Miss Virginia Ritchie, sister of Mrs. Harrison. She had succeeded in having a post-office established at "Lower Brandon" and herself made postmistress. This was done for the convenience of the "Brandons" and the immediate neighbourhood. The proceeds Miss Jennie gave to the "Brandon" church.

Of his visit to "Shirley," his mother's home when she was a girl, and where she was married to "Light Horse Harry," I can find no account written at the time. It is a few hours from "Brandon" to "Shirley" by steamer on the beautiful James, and they arrived there Tuesday, May 10th, and left the following Thursday by steamer for Richmond. So says the *Home Journal* kept at "Shirley." All the country came to see him, and there was a large party to dinner. One of the daughters of the house, then a young girl, says:

"I can only remember the great dignity and kindness of General Lee's bearing, how lovely he was to all of us girls, that he gave us his photographs and wrote his name on them. He liked to have us tickle his hands, but when Cousin Agnes came to sit by him that seemed to be her privilege. We regarded him with the greatest veneration. We had heard of God, but here was General Lee!"

My mother was now at the "White House." I will here introduce portions of a letter of the 9th and 13th of May from her to her daughter in Lexington, telling of my father's arrival on the 12th:

"'WHITE HOUSE,' May 9, 1870.

"Fitzhugh took us on a delightful drive this morning, dear Mildred, to Tunstall's, where we got your letter, and Markie got nine, including yours, so we were much gratified with our excursion. The road was fine, with the exception of a few mud-holes, and the woods lovely with wild flowers and dogwood blossoms and with all the fragrance of early spring, the dark holly and pine intermingling with the delicate leaves just brought out by the genial season, daisies, wild violets, and heart's-ease. I have not seen so many wild flowers since I left Arlington. . . .

"Thirteenth.—I determined, after commencing this, to wait and see your papa, who arrived last evening with Agnes. He looks fatter, but I do not like his complexion, and he seems still stiff. I have not yet had time to hear much of their tour, except a grand dinner given them at Mr. Bennet's. Your papa sends his love, and says he will be in Lexington somewhere about the 24th. . . . There is no news. The country becomes more lovely each day. The locust trees are in full bloom, and the polonia, the only tree left of all that were planted by poor Charlotte and myself. How all our labours have come to naught. The General has just come in. Robbie is riding on his knee, sitting as grave as a judge. He says now 'Markie,' 'Agnes,' and many other words, and calls me 'Bonne Mama.' We expect Rob this morning. . . .

"Yours affectionately,

"M. C. LEE."

At this time my father was persuaded to make me a visit. He had been invited before, when at different times he had been to the "White House," but something had hitherto always prevented his coming; now he decided to come. My "Romancoke" farm was situated in King William County, on the opposite side of the Pamunkey River, and some fifteen miles east of "White House." We arrived there in the afternoon, having come down by the steamer, which at that time ran from " White House" to Baltimore. "Romancoke" had been always a dependency of the "White House," and was managed by an overseer who was subordinate to the manager on the latter estate. There was on it only a small house, of the size usual in our country for that character of property. I had taken possession in 1866, and was preparing to build a more comfortable residence, but in the meantime I lived in the house which had been occupied by the different overseers for about seventy-five years. Its accommodations were very limited, simple, and it was much out of repair. Owing to the settling of the underpinning in the centre, it had assumed a "sway-backed" outline, which gave it the name of the "broken-back house." No repairs had been attempted, as I was preparing to build a new home.

My father, always dignified and self-contained, rarely gave any evidence of being astonished or startled. His self-control was great and his emotions were not on the surface, but when he entered and looked around my bachelor quarters he appeared really much shocked. As I was much better off in the matter of housekeeping than I had been for four years, I flattered myself that I was doing very well. I can appreciate fully now what he must have felt at the time. However, he soon rallied and concealed his dismay by making kindly fun of my surroundings. The next day at dinner he felt obliged to remark on my china, knives, and forks, and suggested that I might at least better my holdings in that line. When he got back to Richmond he sent me a full set of plated forks and spoons, which I have been using from that day to this. He walked and drove over the farm, discussed my plans for improvement, and was much interested in all my work, advising me about the site of my new house, new barns, ice-house, etc. He evidently enjoyed his visit, for the quiet and the rest were very refreshing.

About thirty miles, as the crow flies, from my place, down York River, is situated, in Gloucester County, "White Marsh," an old Virginia home which then belonged to Dr. Prosser Tabb, who with his wife and children was living there. Mrs. Tabb was a near cousin of my father, and as a little girl had been a pet and favourite. His affection and regard for her had lasted from his early manhood. He had seen but little of her since the war, and when "Cousin Rebecca," as we all called her, learned he was to be at the "White House," she wrote begging him to pay her a visit. This he had agreed to do if it was possible.

While at the " White House," we had consulted together as to the best method of accomplishing this trip, and we determined to make it from "Romancoke." So I drove him to West Point, and there got aboard the Baltimore steamer, taking my horse and trap with us. At Cappahoosic, a wharf on the York, we landed and drove the nine miles to "White Marsh," arriving at "supper time," as we still say in Virginia—*i. e.*, about 7:30 P. M.

When General Lee got off on the wharf, so great was the desire of the passengers and crew to see him, that they all went to the side of the boat, which caused her to list so that I was unable to get my horse out through the gangway until the captain had ordered every one to the other side. As the sun went down, it became chilly and I drove quite rapidly, anxious to get my father out of the night air as soon as possible. He said nothing at the time, nor did I know that he noticed my unusual speed. But afterward he remarked on it to several persons, saying:

"I think Rob drives unnecessarily fast."

We were expected, and were met at the door by all the family and guests. A hearty welcome was given us. After supper he was the centre of the circle in the drawing-room, and made the acquaintance of the children of the house and of the friends and relatives of the family who were there. He said little, but all listened eagerly to what he did say, and were charmed with his pleasant smile and gracious manner. "Cousin Rebecca" introduced him to her son-in-law, Captain Perrin, mentioning that he had been wounded in the war and was still lame from the effects. The General replied that at any rate he was all right now, for he had a pair of strong young feet to wait upon him, indicating his young wife.

As was customary in this section of Virginia, the house was full of visitors, and I shared my father's room and bed. Though many a year had passed since we had been bedfellows, he told me that he remembered well the time when, as a little fellow, I had begged for this privilege. The next day he walked about the beautiful gardens, and was driven over the plantation and shown the landscapes and water views of the immediate neighbourhood. Mr.

Graves, Dr. Tabb's overseer, who had the honour of being his coachman, fully appreciated it, and was delighted when my father praised his management. He had been a soldier under the General, and had stoutly carried his musket to Appomatox, where he surrendered it. When told of this by Dr. Tabb, my father took occasion to compliment him on his steadfast endurance and courage, but Graves simply and sincerely replied,

"Yes, General, I stuck to the army, but if you had in your entire command a greater coward than I was, you ought to have had him shot."

My father, who was greatly amused at his candour, spoke of it when he got back from his drive, saying "that sort of a coward makes a good soldier."

That the drive had fatigued him was quite apparent to Cousin Rebecca, who begged him to go and lie down to rest, but he declined, though, finally, at her request, he consented to take a glass of wine. Mrs. Tabb was anxious to give a general reception that day in his honour, so that all the old soldiers in the country could have an opportunity of shaking hands with him, but at the General's request the idea was abandoned.

Several persons were invited to meet him at dinner, among them the Rev. Mr. Phillips, an Englishman, the rector of Abingdon, an old Colonial church in the county. He and his wife were ardent admirers of General Lee, and had often expressed a great desire to see him, so Mrs. Tabb kindly gave them this opportunity. They were charmed with him, and, writing to their friends in England, declared:

"The greatest event in our lives has occurred—we have seen General Lee."

One of his young cousins, in talking with him, wondered what fate was in store for "us poor Virginians." The General replied with an earnest, softened look:

"You can work for Virginia, to build her up again, to make her great again. You can teach your children to love and cherish her."

I was struck with the tenderness of his manner to all these cousins, many of whom he had never seen before, and the real affection and interest he manifested toward them. He seemed pleased and touched by their love and kindness. I think he enjoyed his visit, but it was plain that he was easily fatigued.

To catch our steamer the next morning, an early start was necessary. Arrangements were made the night before, and all good-byes said, for we had to leave the house about five o'clock. That night he was very restless and wakeful, and remarked that it was generally so with him whenever he had to get up at an unusual hour, as he was always uneasy lest he might be late. However, we got off in full time—made the connection with our steamer, and returned immediately to the "White House." I left the steamer at West Point to take my horse home, after which I joined him at the former place.

After a short stay at the "White House," he started for Lexington, stopping over in Richmond for a few days. From there he writes to his daughter Mildred in Lexington:

"RICHMOND, Virginia, May 23, 1870.

"*My Precious Daughter:* I came up from the 'White House' this morning with Agnes, but she threatens to divorce herself from me, and we have already separated. She is at Dr. Fairfax's and I am at Mr. Macfarland's. She promises, however, to see me occasionally, and if I can restore our travelling relations even at costly sacrifice I shall be happy to take her along with me. I find I shall be detained here too long to take the Wednesday's boat from Lynchburg, but, if not prevented by circumstances now not foreseen, I shall take the Friday's boat, so as to reach Lexington *Saturday* morning, 28th inst. If Sam is well enough, and it should be otherwise convenient, he could meet me with Lucy and the carriage or with Traveller. If not, I will get a seat up in the omnibus. Your mother proposes to leave in the boat for Bremo on the 1st proximo, spend one week there, and then continue her journey to Lexington. Agnes has not yet made up her mind whether she will go with me, her mother, or remain for a while. I hope to find you well, though alone. I must reserve all accounts till we meet, which I am very anxious should take place as soon as practicable. I am improving, I think, in general health, but cannot tell certainly as to the difficulty in my chest, as I have been unable to test my progress. I had a pleasant visit to F— and Robert, and enjoyed rest there, which I wanted. Love to Custis and kind regards to all friends. I hope that I shall find all well and doing well. All at the 'White House' send love. Poor Tabb is still sick. Markie Williams is with your mother. Robert came up with us, but returns this evening. I have seen Dr. Houston this morning, and I am to have a great medicine talk to-morrow.

"Your devoted father,

"R. E. Lee.

"Miss Mildred Lee."

CHAPTER XXIII

A ROUND OF VISITS

BALTIMORE—ALEXANDRIA—A WAR TALK WITH COUSIN
CASSIUS LEE— "RAVENSWORTH" —LETTERS TO DR. BUCKLER
DECLINING INVITATION TO EUROPE—TO GENERAL COOPER—
TO MRS. LEE FROM THE HOT SPRINGS—TIRED OF PUBLIC
PLACES—PREFERENCE FOR COUNTRY LIFE

JUDGED by what he says of himself, my father's trip South did him
no permanent good. The rest and change, the meeting with many
old friends, the great love and kindness shown him by all, gave
him much pleasure, and for a time it was thought he was better;
but the main cause of his trouble was not removed, though for a
while held in check.

During the month of June he remained in Lexington, was present at the final examinations of the college, and attended to all his
duties as usual. On July 1st he went to Baltimore in order to consult Dr. Thomas H. Buckler about his health.

While there he stayed with Mr. and Mrs. Tagart.

My mother had returned to Lexington after her visit to "Bremo,"
together with my sister Agnes. To her, on July 2d, he writes:

"BALTIMORE, Maryland, July 2, 1870.

"*My Dear Mary:* I reached here yesterday evening at 9:15 P. M.
Found Mr. Tagart at the depot waiting for me, where he had
been since eight o'clock, thanks to his having a punctual wife,

who regulates everything for him, so that he had plenty of time for reflection. I believe, however, the delay was occasioned by change of schedule that day, of which Mrs. Tagart was not advised. We arrived at Alexandria at 5:00 P. M., and were taken to Washington and kept in the cars till 7:45, when we were sent on. It was the hottest day I ever experienced, or I was in the hottest position I ever occupied, both on board the packet and in the railroad cars, or I was less able to stand it, for I never recollect having suffered so much. Dr. Buckler came in to see me this morning, and examined me, stripped, for two hours. He says he finds my lungs working well, the action of the heart a little too much diffused, but nothing to injure. He is inclined to think that my whole difficulty arises from rheumatic excitement, both the first attack in front of Fredericksburg and the second last winter. Says I appear to have a rheumatic constitution, must guard against cold, keep out in the air, exercise, etc., as the other physicians prescribe. He will see me again. In the meantime, he has told me to try lemon-juice and watch the effect. I will endeavour to get out to Washington Peter's on the 4th and to Goodwood as soon as Dr. B— is satisfied. Mr. and Mrs. Tagart are very well and send regards. The messenger is waiting to take this to the office. It is raining, and I have not been out nor seen any one out of the house. I hope all are well with you, and regret that I was obliged to come away. Tell the girls I was so overcome that I could not get up this morning till 8:00 A. M. Give much love to everybody, and believe me most truly,

"R. E. Lee."

The advantages of early rising my father ever held out to his daughters, so that he knew they would enjoy hearing of his being late in getting down in the morning. During this visit to Baltimore he took advantage of his proximity to many old friends to visit them.

His next letter is from Alexandria to my mother:

"Alexandria, Virginia, July 15, 1870.

"*My Dear Mary:* I arrived here last evening from Goodwood, and was glad to hear from Burke this morning that our Aunt Maria was as well as usual. I wish to get out to Cassius Lee's this afternoon, and will spend to-morrow on the Hill in visiting General Cooper, Mr. Mason, the Bishop, etc.[1] Next week I shall go to Ravensworth and from there think I shall proceed to Lexington. It is so hot that I shall be obliged to forego my visit to Nannie and the 'White House.' It is intensely hot here and I am unable to bear the heat now. I took cold yesterday in the cars or elsewhere and am full of pains this morning, and was unable to sleep last night.

"I have seen Mr. Smith[2] this morning and had with him a long business talk, and will see him again after seeing Cassius. The prospect is not promising. I got your letter at Charles's. Thank Agnes for hers. All were well there and on West River, and sent you all messages of love. I will give all particulars when we meet. I am at the Mansion House, where it is piping hot. I had felt better until I caught fresh cold, but no one can avoid it in such weather. Love to all. I cannot fix yet the day of my return, but it will be the last week in July.

"I hope Custis has got off, though I shall not be able to see him.

"Most truly and affectionately,

"R. E. Lee.

"Mrs. R. E. Lee."

Mr. Cassius Lee was my father's first cousin. They had been children together, schoolmates in boyhood, and lifelong friends and neighbours. He was my father's trusted adviser in all business matters, and in him he had the greatest confidence. Mr. Cazenove Lee, of Washington, D. C., his son, has kindly furnished me with some of his recollections of this visit, which I give in his own words:

"It is greatly to be regretted that an accurate and full account of this visit was not preserved, for the conversations during those two or three days were most interesting and would have filled a volume. It was the review of a lifetime by two old men. It is believed that General Lee never talked after the war with as little reserve as on this occasion. Only my father and two of his boys were present. I can remember his telling my father of meeting Mr. Leary, their old teacher at the Alexandria Academy, during his late visit to the South, which recalled many incidents of their school life. They talked of the war, and he told of the delay of Jackson in getting on McClellan's flank, causing the fight at Mechanicsville, which fight he said was unexpected, but was necessary to prevent McClellan from entering Richmond, from the front of which most of the troops had been moved. He thought that if Jackson had been at Gettysburg the would have gained a victory, 'for' said he, 'Jackson would have held the heights which Ewell took on the first day.' He said that Ewell was a fine officer, but would never take the responsibility of exceeding his orders, and having been ordered to Gettysburg, he would not go farther and hold the heights beyond the town. I asked him which of the Federal generals he considered the greatest, and he answered most emphatically 'McClellan by all odds.' He was asked why he did not come to Washington after second Manassas.

"'Because,' he replied, 'my men had nothing to eat,' and pointing to Fort Wade, in the rear of our home, he said, 'I could not tell my men to take that fort when they had had nothing to eat for three days. I went to Maryland to feed my army.'

"This led to a statement of the mismanagement of the Confederate Commissary Department, of which he gave numerous instances, and mentioned his embarrassments in consequence. He was also very severe in his criticism of the newspapers, and said that patriotism did not seem to influence them in the least, that movements of the army were published which frustrated their plans, and, as an instance, he told of Longstreet's being sent to the Western Army and the efforts that were made to keep the movement secret, but to no purpose, the papers having heralded it at once to friend and foe alike. I also remember his saying that he advocated putting the negroes in the army, and the arguments he advanced in favour of it. My father remarked at table one day that he could not have starved in the Confederate service if he could have gotten bread and milk.

"'No,' replied the General, 'but frequently I could not get even that.'

"His love of children was most marked, and he never failed to show them patient consideration. On the occasion of this visit, his answers to all our boyish questions were given with as much detail and as readily as if we had been the most important men in the community. Several years before the war I remember that my sister, brother, and myself, all young children, drove over to Arlington Mills, and that while going there Colonel Lee rode up on a beautiful black horse. He impressed my childish fancy then as the handsomest and finest horseman I had ever seen—the beau-ideal of a soldier. Upon seeing us he at once stopped, spoke to each of us, and took my sister, then about ten years of age, upon his horse before him, and rode with us for two miles, telling her, I remember, of his boy Robby, who had a pony, and who should be her sweetheart. Often have I seen him on the road or street or elsewhere, and though I was 'only a boy,' he always stopped and had something pleasant to say to me."

The Mr. Leary mentioned here was my father's teacher when a boy in Alexandria. His regard and esteem for him was very high, as is shown in the following letter:

"LEXINGTON, Virginia, December 15, 1866.

"MR. WM. B. LEARY.

"*My Dear Sir:* Your visit has recalled to me years long since passed, when I was under your tuition and received daily your instruction. In parting from you, I beg to express the gratitude I have felt all my life for the affectionate fidelity which characterised your teaching and conduct toward me. Should any of my friends, wherever your lot may be cast, desire to know your qualifications as a teacher, I hope you will refer them to me; for that is a subject on which I can speak knowingly and from experience. Wishing you health, happiness, and prosperity, I am, affectionately,

"Your friend,

"R. E. Lee."

His next letter is from "Ravensworth," where he went after his visit to the "Seminary Hill":

"Ravensworth, Virginia, July 20, 1870.

"*My Dear Mary:* I arrived here yesterday from Alexandria and found Aunt Maria well in general health, but less free to walk than when I last saw her. She is cheerful and quiet, but seems indisposed to try any of the healing baths, or, indeed, any of the remedies resorted to in cases of similar character, and seems to think nothing will be of avail. I hope in time that she will be relieved. Her niece, Mrs. Goldsborough, the daughter of her sister Wilhelmina, is with her. She seems to be a nice little lady—has a big boy of eight months, and is expecting her husband to-morrow, so nothing need be said more on her account. Mr. Dickens was over last evening, and reports all well with him. All the family are to be over this evening, so I cannot say more of them. Ravensworth is looking very well—I mean the house and grounds, but little of the farm seems to be cultivated, and is growing up with pines. I received your letter directed to Alexandria after my return from my visit to Cassius, also Colonel Williamson's. Resolutions will not build the church. It will require money. Mr. Smith did not give so favourable an account of Mr. Price as did Mr. Green. I did not see Mr. P—, for it would have been of no avail without having the plans, etc., and I cannot wait here to receive them. I shall have to send them, or to invite him to Lexington after my return. I propose to leave here, if nothing prevents, on

Monday, 25th inst. If I go by Goshen, I hope to reach Lexington that night, or Tuesday morning after breakfast. I have heard a rumour that the water has been withdrawn from the canal above Lynchburg for the purpose of repairs. If that is so, I shall have to go by Goshen. My cold continues, but is better. The weather is very hot and to me is almost insupportable. At 6:00 P. M. yesterday, the thermometer in Ravensworth hall marked 86°. This morning, when I first went out, it stood at 84°. Thank Agnes for her letter. I cannot respond at this time. The letter you forwarded from Mrs. Podestad describes the sickness her children have passed through. She is now with them at Capon, and Miss Emily has gone to visit Mrs. Barksdale in Greenbrier. Mrs. P—says she will be ready to visit you any time after the middle of August that you will notify her. I am glad all are well with you, and hope the garden will give you some vegetables. I am anxious to get back and see you all. Give much love to the girls, including the Misses Selden. Tell them they must not leave till I return, that I am hurrying back as fast as rheumatism will let me. I have abandoned my visit to Nannie and the boys on the Pamunkey. Tell them it is too hot and that I am too painful. Aunt M— sends love to all. Remember me to all friends. I must leave details till I return.

"Most truly and affectionately,

"R. E. LEE.

"MRS. R. E. LEE."

The building of the church here referred to was the Episcopal church in Lexington, which it was proposed to take down and replace with a larger and better building. My father was a vestryman, and also a member of the building committee.

Dr. Buckler, whom my father had consulted in July, was at this time on a visit to Baltimore, having lived abroad with his family since 1866. When about to return to Paris he wrote and asked my father to accompany him.

This invitation he was obliged to decline.

"LEXINGTON, Virginia, August 5, 1870.

"*My Dear Doctor:* I have just received your letter of the 4th inviting me to accompany you across the Atlantic, and I return you my cordial thanks for your kind solicitation for my health and comfort. There is no one whom I would prefer to have as a companion on the voyage, nor is there one, I am sure, who would take better care of me. But I cannot impose myself upon you. I have given you sufficient trouble already, and you must cure me on this side of the Atlantic. If you are the man I take you for, you will do so. You must present my warmest thanks to your wife for her remembrance of me and her kind offer of the hospitalities of her house. Should I ever be able to visit Europe I shall certainly accept them, but I hope she will soon return to this country and that you will bring her up to the mountains to us. We are all peaceable here now and she will find that we are not as bad as we have been reported to be, and every one will extend to her a hearty welcome, whereas Europe is now convulsed with the horrors of war or the agony of its expectancy, and I fear for a season is destined to feel the greatest calamity that can befall a people. I am happy to inform you that my health is better. I am pursuing your directions and hope that I am deriving benefit from them. I have made my arrangements to visit the Hot Springs, Virginia, on Monday next, as you recommended, and trust I may find relief from them. My rheumatic pains continue, but have diminished, and that in my shoulder, I think, has lessened under the application of the blister. I shall endeavour to be well by the fall. The letter you inclosed to me was from Mrs. Smith on the Hudson—and not from Mr. Henry White, as you supposed. Good-bye, my dear doctor; may you have a prosperous voyage and find your family all well on your arrival, and may your own health be entirely restored. My family unite with me in every kind wish, and I am most truly,

"Your friend,

"R. E. LEE.

"DR. THOMAS H. BUCKLER."

This letter to General Cooper (Adjutant General of the Confederate States Army), written at this time, explains itself, and is one of many witnesses of my father's delicate consideration for old soldiers in distress:

"LEXINGTON, Virginia, August 4, 1870.

"GENERAL S. COOPER,

"Alexandria, Virginia.

"*My Dear General:* Impressed, with all the people of the South, with your merits and services, I have with them admired your manly efforts to support your family, and have regretted that more remunerative occupation, better suited to your capacities and former habits, had not presented itself. This has been a subject of conversation with some of us here, and when in Savannah last spring I presented it to General Lawton, Colonel Cole, and others, and suggested that efforts be made to raise a sum for the relief of any pressing necessity. The idea was cordially, adopted, and it was hoped that an amount would be contributed that would enable you to receive some relaxation. I have received a letter from General Lawton regretting the smallness of the sum collected, $300, and explaining the delay that had occurred, the general poverty of the people, the many calls upon them, and the disposition to procrastinate when facts are not known to them personally. To this sum I have only been able to add $100, but I hope it may enable you to supply some immediate want and prevent you from taxing your strength too much. You must also pardon me for my moving in this matter, and for the foregoing explanation, which I feel obliged to make that you might understand the subject.

"With my best wishes for your health and happiness and for the useful prolongation of your honourable life, I am, with true regard,

"Your friend and servant.

"R. E. LEE."

He remained at Lexington only for a short time, as it was decided that he should go to the Hot Springs, Virginia, where he could try their famous waters for his rheumatism. On the day of his arrival he writes to my mother:

> "HOT SPRINGS, Bath County, Virginia,
> "August 10, 1870.

"*My Dear Mary:* We reached here this morning about 9:30 A. M., Captain White and I, after as pleasant a journey as we could have expected. After taking the cars at Goshen, the old route by Milboro' rose up so strong before me that we determined to adhere to it. Reached the Bath Alum about 4:00 P. M., where we passed the night and were in luck in finding several schools or parts of them rusticating on alum-water. Mrs. Heath was in charge of the detachment from Dr. Phillips's.[3] They presented a gay and happy appearance. This morning we breakfasted at the Warm and had the attention of Richard. There is a small party there, Admiral Louis Goldsborough with his wife and Miss West amongst them. Here there is quite a company. Mrs. Lemmon from Baltimore, her daughter Mrs. Dobbin, Mrs. General Walker, wife of the ex-Secretary of War of the Confederacy, Mrs. and Miss Sivent, etc., etc.

"Dr. and Mrs. Cabell are here, and the Tardys and Mrs. Mac regret that you are not with me. . . I saw Mrs. Maize at the Warm, and her sister from Kentucky, Mrs. Tate. Rev. Mr. Mason and the Daingerfields have a girls' school in the village. The Warm seems to be retrograding. I hope the new man, Edward, has arrived. Tell him to take good care of the cow, and ask the girls to see to her and the garden, etc. I saw Mrs. Caskie at the Baths. She looks very well. Her niece, Gay, is with her, a pretty little child. Mrs. Myers and her children are also there. Mrs. Asher also. Small company, but select. All pleased with Mr. Brown.[4] Tell the girls I have no one to rub me now. Shall miss them in this and other ways much. Dr. Cabell says I must continue my medicines and commence with the hot spout to-morrow. He has great confidence in the waters, and says that 95 out of 100 patients that he has treated have recovered. I shall alternate the spout with the boiler. But he says the great error is that people become impatient and do not stay long enough. I hope I may be benefited, but it is a tedious prospect. I hope that you all will continue well. If you wish to go to the Baths, or to come here, you must do so and write me what you want, if there is anything I can do or get for you. Give love to all the girls and remembrances to all friends. Tell our neighbours that I was so occupied the last days I was in Lexington that I had not time to bid them adieu. If you want more money let me know. God bless you and preserve you all. Good-bye, dear Mary.

"Most truly,

"R. E. LEE.

"MRS. M. C. LEE."

The Richard mentioned had been lately his house servant at Lexington, and Edward was a new man he had engaged for the garden and stable. The letters written to my mother and others of his family from the Hot Springs at this time were frequent, and I give them in full, as they tell all we know now of his visit there:

"HOT SPRINGS, Bath County, Virginia,
August 14, 1870.

"*My Dear Mary:* I received this morning the last letters forwarded by you. The first batch arrived yesterday. I am glad to hear that you all continue well. I hope my letter of the 10th, announcing my arrival, has reached you. It should have done so, it seems to me, previously to your note of Friday. I have but little more to say than I had then. I have taken four baths, Hot Spout, which seems to agree with me very well, but it is too soon yet to look for results. I receive the water on my shoulder, back, and chest. The sensation is pleasant, and so far I have succeeded in preventing taking cold. The atmosphere, however, is damp, and temperature variable. When the sun shines, it is hot; but when it rains, which is the usual condition of the weather, the former the exception, it is cool. Mrs. Sledge and party are here, the former improved. She was much better, went over to the White and Sweet, retrograded, and returned. Will stay here September. Many of our invalids are improving. Society has a rather solemn appearance, and conversation runs mostly on personal ailments, baths, and damp weather. There were some pretty tableaux last evening. The Misses Tardy, Mrs. Dobbin, and the little girls, the performers. Mr. Washington[5] is here. He looks well, is quiet, and has been copying points of scenery in the neighbourhood. I do not know whether he was in search of health or the picturesque. The latter is more easily found in these mountains than the former. Captain White is well and sends remembrances to all. I hope Edward has arrived and is an improvement on the present occupant of the situation. If he does not present himself, retain Henry till I come. I will endeavour to find some one. You do not mention the cow; she is of more interest to me than the cats, and is equally destructive of rats. I am glad the girls are well; what are they troubling about now? I wish they were with me. I find many ladies here for neuralgia. Mrs. General Walker has been much benefited, also others. If little Agnes should desire to try the effects of the waters, tell her to come on, I will take care of her. I suppose Tabb will go with her husband. I am sorry Fitzhugh is complaining. I have written to Rob and Miss Lottie.[6] I heard of Charles Carter's[7] passing up the road to the White, and Mildred preceded him a week. Ella, I hear, is much improved. I shall not go to the White unless specially called by something now unknown, but will remain here till the end of the month, if I find it profitable, and then return to Lexington. I hope the college is prospering. What does Mrs. Podestad say? I understand that Markie Peter[8] and child are occupying her old quarters at the Lomaxes near Warrenton. I have a merry time with my old cronies, tell Mildred. I am getting too heavy for them now. They soon drop me. I am getting uneasy about Edward and Blanche. The reverses of the French, which seem to be light, appear to have demoralised the nation. May God help all in affliction and keep and guard you and all with you, is my constant prayer.

"Truly and affectionately,

"R. E. LEE.

"MRS. M. C. LEE."

"HOT SPRINGS, Bath County, Virginia,
August 19, 1870.

"*My Dear Mary:* I received this morning your letters of the 14th and 18th, inclosing Dr. Buckler's, and was informed by Colonel Turner that he had brought the package to which you referred. He has not yet sent it to me, but, no doubt, will in time. I am sorry that Edward has not kept his engagement, for I liked his appearance and recommendations, though perhaps they are deceptive. You had better retain Henry till I come, unless you fall in with a better. I am glad that you are all well. You have such industrious little daughters that I am sure all will go well. Thank Agnes for her letter and say to her that I have not seen Mr. Vanmeter or Blair, but gave the letter to the former to Colonel White, who will send it to him when he finds out his position. Mr. Thom arrived this morning and Mr. John Johns and family rode over from the Healing. They are there for a sick child. My old friend, Dr. Broaddus, and the Reverend Mr. Jones also presented themselves. . . . I have been trying the Boiler for four days—and the Spout the five preceding. I do not perceive any benefit yet, though some little change in the seat of my pains. I will continue till the middle of next week, the 29th, when, if no decided improvement takes place, I think of going over to the Healing. Dr. Houston thinks that it will be beneficial, whereas Dr. Cabell recommends this. I am obliged to be in Staunton on the 30th ult. to attend a meeting of the Valley Railroad Company, so I shall leave here on the 29th for that purpose. After getting through with that business, I shall return to Lexington. I am sorry that I shall be called away, but I fear my stay here would be of no avail. Colonel White is well and sends regards to all. I am glad that the cow is better. She stands next in my affections to Traveller. . . . I hope that Agnes's neuralgia is better, and as she has not accepted my proposition I presume she declines. Hot bathing is not agreeable to me either in its operations or effects, but I see daily evidences of its good results in others. I wish that it suited your case. You must try and get some one in Sally's place if Tabb, etc., come, and make them all comfortable. If you want more money, let me know in time. Send over to Mr. Leyburn for the flour, when you want it. Mr. Bowie, I suspect, can arrange it for you. I fear Captain Brooks's house will not be ready for occupancy this fall. I hope that General Smith will begin Custis's in time. I heard of him on his way to Edward Cocke's the other day. Mr. Washington is still here. Better, I think. Again love to all.

"Most truly and affectionately,

"R. E. LEE.

"P. S.—Mr. Turner has just sent me the package.

"R. E. L."

To his son Fitzhugh, who was at the "White House" with his family:

"HOT SPRINGS, Bath County, Virginia,

August 20, 1870.

"*My Dear Fitzhugh:* I am very sorry to learn from your letter of the 18th, received this morning, that Tabb is sick. I hope that it will be of short duration and that she will soon throw off the chills. The mountain doctors, however, do not understand them as well as the lowland, and are apt to resort to the old practice. I wish that I could get to the White to see you, but my time is too limited, owing to the late day that I was able to leave Lexington. I propose staying here till the 29th inst., which will only make my sojourn here two and a half weeks, and then going to Staunton, where I am obliged to attend a meeting of the Valley Railroad Company on the 30th. I hope that I shall not be detained there longer than a day or two, when I will return to Lexington, where I hope to find you all. You must tell Mr. and Mrs. Podestad, Mr. Carter, Ella, etc., how sorry I am not to see them at the White, but that I hope they will call at Lexington. I wrote to Ella on my first arrival here, but presume my letter failed to reach her. You did not mention how her health was. I am much concerned at Tabb's indisposition, but am glad to hear that the baby is well. Give my love to both, and I trust you will all be benefited by the mountain air. My personal health is good, but I see no change in my rheumatic attack, which is principally confined to my chest and back. I inclose a note from your mother, transmitted on the supposition that I would write to you. Professor White is with me and I have some few acquaintances, but I am anxious to return. I am glad that Bertus has had a short visit to Orange. He says that he will come to Rockbridge in September. Custis will be there by the first, and we shall all, I hope, be together again.

"Affectionately,

"R. E. LEE."

"HOT SPRINGS, Bath County, Virginia,
"August 23, 1870.

"*My Dear Mary:* I have received your various notes of the 17th and 18th, and I am glad to hear of your well-being. Our good cow will be a loss to us, but her troubles are all over now, and I am grateful to her for what she has done for us. I hope that we did our duty to her. I have written to Mr. Andrew Cameron to inquire about a young cow he has of mine, and asked him to let you know if she is giving milk. If his report is good, you had better send for her. She is, however, young, and will require very gentle treatment. Caution Henry on that point. I have told him, Mr. C—, also, that you would send for the horses, which I wish you would do as soon as you can see that they will be properly cared for. Tell Henry to be particularly gentle and kind to them, or the gray will give him great trouble. He must wash them clean, and not pull out their manes and tails. The girls will have to exercise them till Custis comes. I suppose we may give up expecting Edward. Retain Henry till you can find some one better. You had also better engage some woman or man for a month as a dining-room servant. I think Easter has no intention of coming to us before October, and she will not come then if Mr.—can keep her. You will have so many friends staying with you that you cannot make them comfortable unless you have more servants. As I stated in a previous letter, I shall go to Staunton on the 29th. I hope I shall be detained but a few days. Lest your funds may run low, I send you a check . . . The girls can get it cashed. I may be detained, but I hope to return in time to see our children and friends. I have been here a fortnight to-day. I hope that I am better, but am aware of no material change, except that I am weaker. I am very anxious to get back. It is very wearying at these public places and the benefit hardly worth the cost. I do not think I can even stand Lexington long. Colonels Allan and Johnston[9] arrived this evening on horseback and have given me all Lexington news. Mr. Sledge and his wife, from Huntsville, brother of the Colonel, also arrived, and a Mr. and Mrs. Leeds, from New Orleans, with ten children, mostly little girls. The latter are a great addition to my comfort. I have written to Fitzhugh and Mrs. Podestad. Robert, you know, said he would make his annual visit the first week in September. Tell the girls they must make preparations to welcome all. Mrs. Walker, wife of the former Secretary of War in the Confederacy, is here with her son, whom she says she is anxious to place in college, and wishes to visit Lexington with that view. I have offered my escort and invited her to stay with us. I do not know whether she will go with me. The girls will have to prepare my room for some of the visitors, and put me anywhere. I can be very comfortable in the library. Tell the little creatures they must work like beavers and get a supply of eggs and chickens. Recollect there is flour at Leyburn's mill when you want it. Thank Mildred for her letter. Remember me to all, and believe me,

"Always yours affectionately,

R. E. LEE.

"MRS. M. C. LEE.

"P. S.—I send you an order for the horses. Tell Henry to take with him a bridle and halter. You must write for the cow if you want her.   R. E. LEE."

Mr. Andrew Cameron owned a fine farm near Lexington, and kindly took care of my father's horses when he was away in the summer; also at different times supplied him with a cow and took care of any calf, if there happened to be one, till it was of service. My father constantly rode out to see him, and enjoyed talking farming as they rode together over his fields. His delight in every aspect of Nature was real and ever present. These letters show, too, his care and consideration for animals.

His letter to his daughter Agnes is in lighter vein. His playful moods, so usual with his children, never entirely left him.

"HOT SPRINGS, Bath County, Virginia,
"August 23, 1870.

"*My Dear Agnes:* I have received both of your letters, the last the 17th, and thank you for them as well as for your care of my room and clothes. The former I understand is used for a multiplicity of purposes, and the cats and kittens have the full run of my establishment. Guard me against '*Miss Selden,*'[10] I pray you. I am sorry that you are not with me, as it possibly may have benefited your neuralgia. But if *Miss Belle* is with you, I am sure she will be of greater service, and tell her she must remain till I come, that she may cure me. That you may have some other inducements than your flowers and weeds to take you out of doors, I will write to your mother to send for the horses as soon as she can make arrangements to have them cared for, and then you and Mildred and Miss Belle, the one on Traveller, the other on Lucy, can scour the country and keep us in eggs and chickens. I am sorry for the death of our good cow, but glad that she is out of misery. . . . I do not think any of your friends are here. Mr. Washington has been vibrating between this place and the Healing, but does not seem to be well. Miss Alman, from Salem, Massachusetts, whom you may recollect as having been at the White last summer, is here with her father and mother. Miss Mollie Jourdan left to-day, and Colonel Robert Preston arrived. The Chestnuts and Le Verts are still here. I hope that you are well and that all is well with you. When Custis comes, ask him to see to the horses and the cow and that they are gently treated and properly fed. I know nothing of Henry's capacity in that way. I hope to be home next week and am very anxious to get back.

"Your father,
"R. E. LEE."

CHAPTER XXIV

LAST DAYS

LETTER TO HIS WIFE—TO MR. TAGART—OBITUARY NOTICE IN
"PERSONAL REMINISCENCES OF GENERAL ROBERT E. LEE"—
MRS. LEE'S ACCOUNT OF HIS DEATH

THE following is the last letter that I can find written by my father to my mother. He was back in Lexington early in September, and was never separated from her again while he lived:

"HOT SPRINGS, August 27, 1870.

"*My Dear Mary:* I have received your letter of the 22d. I should remain here a week longer if time permitted, as I have felt in the last few days better than I have yet, but I am obliged to be in Staunton on the 30th, and therefore must leave Monday, 29th. I should not have time to return here. The college opens on September 15th, and I wish to see that all things are prepared. Possibly the little improvement now felt will continue. If not, I shall have to bear my malady. I am truly sorry to hear of Edwin Lee's death.[1] He was a true man, and, if health had permitted, would have been an ornament as well as a benefit to his race. He certainly was a great credit to the name. Give my sincere sympathy to his wife and family. You have never mentioned anything of Dr. Grahame. I have heard that he was in a critical condition. I saw Colonels Allan and Johnston. They only stayed a day, and went on to the White. I have heard of them on their return, and presume they will reach Lexington to-morrow. Mr. George Taylor, who has been a month at the White, arrived here to-day. Both he and his wife are well. The company is thinning, though arrivals occur daily. Mr. Middleton and his daughter and son, from Washington, whom you may recollect, also came. But I hope to see you so soon that I will defer my narrative. I am glad that Mary is enjoying herself and that Rob is so happy. May both long continue so. I will endeavour to get the muslin, but fear I shall not succeed. I trust I may not be detained in Staunton more than a day or two. In that event, you may expect me Thursday, September 1st, but I cannot say as to time. I hope that I shall find you all well. Give my love to Agnes and Mildred, and Custis, if he has arrived. Colonel Turner is very well. Tell his wife that he was exhibited to-day at the Healing as a specimen of the health of the Hot. In my last I gave you my views about the servants and sent you a check for—, which I hope that you have received.   Most truly and affectionately,

"R. E. LEE."

His last letter was written on the morning of the day he was taken ill, September 28th. It was to Mr. Tagart, of Baltimore, at whose home he had stayed the previous summer. Its tone was cheerful and hopeful, and he wrote that he was much better and stronger.

"LEXINGTON, Virginia, September 28, 1870.

"*My Dear Mr. Tagart:* Your note of the 26th reached me this morning, and see how easy it is 'to inveigle me into a correspondence.' In fact, when a man desires to do a thing, or when a thing gives a man pleasure, he requires but small provocation to induce him to do it. Now I wanted to hear how you and Mrs. Tagart were, what you were doing, and how you had passed the summer, and I desired to tell you so. That is the reason I write. In answer to your question, I reply that I am much better. I do not know whether it is owing to having seen you and Doctor Buckler last summer, or to my visit to the Hot Springs. Perhaps both. But my pains are less, and my strength greater. In fact, I suppose I am as well as I shall be. I am still following Doctor B—'s directions, and in time I may improve still more. I expect to have to visit Baltimore this fall, in relation to the Valley Railroad, and in that event I hope to see you, if you will permit me. I am glad to hear that you spent a pleasant summer. Colonel—and I would have had a more agreeable one had you been with us at the Hot, and as every place agrees so well with Mrs. Tagart, I think she could have enjoyed as good health there as at Saratoga, and we should have done better. Give my sincere regards to Mrs. Tagart, and remember me to all friends, particularly Mr.—. Tell—his brother is well and handsome, and I hope that he will study, or his sweethearts in Baltimore will not pine for him long. Captain—is well and busy, and joins in my remembrances. Mrs. Lee and my daughters unite with me in messages to you and Mrs. Tagart, and I am most truly yours,   R. E. LEE.

"S. H. TAGART, Esq."

When my brother Fitzhugh and I reached Lexington, my father was no more. He died the morning of our arrival—October 12th. He had apparently improved after his first attack, and the summoning of my brother and myself had been put off from day to day. After we did start we were delayed by the floods, which at that time prevailed over the State. Of his last illness and death I have heard from my family.

The best account of those last days was written by Colonel William Preston Johnston for the "Personal Reminiscences of General Robert E. Lee," by the Rev. J. W. Jones, published in 1874. Colonel Johnston was an intimate friend of the General and a distinguished member of the faculty of his college. He was also one of the watchers by his dying bedside. I, therefore, give it in full:

"The death of General Lee was not due to any sudden cause, but was the result of agencies dating as far back as 1863. In the trying campaign of that year he contracted a severe sore throat, that resulted in rheumatic inflammation of the sac inclosing the heart. There is no doubt that after this sickness his health was more or less impaired; and although he complained little, yet rapid exercise

VALENTINE'S RECUMBENT FIGURE OF LEE
Washington and Lee University, Lexington, Va.

on foot or on horseback produced pain and difficulty of breathing. In October, 1869, he was again attacked by inflammation of the heart-sac, accompanied by muscular rheumatism of the back, right side, and arms. The action of the heart was weakened by this attack; the flush upon the face was deepened, the rheumatism increased, and he was troubled with weariness and depression.

"In March, 1870, General Lee, yielding to the solicitations of friends and medical advisers, made a six-weeks' visit to Georgia and Florida. He returned greatly benefited by the influence of the genial climate, the society of friends in those States, and the demonstrations of respect and affection of the people of the South; his physical condition, however, was not greatly improved. During this winter and spring he had said to his son, General Custis Lee, that his attack was mortal; and had virtually expressed the same belief to other trusted friends. And now, with that delicacy that pervaded all his actions, he seriously considered the question of resigning the presidency of Washington College, 'fearful that he might not be equal to his duties.' After listening, however, to the affectionate remonstrances of the faculty and board of trustees, who well knew the value of his wisdom in the supervision of the college and the power of his mere presence and example upon the students, he resumed his labours with the resolution to remain at his post and carry forward the great work he had so auspiciously begun.

"During the summer he spent some weeks at the Hot Springs of Virginia, using the baths, and came home seemingly better in health and spirits. He entered upon the duties of the opening collegiate year in September with that quiet zeal and noiseless energy that marked all his actions, and an unusual elation was felt by those about him at the increased prospect that long years of usefulness and honour would yet be added to his glorious life.

"Wednesday, September 28, 1870, found General Lee at the post of duty. In the morning he was fully occupied with the correspondence and other tasks incident to his office of president of Washington College, and he declined offers of assistance from members of the faculty, of whose services he sometimes availed himself. After dinner, at four o'clock, he attended a vestry-meeting of Grace (Episcopal) church. The afternoon was chilly and wet, and a steady rain had set in, which did not cease until it resulted in a great flood, the most memorable and destructive in this region for a hundred years. The church was rather cold and damp, and General Lee, during the meeting, sat in a pew with his military cape cast loosely about him. In a conversation that occupied the brief space preceding the call to order, he took part, and told with marked cheerfulness of manner and kindliness of tone some pleasant anecdotes of Bishop Meade and Chief-Justice Marshall. The meeting was protracted until after seven o'clock by a discussion touching the rebuilding of the church edifice and the increase of the rector's salary. General Lee acted as chairman, and, after hearing all that was said, gave his own opinion, as was his wont, briefly and without argument. He closed the meeting with a characteristic act. The amount required for the minister's salary still lacked a sum much greater than General Lee's proportion of the subscription, in view of his frequent and generous contributions to the church and other charities, but just before the adjournment, when the treasurer announced the amount of the deficit still remaining, General Lee said in a low tone, 'I will give that sum.' He seemed tired toward the close of the meeting, and, as was afterward remarked, showed an unusual flush, but at the time no apprehensions were felt.

"General Lee returned to his house, and, finding his family waiting tea for him, took his place at the table, standing to say grace. The effort was vain; the lips could not utter the prayer of the heart. Finding himself unable to speak, he took his seat quietly and without agitation. His face seemed to some of the anxious group about him to wear a look of sublime resignation, and to evince a full knowledge that the hour had come when all the cares and anxieties of his crowded life were at an end. His physicians, Doctors H. S. Barton and R. L. Madison, arrived promptly, applied the usual remedies, and placed him upon the couch from which he was to rise no more.

"To him henceforth the things of this world were as nothing, and he bowed with resignation to the command of the Master he had followed so long with reverence. The symptoms of his attack resembled concussion of the brain, without the attendant swoon. There was marked debility, a slightly impaired consciousness, and a tendency to doze; but no paralysis of motion or sensation, and no evidence of suffering or inflammation of the brain. His physicians treated the case as one of venous congestion, and with apparently favourable results. Yet, despite these propitious auguries drawn from his physical symptoms, in view of the great mental strain he had undergone, the gravest fears were felt that the attack was mortal. He took without objection the medicines and diet prescribed, and was strong enough to turn in bed without aid, and to sit up to take nourishment. During the earlier days of his illness, though inclined to doze, he was easily aroused, was quite conscious and observant, evidently understood whatever was said to him, and answered questions briefly but intelligently; he was, however, averse to much speaking, generally using monosyllables, as had always been his habit when sick.

"When first attacked, he said to those who were removing his clothes, pointing at the same time to his rheumatic shoulder, 'You hurt my arm.' Although he seemed to be gradually improving until October 10th, he apparently knew from the first that the appointed hour had come when he must enter those dark gates that, closing, open no more to earth. In the words of his physician, 'he neither expected nor desired to recover.' When General Custis Lee made some allusion to his recovery, he shook his head and pointed upward. On the Monday morning before his death, Doctor Madison, finding him looking better, tried to cheer him. 'How do you feel to-day, General?' General Lee replied slowly and distinctly: 'I feel better.' The doctor then said: 'You must make haste and get well; Traveller has been standing so long in the stable that he needs exercise.' The General made no reply, but slowly shook his head and closed his eyes. Several times during his illness he put aside his medicine, saying, 'It is of no use,' but yielded patiently to the wishes of his physicians or children, as if the slackened chords of being still responded to the touch of duty or affection.

"On October 10th, during the afternoon, his pulse became feeble and rapid, and his breathing hurried, with other evidences of great exhaustion. About midnight he was seized with a shivering from extreme debility, and Doctor Barton felt obliged to announce the danger to the family. On October 11th, he was evidently sinking; his respiration was hurried, his pulse feeble and rapid. Though less observant, he still recognised whoever approached him, but refused to take anything unless prescribed by his physicians. It now became certain that the case was hopeless. His decline was rapid, yet gentle; and soon after nine o'clock, on the morning of October 12th, he closed his eyes, and his soul passed peacefully from earth.

"General Lee's physicians attributed his death in great measure to moral causes. The strain of his campaigns, the bitterness of defeat aggravated by the bad faith and insolence of the victor, sympathy with the subsequent sufferings of the Southern people, and the effort at calmness under these accumulated sorrows, seemed the sufficient and the real causes that slowly but steadily undermined his health and led to his death. Yet to those who saw his composure under the greater and lesser trials of life, and his justice and forbearance with the most unjust and uncharitable, it seemed scarcely credible that his serene soul was shaken by the evil that raged around him.

"General Lee's closing hours were consonant with his noble and disciplined life. Never was more beautifully displayed how a long and severe education of mind and character enables the soul to pass with equal step through this supreme ordeal; never did the habits and qualities of a lifetime, solemnly gathered into a few last sad hours, more grandly maintain themselves amid the gloom and shadow of approaching death. The reticence, the self-contained composure, the obedience to proper authority, the magnanimity, and the Christian meekness, that marked all his actions, still preserved their sway, in spite of the inroads of disease and the creeping lethargy that weighed down his faculties.

"As the old hero lay in the darkened room, or with the lamp and hearth-fire casting shadows upon his calm, noble front, all the massive grandeur of his form, and face, and brow remained; and death seemed to lose its terrors, and to borrow a grace and dignity in sublime keeping with the life that was ebbing away. The great mind sank to its last repose, almost with the equal poise of health. The few broken utterances that evinced at times a wandering intellect were spoken under the influence of the remedies administered; but as long as consciousness lasted there was evidence that all the high, controlling influences of his whole life still ruled; and even when stupor was laying its cold hand on the intellectual perceptions, the moral nature, with its complete orb of duties and affections, still asserted itself. A southern poet has celebrated in song those last significant words, 'Strike the tent': and a thousand voices were raised to give meaning to the uncertain sound, when the dying man said, with emphasis, 'Tell Hill he must come up!' These sentences serve to show most touchingly through what fields the imagination was passing; but generally his words, though few, were coherent; but for the most part, indeed, his silence was unbroken.

"This self-contained reticence had an awful grandeur, in solemn accord with a life that needed no defense. Deeds which required no justification must speak for him. His voiceless lips, like the shut gates of some majestic temple, were closed, not for concealment, but because that within was holy. Could the eye of the mourning watcher have pierced the gloom that gathered about the recesses of that great soul it would have perceived a presence there full of an ineffable glory. Leaning trustfully upon the all-sustaining Arm, the man whose stature, measured by mortal standards, seemed so great, passed from this world of shadows to the realities of the hereafter."

A letter from my mother to a dear friend tells the same sad story:

". . . My husband came in. We had been waiting tea for him, and I remarked: 'You have kept us waiting a long time. Where have you been?' He did not reply, but stood up as if to say grace.

Yet no word proceeded from his lips, and he sat down in his chair perfectly upright and with a sublime air of resignation on his countenance, and did not attempt to a reply to our inquiries. That look was never to be forgotten, and I have no doubt he felt that his hour had come; for though he submitted to the doctors, who were immediately summoned, and who had not even reached their homes from the same vestry-meeting, yet his whole demeanour during his illness showed one who had taken leave of earth. He never smiled, and rarely attempted to speak, except in his dreams, and then he wandered to those dreadful battle-fields. Once, when Agnes urged him to take some medicine, which he always did with reluctance, he looked at her and said, 'It is no use.' But afterward he took it. When he became so much better the doctor said, 'You must soon get out and ride your favorite gray!' He shook his head most emphatically and looked upward. He slept a great deal, but knew us all, greeted us with a kindly pressure of the hand, and loved to have us around him. For the last forty-eight hours he seemed quite insensible of our presence. He breathed more heavily, and at last sank to rest with one deep-drawn sigh. And oh, what a glorious rest was in store for him!"

THE END

ENDNOTES

CHAPTER I

[1] My brother's place on the Pamunkey River, where the mare had been sent for safe keeping.

[2] His pet name for my mother.

[3] His third daughter.

[4] His son, Custis.

[5] His appointment of Superintendent of the Military Academy carried with it the temporary rank of Colonel of Engineers.

[6] General William B. Taliaferro, commanding Virginia troops at Harper's Ferry.

[7] Sydney Smith Lee, of the United States Navy, his brother.

CHAPTER II

[1] The Episcopal Convention of the Diocese of Virginia.

[2] Bishop Meade, of Virginia.

[3] His brother, S. S. Lee, C. S. N.

[4] A cousin of Mrs. Fitzhugh.

[5] Miss Martha Custis Williams—second cousin of my mother, afterward Mrs. Admiral Carter, U. S. N.

[6] Major W. H. F. Lee—General Lee's second son.

[7] John Augustin Washington, great-nephew of General Washington, and Mt. Vernon's last owner bearing the name.

[8] Pet names for his two daughters, Mary and Mildred.

[9] Mr. Edward Carter Turner, of Kinloch, my father's cousin.

[10] "Avenel," the house of the Berbeleys, in Fauquier County.

[11] Eldest daughter of John Augustin Washington.

[12] His servant—had been in the dining-room at Arlington.

[13] His horse.

[14] A son of Mr. Edward Turner, of "Kinloch."

CHAPTER III

[1] His cook—a servant from the White House.
[2] Doctor and Mrs. Richard Stuart.
[3] The home of the Fitzhughs, where my grandmother Custis was born.
[4] His two coloured servants.
[5] On account of the Trent affair.
[6] His first grandchild—son of my brother Fitzhugh. He died in 1863.
[7] "Four Years with General Lee."

CHAPTER IV

[1] His nephew.
[2] His daughter Mary, in King George County, within the lines of the enemy.

CHAPTER V

[1] "Fighting Joe" was Hooker's popular sobriquet in the Federal army.
[2] J. E. B. Stuart, commanding cavalry corps.
[3] Two sons and three nephews.
[4] His son, Major General Fitzhugh Lee.
[5] His daughters.

CHAPTER VI

[1] General "Fitz" Lee, and his two brothers, Major John Mason Lee and Captain Henry Carter Lee.
[2] Mr. Charles Carter Lee, the General's brother; Mr. Williams Carter, the General's uncle.
[3] His second daughter.
[4] Longstreet.
[5] A. P. Hill.

CHAPTER VII

[1] An invalid lady, in the yard of whose country place ("Violet Bank") Lee's tents were pitched.
[2] His pet name for my sister Mildred.
[3] His mess-steward.

CHAPTER VIII

[1] Junction of Southside and Danville Railroad.

CHAPTER IX

[1] His old A. A. G.

[2] The "War Governor" of Virginia.

[3] A grandson of Chief Justice Marshall, and Lee's military secretary.

[4] Mrs. Cocke's second son, who lived with his mother at Oakland.

[5] The italics are Dr. Jones's.

[6] Mrs. Cocke's eldest son.

CHAPTER X

[1] Professor E. S. Joynes.

[2] Mrs. Chapman Leigh and Miss Belle Harrison, of Brandon, both very dear friends and cousins of my father.

[3] Mrs. Leigh's.

[4] The father of Professor (or "Captain") White.

[5] Our old pastor of Christ's Church, Alexandria, tha trusted friend of my grandmother and mother, who had baptised all the children at Arlington.

[6] The Virginia Military Institute, a State institution, modelled after the U. S. Military Academy at West Point, was located in Lexington, and its grounds adjoined those of Washington College. Since its foundation in 1839, up to this time, General F. H. Smith had been its superintendent.

[7] The "Brit" mentioned here is Mrs. Britannia Kennon, of "Tudor Place," my mother's first cousin. She had saved for us a great many of the household goods from Arlington, having gotten permission from the Federal authorities to do so, at the time it was occupied by their forces.

[8] Arlington, to that beloved home my mother still hoped to return.

[9] These were the names of some of my sister's pet chickens.

CHAPTER XI

[1] Commander of the canal packet.

[2] My father was not aware, when he wrote such explicit directions about the route, that Colonel Ellis had again put his boat at my mother's service.

CHAPTER XIII

[1] My brother had recently visited Lexington.

[2] The cook.

[3] The cook.

[4] The maid.

CHAPTER XIV

[1] William Preston Johnston, the son of General Albert Sidney Johnston, who fell at Shiloh. He had recently been elected to the chair of History and Literature at Washington College.

CHAPTER XV

[1] Daughter of General W. N. Pendleton, Chief of Artillery of the A. N. Va., and widow of Colonel Edwin Grey Lee, C. S. A.

[2] Daughters of Governor John Letcher—the War Governor of Virginia.

CHAPTER XVI

[1] I had written to him that they had destroyed all my hens.

CHAPTER XVII

[1] Professor Joynes in *University Monthly.*

[2] Her husband.

CHAPTER XVIII

[1] My mother's maid.

[2] The grandson of Nellie Custis, my grandfather's sister, who married Lawrence Lewis, the favourite nephew of Washington.

[3] These relics were restored to the family in 1903 by the order of President McKinley.

CHAPTER XIX

[1] General John C. Breckenridge, of Kentucky, ex-Secretary of War of the Confederate States, had two sons at Washington College at this time. One of them was since United States Minister at the Court of St. Petersburg.

[2] Mrs. S. S. Lee.

CHAPTER XX

[1] Rockbridge Baths.

[2] General Lee's eldest daughter.

[3] His daughter-in-law, Mrs. W. H. F. Lee.

[4] Mrs. Richard Stuart, of "Cedar Grove."

[5] "Yearling" was a term that originated with us just after the war (when many of the students were ex-soldiers), to distinguish the real boys from the "Confeds." From that expression, a professor came to be called a "leader of the herd." It was a form of speech that we had kept up amongst ourselves.

CHAPTER XXI

[1] A Virginian—son of General St. George Cooke, of the Federal Army, who commanded a North Carolina brigade in A. P. Hill's corps, A. N. Va.

[2] "Mrs. Smith" and "Gus" were the names of two of the pet cats of my sister. "Gus" was short for Gustavus Adolphus.

CHAPTER XXII

[1] Miss Mary Stewart, of "Brook Hill," afterward Mrs. Thomas Pinckney, of South Carolina.

[2] Corinne Lawton.

[3] This was the money that came to General Lee from his new edition of his father's "Memoirs of the War in the Southern Department of the United States."

[4] Attorney General in Mr. Davis's cabinet.

CHAPTER XXIII

[1] "Aunt M—" was Mrs. Fitzhugh of "Ravensworth," and "Burke," her coloured servant; Cassius Lee, my father's cousin; General S. S. Cooper, Adj. General of the C. S. armies; Mr. J. M. Mason, Senator in U. S. and C. S. Congress; the Bishop, Bishop Johns of Virginia, all at that time living on the "Hill"—or Seminary Hill—about two miles from Alexandria.

[2] Mr. Francis L. Smith was my father's lawyer. The matter referred to which caused the remark, "The prospect is not promising," was the chance of getting back the estate of Arlington from the U. S. Government. Mr. Smith and Mr. Cassius Lee were my father's advisers in this matter. "Nannie" was the widow of Captain S. S. Lee, my father's brother.

[3] A well-known girls' school at Staunton.

[4] The manager of the hotel.

[5] William Washington, a well-known painter of that day, who was for a short time professor of painting and drawing at the Virginia Military Institute at Lexington.

[6] Miss Charlotte Haxall, afterward Mrs. Robert E. Lee, Jr., who died in 1872.

[7] Charles Carter, of "Goodwood," Maryland, was my father's first cousin. Mildred and Ella, two of his daughters.

[8] Mrs. Peter was a near cousin of my mother, and with her as a little girl our associations had been very near.

[9] Professors Wm. Allan and William Preston Johnston of Washington College. The former afterward principal of the McDonough School, near Baltimore, Maryland; the latter president of Tulane University, New Orleans.

[10] Mildred's kitten.

CHAPTER XXIV

[1] Colonel Edwin Grey Lee was a near cousin. He had distinguished himself in the late war. At its commencement he had volunteered, and was made a 2d lieutenant in the Second Virginia regiment, "Stonewall Brigade." From that rank he quickly rose to be lieutenant colonel of the 33d Virginia, in the same brigade. In 1862 his health, which was very feeble, compelled him to resign, but after a short time he again entered the service, though he never became strong enough to serve actively in the field. General Lee's opinion of his abilities was very high.

SUGGESTED READING

CATTON, BRUCE. *Grant Takes Command.* New York: Book Sales, 2000.

---. *The American Heritage New History of the Civil War.* New York: Barnes & Noble Books, 2001.

CONNELLY, THOMAS L. *The Marble Man: Robert E. Lee and His Image in American Society.* New York: Knopf, 1977.

COWLEY, ROBERT, AND GEOFFREY PARKER. *The Reader's Companion to Military History.* Boston: Houghton Mifflin, 1996.

DAVIS, BURKE. *Gray Fox: Robert E. Lee and the Civil War.* New York: Holt, Rinehart & Winston, 1956.

FELLMAN, MICHAEL. *The Making of Robert E. Lee.* New York: Random House, 2000.

FOOTE, SHELBY. *Civil War: A Narrative.* New York: Knopf, 1986.

FRASSANITO, WILLIAM A. *Grant and Lee: The Virginia Campaigns 1864-1865.* New York: Charles Scribner's Sons, 1983.

FREEMAN, DOUGLAS SOUTHALL. *Lee's Lieutenant's: 3 Volumes.* New York: Scribner, 1944.

---. *R.E. Lee: A Biography, 4 Volumes.* New York: Scribner, 1935.

GALLAGHER, GARY W. *Lee and His Army in Confederate History.* Chapel Hill, NC: University of North Carolina Press, 2001.

GORDON, JOHN BROWN. *Reminiscences of the Civil War.* Baton Rouge, LA: L.S.U. Press, 1993.

GRANT, ULYSSES S. *Personal Memoirs.* New York: Barnes & Noble Books, 2003.

HARSH, JOSEPH L. *Confederate Tide Rising: Robert E. Lee and the Making of Southern Strategy, 1861-1862.* Kent, OH: Kent State University Press, 1998.

JOHNSON, ROBERT UNDERWOOD, AND CLARENCE C. BUEL, EDS. *Battles and Leaders of the Civil War: 4 Volumes.* New York: Century, 1888.

LONGSTREET, JAMES. *From Manassas to Appomattox.* New York: Barnes & Noble Books, 2004.

MCPHERSON, JAMES M. *Battle Cry of Freedom.* New York: Oxford University Press, 1988.

---. *Hallowed Ground: A Walk at Gettysburg.* New York: Crown, 2003.

NOLAN, ALAN T. *Lee Considered: General Robert E. Lee and Civil War History.* Chapel Hill, NC: University of North Carolina Press, 1991.

PFANZ, HARRY W. *Gettysburg—The Second Day.* Chapel Hill, NC: University of North Carolina Press, 1998.

RHEA, GORDON C. *Battle of the Wilderness.* Baton Rouge, LA: L.S.U. Press, 1994.

---. *Cold Harbor: Grant and Lee, May 26 - June 3, 1864.* Baton Rouge, LA: L.S.U. Press, 2002.

---. *The Battles for Spotsylvania Court House and the Road to Yellow Tavern.* Baton Rouge, LA: L.S.U. Press, 1997.

---. *To the North Anna River: Grant and Lee, May 13 - 25, 1864.* Baton Rouge, LA: L.S.U. Press, 2000.

ROLAND, CHARLES P. *Reflections on Lee: A Historical Perspective.* Mechanicsburg, PA: Stackpole, 1995.

SEARS, STEPHEN. *Gettysburg.* Boston: Houghton Mifflin, 2003.

SEARS, STEPHEN W. *Controversies and Commanders of the Civil War.* Boston: Houghton Mifflin, 1999.

SIMON, JOHN Y., E. *The Oxford Companion to Military History.* New York: Oxford University Press, 1999.

SPILLER, ROGER J., ED. *Dictionary of American Military Biography.* Westport, CT: Greenwood Press, 1984.

TAYLOR, JOHN M. *Duty Faithfully Performed: Robert E. Lee and His Critics.* Dulles, VA: Brassey's, 1999.

THOMAS, EMORY M. *Robert E. Lee: A Biography.* New York: W. W. Norton, 1995.

TUCKER, GLENN. *Lee and Longstreet at Gettysburg.* Indianapolis, IN: Bobbs-Merrill, 1968.

U.S. WAR DEPARTMENT. *Official Military Atlas of the Civil War.* New York: Barnes & Noble Books, 2003.

WINIK, JAY. *April 1865: The Month That Saved America.* New York: HarperCollins, 2001.